German antiquity
in renaissance myth

German antiquity
in renaissance myth

frank l. borchardt

THE JOHNS HOPKINS PRESS · BALTIMORE AND LONDON

Art in text adapted from Wilhelm Pleydenwurff's
woodcuts of the "Quaternions" in the *Nürnberg Chronicle* (1493)

The Johns Hopkins Press, Baltimore, Maryland 21218
The Johns Hopkins Press Ltd., London
Library of Congress Catalog Card Number 75-166484
International Standard Book Number 0-8018-1268-2

To give an accurate description of what has never occurred
is the inalienable privilege and proper occupation of the historian.

Oscar Wilde: *A Woman of No Importance*

Höchst reizend ist für den Geschichtsforscher der Punkt, wo
Geschichte und Sage zusammengrenzen. Es ist meistens der schönste
der ganzen Überlieferung. Wenn wir uns aus dem bekannten Gewordenen
das unbekannte Werden aufzubauen genötigt finden, so erregt es eben
die angenehme Empfindung, als wenn wir eine uns bisher unbekannte
gebildete Person kennen lernen und die Geschichte ihrer Bildung lieber
herausahnen als herausforschen.

Nur müßte man nicht so griesgrämig, wie es würdige Historiker
neuerer Zeit getan haben, auf Dichter und Chronikenschreiber herabsehen.

Goethe, *Zur Farbenlehre*

Contents

German antiquity
in renaissance myth

I

Introduction

Readers of older literature and students of history are constantly confronted by the mystery of the universe which housed their authors and documents. Difficulties may arise from simple ignorance of what a Renaissance or medieval author felt, understood, intended when he used this or that word or appealed to this or that frame of reference. Even if a word's denotation is known, it may be accompanied by connotations as complex as the laws that govern the motion of the stars.

A casual visitor to a planetarium in one of the world's great cities can sit in a darkened chamber and watch a monster of electrical wiring, lamps, and lenses project on a dome the night sky as it looked a thousand, or two, or ten thousand years ago. Allowing for a flaw in some lens, error in some calculation, ignorance of some yet undiscovered astronomical law, the visitor can safely assume that the spectacle is a fairly accurate image of the stars on some long-forgotten night.

A student of literature or history can never hope to achieve such accuracy in projecting the image of the universe of his authors or documents. Nonetheless, the attempt is made again and again, sometimes with a sweep across the dome as with a comprehensive theory, sometimes with limited attention to a few square inches, as it were, of a past or alien universe. In these pages I attempt the latter, hoping to contribute some understanding of several words and their connotative backgrounds, to fix their position in the Renaissance, to trace their course through the Middle Ages.

A modern reader of contemporary literature or of chronicles of contemporary events needs extensive knowledge of the philosophical, cultural, and ideological presuppositions of his subject. These, although he lives in the same temporal universe as his subject, may be wholly unfamiliar to him. A different problem is encountered when a modern reader or historian enters a temporal universe different from his own. He does not search first for the presuppositions unique to his author or document, but rather for those common to the era at large, especially in eras when a body of texts and ideas was known to all educated men, a canon as universal as the alphabet. Modern attempts at establishing a canon of learning have consistently met with ridicule from everyone beyond the immediate influence of the canonists. The Middle Ages and the Renaissance, however, needed no committees to compile lists of the one hundred great books. The great books were known, read, distilled, plagiarized, and anthologized. The content and connotation of a word were familiar, and if not, they could quickly be learned from one or another encyclopedic handbook.

Better understanding of the canon itself has recently succeeded in correcting many confused notions, dislodging many formerly authoritative generalizations, and—most importantly—reviving whole categories of thought strange to the modern reader. Access to the canon has been afforded by the revival or discovery of topology and the close study of mythography, patristics, and iconography by those concerned with recreating the medieval and Renaissance universe. Curiously, historical writings of the Renaissance in Germany have largely escaped such scrutiny, and historiography, in the sense of the history of historical writing, has not contributed its share to our knowledge of the canon.

Texts have been within easy reach ever since the publication of Migne's patrologies and the various national *Monumenta*, all of which have otherwise been richly exploited. The rising historical science of the nineteenth century made these sources available but was itself the root of many historiographic problems. One of the most unfortunate and relentless trends in medieval and Renaissance historiography has been, until most recently, the application of nineteenth- and twentieth-century standards of historical accuracy, attempted objectivity, and independence of tradition to works and authors for whom these standards were virtually meaningless. Economic, social, and political historians who have produced excellent studies of the Middle Ages and Renaissance have also, wittingly or unwittingly, harmed their scholarly predecessors in those epochs. Modern histories of historical writing consistently deplore the inaccuracy, bias, and plagiarism of earlier chroniclers, while praising the objectivity and cleverness of some supposed exception whose bias happened to coincide with the historiographer's own or who happened to anticipate modern historical methods. This unhistorical view of historiography has resulted in vast lacunae not only in secondary work but even in the editing of primary sources.

At least as far as primary sources are concerned, the Middle Ages have not suffered seriously under such neglect. The credit lies with the countless editors and compilers of the Bollandist, Stuttgart Literary Society, and Migne series, and similar collections for Italy, England, Byzantine Greece, Scandinavia, and various cities and provinces. The tradition of these compilers is an old and honorable one, extending back into the sixteenth century over such distinguished figures as Muratori, Leibniz, Goldast, de la Bigne, and Schardius. In German-speaking lands the immediate impetus for the nineteenth century's encyclopedic zeal was, however, not this scholarly tradition, but rather the Romantic movement with its glorification of the Middle Ages and infatuation with the national past. German statistical science in the nineteenth century was so closely allied to the Romantic movement that the paradox of Romantic statisticians is rarely noticed as a paradox. Linguistics, education, anthropology, and—not least—history bear the ineradicable marks of their association with the Brothers Grimm, Schlegel, and Humboldt, not to mention Karl Lachmann, the Freiherr vom Stein, and Friedrich Boehmer, one of the early editors of the *MGH* and a friend of Clemens Brentano.

This alliance between Romanticism and academic history explains, in part, the nineteenth century's preference for the Middle Ages and its discomfort with the Renaissance. For a time, the Renaissance was denied admission to Germany by German scholars, even after Burckhardt had dislodged the Middle Ages from the place of honor. Only recently, some specialists have come to regard the Renaissance as a proper category in their investigations of the cultural phenomena of German-speaking lands during the fifteenth and sixteenth centuries.

The Romantic preoccupation with the Middle Ages had further unhappy consequences for Renaissance studies. For example, even the worst and most long-winded epigonic German poets have had the benefit of fine critical editions, while most Renaissance authors remain available only in rare, expensive, and often inaccurate older editions. Considering the scope of the industrious nineteenth-century editing and publishing of old texts, it is astounding to find that the most recent editions of Erasmus and Cusanus are hundreds of years old, with the current critical editions just begun or in painfully slow progress, and that even the most famous neo-Latin poets have reappeared only in anthologies or fragmentary editions, if at all. These deficiencies are now being remedied, slowly. In Germany, greater attention is being paid to the Latin and vernacular monuments of the

Renaissance, although German scholars are still sufficiently under the influence of their Romantic forebears to maintain a polite reserve over against the term, "Renaissance."

It was the opinion of the German Romantics that the end of their beloved Middle Ages spelled the end of the real or imagined unity and harmony of "die Christenheit oder Europa."[1] The popular literature of the age was regarded as a sad decay of a grand tradition and not as a phenomenon to itself or the beginning of something new. What was undeniably excellent or influential appeared as a medieval survival. Luther then became one who purged Germany of the decadent Renaissance spirit (which presumably had not reached across the Alps in the first place) and restored "die Christenheit oder Deutschland."

This hopelessly myopic view was and is shared by scholars far less cordial to Germany. For them, however, Germany is not an admirable late stronghold of the Middle Ages, but rather a somewhat backward island in a sea of Renaissances. This distortion, whether cordial or hostile to Germany, rests on a simple misinterpretation: the medieval revival in Renaissance Germany has been labeled a "survival." From the disrupted historiographic tradition to the similarly disrupted heroic-literary tradition, all has been seen as a continuity. Had indeed such a continuity prevailed, we should have today more than a single, unique manuscript of the epic *Gudrun*. It is well known that Emperor Maximilian I ordered and richly subsidized the transcription of medieval literary monuments, but he was hardly an epigonic medieval emperor. One has only to see the graphics he commissioned and the artistic projects he left unfinished to realize that he was a Renaissance prince in the best Italian manner. His revival of medieval conventions was just that, a revival. A style-conscious craftsman of today may fashion an implement antique in appearance. This does not make him or the implement either antique or necessarily atavistic. On the contrary, the implement and the craftsman's consciousness of style reveal a characteristic of the present: an awareness of generation, a certain nostalgia for something known only vicariously. Was the Renaissance much different in awareness of its past? Even in Italy, medieval literature was not ignored. The Renaissance, after all, assumed the task of providing Italy with great medieval epics. Had it been left to the Middle Ages, Italian literature would have been deprived of its

---

[1] Much of the discussion here and in the following comments on the Renaissance is deeply indebted to the pioneer introduction to "German Renaissance Literature" by Harold Jantz, *MLN*, LXXXI (October 1966), 398–436.

Ariosto and Tasso. The Italian medieval revival has been regarded, since Burckhardt, as a Renaissance phenomenon. The German equivalent, partially derivative and partially independent of Italy, is not less so.

Burckhardt is perhaps the least obstinate of the nineteenth-century historical scientists (and their many descendents) in refusing to consider the mythical, the legendary, and the symbolic as a legitimate part of history. This limitation has resulted in such regrettable practices as the edition of medieval chronicles omitting the earlier sections because of their "unreliability" or "fantasy." These practices are by no means vices only of the past. Some positivistic historians have chosen a most anachronistic point of view for evaluation of their medieval precursors. The chronicles are considered important insofar as they meet the standards of post-Ranke historical writing. This lack of logic extends into formal historiography and is most villainous in its influence on Renaissance studies. For example, in modern interpretations of the Italian Renaissance, a statement on Italy's rejection of the Holy Roman Empire is virtually inevitable. Dante's *De Monarchia* appears as an abiding embarrassment. Petrarch's and Rienzo's dramatic appeals to Charles IV are regularly discounted as formulaic or opportunistic. But were they? The Empire was undeniably an antiquated and impotent political institution, but in prestige it was second only to the papacy. Despite Bruni, Machiavelli, and Guicciardini, *Realpolitik* is an invention of the nineteenth century. Neither Dante nor Petrarch nor Rienzo was *Realpolitiker*, and political realities meant little to their idea of the Empire. The Renaissance, like the Middle Ages before it, accepted myth, magic, sacrament, and symbol as realities at least as immediate and concrete as other normal, everyday experiences. Positivistic history and hard-nosed politics by themselves are thoroughly anachronistic tools to use in dissecting the thought of the Renaissance.

This is not to say that some Italians did not reject the myth of the medieval Empire. Certain Italians did. Others, however, did not. And some did both. In any case, the mere rejection of the imperial myth ought not to be a criterion for judging a thinker to be of the Renaissance and hence "modern." The very exercise of seeking "modernity" in the Renaissance betrays anachronism, as does the notion that modern political thought is somehow more rational and realistic than that of the benighted past. Nationalism, not to mention the even more unfortunate political slogans of the twentieth century, is quite as rooted in the irrational, impractical, and indefensible as were the theoretical ambitions of the Ghibellines. The whole category of "realism" in political history needs to be tempered with the categories of the unreal or the unrealistic. Recent historiographic work, rejecting the categories of myth, reacts in parts to the specter of *Geistesgeschichte*, which haunts the study of history not less than the study of literature. This, however, does not pardon the omission of myth, imagination, legend, and symbol as an intrinsic constituent of the intellectual life of the Renaissance.

Almost all questions which this book asks and seeks to answer lie within the elusive boundaries of the unreal, the unrealistic, and the connotative. They concern the myths of the German past, what they were in the Renaissance, where they came from in the preceding eras, what values they implied. When a Renaissance man used the words "German," "Swabian," "Frank," "Swiss," "Prussian," or "Bavarian," he made more than a simple geographic or ethnic distinction. In America today, for example, the word "Bavarian" is likely to suggest "beer," even if the issue is Bavarian politics, a Bavarian monastery, or the Bavarian State Library. Similarly (or dissimilarly), a Renaissance man assumed certain frames of reference when he wrote of the German Empire, of the piety or superstition, the virtues and vices of German men and women; and these frames of reference had visible sources in tradition. There is no question but that the connotations are radically different today and that the frames of reference have been almost entirely shifted.

The major secondary literature dealing with the Renaissance myths of the German past is discussed in the bibliographical appendix. The literature poses many of the questions concerning these myths, but nowhere has the tradition handed down from the Middle Ages been satisfactorily presented. Nowhere have the various branches of the tradition—learned and popular, Latin and vernacular, famous and little known—appeared synoptically. The secondary literature and the primary texts discussed in it are usually the exclusive property of historians. In recent times, they have seen in this tradition—and stressed—glimmers of modern historical writing. The present work, while not completely ignoring the "modern" elements in these old texts, regards them in a very different light. It searches less for the accurate and factual, and more for the imaginative and fantastic.

In the age of Goethe, critical historians decided that the Roman legend of Lucretia was without foundation, not credible, not factual—and that this was the truth of the matter. Goethe commented: "Was sollen wir aber mit einer so ärmlichen *Wahrheit?* Und wenn die Römer groß waren, so etwas zu erdichten, so sollten wir wenigstens groß genug sein, daran zu glauben." [2] What are we to do with such an impoverished *truth?* If the Romans were grand enough to conceive of such a thing, we should at least be grand enough to believe it. In a similar spirit, this study is not concerned with the historical "truth" about remote Germanic antiquity, but rather with what Renaissance and medieval men were "grand enough to conceive." Belief is left to the discretion or inclination of the reader.

Up to now I have employed terms such as "Renaissance," "Middle Ages," "myth," "German," and "past" without definition. There is no satisfactory consensus about the meaning of several of these basic expressions. For example, the use of the word "Renaissance," among Germanists at any rate, is most curious. As often as not, the literary historians try to avoid it by using "humanism and Reformation" instead. This circumlocution is inadequate. What is to be done with works that are clearly not humanistic, not directly involved with the Reformation, but certainly no longer medieval? A text like the anonymous *Koelhoffische Chronik* (1499) is a case in point. Its author was a contemporary of Reuchlin, Celtis, Bebel, and other German humanists of European reputation. The author was, however, by no stretch of the imagination a humanist. His command of the newly discovered texts of antiquity was minimal, his involvement with learning for its own sake hardly discernible, his employment of the new Latin style nonexistent (he wrote in German). Nor did he, like many humanist historians, emerge as a distinct personality through his work. On the other hand, it would be inaccurate and anachronistic to classify him as "medieval," for he subjected his sources to a form of critical examination that was untypical of the Middle Ages. His critical approach, held in common with the humanists, was truly as characteristic of the Renaissance as it was uncharacteristic of the Middle Ages.

The discussion of the texts proper in the next chapter begins with a work from the year 1418, the *Cosmodromium* of Gobelinus Persona. As well as I can determine, this was the first Latin universal history

---

[2] From a conversation with Eckermann, 15 October 1825: Ernst Grumach, ed., *Goethe und die Antike*, 2 vols. (Berlin, 1949), II, 864–65. Cf. Mario Krammer, "Die Legende als Form geschichtlicher Gestaltung," *Geist und Geschichte*, III (Breslau, n.d.), 24.

with any widespread distribution in Germany since the chronicle of Martinus Polonus almost a century and a half before. In the time intervening between these two works, a number of people and events took their places in history: Dante, Petrarch, Boccaccio; Petrarch's and Cola di Rienzo's sojourn in Germany; the founding of the University of Prague by Charles IV and his humanist circle; and, finally, the Council of Constance (1414–18), which brought so many Italian scholars to German lands. Gobelinus Persona wrote at the conclusion of the Council, following the first great wave of the new learning that had reached Germany. Whatever his sources and tradition, he did not remain uninfluenced by the ferment about him. Gobelinus felt a need to describe the world and its history, and felt that the medieval chronicles were no longer satisfactory, at least not without his intervention. Gobelinus as a humanist figure does not, however, deserve a place even near an Aeneas Sylvius or a Nicolaus Cusanus. As with the *Koelhoffische Chronik*, the most sensible term to use in describing the new—but not humanist—phenomenon of Gobelinus Persona is "Renaissance."

Looking even farther back in time, one finds in the fourteenth century developments that clearly led to the Renaissance in Germany. Political and religious strife brought to German lands ideas of Marsilius of Padua and William of Occam that challenged the traditional conceptions of imperial crown and papal tiara. The Empire and the Church had been weakened by decades of feuding and corruption, and the cry for reform became more articulate as the period advanced. The Empire replied with an introverted policy, attempted to consolidate its unrealistically inflated hegemony, and thus placated enough forces for the institution to survive, however feebly, without the laceration the Church was to endure. The Church, by delay, refused to reply. Mysticism gave way to fanaticism, and heresy could hardly be distinguished from piety. The soil of Bohemia from which Jan Hus had sprung was rich in both heresy and piety.

On that same soil, a generation earlier, the first university in the imperial north found a home, when it was chartered in Prague by Charles IV in 1348. At the University and in the imperial chancery at Prague the early Italian Renaissance received a warm welcome. Humanist learning and style began to play an important role in the work of politicians and scholars. Petrarch and the Roman Tribune Rienzo visited Prague, met the Emperor and his Chancellor Johannes von Neumarkt there, and left an indelible mark on the city and the culture that sprang from it.

Strict humanism, however, with its elegant Latin style and self-conscious revival of classical antiquity, was only one aspect of the Renaissance, even in its early stages. A resurgence of vernacular literature also belonged to this period—witness the *Canzoni* of Petrarch or the *Decameron* of Boccaccio—and it is the most compelling reason for using the term "Renaissance" in reference to fifteenth- and sixteenth-century German letters. It should help avoid the pitfalls of some of the more general works that, confined to the term "humanism and Reformation," have passed over the vast bulk of a vernacular literature at least as varied, and often as influential, as its Latin counterpart.

The field of popular vernacular literature is, after a hundred and fifty years of Germanistic studies, still largely unexplored. There are gratifying exceptions, but they are insufficient in number to warrant complacency. Too much has been left undone. Even the outstanding literature of translation, which antedates Luther by several hundred years, has never been truly incorporated into the greater picture of the period in Germany. Far too little from these various writings has entered the corpus of learning expected of an educated European or even of an educated German. These gaps would be less disquieting if they were the result of a long tradition of intense study and not the effect of outdated preconceptions. The condescension which greets this whole vernacular literature, even among Germanists, indicates a need for the hand of a daring revisionist. Such, alas, cannot be expected to appear within the scope of this book. But perhaps a legitimation of the term "Renaissance" for German vernacular letters might make way for the much-needed revision.[3]

The term "Renaissance," then, is used here with fairly standard connotations, to represent a historical period when there flourished a revived interest in the learning of classical antiquity, in the past of nations, and in the discovery of whatever could be learned. When I use the word in connection with Germany, I define it as a period characterized by a distinctive world view and spanning the time from the Council of Constance to the decline of the Reformation, preceded by a transitional period that began about 1350 when the Prague Chancery flowered.

My investigation stops short of the fully developed Reformation,

---

[3] Objections to the term "Renaissance" in English studies as "an imaginary entity responsible for everything the speaker likes in the sixteenth century" are expressed by C. S. Lewis, *English Literature in the Sixteenth Century* (Oxford, 1965), p. 55. Would that the term had been so abused in German studies!

but this is not to imply that I concur with the opinion that Renaissance and Reformation are incompatible. It is rather a matter of convenience to limit the texts to a reasonable number, for after about 1531 the bibliography is quite overwhelming. New sources, first and repeated editions, old and new commentaries become so numerous that a single work dedicated to a comprehensive bibliography is necessary before any large-scale interpretive work can be contemplated. The historiographers, for whom the task is more immediate, have avoided the problem; so have the literary scholars, whose interest in these sources is secondary.[4]

By limiting this study to the period preceding the widest spread of the Reformation in Germany, I hope to avoid the problems involved in untangling polemic from the joy of invention, propaganda from what was considered real learning. As the sixteenth century advanced, the study of the German past took on distressingly "modern" and critical overtones. Beatus Rhenanus may be said to have initiated this new criticism in his *Rerum Germanicarum Libri III* (Basel, 1531). Creative speculation, that is to say, unbridled fantasy, went into a definite decline following the publication of this work which consolidated, for the first time, the more reputable learning concerned with the history of Germanic antiquity. Later in the century, new editions of earlier speculations appeared, such as Simon Schardius's *Historicum Opus* (Basel, 1574), which contained texts of Bebel, Wimpheling, Trithemius, and Münster, among others, but nothing substantially new. The investigation of Germanic antiquities was, temporarily, becoming remote, as not the antiquities but their interpretations were studied. As to my own study of these interpretations, I wish to conclude it before it need leap off into one further degree of removal.

Because the term "Renaissance" encompasses approximately one hundred and fifty years in one of the most revolutionary periods in history, it must cover a multitude of sins. Nonetheless, it does not need to cover anywhere near the multitude of sins covered by the terms "Middle Ages" and "medieval." The Middle Ages, encompassing some thousand years from around the fall of Rome to the beginnings of Italian humanism, is a period so vast that one can say almost any-

---

[4] The best accomplishment in this area is Gerald Strauss's *Sixteenth-Century Germany* (Madison, Wis., 1959), but even this is only a beginning.

thing about it and not be entirely wrong. Something may be true of one century and not of another, or of one place and not of another. Contradictory statements may even be true and complementary. One scholar writes that medieval historical writing was "focused regionally on cities, bishoprics, monasteries, and dynasties."[5] Another writes, "medieval historiography was in its purview thoroughly universal."[6] Otto von Freising's chronicle of the "two cities" is clearly universal; his history of the deeds of Frederick is clearly dynastic. Despite such merely apparent difficulties, these terms have found a far more satisfactory consensus than "Renaissance," and it is not necessary to redefine them.[7]

The medieval or renascent characteristics of the Middle Ages or Renaissance—all possible combinations have been defended—have been a matter of much heated discussion in the last decades.[8] I have no intention of contributing to that discussion. The lacunae in the secondary literature, however, require a statement of position, since they include the failure to examine with any caution the weighty influence of medieval learning upon the Renaissance myths of the German past.

Renaissance historians delving into the German past unquestionably knew and read the standard medieval chronicles, rediscovered those not standard, studied medieval canonists and publicists, and otherwise indebted themselves to the immediately preceding age. Even the most superficial glance at a list of publications by such an unequivocally Renaissance figure as the Parisian printer Jodocus Badius Ascensius or a list of the sources used by the great Viennese humanist Johannes Cuspinianus reveals the vivid interest northern humanists had for

---

[5] Richard Kuehnemund, *Arminius or the Rise of a National Symbol in Literature,* University of North Carolina Studies in the Germanic Languages and Literatures, VIII (Chapel Hill, 1953), p. xxiv.

[6] Richard Buschmann, *Das Bewußtwerden der deutschen Geschichte bei den deutschen Humanisten* (Göttingen, 1930), p. 5.

[7] What I suppose to be the standard defense of the "scientifically preposterous" term "Middle Ages" is to be found in Ernst Robert Curtius, *European Literature and the Latin Middle Ages,* Willard R. Trask, trans., Bollingen Series, XXXVI (New York, 1953), pp. 20ff.

[8] The dispute has been surveyed by August Buck, *Das Geschichtsdenken der Renaissance,* Schriften und Vorträge des Petrarca-Instituts Köln, IX (Krefeld, 1957), and more briefly by the editors of *The Johns Hopkins Magazine,* XVIII (Spring 1967), 1–6. Extensive selections from the dispute have been edited by Karl H. Dannenfeldt, *The Renaissance: Medieval or Modern?* (Boston, 1959), with further bibliography.

their medieval precursors.[9] Some awareness of this connection has emerged in studies of the early history of printing, but these shed light on areas outside of historiography.[10]

The survival and revival of medievalia in Renaissance Germany demonstrate the organic continuity of one age out of another, and that alone suffices to explain a large part of the medieval interests of Renaissance Germans. But even more identifiable forces are at play. In their search for a national past, the Italians understandably turned to classical antiquity. Inspired by the Italians, the Germans, too, turned to classical antiquity; needless to say, they failed to find there a satisfactory construct of a German national past. German Renaissance writers turned therefore to the only other authoritative literary tradition available to them, that of the Middle Ages. Their attention to Jordanes, Einhard, Otto von Freising, and Alexander von Roes, for example, does not attest to Germany's recalcitrant adherence to medieval standards, but implies the same curiosity about the national past as had pointed the Italians in the direction of classical antiquity.

It is perfectly defensible to maintain that this period in Germany was remarkably medieval, but only by maintaining that it was remarkably "Renaissance" as well. An analogue to this tame paradox became the compromise solution to the medieval–Renaissance dispute of the 1940's. Konrad Burdach had reached the same conclusion much earlier, in 1913, when he wrote that "the Middle Ages were far more humanistic, the Renaissance far more medieval than general scholarly awareness assumes."[11]

---

[9] Cf. P. Renouard, *Bibliographie des impressions et des oeuvres de Josse Badius Ascensius . . . 1462–1535*, 3 vols. (Paris, 1908), I, 76, 79, 81, 85, 92; II, 37, 66, 177ff., 460–61, 477ff.; III, 9, 120–29, 249, for Badius's publication of the works of Eusebius, Gregory of Tours, Paul the Deacon, Liutprand of Cremona, Aimonius (or Annonius), Geoffrey of Monmouth, and Saxo Grammaticus. Hans von Ankwicz-Kleehoven, *Der Wiener Humanist Johannes Cuspinianus* (Graz and Cologne, 1959), pp. 309ff., mentions Cuspinianus reading, among others, works of Einhard, Pseudo-Turpin, Gotfried of Viterbo, Otto of Freising, Regino of Prüm, Ekkehard of Aura (i.e., the chronicle of Ekkehard and Frutholf), Sigebert of Gembloux, Liutprand of Cremona, Hermann of Reichenau, Vincent of Beauvais, Dietrich of Niem, and Martinus Polonus.

[10] See Curtius, *European Literature*, p. 27 and note 23; also Jean Seznec, *The Survival of the Pagan Gods*, trans. Barbara F. Sessions, Bollingen Series, XXXVIII (New York, 1953), p. 225; also Ernst P. Goldschmidt, *Medieval Texts and their First Appearance in Print*, Bibliographical Society Transactions, Supplement XVI (London, 1943), pp. 73ff. and passim, on whom both Curtius and Seznec depend. Goldschmidt is, however, the first to admit that his work is not comprehensive: *Medieval Texts*, pp. 70–71.

[11] "Denn das Mittelalter war viel humanistischer, die Renaissance viel mittelalterlicher, als das allgemeine gelehrte Bewußtsein annimmt." Konrad Burdach, *Rienzo und die geistliche Wandlung seiner Zeit* (Berlin, 1913–28), p. ix.

"Myth" is, unfortunately, also an overburdened term. Now it is used to mean a simple imaginative fable, now to describe the archetypal, fundamental, and final truths common to all peoples. The tales and notions studied here share to some extent in both extremes. The simple fictions in Renaissance and medieval speculations about the past require no comment at this point. Archetypal implications, now hardly avoidable in the usage of "myth," appear in the stories of ethnic, national, tribal, or civic origins. Divine or heroic descent crosses all cultural boundaries, and survives today in the honor accorded to real or suppositious ancestors, be they kings or princes, founding fathers or sainted pioneers. Archetypal are also the stories of heroes, the strong, the wise, the just, and the brave, representing concretely the highest ideals of a culture and ranging far beyond the limits of this book.

Instead of a special definition, I shall suggest a general description of myth as the term is used here. Myths share several characteristics with saga, legend, fairy tale, and kindred genres—such as narrative form and contents fixed in prior time but related to events, persons, processes, or institutions of present importance to the intended audience. Veneration of the past, moral lessons, or explanation of otherwise inexplicable phenomena are, however, rarely the primary functions of myths, as they may be of saga, legend, and fairy tale. Myth is rather a means by which a culture organizes, interprets, and gives authority to its most cherished assumptions about itself and the world. The validity of those assumptions depends not on any conformity with empirical reality—they may or may not be supported by the evidence of the senses—but on broad acceptance of the assumptions by the constituents of the culture. Myth has its primary reality among those who believe it to be a true explanation of significant affairs, who emotionally accept the explanation as operating in the world regardless of other possible explanations. It is, I suggest, almost unrecognizable in present time and place. Even if it can be recognized as based upon or containing an unverifiable assumption, its practical consequences still cannot be avoided. Myth is recognizable primarily when it has lost its validity. This feature of myth underlies the popular usage of the term as a disparagement of claims one dislikes or believes untrue. There myth is equivalent to fiction or untruth and can refer to present events. But the usage is imprecise. We can recognize the myth of the Golden Age in the Renaissance,[12] but we are unlikely to identify our

---

[12] Harry Levin, *The Myth of the Golden Age in the Renaissance* (Bloomington, 1969), p. xiii.

own conviction of imminent perfection or destruction or change as an unverified assumption. Even if we could call it a myth, we cannot act free of its implications.

Myth is based on feeling, but is expressed rationally in the visible world. Changes in reality do not, by themselves, change myths. The visible world is, on the contrary, more likely to be subordinated to the whims of myth than vice versa. The basis in feeling and the rational exterior make myths as influential as they have always been. But as feelings change, this exterior may survive and become a curiosity. Only then it becomes recognizable as myth.

It would be possible to add many more descriptive limitations to the term, but that would defeat the very purpose for which I have chosen it: even after restriction, it remains happily suggestive. To attempt a more precise definition would also ensnare the discussion in problems of method, which normally solve themselves in the course of investigating a large body of evidence. Let this, then, suffice. In any case, the sense in which I use "myth" should grow clear from the treatment of the texts.

Although the word "German" has the good grace today to refer specifically to the speakers of one modern European language and their lands, it had to bear far heavier responsibilities in the Renaissance. Ideally, the word ought to be used here to denote those tribes in antiquity and those provinces later on that were to become Germany. This is, however, impossible. The Renaissance had little notion of German nationality and identified as German what we today classify as Germanic, or even Celtic and Slavic. Renaissance Germans were clearly aware that Germanic tribes had migrated across the whole of Europe, leaving their names to France, England, Normandy, Burgundy, and Lombardy. Where they may have failed to recognize (V)Andalucia, they invented "Gothi-Alania" for Catalonia. Not only did they lump under "German" virtually everything we recognize today to be Germanic, but they also claimed the not always reputable achievements of the Phrygians and Scythians, the antiquity of the Celts, and the lands of the Slavs. "German" is then used here in the same broad sense, extended to include Germanic and its exaggeration beyond Germanic.

The last term requiring definition is "past." This is the vaguest term, and the easiest to limit. The initial point is the time of Adam, or perhaps slightly earlier, in the age of Demogorgon. There is, conveniently, a propagandistic myth about Adam's being German, and one no less propagandistic about the Demogorgon's special relationship to the Germans. The concluding point must remain movable. The Renaissance in Germany rarely applied mythical import to events much later than the Great Interregnum (1254–73). There are isolated exceptions. Imperial coronations always brought out strongly colored claims. Cola di Rienzo's Roman revolution (1347 and 1354) made a remarkable impression on Germany; however, I have been able to discover only one claim tracing the descent of an Ulm family from Rienzo to connect him to Germany in any mythical way.[13] Emperor Maximilian I became a myth in his own time, and to no small extent by his own deliberate doing.[14] However, 1519 is somewhat too close to be a "past" in relation to the Renaissance in Germany. The Great Interregnum then stands as an approximate concluding terminus for the term "past."

The first materials for this study are certain Renaissance texts. Many of them are relatively obscure. The better-known ones are to be discussed from a new point of view. They move freely between Latin and vernacular, chronicle and polemic, poetry and journalism. The guideposts are those details and narratives that may be called "myth" as characterized above. The social, economic, or political history of Germany reflected in the texts will not be examined specifically. I do not attempt a complete survey of all regional myths or of myths attached to minor cities, provinces, or princely houses, though typical instances of each will appear, some at considerable length. A complete survey does deserve to be made, for there are some fine stories, even in the most peripheral texts.

Once the Renaissance myths of the German past can be identified, their sources are at issue. A cursory review of the sources from classical antiquity is necessary because a substantial portion of Renaissance inventions about the German past is rooted in ancient texts that were not widely known in the Middle Ages. Some Renaissance fabrications

---

[13] A close contemporary reports in 1349 Rienzo's victory in Rome: Franz Karl Grieshaber, ed., *Oberrheinische Chronik* (Rastatt, 1850), pp. 37–38. Jakob Twinger von Königshoven (1400/1415) believed Rienzo ultimately victorious: Karl Hegel, ed., *Chroniken der deutschen Städte*, IX (Leipzig, 1871), 586–87. Johannes Naucler's *Chronicon*, first published posthumously in 1516, gives an extensive report on Rienzo, calling him "a lover of liberty." I use the 1584 Cologne edition, II, 391–94.

[14] Cf. Glenn Elwood Waas, *The Legendary Character of Kaiser Maximilian*, Columbia University Germanic Studies, XIV (New York, 1941), pp. 88, 156, and passim.

exploited the newly discovered classical texts. The very similarity between the fabrication and the authentic source was used to corroborate the veracity of the fiction. Used to the same end was the dissimilarity between the fiction and medieval sources. Some examination of ancient texts may also be necessary to point out a few connections that seem to have escaped the attention of modern readers. The review is brief, however, because the vast majority of the contributions of antiquity are to the credit of Tacitus; and Tacitus's influence on the northern Renaissance is well known.[15]

From classical antiquity, the search turns to pertinent sources in the Middle Ages. Several Church Fathers offer material for these myths, and then the major texts will be histories, chronicles, annals, polemics, and poems from the dawn of the Middle Ages to the time of the Great Interregnum. The period from the Interregnum to the Council of Constance requires a separate consideration because of the extraordinary changes and consolidations that mark those years of transition. All texts are examined in a succession as close to chronological order as logical order permits.

Finally, the myths are to be classified according to their origins or originality, that is, whether they were rooted solely in classical antiquity, solely in the Middle Ages, were of mixed origins, or were without visible tradition altogether. In the discussion of medieval or mixed origins, the dependence on the Middle Ages of Renaissance ideas will be the implicit issue. The last sections discuss the survival of the myths, of the mythical disposition in history, and of the coincidence of the historical and literary imagination.

To make the work at all manageable, certain limitations have been imposed on the texts introduced to the study. Medieval *vitae* and *legenda*, translations of relics, reports of the founding of churches, bishoprics, etc., canon, civil, and public law, Byzantine and Jewish literature, Eddic texts, local or national chronicles not known to the Renaissance had to be omitted, although some isolated cases must be mentioned. The basic reservoirs for the Renaissance myths of the German past are histories and polemics, but even these have been limited as categories. Insofar as medieval traditions were ignored by the Renaissance, they are omitted here. An attempt is made to reconstruct

---

[15] Paul Joachimsen, "Tacitus im deutschen Humanismus," *Neue Jahrbücher für das klassische Altertum*, XIV [XXVII] (1911), 695–717; also Hans Tiedemann, *Tacitus und das Nationalbewußtsein der deutschen Humanisten am Ende des 15. und Anfang des 16. Jahrhunderts* (Berlin, 1913); and most recently, Else-Lilly Etter, *Tacitus in der Geistesgeschichte des 16. und 17. Jahrhunderts*, Basler Beiträge zur Geschichtswissenschaft, CIII (Basel and Stuttgart, 1966).

only those myths that found a reception among German Renaissance men rather than to deal with all the myths about Germany and its past. It would be quite erroneous to assume that the Middle Ages were as uniformly receptive to German antiquities as the later age leads one to believe.

The selection of texts was also influenced by accessibility. My findings lead me to believe, however, that the less accessible sources harbor few myths that would not fit comfortably in the general patterns established by the available materials. Throughout the book I have plundered translations, where they have been available, but regularly I have compared them with originals. In certain cases, Renaissance translations, redactions, and studies of older works are so idiosyncratic that they reflect little of their purported models—but then they reveal a great deal about their own time. In citing, I have taken the liberty of referring to originals or translations indiscriminately, generally in such a way as to ease the reader's proof of the reference, whether or not he has the same edition at hand. Where I have been forced to make my own English translations, I have done so, but they are meant to be glosses rather than examples of the translator's considerable and undervalued art.

The Renaissance myths of the German past and their sources are treated here in a series of categories: origins, fabulous and real; heroes, fabulous and real; ancient religion, fabulous and real; ancient virtue and vice, in peace and war; and the *Imperium*. Although these categories became apparent only toward the end of my work and are hence inductive, they will be applied deductively to the matter as an ordering principle. To make them more useful, I present a concrete illustration of the myths that fill them. In keeping with my resolve to restrict documentation to the absolute minimum in this introduction—the remainder of the book is, to compensate, over-documented—I omit citation of sources here. Each myth will be identified according to its source when it appears in the subsequent chapters.

German Renaissance men were greatly concerned with the origins of their ancestors. Their conjectures may have been motivated by vanity, national pride, simple curiosity, or an intense interest in the past. Whatever the motive, they were faced with a frustrating paucity of reliable authorities. Hence they conjectured, for example, that the Germans originated with Adam, which in itself is not extraordinary. But the Germans, as it seems, had left Babel before the confusion, and thus preserved their ancestry from Adam intact, while all other nations are derivative in language and culture. The Demogorgon existed out of time but, others maintained, the Germans stem from him, so called because they used to live in such fraternal harmony [sic!]. Still others believed that the Germans got started with Japhet, son of Noah, when he came to Europe after the flood. Yet others held that the Germans descended more immediately from Gomer, Gog, or Magog, sons of Japhet. There were also reports that Noah's later sons, those born to him after the flood, included Tuyscon, who gave his name to the Germans—"Teutsch."

Tuyscon gives the clue that Renaissance genealogic mythographers hardly felt bound by the most famous traditions. Their inventive ambition became impressive indeed when they began to seek origins in the generations after Noah. His grandsons, the sons of Tuyscon, include Suevus, Vandalus, and Prutus, who gave their names to the Swabians, Vandals, and Prussians. Another son of Tuyscon is said to be Hercules Alemannus, who is father of the Bavarians. Others say that Bavarus, who led the Bavarians out of Armenia after the flood, is their first ancestor and gave them their name. Some slanderers say that their name comes from an attempt to disguise, by the purchase of an initial "B," the name others called them, "avari," greedy. The Franks have, as it appears, more recent origins. They stem from Priam, grandson of Priam the Great, or, according to others, from Francio, who left Troy with Aeneas after the fall of that city. It is because Aeneas called the Franks his brothers, "germani," that the Germans have their name. Yet others believe that the Franks descend from the Bavarian king Francus, who flourished at the time when the German queen Amär destroyed Ephesus.

The origin of the Saxons is even more recent. They originate with the survivors of Alexander the Great's army, who fled the conquered lands after the death of their leader. Their name comes from the *Saxum Marpesiae* on the Caucasus, where they sojourned en route to northern Europe. (This rock had been named after the Gothic queen Marpesia, who founded the Amazons.) However, others say that the Saxons came from Britain. The Swiss are perhaps the youngest of all these nations. They are the Swedes who fled their homeland during a great famine. One of their leaders was called Switerus, and presumably he gave them their name. Others say that the Swiss came from cowardly Saxons whom Charlemagne left to guard the Alpine passes while he marched to Italy. These calumniators say that the Saxons told the Emperor, in order to gain his favor, that they would sweat ("switten") it out. For this reason they are called Swiss, considering the pronunciation differences between Saxon and Upper German. The

Swiss are also supposed to stem from Huns and Goths. The Goths and Langobards originate from the island of Scandinavia in the Northern Ocean.

Only the last two origins given by our Renaissance authors—for Goths and Langobards—seem to reflect a real state of affairs. All the others are but a few versions of the fabulous origins of the German nation and its tribes. The myths of origins overlap with the myths surrounding the fabulous heroes, for many of them are given as the founders of cities or states.

The very word for hero in German, "Held," comes from the Bavarian prince Helto. One of the earliest men properly to carry this honorific was Trebeta, son of Ninus and Semiramis of Assyria. After the death of his father, Trebeta fled his notorious mother and her illicit designs on him. He eventually came to the river Mosel, where he founded and named the city of Trèves or Trier. One of Trebeta's companions, Tyras of Trier, founded the city of Tyrasburg, which by lapse of the "y" and addition of an initial "s" became known as Strassburg. All of this had occurred long before Romulus founded Rome. Somewhat later, Basanus the Great was King of the Franks. He lived from 284 B.C. until his mysterious disappearance in 240 B.C., and brought law and justice to his people. His deeds were related by the historian Hunibald, who stood in succession with Wasthaldus, Amerodacus, and Salagastald, men of learning in that nation. Wasthaldus flourished in 410 B.C. and produced twelve books on the origins and history of the Franks. Bardus, a German king in Gaul, discovered poetry and song. Men of learning and justice found an important place among the fabulous heroes, as well as among those with firmer footing in historical reality.

Among the latter belongs Theodoric, who took the mantle of the Roman Empire after the failure of Augustulus. The Pippins, Charles Martel, Charlemagne, the Ottos, the first and second Fredericks, in their piety and virtue served the Church with an excellence unparalleled elsewhere. Some maintain that Theodoric and Frederick II oppressed the Church, and go so far as to say that neither of them ever died properly: Frederick is supposed to return one day and harass the Church. Nevertheless, Frederick was known to be a pious and learned monarch, and he was not the only learned man among imperial rulers. Charles the Great was also an important patron of learning. In his time and shortly afterward, Hrabanus Maurus and Walahfrid Strabo flourished. Otfried von Weissenburg and Hugh of St. Victor are memorable among the men of learning, and Hrotswitha von Gandersheim and Hildegard von Bingen among the women.

The emphasis on the learned might seem to be a humanist idiosyncrasy, but this is not entirely the case, for there are strong medieval precedents. Similarly, it might seem that a Roman-Germanic syncretistic theology in the Renaissance would also be a humanist confabulation. This is also, surprisingly, far from true.

As the stories have it, the ancient Germans worshiped among their gods Mars, Hera, and Hermes. This can be seen in the name of the town Merseburg, which is variously explanined as Mars-burg, "tom" Hera-sburg ("at the" Herasburg in Low German), or Her(m)esburg. They also worshiped Mercury, Hercules, Isis, Pallas, Ceres, the Moon, the Sun, and others. Wotan is said to be the equivalent of Mercury, Freia of Venus. The Swabian goddess Zise is supposed to represent Ceres; others make her into a Swabian version of Venus Cypria. The report of the worship of the moon and the sun is explained as a later confusion of ancestor worship: Tuyscon's son Mannus and Mannus's wife Sunno were venerated by the ancient Germans, and only later were "der Mond" and "die Sonne" attached to their names. The ancient Germans let pious women dedicate their virtue and lives to the service of religion. One report indicated that the Vestal Virgins of Rome were actually Westphalian nuns. Their priests were Druids who had found sanctuary in Germany. They were exceedingly learned, knew Greek, and were expert in augury. They conducted worship in oak groves and did not build churches. There was a time of human sacrifice, but this practice was corrected. The real ancient religion—however little is actually known of it today—provided some of the myths, but these were hopelessly confused with later additions. Of all this information, which the Renaissance firmly believed, only the names of Wotan and Freia with some details of worship and sacrifice seem to reflect ancient Germanic religion as we understand it today.

The piety implied by their religion and its purported simplicity was thought to be among the greatest virtues of the ancient Germans. Their simplicity was further reflected in their cuisine. Wine, for example, was forbidden them except at the winter festival, which is why Christmas is called "Wein-nachten." Others report that they were not so restrained in food and drink, but that seems more appropriate to the later rather than to the early Germans, or so the Renaissance thought. Renaissance men in Germany shared with their Italian mentors (and with the common heritage from imperial Rome) a peculiarly enthusiastic, "soft primitivist" view of the ancestral past. The Renaissance saw the devotion of ancient Germanic women reflected in all their activities and sang the praises of their unquestioned honor and gallantry. Their men were brave and warlike, never defeated.

Even Alexander the Great feared them and recommended that they be avoided. Some say that they tasted defeat at the hands of Caesar, but only because he was aided by other Germans. They were avenged when the Roman general Quintilius Varus was defeated with the loss of three legions, whence Emperor Augustus's cry, *Quintili Vare legiones redde!*—"Quintilius Varus, give me back my legions!"

Now the Emperors are German. This was prefigured when the ancient Germans aided the first Caesar in his victory over Pompey. This secular prefiguration was complemented by a religious one, when St. Peter sent his staff, the emblem of power, to raise St. Maternus from the dead. The staff remains in Germany, and to this day the popes do not carry staffs. This shows as well that the specifically sacred mission of the Empire had always been intended for the hands of the Germans. The activities of the pious rulers demonstrate the fulfillment of the intention.

The above examples ought to suffice as illustrations of the categories of origins, heroes, virtue and vice, and the *Imperium*. Their confusion, ingenuity, extreme provincial pride, and variety should make it clear that a chasm separates the twentieth century from the historical imagination of the Renaissance in Germany. The vast majority of these stories, particularly the least realistic of them, occupied the Renaissance mind as securely as the winter at Valley Forge or the Battle of Gettysburg occupies the historical imagination of a present-day American.

Our preview of the subject matter reveals at least one additional problem. Because of the great number and variety of the myths and the multiplicity of their traditions, it would be unrealistic to present them as an even relatively cohesive mythology. This they were not, nor did they become so. Many individual myths survived the Renaissance. Several of the most fabulous ones survive in modern times. But their very proliferation, especially in the Renaissance, condemned most of these myths to extinction—although not before they entered the reservoir of literary allusion. There they passed into the hands of those who had no need to be embarrassed by using them. The curious technique which Renaissance historical writers employed to create new myths—but which succeeded in destroying almost all of them—will be discussed in the next chapters. It is called *anasceua*, the topos of critical rejection, and will be dealt with as the need arises in the texts. The presentation of the myths is not intended specifically for application to any one or several works in the subsequent literature. I present the myths primarily for whatever value they have in themselves, then to illustrate some patterns in the creative imagination of the past, and finally to reconstruct a part of the Renaissance and medieval universe.

The attempt to reconstruct a medieval or a Renaissance universe assumes the existence of such a universe. By comparison with the present, this assumption may seem preposterous. No one can pretend to the knowledge of some corpus of patterns and traditions that underlies contemporary literature in the way that Ptolemaic cosmology, for example, underlies literary expression from the age of Virgil to that of Goethe. But studies in older literature have shown beyond a reasonable doubt that a corpus of common assumptions does, in truth, extend well into modern times. Who is to say whether future generations of scholars will not find a similar corpus underlying the literature of today? We may now be too close to observe it. If someone were to observe and describe it, he would certainly cause considerable annoyance in a literary world which postures with originality, isolation, idiosyncrasy, and emphatic denial of common assumptions. This posture was not unknown to older thought, particularly in the Renaissance, but never did or could prevail. The influence of the established patterns was irresistible. To seek the basic assumptions and universal features of the medieval and Renaissance world is not a meaningless or hopeless enterprise.

As for the myths of the German past, there is no other possible avenue of investigation and interpretation than within the framework of this universe. The tradition of learned historical speculation in the Middle Ages was available to the Renaissance in all conventions of transmission. To the availability should be added the probability of use by Renaissance German historians. They had on hand few or no other sources for the reconstruction of dim antiquity. The oral history of the Germanic peoples had long ago collapsed under the pressures of literacy and christianization; the fragments that remained in heroic literature were confused and unauthoritative. The collection of inscriptions and similar documents was in its infancy, wholly without a scientific method for evaluation. This left little but what was available of the historiographic tradition.

The majority of historical myths in the Renaissance came directly from the medieval chronicles. A smaller but very important part came from writers of classical antiquity. Few myths had no direct ancient or medieval antecedents, but even these appeared in traditional forms.

The myths of origin show all variations of dependence. The tradition, in unconscious parody of the major constituents of western European culture, created three acceptable nurseries of nations: the biblical, the Germanic, and the classical. For the new nations, the earliest records to survive take the biblical option. The Church Fathers considered the invading Goths a scourge of God and found Gog and Magog in Old Testament prophecy to explain their origins. It was hardly a flattering explanation, and it remained confined entirely to ecclesiastical writing. But it set the precedent of origins in the first generations after Noah, a most logical choice in view of the demands of sacred history. In the Middle Ages, most writers were satisfied to know that the European peoples all descended from Japhet. Some required more explicit and exclusive genealogies. The Bavarians took the biblical option with their myth of Armenian origins, anticipating the Renaissance's more enthusiastic use of the children of Noah. Sacred history also provides Trier's origins in the age of Abraham, with Trebeta's flight from Babylon.

The Germanic option entered the tradition not long after the biblical, with the theory of Gothic origins in Scandinavia. These were somewhat elaborated with the Langobard parallel, which added to distinguished leadership and battles with the invaded nations the important features of starvation in the land and selection of the refugees by lot. The convention was widely imitated and served several nations: the Hungarians, who are not at issue here, the Swabians, and very much later, the Swiss. By all appearances, the myth is more or less historical. There does seem to have been a natural disaster or deterioration of climate in Scandinavia around the turn of the eras, which may account for the start of the Germanic migrations. Furthermore, the first learned reports specifically appeal to the oral history of the Goths as an authority. And this is supported by the likelihood that the Latin report of the Langobard myth was a close translation of an unwritten Germanic original. This comfortable, if tenuous, body of evidence was entirely upset by Herodotus who, in the fifth century B.C., described the identical sequence of events for the Tyrrhenians. Even more disturbing is the location of Tyrrhenia in the Italy invaded successively by Goths and Lombards. The Scandinavian myths entered learned tradition in the same succession. These facts admit of several reasonable interpretations. The learned record of barbarian myths presumes the contact which invasion represents. So it may be that the Germanic peoples preserved some memory of their historic cataclysm in the North, that the Latin historiography merely reports the memory, and that the similarities to Herodotus are pure coincidence. It may, however, also be that the Germanic peoples shaped their myths after models found first among the conquered nations.

The latter is certainly the case for the classical option. The Trojan origins myths of the Franks are unthinkable without contact with the Roman world. But even here, the genesis of the myth is ambiguous. It appears that non-Roman peoples in the lands conquered by the Franks claimed Trojan origins long before the conquest. The seventh- and eighth-century reports may thus be purely a learned fabrication on the model of Virgil, or a record of popular beliefs adopted by the Franks from the conquered peoples, as they adopted their language and religion. The Macedonian origins theory, associated with the Saxons, admits no source other than Mediterranean cultural tradition. The fame and military prowess of Alexander may, however, have captured the popular imagination of the warlike Saxons in their contact with the Roman world, quite apart from any single historical or literary tradition. In any case, they chose him as a founding father long before he was appropriated by the medieval North in the vernacular Alexander Romances.

One troublesome aspect of all these myths is the consistent glorification of flight and exile, in open defiance of the warrior ethic, where victory is the right and an exile the criminal. But many medieval heroes were exiles—Dietrich, Hildebrand, Havelok, Tristan—and many were glorified in their defeats—Siegfried, Hagen, Roland, Arthur. It seems analogous to the now mythical origins of Americans and Australians from malcontents, ne'er-do-wells, and convicts. The patterns suggest historical archetypes that both underlie and transcend the single examples of origins myths. There seems to have been a sense of poignancy or tragedy or possibly simple pride in the overcoming of terrible obstacles in the forming of nations. However, this leads to unverifiable conjecture and, worse yet, to a psychology of history.

The tradition supplied all these patterns—the biblical, the Germanic, and the classical—and all the origins myths betray some dependence on them. The Bavarian, Gothic, Frankish, and Saxon myths, among others, came into the Renaissance substantially unchanged. Some national, dynastic, and civic origins myths were neologistic, and hence without detailed precedents in the tradition. But, as in the case of the Swiss, it is probable that only the names were changed to conceal the plagiarism of an available myth. The most extravagant myths —a German Adam or a German Demogorgon—do defy the search for antecedents, but even they are Renaissance extensions of a traditional principle that confuses distinction with antiquity.

The greatest number of neologistic myths in the Renaissance is traceable to the rediscovery of Tacitus. They seem to represent the choice of classical origins, predictable for Renaissance humanism. As usual, matters are not so simple. A certain school of patriotic humanists, including Ulrich von Hutten, recognized the value of Tacitus for historical and propagandistic purposes, and used him to those ends. But far more influential than the works of Tacitus themselves was their appearance in the forgery published under the name of Berosus. It tied the classical option to the biblical, placing the Germanic antiquity of Tacitus in the context of the children of Noah. This was perhaps not as "modern" as the services rendered by Hutten, but it was far more typical of the Renaissance. The forgery and the fusing of classical and biblical was, significantly, not of German but of Italian provenance.

My emphasis on the tradition and its manifestations in Germany leaves unexamined crucial differences between medieval and Renaissance practice, and crucial similarities between Germany and its European neighbors. Since Germany, all by itself, supplies an unwieldy body of myths, this study has little room for the pursuit of the mythical past in other countries. But this is not to imply that others were spared the same folly or that they courted it with less gusto. No one was immune. The literary fruits of the pursuit are, in fact, more evident outside Germany, in the *Franciade* of Ronsard, for example, or the antiquarian plays of Shakespeare. Even the Italians, with a strong bent toward scientific history, preserved and invented a quantity of historical nonsense, e.g., Aeneas Sylvius Piccolomini from Aeneas and Sylvius of Roman antiquity. But the Italian contributions overall have far greater significance than their incidental lapses into more typically northern myth-making.

The Italians also made myths, but theirs was a formidable structure. For every sentence the German patriots could extract from Caesar, Tacitus, or the medieval chronicles, the Italians had a library of historical traditions with the unimpeachable authority of classical antiquity. They displayed interest in the past somewhat earlier than their German equivalents did, more or less independently, in the late fourteenth and early fifteenth centuries. The Italians' turn to the past was comprehensive, included an entire culture rather than only history, and had an elaborate and knowable object. By contrast, the Germans' turn to the past was confined predominantly to history and, later, theology. Even today, their historical object seems sketchy and difficult to describe, although their religious revival is comparable in its successes and failures to the Italians' revival of classical antiquity.

The Italians clearly set the tone and, in humanism, provided the model. It was this massive orientation to the past, I believe, as much as any other single feature, that distinguished Renaissance from medieval historiography, at least in Germany. The chronicling of contemporary events certainly did not suffer from this turn; on the contrary, it seems to have benefited. But the immediacy and color of these reports represent a continuity from the medieval anecdotal history of the legends and the first-hand reports of diplomats and travelers. It is the study of past as opposed to present history that assumes a new importance in the Renaissance.

The wild fantasy of the Renaissance historians seems to me a sign of the new attitude. They pursued impressionistic etymology, for example, with a vigor that almost, but not quite, put Isidore of Seville to shame. Precisely in this unscientific practice, common to medieval and Renaissance historiography, are the differences revealed. For the medieval tradition, etymology explained the present form of a word or place name, why it was now this and no other: the past was wholly subordinated to the present and, in fact, hardly distinguished from it. In Renaissance practice, etymology took a place beside the recovery of medieval chronicles, Tacitus, forgery, and free distortion of classical antiquity to assemble a comprehensible and detailed picture of the remote past, different from today, usually a reproach for today, sometimes a consolation that today was better, but always different in some way. I suggest that medieval historigraphy blurred the differences because it regarded the past as present. The Incarnation, the central event of history for the Middle Ages, was never distant and ever present, renewed daily in the divine liturgy. It is perhaps significant that some of the Reformation changes made the liturgy into a commemoration of the divine sacrifice rather than a recreation of it or, in human terms, past and unique rather than present and abiding. These generalizations admit countless exceptions, but nonetheless suggest themselves repeatedly in comparing medieval and Renaissance historiography.

This awareness of the past collaborated with a progressively more scientific method, basically philological, to discourage the anarchic speculation of Renaissance historians about their antiquity. When the forgeries and fabrications were printed later in the sixteenth century, the reader was not expected to believe the text blindly, but rather to question it. Anarchic speculation could not long survive in such an atmosphere. A further discouragement to the myths of the German past in their historiographic transmission came with the new concerns of Reformation historians, to whom the religious rather than the secular past was of prime importance. By the middle of the sixteenth century, Renaissance mythical antiquity had largely passed out of historiography and into literature, where it enjoyed an honorable and not altogether idle retirement.

The passage of the myths into literature should not, however, imply a great liberation of historiography from the mythical disposition. On the contrary, the absence of a confined, obvious, and relatively harmless field of wild conjecture has left the whole span of history open to myth-makers. The growing sophistication of historical method is as available to them as to serious historians, which makes the myths more true, only more difficult to detect. Indeed, the energies the Renaissance expended in mythologizing the past seem today expended in mythologizing the present. One wonders whether this is an improvement. To help the reader decide for himself, we turn to the Renaissance myths of the German past.

II

T̶ḫe renaissance myṭḫs of
t̶ḫe german past in
t̶ḫe fifteenth century

For our purposes, the fifteenth century begins somewhat tardily, at the end of the Council of Constance. While the Italian visitors to the Council scattered across Germany, relieving the monasteries of their excess of ancient texts, several German scholars were continuing a process of historical understanding which would help their successors to follow in the footsteps of the Italians—with intense regrets for having dawdled. This process took many shapes; one was the development of patriotic historical writing within the tradition of universal history. It is with this development that we begin.

GOBELINUS PERSONA (1358?–1421?) studied at the University of Erfurt in its earliest years (1392–94). Shortly after the Council of Constance, he produced a world history, the *Cosmodromium*, which begins with the Creation and continues through 1418. His work was not printed until 1599, but was nonetheless relatively well known prior to that. He was widely quoted in the fifteenth century, and several of the following myths entered Renaissance tradition in his wording. A manuscript survives from 1471. The *Cosmodromium* was an important source for the more renowned North-German historian, Albertus Krantz (died 1517).[1]

Gobelinus's course through the cosmos runs over some 300 folio pages which, it is generally agreed, contain a great many reliable and original observations (Potthast, p. 532). He does not hesitate to inject personal experience and to use first-hand observations in assuring the reader of the accuracy of his assertions. By and large, this accuracy is of no interest here. It is only important to indicate Gobelinus's independence of written tradition in certain areas—presumably a Renaissance characteristic in this ignored historian. Gobelinus does, on the other hand, quote freely and fully from older authors. But even here he breaks away from tradition. Many of his borrowings are accredited in the text after the manner of the canonists, even though it is widely believed that this practice did not penetrate historical writing in the North until late in the sixteenth century. In any case, such accreditation is a distinctly-not-medieval practice in the writing of history. Gobelinus's debt to his medieval predecessors was nonetheless considerable, although it is not the issue here. The myths which Gobelinus created or transmitted fall into the above-suggested categories of origins, heroes, religion, and the *Imperium*; the category of ancient virtue and vice in peace and war seems to have been less important.

The second area of the world after Asia, he tells us, is Europe. The first region of Europe is Lower Scythia, which lies between the Maeotian swamps, the Danube, and the Northern Ocean, and is next to Germany. Lower Scythia is divided into Alania and Dacia or Gothia. The latter separates Germany from Russia. After Lower Scythia, the second region of Europe is Germany, so called because of its ever increasing population. Germany is bounded by the Danube, the Rhine, and the Ocean. The region has many provinces. Some but by no means all have been described by ancient authors. For this reason and because it seems the Germans did not study letters before they accepted Christianity, it is difficult to explain the origins of the provinces' names. Among their lands are Livonia, Prussia, Holstein, Frisia, and Saxony, of which the part between the Rhine and the Weser is called Westphalia. Slavs, that is, Vandals, live across the Elbe. Those in the

---

[1] August Potthast, *Bibliotheca Historica Medii Aevi*, 2 vols. consecutively paginated, 2nd ed. (1896; reprinted Graz, 1957), I, 532–33 [henceforth "Potthast"]; also Henricus Meibom, Jr., ed., *Rerum Germanicarum Tomi III* (Helmstedt, 1688), I, 59 [vol. I of this collection henceforth simply "Meibom"]; cf. also Arno Borst's monumental *Der Turmbau von Babel*, 6 vols. in 7 (Stuttgart, 1957–63), on Gobelinus: III.i, 1021–22.

neighboring lands, Cracovia, Polonia, Bohemia, and Sclavonia, speak Gothic, that is, Sclavonic.[2]

With this as geographic and ethnic background, we may turn to those names and peoples whose origins are known. The Langobards left their island in the Northern Ocean, Scanzia, about the time of the fall of Rome. Their king was known as Agelmund when they still bore the name Winuli. The leaders of the expedition from Scanzia were two brothers, Ibor and Agio. They did battle with the Vandals and Huns upon reaching the mainland. To deceive the enemy, they disguised their women as men by tying their long hair about their faces. Thus the people were called long-beards or Langobards. Some say they received their name personally from their god, Godan, who is the same as Mercury. Those who settled in Rhaetia spoke Greek, but the majority spoke German, that is "Deudsch" in Upper German, "Dudesch" in Lower German. At the time of the exodus, a woman gave birth to seven babes and left them in a pond to drown. The younger Agelmund, son of Agio, rescued the strongest and adopted him, because the infant had grasped his spear. This foundling too was named Agelmund and became king after the death of his adoptive father (Gobelinus I.5 and VI.24, in Meibom, pp. 69 and 217).

The Goths are direct descendents of Magog, son of Japhet and grandson of Noah; Magog's brother Gomer is father of the Gauls and Galatians (Gobelinus II.2, in Meibom, p. 77). Geographically, the Goths originate in Scanzia like the Lombards. About the time when Joseph was in Egypt, the Goths had so increased in number that they were obliged to find new homes. Under their king Berig, they invaded the lands of the Vandals. After his death, they proceeded to Scythia. The Gepidae are the Goths who were too slow and thus were left behind. After the death of King Filimer, Taunasis ruled the Goths and led them to Pontus. Verosis, King of Egypt, instigated a war with the Goths. Taunasis took his men and subjugated all of Africa. In the absence of the men, the women banded together to defend themselves. They elected Lampeto to guard the borders of the homeland and

---

[2] The above paragraph is a loose translation of a section of Gobelinus's Book I (*Aevum Primum*), ch. 5 in Meibom, pp. 66–67. Gobelinus still uses the traditional division of history into the six ages of the history of salvation. His markedly secular interests are not wholly harmonious with the traditional theological conception of history. Readers who are disturbed by the general familiarity of the chorography may be comforted until ch. 4 of this study by the knowledge that Gobelinus cites Isidore of Seville as his source. I generally suppress such information, even when the Renaissance author explicitly acknowledges his debt, in order that I may reserve the medieval tradition for more organic treatment in the later chapters and not present it here in disconnected fragments.

Marpesia to lead an army. The latter marched off to Africa, where she won many victories. En route she and her army delayed in the rocky Caucasus, and there gave her name to the *Saxum Marpesiae*. These are the Amazons whose realms included Ephesus with the temple of Diana famed for its beauty. Gobelinus also describes Penthesilea's arrival at Troy after the death of Hector, and her death and dismemberment at the hands of Pyrrhus (III.18, in Meibom, pp. 109–10).

The origin of the Huns, too, is associated with the Goths. For in the reign of King Filimer, son of Gandaric the Great, the Goths entered Scythia to make war. Some monstrous women, witches, called in the Gothic tongue "Alirunae," fled before the Goths into the woods. They mixed with satyrs and fauns. The resultant offspring were the ferocious Huns. Before their mothers weaned the Hunnish babes, they wounded them to teach them cruelty (Gobelinus III.18 and VI.16, in Meibom, pp. 109 and 205).

The Saxons were the faithful remnants of Alexander the Great's army. After Alexander's death, they despaired of ever returning to their homeland. These Macedonians migrated to the Caucasus. There they sojourned at the *Saxum Marpesiae*, which is the reason they are called Saxons. With three hundred ships they planned to cross the sea. All but a few perished. Of the ships which arrived safely across the waters, eighteen entered Pruzia, and twelve Rügen. Twenty-four came to the mouth of the Elbe, and they are the fathers of the Saxons (Gobelinus V.11, in Meibom, p. 158).

Although Saxon origins seem to be younger than others, the language is foremost among the German tongues. Just as Hebrew is gutteral, Latin dental, and Greek—the foremost of the three sacred languages—palatal, so is High German gutteral, Middle German dental, but Saxon—the foremost of the Teutonic languages—palatal (Gobelinus V.11, in Meibom, p. 159).

The British are known to stem from Brutus, a bastard son of Priam the Great, who fled Troy with a multitude of Trojans. England, however, has its name from a Saxon duke. Hengist and Horsa, who led the Saxons to victory in Britain, were sons of the Duke of Engere or Angaria in Saxony. The variation between "l" and "r" is well known in the Westphalian tongue, as for example between "Engelschen" and "Engerschen." This indicates how England could be named after Engere or Angaria. Others say that this Duke had a daughter called Enghele or Angela, and that England is named in her honor (Gobelinus VI.23, in Meibom, p. 216). The Saxons also gave Burgundy its name, for "Bürge" is a Saxon word, and the Gauls used it to name the Saxons (VI.18, in Meibom, p. 208).

The one certainty about the origin of the Franks is that they come from Troy. All question is removed by the knowledge of Charlemagne's descent from Dardanus. Some say that Phrygas, a brother of Aeneas, fled Troy with a group that elected Francio its leader and named themselves after him (Gobelinus III.21, in Meibom, pp. 113–14). Others say that, after the fall of Troy, they left Phrygia for Pannonia, where they were called Sicambri. There they were pressed into slavery by the Romans. Subsequently, they left Pannonia under their elected king, Priam, and settled along the river Main. They were given their liberty by Emperor Valentinian and so received their name "Franks," that is, the free (VI.16, in Meibom, p. 205).

These are the myths of origin as recounted by Gobelinus Persona. They are all of the fabulous type, with the following exceptions: Gothic and Langobardic origins in Scandinavia, the battles with the "Vandals" upon reaching the mainland, and the general direction of Gothic migration south through "Scythia," Great and Little Russia, to the Black Sea. The Vandals in question are naturally not the Germanic tribe that devastated North Africa in St. Augustine's time. They are rather a hopelessly confused misunderstanding for "Wends," the Slavic people still represented in the Spree forest and the Lausitz province south of Berlin. Vandals, Venedi, and Venethi, among others, in their similarity to "Wendish" aid the confusion which prevails throughout this period. Historically reliable sources tell of numerous battles between Germanic invaders and Slavic inhabitants in the territories east of the Elbe. The reader's attention is also called to the first myth about the origin of the Prussians with the eighteen ships of the Macedonians.

In the fabulous, non-historical category, there are no heroes of any consequence who had not appeared in the preceding discussion of origins. Several heroic figures from the dawn of relatively certain Germanic history are mentioned by Gobelinus, although he makes no distinction between the real and the fabulous. He tells us that Julius Caesar, who is real enough, founded the city of Jülich between Cologne and Aachen (V.18, in Meibom, p. 171). Caesar apparently had enough time to urbanize the larger part of the Rhine at his leisure. Gobelinus has a peculiar sensitivity to the hybrid of mythical and real history as it appears in Caesar's founding of cities. The hybrid flourished particularly in the history of the Mediterranean Germans of late antiquity. Gobelinus expresses considerable interest in this period, stimulated partly no doubt, by the availability of sources. But his interest may have an additional explanation. For a fifteenth-century historian, Gobelinus is an extraordinarily alert observer of vernacular phenomena; he is exceptional indeed in reporting in learned Latin what he heard in vulgar German. It happens that the vernacular of the fifteenth century provides a disproportionate number of surviving Germanic heroic epics. The so-called *Heldenbuch* was in wide circulation in the period. It contains degenerate forms of ancient song cycles about Theodoric, Clovis, Walther of Aquitaine, and Attila, as well as themes of Ostrogothic, Frankish, Visigothic, and Burgundian provenance, not to mention Norse, Celtic, Russian, and oriental elements. Gobelinus was surely familiar with these tales, although he may have rejected them as too confused and fantastic. The kernel of truth in them springs largely from the history of southern Germanic tribes in the fourth through sixth centuries: the Burgundians, the Goths, and the Franks, in their difficulties with the Huns and among themselves. Gobelinus may well have detected the importance of these events to the poetic-historical imagination of his countrymen.

He tells of the Gothic king Hermanricus, who was in his time favorably compared to Alexander the Great and whose bravery kept King Balambus of the Huns from attacking the Goths—an assault they dared only after the death of Hermanricus (Gobelinus VI.16, in Meibom, p. 205). The line between pure fantasy and uncertain early history passes through the Merovingian family tree at the point where Marcomir, who seems to be historical, appears as the son of Priam, who seems to be imaginary. Marcomir is supposed to have ruled the Franks in the time of Theodosius, 379–95 A.D. (VI.1, in Meibom, p. 210). From this time forward, Germanic nations came into such painfully close contact with the civilized world that few ancient historical writers could ignore their presence altogether. Heroic figures, whose reality we cannot but whose heroism we might question, began to appear with regularity. From these reports, Gobelinus takes the activities of Alaric of the Visigoths, Gunder of the Vandals, Ermanric of the Swabians, and their battles with Rome.[3] Faramundus, Clodius, Merovingus, and Hilderic of the Franks, and Thorismund and Theodomer of the Goths, among many others, appear in the chronicle, but are of lesser importance than Theodoric the Great (VI.23–24, in Meibom, pp. 215–18).

---

[3] Gobelinus VI.22, in Meibom, p. 213. It is exceedingly difficult to evaluate the interminable reports, both in Gobelinus and elsewhere, about the interminable wars between Rome and the Germanic invaders. Apparent preoccupation with these hostilities is best explained by the simple fact that Germanic history was non-existent for the Middle Ages outside Germanic confrontation with the Roman world. To write about the ancient Germans was to write about their wars with the Romans. Further extrapolations are hazardous in the extreme.

In addition to the vernacular traditions, a dual Latin evaluation proceeded from late antiquity to preserve the memory of Theodoric. One was a fairly objective part of secular history; the other, a traumatic recollection of a powerful Arian heretic and Germanic monarch by orthodox and Roman religious history. Gobelinus preserved them both. While Zeno was Emperor in the East, the Goths were devastating Illyria and Thrace. Zeno made a peace with Theodoric, King of the Goths, and sent him against Odoacer in Italy. Theodoric was victorious and established his capital in Ravenna (Gobelinus VI.24, in Meibom, pp. 217–18). This represents the secular history with a slight admixture of the vernacular traditions. The religious viewpoint appears when Gobelinus judges Theodoric as an enemy of orthodoxy. He had the great Boethius murdered, as well as the Roman Patrician Symmachus and Pope John. Shortly after all his murders, Theodoric himself died; later, a saintly man, Solitarius by name, saw Theodoric's soul cast into the mouth of a Sicilian volcano, while Symmachus and John looked on (VI.26, in Meibom, p. 220).

Gobelinus's early history then moves on to the Franks with remarkable insight into their importance for the development of the Christian West. A contemporary of Theodoric was Clodovaeus, son of Hilderic and King of the Franks. Clodovaeus (Clovis) held all of Thuringia and Franconia, that is East Francia, and a large part of Gaul, that is West Francia. From Chilperic, King of Burgundy, Clodovaeus received the royal daughter Dochilt to wife. She was Christian, and on her account the King and all the Franks were converted to Christianity (Gobelinus VI.24, in Meibom, p. 218). The Franks were, of course, already nominally Christian, but of the Arian variety. The epoch-making significance of this conversion has been recognized. The Franks were no longer in religious conflict with the heirs of Roman culture in the conquered lands. The decay of Germanic power in the rest of Roman Europe was attributable in part to the disharmony between Arian conqueror and orthodox substrate. Roman orthodoxy and Frankish ambition supported one another and laid the political foundation for medieval Europe, at least on the continent. Without the Franks, Roman orthodoxy might not have prevailed in Europe; without Roman orthodoxy, the Franks might have gone the way of the Goths, a historical memory but not a formative historical force.

An intuitive grasp of this underlies Gobelinus's description of the increasing power of the Franks. Chilperic, and after him Carloman, led the nation. Carloman subdued Brabant. His son Pippin is ancestor of the dukes of Brabant. In the meantime, the Langobards in the company of the Saxons marched into Italy. Later, the Langobards inter-married with the Bavarians (Gobelinus VI.27–29, in Meibom, pp. 221–23). All the while, the Franks were consolidating their gains in the North, until Charles Martel held sway over the Saxons, Bavarians, Swabians, Frisians, Burgundians, and—despite the patent anachron-ism—Lotharingians. At this time, St. Boniface preached in Germany (VI.37, in Meibom pp. 233–34).

Charlemagne, Charles Martel's great descendant, among his other deeds named Frankfurt on the Main. While in retreat from the pagan Saxons, he forded the Main with his Frankish army, whence Frank-furt. When criticized for his withdrawal, Charlemagne announced that it was better to say that Charles fled before his enemies than to say that he was killed by them (Gobelinus VI.38, in Meibom, pp. 236–37). Charlemagne finally conquered the Saxons for Christianity. In order to maintain their orthodoxy, he established in Westphalia a secret court called "Frigeding" ("Fehmgericht," kangaroo court). This court could try, condemn, and execute reverted pagans without their ever learning the judgment.[4] Charlemagne performed notable services also for learning. He transferred the *Studium* to Paris from Rome, whither the Romans had brought it from Greece. The great Charles was hon-ored by princes from all over the world for his power and achieve-ments. Aaron, King of the Persians, for example, sent an elephant among other magnificent gifts to Charles at Aachen (VI.40, in Mei-bom, p. 240). The Aaron in question is Harun al-Rashid, Caliph of Baghdad.

The history of the Empire records the glory of the Carolingians and Ottonians that rests on the learned flowering represented by Einhard and Hrabanus, on the ecclesiastical reforms of Louis the Pious, and on the military victories of the Ottos (Gobelinus VI.41, 48, in Meibom, pp. 241–42 and 248ff.). Gobelinus moves through his imperial history chronologically, attaching no unusual mythical aura to the Emperors before Frederick II Hohenstaufen. He calls him *Draco Magnus*, the Great Dragon, and Antichrist and places on his lips the story of the three impostors, Moses, Mohammed, and Christ (VI.64, in Meibom, p. 278); but more of that later, in connection with other authors and other works.

These then are some of the heroes, fabulous and real, whom Gobe-linus takes out of the mythical past to people his history of the world.

---

4 Gobelinus I.5, in Meibom, p. 67. On the subject of the *Fehmgericht*, cf. Jacob Grimm, *Deutsche Rechtsaltertümer*, 2 vols., 4th ed. (1899; Darmstadt, 1965), II, 457–59, and bibliography, p. 685 s.v. "Wigand." It is known to musicology in the form of an opera by Berlioz.

It was, of course, necessary for him to dwell on the deeds of Charlemagne. One detects, however, some regret that it had to be the Saxons whom Charles had defeated, for Gobelinus was obviously quite partial to them. When discussing the ancient religion of the Germans, Gobelinus mentions only the customs of the Saxons or uses Saxon forms of wider German practices.

The weekdays, he tells us, reflect the ancient Germans' belief in the planets as gods. The days of the sun and of the moon, "Sunnentag" and "Manentag," show that these celestial bodies were worshiped. The day of Mars is called "Dingestag." Among the ancient Germans "Ding" meant judgment, as is apparent in words such as "Frigeding." Since Mars was thought to be the executor of capital punishment, he was honored in the name of "Dingestag." The day of Mercury is called "Godensdag" or "Wodensdag" or, by syncope, "Woanstag." (This philological term is Gobelinus's and not mine.) We know that among the Langobards Mercury and Wotan were equivalent. When the Saxons returned from their Italian sojourn with the Langobards they brought this usage back with them (cf. Gobelinus VI.24, in Meibom, p. 217). Jove's day is called "Donnerstag," in honor of Jove's thunderous activity. Venus's day is called "Fritage" because Freyge (or Freia) was the same as Venus among the pagan Germans. Gobelinus knew the word "frien" ("freien," in modern times more or less an equivalent of English "to woo"), which seemed to have referred to Venus's favorite pastime. The day of Saturn is variously called "Sonnenavend," by corruption "Sunnavend," and "Sambstag" or "Satertag." The former names indicate an honoring of the sun even on the eve of Sunday. The latter names contain the name of Saturn (II.4, in Meibom, p. 81). Gobelinus was a better philologist than he could have known. His explanations were sound, except that they said nothing accurate about ancient Germanic worship. His critical and receptive ear to dialect variations was most unusual. He must have learned this from personal experience, since it is difficult to imagine a written authority in this period who would have bothered with such information. Gathering of first-hand evidence for a description of the remote past is not in the manner of a medieval historian, even though Gobelinus is strongly indebted to traditional historical writing. Like any real transitional figure, he straddles the two eras with unqualified adherence to authority binding him to the Middle Ages and free expansion of knowledge from personal observation binding him to the Renaissance.

To return to the religion of the ancient Germans, or more properly Saxons, Gobelinus reports that the Saxons celebrated a pagan ritual in the autumn to honor their fallen dead. This usage was taken over into All Saints and All Souls days (Gobelinus V.11, in Meibom, p. 159). What an extraordinary observation for Gobelinus to have made! During the wars on the pagan Saxons, Charlemagne captured and destroyed a sanctuary of theirs called "Irmenseul," that is, the column or image of Hermes. Hermes is the Greek form of Mercury, which along with the palatal character of the Saxon language proves their Greek origins from Alexander's army. In a rather funny and slightly bawdy linguistic excursus, Gobelinus explains how "Heresberg" and "Mersberg" reveal the Saxons' cult of Hermes and Hera, the Greek Juno. The differences between the Greek and Saxon forms result largely from tintinnabulation and corruption (the terminology is again Gobelinus's). Hera's "berg" can be discovered in "Mersberg" by observing the phrase, "Ick ga tho dem Eresberge," which can easily slide into "Ik ga tho dem Mersberge."[5]

The linguistic observations of Gobelinus are tantalizing in their originality and quasi-correctness; but his account of ancient Germanic religion leaves more to be desired. The only approximately accurate details known to him were the names of Wotan and Freia. Perhaps it is exceptional enough for even these to have survived the storms of Christianization. Gobelinus has forgotten that there is a separate identity for the god of thunder. On the other hand, his explanation for Tuesday comes remarkably close to modern theory. In "Ding" recent philologists see a reference to an attribute of Mars understood as German Tiu, the god who presided over the "Thing," the diet, which was both council and court of judgment.[6]

Gobelinus is not quite so moralizing an author as many others. He normally does not state his views on ancient virtue and vice outright. In consequence, implications must be drawn from his descriptions. There is little other than his praise for the Saxon language to indicate whether he approves or disapproves of anything he describes. He characterizes ancient German-Germanic activity as warlike, and that seems to be the most important quality common to all the old Germans. The first fuller description of Germans in the "Sixth Age" covers the attack of the Germans and Alani during the reign of Valerian (253–59 A.D.), when the Germans took Gaul and came as far as Ravenna (Gobelinus VI.11, in Meibom, p. 197). We may assume that Gobelinus considered this "virtuous." He certainly considered virtuous

---

[5] Gobelinus VI.38, in Meibom, p. 235–36. This is surely one of the earliest instances of transformational grammar, not, however, of the questionable practice of employing descriptive linguistic laws to prove ethnic relations.

[6] R. Priebsch and W. E. Collinson, *The German Language*, 6th ed. (London, 1966), p. 30.

the freedom implied by the name of the Franks (III.21 and VI.16, in Meibom, pp. 113–14 and 205). Peaceful virtue was seen by Gobelinus, if anywhere, only in the suffering of the 11,000 virgins martyred by the Huns at Cologne, although he seems to cast some doubt on the literal truth of the legend (VI.23, in Meibom, p. 214). Gobelinus may have disapproved of the German ignorance of letters before Christianity and may have disapproved of it sufficiently to think of it as a vice (I.5, in Meibom, p. 66). But he says even less of vice than he says of virtue.

The myth of the *Imperium* is a more complex issue in Gobelinus than his myths of origin, heroes, or ancient religion. It has in common with the myths of virtue and vice that it is implicit in the text. It is, however, much more pervasive. Gobelinus is not at all a theoretician of the Empire, but one who simply accepts the myth as an everyday reality. He ignores the opportunity taken by others of associating the alliance of Rome with Germanic tribes against the Huns (Gobelinus VI.23, in Meibom, p. 214) with the later possession of the *Imperium* by the Germans. Nor does he see any contradiction in declaring on the one hand that Augustus's Empire perished with Odoacer's defeat of Augustulus (VI.24, in Meibom, p. 217), and on the other that Augustus's Empire was very much alive at Charlemagne's coronation by Pope Leo (VI.38, in Meibom, p. 239). Gobelinus knew that there was no difference between Augustus's Empire and the medieval Empire, except that the Franks held what the Romans, or later the Greeks in Constantinople held. With Otto the Great, Gobelinus declares that the *Imperium Romanum* was transferred to the Saxons. It was, in any case, the Roman Empire, and it was, in any case, in the hands of the Germans (VI.48, in Meibom, p. 250).

Among the activities of the Emperors was their waging war on pagans or other enemies of the Church, be they Lombards or Slavs (Gobelinus VI.42 and 48, in Meibom, pp. 243 and 249–50). Otto III, Gobelinus believed, established the College of Imperial Electors. It contained the lay Electors: first, the Margrave of Brandenburg, who was Imperial Chamberlain; second, the Palatine Duke of the Rhine, who was Imperial Steward; third, the Duke of Saxony, who was Imperial Sword-bearer and Marshal; and fourth, the Duke and later King of Bohemia, who was Imperial Cup-bearer. The remaining members were the ecclesiastical Electors: first, the Archbishop of Mainz, who was Imperial Chancellor for Germany; second, the Archbishop of Trier, who was Imperial Chancellor for Gaul; and third, the Archbishop of Cologne, who was Imperial Chancellor for Italy (VI.50, in Meibom, pp. 252–53). One must be sure to understand that these chancellery titles did not indicate ambassadors to the territories named, but rather ministers or plenipotentiaries who, at least theoretically, wielded real power over their countries. Occasionally, the power was more than theoretical, but that is unimportant here. What is important is Gobelinus's clear acceptance of the *Imperium* as a political institution which transcended nations.

In sum, Gobelinus must have felt about the Empire, first, that there was no fundamental difference between Frankish or Saxon possession and Roman or Greek possession, second, that it was now in German hands, third, that its function was largely religious, and fourth, that it was superior to nations. The skeletal pattern of these views will reappear and fill out as we progress through the century. Actually, the myths had been fully and finally established well before Gobelinus and any of the authors discussed here who either used them or simply lived with them.

At least one aspect of the myth of the *Imperium* is highlighted by Ulrich von Richental (died after 1438), a contemporary and close analogue to Gobelinus. Ulrich's spirited chronicle of the Council of Constance gives us a brief report about the Imperial Electors, including their weighty titles. The Archbishop of Cologne, for example, appears as Arch-Chancellor of the Holy Roman Empire for Italy, Lombardy, the Empire of the Greeks, and the kingdoms beyond the sea: ". . . to him they owe fealty, should the Empire suffer dangers."[7] Ulrich was no propagandizer of the Empire and its myth; his reports are distinctly naive and unprogrammatic. He simply relates what seem to him to be the facts. The Holy Roman Empire's suzerainty over other kingdoms and even empires is the way of the world for Ulrich.

The supremacy and, what is more important, the sanctity of the Empire permeate a lengthy historical song by a contemporary of Ul-

---

[7] Michael Richard Buck, ed., *Ulrich von Richenthal: Chronik des Constanzer Conzils, 1414–1418,* BLVS, CLVIII (Tübingen, 1882), pp. 15–16. The Council must have been a magnificent assembly, with representatives as exotic as the Duke of Smolensk, not to mention the Archbishop of Kiev. And all of this in what was, after all, an Alpine village. See pp. 138–41 for a fascinating eye-witness account of the celebration of the Byzantine liturgy at an inn near Constance. The chronicle is most famous for its description of the executions of Jan Hus and Jerome of Prague (pp. 76–83). The chronicle survives in several manuscripts and was thrice printed in the Renaissance, in 1483, 1536, 1575 (cf. Potthast, p. 1080).

rich: "Des conzils grundveste," written in 1418 by one THOMAS
PRISCHUH of Augsburg. He is thought to have been a minstrel, but if
so, then one with a scholar's command of the magic and apocalyptic
literature of his age, a literature in which the myth of the Empire
plays a vital part.[8] Prischuh reports the prophecies of Brother Lucas,
General of the Order of St. Bridget. Among them is one saying that
Sigismund would win the Holy Sepulchre ("Grundveste" ll. 483–500).
This is a prerequisite for the end of the world as it was regarded in
this period. The task is significantly placed in the hands of the reigning Emperor. Prischuh makes it clear that the Emperor is the captain
of Christendom. His duty and power permit and require him to sum-
mon a council to heal the breach in the Church (ll. 53–58). Of all the
kings and their representatives, the Roman King is first (ll. 719–88).
The majesty of his kingship is the highest in the world (ll. 1499–1503).
His prime desire and responsibility is the restoration of unity on earth
(ll. 115–18, 789–94). Sigismund is to accomplish this with the revival
of the law which forbids the election of a pope without the consent
of the Roman King (ll. 1494–98). In his encomium of the Emperor,
Thomas Prischuh compares him to the Good Shepherd (ll. 1555–58).
In his prayers for him, the minstrel calls upon God to give Sigismund
the various virtues of Abraham, David, Moses, Joshua, Gideon, Judas
Macchabeus, and—without any transition or distinction—Charlemagne (ll. 1615–24). The sanctity of the Empire could hardly be more
emphatically expressed. At the time of the Council of Constance something had to be sacred, since the Church could hardly have been
expected to fulfill that function with its many political troubles.

The next great gathering of Christendom, at Basel in 1431 (lingering
on to 1449), was the occasion for a document that dealt intensively
with the problems of the Empire, revealing, among other things, more
about the myth of the *Imperium*. NICOLAUS OF CUSA (1401–64), the
first German humanist of European reputation, wrote his *Concordantia
Catholica* in Basel from 1431 to 1433. His humanist credentials include the discovery of a Plautus codex and possible involvement with

---

[8] Rochus von Liliencron, ed., *Die historischen Volkslieder der Deutschen vom
13. bis 16. Jahrhundert*, 4 vols. and Appendix (Leipzig, 1865–69), I, 228–57. Thomas
Prischuh knows of the magic book of Solomon (ll. 581–612), of various "-mancies"
(ll. 617–42), of the alchemy of Arnald of Villanova (ll. 673–81), of the prophecies of
Joachim of Fiore (ll. 141–48, 997–1018), and of Hildegard of Bingen (ll. 1266–69).
Cf. Ulrich Paul, *Studien zur Geschichte des deutschen Nationalbewusstseins im
Zeitalter des Humanismus und der Reformation*, Historische Studien, CCXCVIII
(Berlin, 1936), p. 16 [henceforth "Paul, *Studien*"].

the discovery of Tacitus.[9] Cusanus enjoyed a high reputation even among the Italians of his time, a rare accomplishment for a German. He is a fascinating figure, and his writings are varied and complex. Here, however, we consider only a fragment of his thinking, letting the texts speak for themselves. Since his political and historical suggestions are, generally speaking, traditional, they may be regarded as typical of the historical imagination of northern humanism.

Cusanus's presentation would also be a particularly felicitous introduction to the myth of the Empire. Not only the authority of so distinguished a figure as Cusanus but also the extremity of his position dramatize for a modern world weaned on *Realpolitik* the meaning and importance historical myth in general and the Empire myth in particular had for the past.[10] Behold, the Emperor of the Christians is vicar in the office of Christ, as King of Kings and Lord of Dominions, and his Empire surpasses all others for it is closest to God (*Concordantia* III.5.341–42, in Kallen, pp. 354–55). In antiquity, the Emperor enjoyed the title of *Pontifex Maximus* because of his concern for religion; the concern, if not the title, carries into the present. Just as the Pope exerts power first over Rome as its Bishop and then over the Universal Church as Patriarch, so the Emperor rules immediately over those subject to the Empire and then through kings and princes who must acknowledge his primacy (III.7.349, in Kallen, pp. 360–61). The Emperor is the Prince and Lord of the world, and everything is in his power—indeed even the Pope is not above him in matters of the Empire (III.5.340, in Kallen, p. 353). Correspondingly, the Empire is advocate of the Universal Church and has the responsibility of maintaining law and guarding the orthodox faith (III.7.351, in Kallen, p. 361). The Emperor is Constantine reborn, the successor of Justinian, the protector of the faith, and the protector of the law (III.7.354–56, in Kallen, p. 363). The success of the Empire's sacred

---

9 Andreas Posch, *Die "Concordantia Catholica" des Nikolaus von Cusa*, Görresgesellschaft ... Sektion für Rechts- und Staats wissenschaft, LIV (Paderborn, 1930), p. 16. A spirited biographical sketch of Cusanus, one which, however, merits the traditional "cave!" is Ludwig Pralle, *Die Wiederentdeckung des Tacitus: ein Beitrag zur Geistesgeschichte Fuldas und zur Biographie des jungen Cusanus*, Quellen und Abhandlungen zur Geschichte der Abtei und der Diözese Fulda, XVII (Fulda, 1952), pp. 16ff., 65, 68, 70, 84–85, 92. Cited as "Kallen" is the new critical edition in progress, Gerhardus Kallen, ed., *De Concordantia Catholica*, Nicolai de Cusa Opera Omnia, XIV (Hamburg, 1959–65). Only Book III is used, which formulates the theory of the Empire.

10 Even a study as cautious as Morimichi Watanabe's *The Political Ideas of Nicholas of Cusa with special reference to his "De Concordantia Catholica,"* Travaux d'Humanisme et Renaissance, LVIII (Geneva, 1963), pp. 115ff. and passim, insists on judging the Empire in terms of "Realpolitik," suggesting anachronism for other opinions.

mission has been illustrated in the conversion of the Hungarians, Danes, Bohemians, and Prussians, all of whom came into the Church because the Empire acknowledged its custody of the faith (III.26.485, in Kallen, p. 427). As the *Sacerdotium* is the soul of Christendom, the *Imperium* is its body, and the head of the body is the Emperor (III.1.292 and III.41.580, in Kallen, pp. 327 and 466–67). Thus Cusanus begins and ends his book on the Empire in the *Concordantia Catholica*.[11]

Four elements, as I have suggested, combine to make the myth of the *Imperium*: the medieval Empire *is* the Roman Empire of antiquity; it and its functions are sacred, almost sacramental; it is now in the hands of the Germans; and the Emperor is the first monarch of the world, and the Empire is above all realms. Cusanus affirms the initial component, at first tacitly, by failing to distinguish in any way between the *Imperium Romanum* and the medieval Empire. One major problem of the tract expressly betrays acceptance of the identity of ancient and medieval Empires: was the *Imperium Romanum* in truth transferred from the Greeks to the Germans in the person of Charlemagne? Cusanus assures us that it is a most popular opinion (*opinio vulgatissima*) that Charlemagne received the Empire. Some say that he was hailed Emperor. The fact of the matter is that he was called *Patricius* (*Concordantia* III.3.313, in Kallen, pp. 337–38). The first in recent times properly to be called Emperor was Otto I, who won the title basically by force of arms and by the will of the Roman people (III.3.322, in Kallen, p. 343). Charles or Otto in either case— it was the *Imperium Romanum* which changed hands. The same issue affirms the second component of the imperial myth, for in either case, the Empire was received by Germans. Cusanus goes so far as to call it the *Imperium Germanicum* (III.32.507, in Kallen, p. 438).

The reasons for the Cardinal's views on Otto include an anticipation of the argument that the Empire was granted by papal donation. It was a weighty canonical argument, and Cusanus had to confront or evade it in order to guarantee imperial independence of the papacy. Independence of the papacy did not, however, imply independence of the *sacerdotium*, as witness imperial proselytizing of pagan peoples and imperial custody of the faith. These were intended by Cusanus to affirm the sacred duty of the Empire. His statement on the primacy of

---

[11] Andreas Posch's commentary on the above material is most helpful, esp. pp. 180, 187, 205–206. My own presentation of the imperial myth in Cusanus is intentionally one-sided. The Cardinal knew that the Empire was in serious difficulty and not at all living up to the ideals he described (III.32.507, in Kallen, p. 438). For the complementary historian's view cf. Watanabe, pp. 136–44.

the Empire and on the Emperor as *caput mundi* is almost too un-equivocal to require comment. His view of the social structure of the world permits nothing but this conclusion: social order ascends through counts, marquises, dukes, and kings *usque in caesareum caput*, up to the imperial head (III.1.292, in Kallen, p. 327).

The great Cardinal's opinion of Otto as the first German to be invested with the Empire is not unique and has an old tradition. His position is, however, a minority one. As far as most medieval and Renaissance men were concerned, Charlemagne was the first to rule the Empire in recent times. Since most Germans considered Charlemagne a countryman, this in no way diminished the German character of the Empire. In his zeal to confirm the sacred stamp of the Empire, Cusanus again joins a minority tradition in regarding Frederick II as a warrior for the Church and worthy of praise for his defense (*propugnatio*) of the faith (*Concordantia* III.41.576, in Kallen, p. 465).

Although this discussion has centered on the myth of the *Imperium*, Cusanus's work touches in passing on several other myths of the German past. He clearly saw in the German winners of the Empire the virtues of warlikeness and piety, which made them fit defenders of both the Church and the Empire. Nothing of the ancient religion of the Germans appears and little of the fabulous heroes of the German past.[12] He recognizes, however, many of the real mythical heroes: Charlemagne, Otto I, and Frederick II have already been mentioned. On all of them Cusanus imposes a strong charismatic aura. He also touches on Hugh of St. Victor, claiming him for Germany, *noster excellentissimus Saxo* (*Concordantia* III.39.558, in Kallen, p. 456), so that not all heroic figures be political, but that a man of learning take his place among them.

While maintaining the supra-nationality of the Empire, the *Concordantia Catholica* is, in a sense, a nationalistic work. Few Germans of the Renaissance could distinguish between the notions of a national German state and an international Empire. Patriotism, thus, expressed itself paradoxically in provincialism as well as the traditional affirmation of the Empire. Cusanus is the first in the Renaissance to relate the story of the founding of Trier, the metropolis of his native district.

---

12 Cusanus, like many of his predecessors, mentions Prester John (III.6.345, in Kallen, p. 358), but Prester John is not German or, let us say, only few claims to that effect can be found. Cf. ch. III of this study, under the Alsatian Anonymous and Naucler. Prester John appears in the historical writing as often as any unquestionably historical figure following his debut in Otto of Freising's chronicle on through the Renaissance. Watanabe, p. 132 note 12, mentions recent bibliography on the subject.

After the death of Ninus, King of the Assyrians, Semiramis, his Queen, took the reins of the state. Fearing the illicit designs of his step-mother, Trebata the son of Ninus, fled to Europe and founded Trier. This occurred in the forty-second year after the birth of Abraham (*Concordantia* III. Prooemium.280, in Kallen, p. 320). The emergence of a form of national self-consciousness is one of the primary characteristics of the Renaissance in Germany. It lies at the roots of the flourishing interest in the mythical past. Cusanus is not nationalist in the sense of the next generation of German humanists—Wimpheling, Celtis, and Bebel, for example. But his political awareness faces the same dilemma, and, like the more strictly patriotic authors, he grasps both horns, the Empire and the province, leaving the idea of a German national state in a limbo between the two.

This all too brief survey of Nicolaus Cusanus's contributions to the myths of the German past shows little that is unusual. His mention of Prussia, its supposed conversion under imperial auspices, and the implication of its absorption into the Empire reflect German interest in the East, characteristic of middle-European politics since the days of Charlemagne and particularly the Ottos. If his argument represents awareness of this trend, it is a sign of considerable historical sophistication. Cusanus also appears to be exceptionally incisive when he argues for the Ottonian succession to the Empire. From the viewpoint of modern political geography, the medieval Empire is more directly traceable to Otto than to Charlemagne. In both cases, as to the "Ostpolitik" and the foundation of the Empire, Cusanus seems to be well ahead of his time. However, to see him so would be a serious misinterpretation. He discusses both issues in the unconditional service of the papal–imperial dispute, obviously on the side of the medieval Empire. Cusanus shares this preoccupation and partisanship with the majority of his German contemporaries.

Cusanus does point to the future of German historical writing in another way, not involving content so much as method. When he defended the Ottonian succession to the Empire, he attacked as most popular, with a hint of "common" or "unlearned," the belief in the Carolingian succession. The critical rejection of one myth in order to support and give greater credibility to another becomes one of the most common techniques of Renaissance historical writing in the North. The rejection is usually more heated than this example from Cusanus. The old myth, in the opinion of the critic, was normally not only wrong, but positively nonsensical. To a modern reader, however, the new myth may be as nonsensical as the old one, or more so. This is the practice to which I referred in the introductory chapter as a factor in the proliferation and eventual demise of most Renaissance myths of the German past. For the sake of simplicity I shall call this conventional practice "the topos of critical rejection" or, by its medieval name, *anasceua*.[13] It seems to be one aspect of the presumably new and presumably more rational standards which the Renaissance is supposed to have applied to its world. It happens not to be altogether new. And for whatever rational implications it might have had, the topos and the assumptions behind it more clearly demonstrate the exercise of imagination than that of critical reason.

It is precisely fertile imagination that characterizes the minor texts and authors whose contributions complement the opinions of Cusanus and prepare the way for the more comprehensive mythical view of Cusanus's friend in humanism, religion, and reform, Aeneas Sylvius Piccolomini. The provincialism which Cusanus seems to have heralded in his story of the founding of Trier was, in fact, one voice in a vast chorus. Gobelinus Persona's predilections for Saxony represent the same inclination even though, like Cusanus, his proper object of study was more universal. Alongside Gobelinus and Cusanus stand a numerical majority of German historical writers whose interests are solely provincial. One such is NICOLAUS GRILL who, writing about 1428, described for the first time in our period the fabulous origins of the Bavarians. After the deluge, their nation left Armenia under the leadership of their prince Barbarus. They moved west and drove out the inhabitants of the new land which they eventually settled. It was named "Barbariaz," in honor of their prince.[14]

ANDREAS VON REGENSBURG, once called the "Bavarian Livy" (died after 1439), confirms the Armenian origins of the Bavarians in much the same manner as Nicolaus Grill. Andreas adds that the district was only later called Noricum, after Hercules's son Norix, who founded Regensburg. An alternate version names Boamund and Ingram as the heroes who led the nation out of Armenia. Their immediate successors were the princes Adelger and Theo. The Bavarians were without a king until Garibaldus, who flourished in the reign of the second

---

[13] See my "The Topos of Critical Rejection in the Renaissance," *MLN*, LXXXI (October 1966), 476–88.

[14] K. T. Heigel, ed., "Mühldorfer Annalen," in *Chroniken der deutschen Städte*, XV (Leipzig, 1878), p. 381.

Tiberius (581 A.D.).[15] Andreas informs us also of the origins of the Franks, that they stem from Troy and moved west over the Maeotian Swamps. For aiding Emperor Valentinian against the Alani, they were granted ten years of freedom from tribute, whence they are called Franks, that is, free (*Andreas*, pp. 441–42). The fact that Charlemagne's forefather Angisus, father of Pippin the Fat, was named after Aeneas's father Anchises also attests to the Trojan origin of the Franks. Many Bavarian princes trace their lineage from this Angisus (*Andreas*, p. 511). This is a clear case of inter-provincial borrowing. Andreas repeatedly taps the traditions of the Franks, not in their honor, however, but in the service of Bavarian mythical history and the interests of the Empire. Like Cusanus, Andreas clings to the horns of the provincial and the imperial.

His heroic figures, regardless of their provenance in the tradition, are somehow related to the Bavarian line. These include fabulous and real heroes whose names are, again, more easily associated with the Franks. An example is Salegast, who formulated Salic Law (*Andreas*, p. 10). Charlemagne's ancestors perform similar roles in Bavarian history, when Andreas relates the story of Charles Martel's birth. A messenger brought Pippin the happy news with the words: "Vivat rex quia karolus est," which translates, "Long live the King for he is a robust man." "Karolus," Andreas assures us, means "robust man." By this Pippin knew that he was father of a son, and he thought it a good name to give to his heir (*Andreas*, p. 19 and note 1). The etymology is, incidentally, accurate.

Of ancient religions, Andreas mentions only the worship of Cycza near the city of Augsburg. An idol had been dedicated to her there. Andreas is convinced that the curious name of the goddess conceals the Roman goddess of love in her epiphany as *Venus Cypria*. His derivation seems to be less successful this time.[16] The vicinity of Augsburg is said also to be the setting of the great defeat of Quintilius Varus (*Andreas*, pp. 6–7). Like Gobelinus, Andreas of Regensburg ignores the questions of virtue and vice in historical matters.

As with all the present authors, the aura of the *Imperium* hovers

---

[15] Potthast, p. 44. Georg Leidinger, ed., *Andreas von Regensburg: Sämtliche Werke*, Quellen und Erörterungen zur bayerschen und deutschen Geschichte, N.F., vol. I (Munich, 1903), pp. 507–8 and 592ff. Cf. Borst, III.i, 1031.

[16] *Andreas*, p. 7. On this goddess, see Jacob Grimm, *Deutsche Mythologie*, 3 vols., 4th ed. (1875; reprinted Darmstadt, 1965), I, 242–48. There seems indeed to have been such a goddess, Slavic in origin, however, not Germanic, and in truth a patron of grain: W. Sturmfels, *Etymologisches Wörterbuch deutscher und fremdländischer Ortsnamen*, 2nd ed. (Bonn, 1930), p. 155, s.v. "Zeitz."

over the whole of Andreas's conception of the history of government. His chronicle of the Emperors naturally begins with the first Caesars, Julius and Augustus (*Andreas*, pp. 5ff.), and continues through Charlemagne and the Ottos (pp. 29ff.). If this alone does not satisfy the continuity of ancient and medieval Empires, Andreas's treatment of the history of Augsburg does. For Tiberius and Charles IV are considered without distinction of title in connection with the privileges of that Bavarian city (p. 8).

The question of the German possession of the Empire is in Andreas both simple and complex. He harbors no doubt that the Germans now hold the Empire, but he joins Cusanus in the minority tradition that they did not receive it until Otto I. In contrast to Cusanus, Andreas avoids the title *Patricius* and suggests a line of transfers of power—*translationes*—preceding Otto: from the Greeks to the Franks, from the Franks to the Italians, from the Italians to the Gauls, and from the Gauls to the Germans (*Andreas*, pp. 29–30). Andreas's description is far more accurate than the traditional notions of the translations of the Empire. It reproduces the main lines of Carolingian imperial politics, from the coronation of Charles, past the division of the Empire, to the death of Berengar (962 A.D.). Despite its accuracy, this version was eventually suppressed in Germany, since it implies that Italian and "Gallic" claims to the Empire could be as firmly rooted as the German. Andreas himself probably intended no such interpretation. If anything, he saw in the history of the *translationes* the eventual suzerainty of the Empire over Gaul, Italy, and Germany, as mirrored in the titles of the ecclesiatical electors. An apparent ambiguity remains in the terms "Franci" and "Gallici." They are perhaps best translated as "Frankish" and "French." For Andreas, the Empire came to the Franks with Charlemagne, and later went to the French. If the western branches of the Carolingian family are considered French, his observation is accurate. In no case would he call Charlemagne French or Gallic. This is almost unthinkable for a fifteenth-century author with national or provincial self-consciousness sufficient to write a chronicle of Bavaria. Andreas excludes any possibility of misinterpretation by giving Charlemagne a German birthplace, Ingelheim (p. 31). The complexity of the national pseudo-issues are eventually driven out by the simplicity of the imperial myth: whatever the meanderings of the genealogy, the line of the Emperors was ultimately German.

The sacred mission of the Empire confronts fewer difficulties of interpretation in Andreas, since he simply describes the efforts of the Emperors as defenders of the Church. Otto III, for example, won by his victories against the infidel the title, "pale death of the Saracens."[17] The Empire's final efforts in behalf of the Church also find a place in Andreas's writings. The Empire will not only survive until the end of the world, the end of the world depends on the life-span of the Empire. The same number of years remains to the world and to the Empire. As given in the Middle Ages and the Renaissance, this number is usually not very great, and the Empire thus assumes more immediate importance to the life of the pious. The last man to rule the world will be a Roman Emperor, and his name will be Frederick, says the Sibyl (*Andreas*, pp. 481 and 577). His deeds will include the winning of the Holy Land and the reform of the Church. No one knows which Frederick this will be. The almost mystical significance of the Empire begins to emerge: in Cusanus, the Empire was closest to God and complemented His Church; in Andreas, the mysterious Sibyl reveals its eschatological function.

The place of Andreas in fifteenth-century German historiography is quite important, although he hardly deserves the honorific "Livy," either Bavarian or any other kind. He is indeed the father of Bavarian historical writing and has distinguished heirs, not the least of whom is Aventinus. Andreas himself is, however, neither as innovating as Gobelinus Persona, nor as important a milestone as Cusanus. He is rather a completely typical example of popular historical conventions in the fifteenth century. The chronicle is generally dependent on medieval historical writing, although Andreas may have been the first to have gathered so many disparate sources for the purpose of a provincial history. There are, nonetheless, many chroniclers like him, and they and he together represent the historical tradition which humanist criticism, with dubious success, attempted to correct.

Popular historical conventions were not so fixed as to demand conformity to a historical production like Andreas of Regensburg's. Some works were even more tradition-bound, never abandoning the most limited canon of medieval chronicles. Others could be quite daring, seeking information from all possible sources, even oral tradition as Gobelinus ventured to do. However undefined the boundaries were

---

[17] *Andreas*, p. 529. In fact, Otto III did nothing effective against the Fatimids. The title seems to be a late tradition in its attribution to Otto, going back perhaps to the twelfth century. Possible roots may lie in Byzantine influences in Rome during the reign of the Ottonians. Theophano, a Byzantine princess, was Otto III's mother and regent during his minority. The title was used of the Byzantine Emperors, and this was known in the West in Otto's time.

between literature and history in this period, they seem to have been certain enough to preclude extensive borrowing from the richly historical vernacular poetry of the fifteenth century. Very few works dare to cross the genres. One such a work is the Thuringian chronicle of JOHANNES ROTHE (fl. 1434), chaplain of Princess Anna of Eisenach. It is all the more interesting for its daring. Rothe is of course in debt to many of the same sources as the authors already seen. Like them he is subject to the provincial–imperial dilemma. He knows of the prophecies about Frederick and the Empire at the end of the world. But Rothe's work reads more like a slightly confused novel than an attempt at history. Even by the standards of fifteenth-century historical writing in the North, his chronicle is somewhat on the imaginative side. Both in its fiction and the extent of its fiction it has no real equal until the *Compendium* of Frankish history by Trithemius in the second decade of the sixteenth century.

The very first German to appear in history, Rothe informs us, was Ninus of Babylon, who founded Trier 784 years after the flood, when Abraham was 7 years old.[18] The Trojans appear on the scene somewhat later. Priam, nephew ("swestersun") of Priam the Great, and Anthenor flee fallen Troy. Anthenor and his son, Senno, move toward Hungary and build "Sytambria," while Aeneas and Priam proceed over Africa to Italy. Priam alone continues on to the Rhine where he and his followers confront a nation of great women called *Theotonica*, who are a race of giants. Priam's men and the Teutonic women intermarry, and of these unions are born Seifridt, Hagin, and Krimehilt, of whom we have many songs. The name "German" comes from the fact that Priam and Aeneas were of one nation, brothers, hence *Germani* (*Rothe*, pp. 37–38). While Saul was King in Judea, Senno, son of Anthenor, left Sytambria and came to Germany. Senno and his son, Marcomedt, became the first kings of Thuringia (*Rothe*, p. 38). An anonymous Latin chronicler of Erfurt, thought perhaps to be Rothe, suggests alternative origins with the Saxons and Westphalians stemming directly from Japhet, and the Franks and Thuringians following them in time. He derives the name of the Franks from "feroces" and that of the Thuringians from "duri."[19] These last etymologies are slightly unusual in that they are not eponymic, but supposedly reflect the character of the people.

---

[18] Potthast, pp. 985–86. Borst, III.i.1022–23. Rochus von Liliencron, ed., *Düringische Chronik des Johann Rothe*, Thüringische Geschichtsquellen, III (Jena, 1895), p. 30.

[19] Text in Johannes Pistorius, *Illustrium veterum scriptorum ... tomus unus* (Frankfurt, 1583), p. 908. Cf. Potthast, p. 103, s.v. "Anonymi Erphesfordensis."

Besides the heroes connected with the origins of the Germans, Rothe mentions "Brennie," a German King who took Rome (*Rothe*, pp. 46–47). Julius Caesar seems to be granted German citizenship in the light of all his accomplishments in the North. They include the building of a great many towns and fortresses, not the least of which was "Kufhusen" (Kyffhäuser). Rothe etymologizes the name out of Latin "confusio," as does the anonymous Latin chronicler, who adds that the name seems to be Gallic (Pistorius, p. 909). Caesar, according to Rothe, also built Homburg, Jülich, and Lüneburg (*Rothe*, p. 54 and cf. p. 9). The anonymous Latin chronicler specifies that the latter town was so named because Caesar forced the Thuringians to worship *Luna* according to Roman usage (Pistorius, p. 909). The Anonymous adds to the list of heroes Merwygus, King of the Franks, who named the Merwesburgk in Erfurt, and who re-established the Kingdom of Thuringia in the year 426 while the Empire rested in the hands of Theodosius (Pistorius, p. 910).

The mythical heroes in Rothe's chronicle are predominantly the product of the learned historical tradition. He does, however, abandon this tradition altogether for a short while, or rather, he joins to it popular literary utterance. Among the more recent heroic figures, legendary, partially legendary, and real, Rothe includes Meister Klingsor of Hungary, Heinrich von Ofterdingen, and Wolfram von Eschenbach. These were involved with Satanic forces in the great battle of song, the "Wartburgkrieg" (*Rothe*, pp. 332ff.). This poses for the first time in our texts the thorny problem of the relationship between "story" and "history" in the minds of Renaissance authors and their audience in the North. The problem is compounded here by the historical reality of the combatants in the fictitious battle of song. Wolfram von Eschenbach is no less certainly real than the purportedly German Brennus or the founder of the Merovingian dynasty. The standards implied by Rothe's discussion of the "Wartburgkrieg" seem to exclude, or at least evade, the accepted conventions of historical writing in his period. Those events of sufficient importance to be recorded in the collective memory of his audience deserved entry into his chronicle. Historical reality was beside the point, and learned authority was not the exclusive source of historical knowledge. A "story" originally composed under the fiction of a historical reality lost the quality of fiction and became "history." The process is a simplified version of the entire problem of myth in history; but we shall turn to this again when the texts will suggest the occasion.

The prime mythical entity with penetrating historical reality for Rothe and his contemporaries was the *Imperium*. Like other authors who felt no need to defend the Empire but merely accepted it, Rothe contributes to the myth fragmentarily. The fragments are nonetheless most suggestive and enlightening. For example, Charlemagne, who was born in Ingelheim, received his sword directly from heaven (*Rothe,* p. 159). This very sword was believed still to be in the imperial regalia. Charles had received the *Imperium* and brought it to the hands of the Germans for his services to Pope Leo. The Pope's enemies had blinded him and cut out his tongue. He cried out to Charlemagne for aid, after a miraculous restoration. In return for the vengeance exacted upon the enemies of Pope and Church, Charles was rewarded with the Empire. When he died, his remains were brought to Aachen as sacred relics (pp. 162–63).[20]

The might and the sacred character of the Empire are further exemplified in Frederick I's special service to the church of Cologne. He had his chancellor for Italy, Rainald, Archbishop of Cologne, bring the relics of the Three Magi from conquered Milan to the metropolis of the Rhine (*Rothe,* p. 300). This Rainald is the famed patron of the Archpoet and a rare example of the very real power that an Imperial Chancellor could wield. Rothe's chronicle provides an instance of the same eschatological aspect of the Empire apparent in Andreas of Regensburg's work. To the year 1261 Rothe reports the appearance of a false Frederick II. He adds that in his own time stories were current to the effect that Frederick had never died and now lay hidden in the Kyffhäuser (built by Caesar!). Frederick, as the story goes, lets himself be seen every now and again. When his time comes he will be most powerful, make peace among the princes, win back the Holy Land, and reign as the final Emperor before the coming of the Last Day (pp. 462–63). In 1285, yet another man appeared claiming to be Frederick. He was burned for his troubles in the town of Wetzlar at the instigation of Rudolf of Hapsburg (p. 446).

These evidences of the imperial myth appear here as isolated items largely removed from context, but in Rothe they reside in harmony

---

[20] A document dated Rome, 20 March 1452, concerning Frederick III's coronation reads in part: "Item nun hetten die von Nürnberg gen Rome pracht das hailig wirdig hailtüm, des hailigen, hohen himelsfürsten kaiser Karls cron, die da vol wirdigs hailtüm ist, und *das hailig schwert, das der engel im vom himel pracht,* mit demselben schwert er manigfaltigclich gestritten hat und cristenglauben gemert" [italics mine]. Item: the Nürnbergers bore to Rome the holy, noble relic, which is the crown of the holy, high, heavenly prince Charles, and which itself is filled with magnificent relics; they brought also *the holy sword, which an angel took to him from heaven* and with which he often did battle and spread the Christian faith. This was written by Caspar Enenkel, imperial counselor: Fr. Roth, ed., in *Chroniken der deutschen Städte,* XXII (Leipzig, 1892), pp. 307 and 321.

with a great many other facts and fables. Precisely because these extraordinary notions appear in ordinary context, do they illustrate the
basic premises Rothe assumed for himself and his readers. The divine
origin of Charlemagne's sword, the removal of the relics of the Three
Magi to Cologne, the survival of Frederick, and his possible return as
"Endkaiser," all these were not used to prove the sanctity and power
of the Empire, but rather revealed what everyone knew to be its
character. Rothe had no need to dwell on the German possession of
the Empire, although he implies it in connection with Charlemagne's
birthplace. Nor did Rothe have to draw openly the associations obvious to his readers between, on the one hand, the establishment of
the Kyffhäuser by Caesar, the first Emperor, a Roman, and on the
other hand, the concealment in the Kyffhäuser of Frederick, the last
Emperor, a German. And Rothe did not have to state that the Empire
was above all kingdoms. He assumes it. The Empire was Roman and
German, sacred and supreme, and that was that.

The myth of the Empire as an immediate and palpable reality
emerges from some fifteenth-century journalistic chronicles which report a funeral observance for Emperor Sigismund celebrated in Nürnberg in 1438. The texts in question are two contemporary accounts,
one anonymous, one from the hand of the Nürnberg patrician Endres
Tucher. In both documents the dignity of the deceased monarch is,
of course, respected. But the most important item, that which left the
strongest impression on contemporaries as witnessed in these reports,
was the presence of the imperial regalia, identified as Charlemagne's.
They included the orb and sceptre, the diadem, and the sword.[21] The
vital role these implements played in medieval history is known to
any student of the origins of the Guelf-Ghibelline dispute or the life
of Walther von der Vogelweide. The reasons that eye-witness accounts
would dwell on the signs of Charlemagne's imperial power are clear:
they were ceremonial, hence virtually sacramental reminders of the
person of the great Charles, his winning of the Roman Empire for
German hands, and his power over a united Christendom. Beyond
being reminders they were the living implements of power without
which no prince could assume the imperial dignity. The imperial
regalia reposed with the burghers of Nürnberg, who brought them

21 Theodor von Kern, ed., "Chronik aus Kaiser Sigmund's Zeit bis 1434,"
Chroniken der deutschen Städte, I (Leipzig, 1862), p. 400. Theodor von Kern, ed.,
"Endres Tucher's Memorial, 1421–1440," *Chroniken der deutschen Städte*, II,
(Leipzig, 1864), p. 28.

forth only for such occasions as imperial funerals or coronations. The imperial regalia were perhaps the most concrete myth of the German past in the Renaissance.

These relatively unsophisticated expressions of historical conscious-ness dominate the picture of German historiography in the fifteenth century. The picture is, however, incomplete without the urbane and erudite contributions from abroad, particularly from Italy, and most particularly from the pen of AENEAS SYLVIUS PICCOLOMINI (1405–65), later Pope Pius II. Although Aeneas's historical criticism hardly com-pares to that of a Leonardo Bruni, his and not Bruni's histories be-came normative in Germany. As prime apostle of humanism in Germany, he and his influence are well known, and many of his con-tributions have been examined elsewhere.[22] I shall touch on a few which complement from a mythical viewpoint those findings made from a more practical approach.

In 1446, while still an anti-curialist, Aeneas Sylvius wrote *Libellus de ortu et authoritate imperii Romani.*[23] Early in his discussion, Aeneas refers to the movement of the four world empires from As-syrians to Medes and Persians, to Macedonians with Alexander the Great, and finally to Romans with Julius Caesar (Schard, p. 316). The imperial power of Rome clearly received a special sanction not granted to other empires: Christ chose of all times in history to come at the time of Augustus's census, thus submitting Himself to Roman im-perial authority at His very birth; He declared as well that one ought to render to Caesar the things that are Caesar's (pp. 316–17). Further-more, scripture reveals (II Thess.ii.7) that Antichrist cannot appear as long as the Empire holds (Schard, p. 318). This Empire, with these special functions, was transferred from the Greeks to the Germans in the person of Charlemagne, King of the Franks, by nation a German, because of his services to the Church, particularly his defense of the Holy City (pp. 319–20).

Elsewhere Aeneas touches on Charlemagne and his German nation-ality. He was born in Germany and placed his imperial capital at Aachen, which is a German city. The Empire since his time was ever

---

[22] Ulrich Paul, *Studien,* p. 26, calls Aeneas Sylvius the "unwitting father of Ger-man national self-consciousness." Paul's work is a comprehensive view of Aeneas's influence on the historical writing of Renaissance Germany. More recent bibliog-raphy is available in Berthe Widmer, ed., *Enea Silvio Piccolomini Papst Pius II* (Basel and Stuttgart, 1960), pp. 471–74.

[23] See Potthast, p. 23. I use the edition by Simon Schard in his *De iurisdictione, autoritate et praeeminentia imperiali* (Basel, 1566), pp. 313–28.

in the hands of the Germans. The assertion that the Empire came to the Germans with Otto I means only that the Empire was inherited by the East Franks. They are properly called Franks, whereas the West Franks are properly called French—"Francigenae."[24] The meaning of Aeneas's distinction for the succession of the Empire is somewhat obscure.

All people and powers are under the Roman Emperor in temporal matters as they are under the Pope in matters spiritual. Those err who claim that they owe the Empire nothing (Schard, p. 319–20). These remarks of Aeneas require no comment. Like Cusanus, Aeneas Sylvius maintains all aspects of the myth of the *Imperium*: it is the Roman Empire; it is now German; it has extraordinary religious responsibilities; it is above all worldly monarchies. However, unlike Cusanus, who seems to have supported the myth consistently, Aeneas was forced by political circumstance to suppress some of the more extreme implications of the myth.

Whatever his politics at the moment, Aeneas would hardly forgo the opportunity of a witty criticism at the expense of an Emperor. His book on illustrious men describes a meeting between Emperor Sigismund and Pope Eugene IV. If it is historical, it must have taken place during the Emperor's Roman visit of 1433. "There are three things, Most Holy Father," the Emperor said, "in which we differ, and again three in which we are alike. You like to sleep late, I rise before dawn. You drink water, I wine. You flee the women, I chase them. But we are alike in these: you generously spend the wealth of the Church, I keep nothing to myself; you have sick hands, I have sick feet; you are destroying the Church, I the Empire."[25]

Aeneas contributes substantially to the myths of origin and fabulous heroes, first by gathering a good many stories and then by giving them the stamp of his considerable authority. By becoming Bishop of Ermland about the year 1457, he joined the Prussian hierarchy. He assures us that the Prussians stem from those Goths who remained behind in

---

[24] *De statu Europae sub Frederico III Liber,* c. XXXI, "De Francorum origine et Franconia," in Marquard Freher and Burkhard G. Struve, eds., *Rerum Germanicarum Scriptores,* 3 vols. (Strassburg, 1717) II, 129 [henceforth "Freher/Struve"].

[25] Aeneas Silvius, *De viris illustribus,* BLVS, I.3 (Stuttgart, 1843), p. 65. Glenn Elwood Waas tells a similar story about Maximilian in his *Legendary Character of Kaiser Maximilian,* Columbia University Germanic Studies, XIV (New York, 1941), p. 139: Luther explained in 1536 why Maximilian had been known to laugh: it was in the Emperor's contemplation of the divine arrangement of the spiritual and temporal orders—the one had been placed under a drunkard—Julius II; the other, under a chamois hunter—himself.

the land of the Ulmerigi after the Goths left "Scandavia."[26] In the footsteps of Cusanus and Rothe, Aeneas reports the mythical origins of the city of Trier. In his extensive praise of German cities, the story appears that Atreba (Trebata), son of Ninus and Semiramis, founded Trier 1300 years before the founding of Rome. It is said that, even as St. Peter lived, Trier accepted the religion of Christ.[27] Elsewhere Aeneas challenges the story that the Saxons or Thuringians are supposed to have arrived from Macedon by ship (Freher/Struve II, 119). But in the same work Aeneas explains how the Franks came from Troy (II, 127ff.). Priam, nephew of Priam the Great, left fallen Troy, crossed the Euxine Sea and the Maeotian swamps, whence he entered Scythia. There he founded the city of Sicambria, which is why his people were called the Sicambri. Emperor Valentinian, when threatened by the Alani, promised ten years' freedom from tribute to whoever would defeat them. The Sicambri came and did just that. They were granted their freedom from tribute, and their name was changed to "Franci," which in Attic means "fierce" or "noble," and which Italians call "free." Aeneas proceeds through the now Frankish Priam and Anthenor, over Marcomir and Sunno, Faramundus and Clodius, to Clodavaeus and Merovaeus and thus to the dawn of real Frankish history.

Aeneas's denial of the fabulous stories of the Saxons or Thuringians and acceptance of the fabulous origins of the Franks is the general situation for the topos of critical rejection. Here, however, it is unclear whether he is employing the denial in support of the acceptance. Such employment is an essential characteristic of *anasceua*. A clearer example suggests itself in Aeneas's explanation of the name of the Germans: it is nonsense to say that the name comes from their brotherhood with the Gauls, as some maintain, for the two could not have been more different; actually, the name comes from "a germinando," because of the great growth of the Germans (*Germania* II.6, in Schmidt, p. 49). Here the rejection of the one myth is in unequivocal support of the other, and of course in similar support of the author's critical acumen and credibility.

Aeneas does not pass over, as we shall, the real mythical heroes of the Germans, such as the Ottos and Fredericks (*Germania* II.29, in Schmidt, pp. 66–67). In Aeneas's thoughts on the *Imperium* and the fabulous origins of the Germans, sufficient numbers of heroic figures

---

[26] Theodor Hirsch, ed., "Aeneas Sylvius: Preussen betreffende Schriften," in his *Scriptores rerum Prussicarum* (Leipzig, 1870), IV, 212–13, 218–19.

[27] Adolf Schmidt, ed., *Aeneas Silvius: Germania* (Cologne and Graz, 1962), p. 51, covering Aeneas's Book II, ch. 8. Cf. Borst, III.i.969.

have been presented to understand this aspect of his myths of the German past. Ancient religion and morals have not yet been mentioned, but they are important to Aeneas. The future Pope makes it transparent in his *Germania* that the Germans are in heavy debt to Rome. Whatever prosperity and fame they now have comes directly from their liberation from barbarism by the Roman Church. In ancient times, the Germans were ill-clothed, ill-fed, ill-housed, no matter how brave and warlike they may have been (II.2ff., in Schmidt, pp. 46ff.). Their religion was primitive and barbaric. The major deities were only what they could see: sun, fire, moon. No cruelty was left uncommitted in their worship. They honored Saturn, Jupiter, Mercury, Bacchus, Ceres, Diana, Venus, and other monsters. Only through the Church were they liberated from this vice. Indeed, before their conversion, there was nothing more disgusting than Germans (III.7–8, in Schmidt, pp. 75–76). On the other hand, the ancient Germans had the advantage over the moderns in bravery, generosity, zeal, justice, and—above all—unity (II.33, in Schmidt, p. 69).

Virtually everything Aeneas wrote about Germany, good and bad, found strong response among his disciples and successors in the North. Ulrich Paul (*Studien*, pp. 56–57) enumerates no less than thirty-nine motifs and issues that found proponents and attackers after Aeneas. His influence is incalculable, perhaps even out of proportion to his actual talent. The Apostle of Humanism in Germany left his mark not only on historiography, but on literature and politics as well. In the face of his heritage, the chimera of perpetual Middle Ages in Germany loses even its apparent substance. The above paragraphs have hardly done justice to Aeneas, even in his limited function as transmitter of myths of the German past. His historical thought is complex, in fact convoluted. Here only some of the main threads have been drawn out of the tangle.

It is not necessary to simplify, as has been the case with Aeneas Sylvius, the contributions of the obscure and not untalented poet who called himself "Der Küchlin." Between the years 1437 and 1442, this poet produced an uncomplicated versified account of the origins and early history of Augsburg.[28] He describes the Trojan origins of the

---

[28] F. Frensdorff, ed., "Die Reimchronik des Küchlin," *Chroniken der deutschen Städte,* IV (Leipzig, 1865), pp. 333–56. Cf. Potthast, p. 702; Borst, III.i, 1033; Paul Joachimsohn [sic], *Die humanistische Geschichtschreibung in Deutschland: Die Anfänge—Sigismund Meisterlin* (Bonn, 1895), pp. 12–16 [hereafter cited as *Meisterlin*].

Germans at large and the Swabians in particular, much as the fable appeared in Rothe's chronicle and, as it seems, from the identical source. After a précis of Homer's *Iliad* in no more than thirteen lines ("Reimchronik" ll.58–70) of thoroughly charming doggerel, Der Küchlin explains ("Reimchronik" ll.71–75):

> doch blieb des geslechts ein sam
> des kunigs enklin mit sinem nam
> Priamus der junger genant
> zů dem noch einer was bekant
> Eneas, desselben stams ein held.

[but of the royal house one seed remained/ the grandson of the King, called with his name/ Priam the Younger/ in addition to whom one other was known/ Aeneas, hero of the same house.]

These two wandered through Africa to Italy. Young Priam continued to the Rhine, drove out the natives there, and joined forces with the ancient city of Trier ("Reimchronik" ll.76–96). At Cologne, Priam and his men found a nation of beautiful women whom they took as wives (ll.97–104). Of the naming of Germany, Der Küchlin relates (ll.105–115):

> Eneas der schriebe Priamo
> in allen brieven germano,
> darumb das sie von einer samen
> geboren waren mit kunigs namen;
> die schrift die schal durch das lant,
> das die edeln würden alle genant
> Germani, und was sie hetten inn
> oder hernach möchten land gewinn,
> die hießen nach in Germania,
> das sind teutsche land, verr und na,
> die gemeinlich den namen tragen.[29]

[Aeneas wrote to Priam/ in all his letters, "brother,"/ for they were of the same seed/ born with royal name;/ the writings spread throughout the land/ so that the noble people all were called/ "Germani," and what they possessed/ or later won of the land/ was named after them Germania,/ these are German lands, far and near,/ which bear the name in common.]

---

[29] The vitality of this tradition is demonstrated by the fact that the Trojan origins of the Swabians appear almost twenty years later in everyday correspondence, and not only in chronicles: Letter from Hieronymus Rotenpeck of Rebdorf to Sigismund Gossembrot, dated in Rome, 1458, in Paul Joachimsohn, ed., *Hermann Schedels Briefwechsel 1452–1478*, BLVS, CXCVI (Tübingen, 1893), p. 21.

Of these "Germani," one group left the Rhine and founded a city named "Zisaris" in honor of their idol "Zise," for whom they built a temple on what became known as the "Zisenberk" (ll.116–44). By this time, Der Küchlin is calling the nation "Germani und Swaben." The poet explains that the national city, "Zisaris," is older than Rome (ll.145–72), presumably because Priam and his descendents went about the business of founding a city before Aeneas and his descendents got around to it.

Rome nonetheless has considerable influence on the fate of the Swabians and their city ("Reimchronik" ll.173–77):

> Als nu Augustus Octavian
> kieserlichen gewalt gewan
> und hort, das die edeln Germani
> überall wollten sitzen fry,
> da schickt er uß dri legion. . . .

[When Caesar Augustus/ won the imperial might/ and heard that the noble Germans/ wished to reside in freedom everywhere,/ he sent out three legions. . . .]

Of the three legions, one came from Rome under the praetor Varus and was called "Martia"; two others were sent from Macedon, under the royal son Aver. They all made camp before the various gates of the city. While the inhabitants were worshiping their goddess within the walls, their armies came from without and took the Macedonian legions by surprise, annihilating them except for the young King Aver (ll.229–34):

> der ward geantwort nach dem sig
> in künges kleider lebendig;
> die herren da hetten kein erbärm
> und wöllten keim sin bāt gewärn,
> sie ließen in metzgen als ein ků
> und begraben in dem veld darzů.

[he was captured after the victory/ alive, in royal garb;/ the lords had no mercy/ and refused him every plea,/ they had him butchered like a cow/ and buried him in the open field.]

Since he was Greek ("Krieg-") and called Aver ("-haber"), the place in which he was buried is to this day known as Kriegshaber ("Reimchronik" ll.235–38). Folk etymology can be as complicated as anything a nineteenth-century philologist could invent. The Romans came too late to the aid of their allies, but attacked the city and killed two of its princes, Habin and Kackus, who thereby gave their names to Havnerberg and Keckingen (ll.239–59). The Romans pressed hard on the city and would surely have won it, had not the Swabian armies again come to the rescue. They now annihilated the Romans, whence Perlach receives its name, "perdita legio,"—"lost legion" (ll.260–76). Varus escaped in cowardice, was captured, and eventually executed (ll.277–88).

The Germani and Swabians rejoiced in their victory. In Rome there was considerable gloom, particularly in the household of the Emperor ("Reimchronik" ll.289–96). Of Emperor Augustus Der Küchlin says (ll.297–304):

> sin hertz und gemůt was leides vol
> und klagt anders, dann ein keyser sol;
> er ward von leid der sinn beraubt,
> das er slůg an die wand sin haupt,
> die kleider zart er ab dem lib,
> vil ungeperd sach man in trib,
> er schrei: ach Rom und Macedon,
> Varre gib wieder die legion!

[his heart and spirits were full of misery/ and he lamented, not a fitting pastime for Caesar./ He lost his mind with misery/ and so beat his head against the wall/ and tore his clothes from off his body./ He was seen to act unseemly,/ he cried: O Rome and Macedon,/ Varus give me back my legions!]

The Swabians rejoiced in direct proportion to the mourning of the Romans. To commemorate their victory they renamed the city Vindelica after a nearby stream which had served as a crucial advantage in the battle ("Reimchronik" ll.305–16). Subsequently, Drusus and Claudius came and subjugated Gaul and Germany. They killed so many Germans and Swabians that these lost their freedom. Drusus renamed the city yet again, this time after Augustus, and it remained in Roman hands until the coming of Christianity in 241 A.D. (ll. 317–66). Der Küchlin concludes the poem as he began it, with a petition to the Trinity to come to the aid of the poet and his poem.

The liberty I am taking in quoting extensively from this poem and describing it rather fully may need some defense. Der Küchlin is without question far less important than the Italian and German humanist historians represented in Aeneas Sylvius and Sigismund Meisterlin. His purported unimportance is the first reason for my attention:

Aeneas and Sigismund have received ample monographic appreciation, whereas few scholars have ever heard of Der Küchlin. Secondly, the few times he is mentioned at all, it is to divert attention from him and toward vastly more boring and presumably more significant monuments. Der Küchlin's poetic economy, his ear for rhythms, and his unaffected narrative directness place his work far above most versified histories and historical songs of the period, which are generally prose forced into verse. He is neither blessed nor burdened with the art of the Meistersinger. If his work were better known, students of German might be inclined to look beyond the handful of names associated with German vernacular literature in the fifteenth century. While the poem is hardly a glory of world literature, it is certainly one of the little pleasures of which Germanists, if no one else, should not be deprived.

Yet another historian of Augsburg and the first, according to one critic, to bring humanism to the writing of history among Germans was SIGISMUND MEISTERLIN.[30] A sign of the new criticism is no doubt to be found in that Sigismund rejects out of hand all the nonsensical stories of Trojan origins for the Swabians. The fact of the matter is that they stem directly from Japhet. They are therefore indigenous to the land. Their first appearance in history comes with their defeat at the hands of the Amazons some 550 years before the founding of Rome. Their city, which was to become Augsburg, is at least that much older than Rome, and who is to say how much older than that it may be (*Meisterlin*, pp. 34–35 and 290)? The Swabians' Trojan origins are to be rejected, not only because they lack proper historical evidence—the real evidence points to their being older than Troy— but because it is undignified to stem from a lot of refugees. The Franks on the other hand might stem from the Trojan prince, Franco (pp. 27–29). The new criticism seems to bring, in advance of major historical sophistication, another and more striking example of *anasceua*, the topos of critical rejection.

Among Meisterlin's heroes are Brennus, the Swabian, who led his men to triumph over Rome. Antiquity also reveals the unprecedented valor and modesty of the Teutonic women in the battle against Marius at Aquae Sextiae (*Meisterlin*, pp. 35–36). The Swabians' great zeal for battle can be read in their very name, "Suevi," which also

---

[30] Joachimsohn, *Meisterlin*, Foreword. Meisterlin's *Chronographia Augustensium* was produced about 1456; see Potthast, p. 783. For a brief and useful sketch of Meisterlin's activities, see Paul, *Studien*, pp. 33–34; cf. Borst, III.i, 1033–34.

appears as "Sevi," and means "brutal" or "gruesome." This etymology was as current as the fable of the Trojan origins of the Germans.[31] Meisterlin relates how the ancients complained about the rage of the Cimbri and the fury of the Germans.[32] He attributes these qualities of the Cimbri in particular and the Germans at large directly to the Swabians. Rage is then numbered among the virtues of the ancient Germans, along with the talents of the smith and the carpenter, and the labor of the farmer, hunter, and butcher (*Meisterlin*, p. 298). Some connect gluttony and lust with the goddess Ceres, but actually the Swabians worshipped her on account of the fertility of the land, for she was the goddess of grain. Since Germans habitually mispronounce Latin, Ceres became "Ciza," and Cereres, "Cizaris" (p. 294). Meisterlin's myths appear in virtually all the categories: origins, heroes, virtue, religion. I pass over the *Imperium* here; it will be considered when we return to a later work of Meisterlin's.

This brief, superficial, and highly selective account of Meisterlin's contributions to the ancient history of the Germans does not allow a major distinction between him and the popular historians such as Andreas and Der Küchlin. He is nonetheless considered a pioneer in the North of the new form of historical writing. This may or may not be the case, and these pages are most certainly not the place to challenge Joachimsen's theory. Whether it is substantially correct or not, Meisterlin's writings clearly preserve select popular traditions, rather like Aeneas Sylvius's. This may be explained as a gradual separation of the popular and learned traditions. The innovations could not wholly break from the accepted manner of history. Such an explanation is generally satisfactory, but I should like to suggest a complement or alternative. The fifteenth century was largely incapable of conceiving a culture other than its own, least of all a culture without the Roman constituent. German historians of the period were equally unprepared to admit wholesale Germanic barbarism. They were thus obliged to imagine Germanic antiquities as an analogue to Roman antiquities. This obtained for humanist as well as popular historians. Only in the sixteenth century, a substantially different culture could be imagined by a rare few historians. This ability to escape contempo-

---

[31] *Meisterlin*, pp. 290–91 and *Hermann Schedels Briefwechsel*, p. 20.

[32] The *furor Teutonicus* was a common complaint and was rarely considered a virtue as it was by Meisterlin. The Italian humanist Bartholini is also exceptional when he praises German valor specifically in these terms: "Victaque Teutonicis Romana furoribus arma." His poem was, however, written in honor of the German Emperor: Justus Reuber, *Veterum Scriptorum ... Tomus Unus* (Frankfurt, 1584), p. 473. On the whole issue cf. Ernst Dümmler, "Uber den furor Teutonicus," *SB der königlichen Preussischen Akademie der Wissenschaften zu Berlin, philosophische-historische Classe*, no. IX, (18 February 1897), pp. 111–26.

rary standards and dispositions may be more a sign of "modernity" among these historians than the ineffectual beginnings of critical historical analysis or even the hunt for new and better sources.

The distinction between popular and humanistic history in this period is at best tenuous. If Meisterlin is humanist, then his imitators should be also, to the extent of the success of their imitation. Unequivocally dependent on Meisterlin and widely imitative of him is an anonymous chronicle of Augsburg, from the founding of the city to the year 1469.[33] Even with the best of will, one cannot find the remotest trace of humanism in this work. The anonymous chronicler plunders Meisterlin for details, but ignores any trace of criticism and any suggestion to read the newly discovered texts of antiquity. He even challenges Meisterlin on some of the details. In contrast to his model, the Anonymous has the city of Augsburg founded a mere 150 years before the fall of Troy, which is approximately the time that the Swabians fled to Alemannia. Plinius and Schgolopotius [sic] had, as it seems, defeated a Gothic army, and the Gothic women had established another army of their own to seek revenge. They elected "Lampode" and "Mersopia" their leaders and set about devastating the world. In the course of these Amazon rampages the Swabians, too, were attacked. When the Swabians could return to their city, they built a temple to their goddess Zisa, who is supposed to be Ceres. All of this can be found in Ovid and Horace, the anonymous author assures us ("Chronik," pp. 280–83). Lest the Swabians be thought cowards, let it be remembered that their very name means "cruel" or "severe," that their leader, "Prenno," attacked Rome, that Julius Caesar could only conquer them with kindness, that later they dealt a grave defeat to the Roman legion *Martius* under Varus near Ausgburg (pp. 280, 283–86).

The Anonymous touches on the myth of the *Imperium* when he explains that the Roman Empire passed from Constantinople to "Franckreich" with Charlemagne, and later to the Germans ("Chronik," p. 294). In 1469, "Franckreich" could not have meant anything but France. It is as surprising as it is probable that the Anonymous considered Charlemagne French. While disturbing and anomalous, this supports the generally accepted notion that German national self-consciousness was, long into the sixteenth century, restricted to the

---

[33] F. Frensdorff, ed., "Chronik von der Gründung der Stadt Augsburg bis zum Jahre 1469," *Chroniken der deutschen Städte*, IV (Leipzig, 1869), pp. 265–332.

humanists. Despite his great learning, and despite his pretentious and usually erroneous references to classical antiquity, the Anonymous was no humanist. The heated humanist defenses of Charlemagne's German nationality would not have been necessary without the formidable minority tradition which the Anonymous's thoughts represent. The myth of the *Imperium* remains intact, nonetheless, since the Anonymous affirms that the Empire was transferred to the Germans, if only somewhat later.

This Augsburg chronicle conceals another piece of the puzzle of Emperor Frederick. In 1155 [sic], Frederick II is supposed to have told Heinrich, Landgrave of Thuringia, that three men had seduced the whole world: Moses the Jews, Christ the Christians, and Mohammed the heathens ("Chronik," p. 303). This is troublesome talk for the future "Endkaiser," and very much reflects the memory of Frederick II as Antichrist, as we saw it in Gobelinus Persona. Yet another difficulty arises in this particular incidence of the "three seducers" story. The tradition is approximately two hundred years old and is consistently associated with Frederick II. The Anonymous correctly puts the words in the mouth of Frederick II and correctly makes the listener Heinrich of Thuringia, but he transports the events into the time of Frederick I Barbarossa. To make matters worse, a Heinrich Landgrave of Thuringia (surnamed Raspe, just like Frederick II's interlocutor) flourished in Barbarossa's time. Visible here is a confusion of the two great Hohenstaufen. Precisely this confusion gave form to the elaborate myth of Emperor Frederick as it was to survive beyond the Renaissance.[34]

More myths of Augsburg and the Swabians will appear as we move on through the Renaissance. I have taken some liberties with chronological order to gather together the myths of the mid-fifteenth-century Swabians and should perhaps summarize the results before moving to Swiss texts of the same period. The Swabians have been seen to originate from Japhet or more recently Troy. They are known to have battled with the Amazons. Among their heroes are Brennus, who challenged Rome, and the valorous women who challenged Marius. Their worship centered on Ciza, who is the same as Ceres. Their greatest virtue is reflected in their name, severe, although they were also fine

---

[34] An attack on Emperor Frederick III, dated 1470, seems to confuse the first two Fredericks completely: Hermann Grauert, "Zur deutschen Kaisersage," *Historisches Jahrbuch*, XIII (1892), 141. The same confusion prevails in a patriotic tract from the year 1495: Paul, *Studien*, p. 118. The modern form of the confusion is preserved by the Brothers Grimm, *Deutsche Sagen*, 3rd ed. (Darmstadt, 1960), pp. 49–50, no. 23.

craftsmen. This suspiciously resembles the dawn of middle class self-consciousness in northern historical writing. Of the myth of the *Imperium*, its German character has been affirmed, and some mystery has been added to its heroic figure, Emperor Frederick.

The Renaissance historical myths connected with Switzerland may be attributed largely to FELIX HEMMERLIN and EULOGIUS KIBURGER. In a dialogue between a nobleman and a rustic (ca. 1448/1450) Hemmerlin developed an elaborate fable to explain the origin of the Swiss name. There were some exceptionally difficult Saxons whom Charlemagne had forced into exile. Some of them wandered into what was to become Canton Uri, others into Wallis. There they were told to guard the passes when Charles marched into Italy. In order to win the favor of the great king who had been pursuing them, they willingly acceded to his request. They said, let us sweat here, "wie wellen hie switten," which is why they came to be called Schwyzer. Such remarks succeeded in annoying the Swiss and, when Hemmerlin lost the protection of the Austrian princes, cost him his freedom.[35] Even though this invention found an echo in subsequent years, the more popular thoughts on the origin of the Swiss appear in the work attributed to one Eulogius Kiburger.[36]

In his "Vom Herkommen der Schwyzer und Oberhasler," Kiburger tells us that, while Cisbert was King in Sweden and Christoffel was Duke in East Frisia, a great famine prevailed in the North. A council was convened and a decision made that lots should be drawn. Regardless of status or condition, those selected could leave. Six thousand Swedes and twelve hundred Frisians left and came up the Rhine (Baechtold, pp. 180–82). This much can be read in the chronicle of Pliny.[37] The French ("us Frankrich") princes Priamus and Peter von Moos tried to stop them. To protect themselves, the refugees elected three captains, Swicerus and Remus of Sweden and Wadislaus of Hasnis (Hafnia—Copenhagen?), a city between Sweden and East

---

[35] Jakob Baechtold, ed., *Die Stretlinger Chronik*, Bibliothek älterer Schriftwerke der deutschen Schweiz, I (Frauenfeld, 1877), p. LXXVIIf. [henceforth "Baechtold"]. Hemmerlin's doctoral diploma is, incidentally, the oldest of its kind still extant: Richard Feller and Edgar Bonjour, *Geschichtsschreibung der Schweiz*, 2 vols. (Basel and Stuttgart, 1962), I, 68.

[36] Baechtold, p. LXX, but cf. Feller/Bonjour, I, 97–98.

[37] Exactly what Eulogius Kiburger had in mind when he said Pliny was an authority for Swiss origins is uncertain. It is either an example of fictitious authority, or in truth resided somewhere in Pliny's lost books. The former is of course more likely.

Frisia. The refugees attacked the French ("Franzosen") quickly, in unity, and with high spirits, despite the fact that they were outnumbered four to one. The refugees had good luck and won the day, putting to flight those whom they did not kill. After dividing the booty equally, they proceeded up the Rhine until they reached the Duchy of Austria (Baechtold, p. 183). Eventually they reached the Alps and asked the "Haptsburg" Duke for permission to settle the land. It was granted (p. 184).

Because of military services rendered to Pope Zosimus and Emperors Honorius and Theodosius, the privilege of responsibility to Pope and Emperor alone was granted to Switerus, Remus, and Wadislaus (Baechtold, pp. 188, 195). Others say that such rights were won by valorous conduct in battle with the Saracens, Huns, and Vandals. Yet another source claims that four leaders took the Swiss from Sweden: Schwyter and Schweyg for Schwyz, Rumo for Unterwalden, and Resti for Hasli (Baechtold, p. lxiv). The Swedish origins theory appeared again in 1478 and is the one that eventually prevailed (p. lxxxi). In 1531, prayers were ordered throughout Switzerland to commemorate the exodus from Sweden (p. lxxxii). There are yet other myths of Switzerland, also quite widespread, but their earliest appearance in this period follows Kiburger by some years.

As has largely been the case elsewhere, the Swiss myths of origin comprise many of the myths of fabulous heroes. To those already mentioned may be added Alfonsus of Frisia, historian and man of letters whom Kiburger claims as his source for the story of Swiss origins (Baechtold, p. 182). On the presumption that Alfonsus of Frisia is a fiction, he is chronologically the first of a small but very distinguished group of Renaissance inventions, all conjured up to verify the unverifiable. Kiburger made a great virtue of Swiss warrior qualities and the political and religious freedom these qualities won. Nothing appears about the ancient religion of the nation. The myth of the *Imperium* is fully corroborated by the responsibility to Emperor alone. It was meant to indicate that the Swiss were subject to no ducal or princely family, but only to the man who might be Emperor at the time. That the privilege was supposed to have been won under the Emperors Honorius and Theodosius and now was to be exercised under, let us say, Frederick III, demonstrates that the myth allows of no interruption in the continuity of the Empire.

Switzerland not only housed a flourishing folkloristic historical tradition, but the intellectual seeds of some of the most progressive thought in the Northern Renaissance. Paradoxically, this thought allied itself with some of the most traditional political notions in currency. The alliance is of great importance to our subject because it represents the view of national history that was to be held by the most distinguished figures of the Northern Renaissance. It is in this alliance that learned and popular history find the greatest common ground. The traditional political notions were ingrained in the popular mind. When the German humanists began programmatically to develop a kind of national self-consciousness, the popular traditions were as fertile an area for their exploitation as any other available to them.

An important example of this similarity is to be found in a learned forerunner of the more famous Upper German humanists, HERMANN PETER AUS ANDLAU.[38] The first vice-chancellor of the University of Basel, teacher of Sebastian Brant and Jacob Wimpheling, dedicated his work of 1460 on the imperial monarchy to Frederick III. The identity of Germany and the Roman Empire was so complete in the mind of Hermann Peter that his essay suffers from a disproportion of material specifically concerning Germanic antiquities over against the imperial myth. The publicistic requirements of his subject moved the jurist to show that the Germans were worthy successors to the Empire on account of their antiquity co-eval to that of the Romans, their close relationship to Rome, the ancient apostolic prefiguring of their possession of the Empire, and even their own virtue.

Hermann Peter's chapter on the excellence of the German nobility and on the antiquity of its origins was written explicitly to demonstrate the propriety of German possession of the Empire. There the publicist presents the Trojan origins of the Germans much as they appeared in Rothe and Der Küchlin, and almost certainly using the same source. The younger Priam led his people to the Rhine where they founded another Troy, now called Xanthen. They met and married the Teutonic women, and their issue spoke Teutonic. This whole people befriended the nearby people of Trier, the oldest city in Europe. The descendents of Priam became known as Germans because Aeneas's men in Italy called their allies in Gaul and Teutonia "Germani," that is, "sprung from the same seed" (Hürbin, XII, 94–95). Hermann Peter challenges one of Isidore of Seville's explanations of

---

38 Joseph Hürbin, ed., "Der 'Libellus de Cesarea monarchia' von Hermann Peter aus Andlau," *Zeitschrift der Savigny Stiftung für Rechtsgeschichte*, Germanistische Abtheilung, XII (1891), 34–103, contains Book I; XIII (1892), 163–212, contains Book II [reprint Leipzig, 1964]. Cf. Hedwig Riess, *Motive des patriotischen Stolzes bei den deutschen Humanisten* (Berlin, 1934), p. x–xi.

the German name, which connects it to the Germans' ferocity and endurance (XII, 96).

The tale is continued into the time of Valentinian, when a great army of Trojan blood under Marcomer, Sunno, and Genebald came out of Sicambria and the Maeotian Swamps. In the time of Pharamundus, this nation had a series of unpleasantnesses with the Roman Emperor. Their bravery in these encounters gave them the name "Franci," which in Attic means "fierce." The Franks and the Germans were and are of one nation. Those that married with the Gauls are called French—"Francigenae." The Germans were known for their joy in battle even from oldest times, and the women seem to have shared this quality. Boccaccio of Florence, Hermann Peter reports, tells us of the Teutonic women who fought the Consul Marius after the defeat of their men, and who, themselves defeated, sought to become vestal virgins. When denied, they killed their children and themselves, prefering death to dishonor (Hürbin, XII, 95–97).

Because of their great valor, not to mention their service to the Church against the heathen, the Germans received the Empire. Hermann Peter had mentioned earlier (Hürbin, XII, 53) the migration of the world *Imperium* westward from the Babylonians to the Romans, and now he notes the continuity of this westward movement in connection with the possession of the Roman Empire by Greeks and Germans (XII, 86–87):

> Unde cum annis tantum CCCCXV sacram imperii arcem tenuisset Grecorum potencia, rursus ab Oriente in Occidentem, a Grecis in potentissimos Germanos non sine superne disposicionis fato Romanum imperium translatum est.

> [And then, when the power of the Greeks had held the sacred summit of the Empire for only 415 years, the Roman Empire was transferred again from the east to the west, from the Greeks to the most powerful Germans, not without divine ordainment of the new state of affairs.]

While perhaps not quite a historical law, this movement of the *Imperium* is one of many pieces of evidence Hermann Peter gathers to show that the Germans had been predestined for the Empire. Caesar subdued all of Gaul and Germany, and established fortifications at Trier, Cologne, and Mainz (XII, 95). This was certainly to reflect the later patterns of imperial power in German hands.

An even clearer prefiguration rests on religious history. Saint Peter sent saints Valerius, Maternus, and Eucharius to Alsatia to convert the pagan. Maternus died upon arrival there. The two others returned, having buried Maternus. In Rome, Saint Peter gave them his staff—"baculus"—and told them to raise Maternus from the dead. And so they did. To this day the pope does not carry a staff. The custody of the staff of Saint Peter among the Germans shows that they were chosen above others for the governance of the Empire, and that they and the Empire in their possession were to be patrons of the Church (Hürbin, XII, 93–94):

> Hunc itaque baculum beatus Petrus Romanus episcopus per Eucharium et Valerium transmisit in Germaniam, dum pontifex Romanus in persona magnifici Karoli Romanum imperium de Grecis transtulit in Germanos.

> [And so, just as the blessed Peter, Roman bishop, transferred his staff to Germany through Eucharius and Valerius, did the Roman pope transfer the Roman Empire from the Greeks to the Germans in the person of the magnificent Charles.]

German protection of the Church coincides with the very beginnings of German possession of the Empire. Charlemagne's defeat of Desiderius, the Lombard king, had been to avenge the Pope (Hürbin, XII, 88–89). The Pope then raised Charles to the Empire, and when the coronation took place in Rome, the cry went forth (XII, 90):

> Karolo Augusto a Deo coronato magno et pacifico Imperatori Romanorum vita et victoria.

> [To the august Charles, crowned by God, the great and peaceful Emperor of the Romans, life and victory!]

The new Emperor had been crowned by God. Charles as King of the Franks was German, for the Franks' seat was first in Germany, and Charles himself had been born there. Charles combined three noble lines, in that he had Roman, Greek, and German ancestry. It is said of his parentage that he was *Romuleus matre, teutonicus patre*—"of Rome by his mother and a German by his father." "Romuleus" implies both old Rome and new Rome (Hürbin, XII, 92–93). The abiding piety of Emperors is exemplified by the religious Otto I and the generous benefactor of the Church Frederick II, and most importantly by the oath of the Emperor who swears to defend the Church from all enemies (XIII, 164, 175–76).

The intimate association of Church and Empire has roots in the very foundation of both. Christ Himself sanctified the Empire by choosing to come at the time of the universal peace engendered by the Roman imperial authority (Hürbin, XIII, 63). One cannot forget that Christ commanded that the things that are Caesar's be rendered to Caesar (XIII, 183). The special relationship of Church and Empire is further illustrated by the power which the Emperor alone, like no other ruler, wields over the Church (XIII, 184–85). Perhaps the most significant indication of the Empire's special function is that Antichrist cannot come as long as the Empire stands. When finally the great battle of Christ and Antichrist is complete and the last and perfect age come, then the world monarchy, that is, the Roman Empire, will become the *maximum triumphantissimumque imperium* (XIII, 219).

All questions fall away concerning the continuity of the ancient and medieval Empires, the German possession of the same, and the sanctity of the *Imperium*. The primacy of the Empire is also demonstrable. The immediate suzerainty of the Emperor receives visual confirmation in the three coronations: first by the Archbiship of Cologne in Aachen, then—with the Iron Crown—by the Archbishop of Milan in that city, and finally by the Pope in Rome.[39] The Emperor holds immediate power over Germany, Lombardy, and Italy. However, his rule extends well beyond those bounds.[40] The superiority of the authority of the Emperor of the Romans over other kings is shown in three ways: he is superior in dignity and power because he was approved by Christ Himself, because he holds special prerogatives with the Church, and because the imperial insignia are his. The diadem, the sword, the sceptre, and the globe are the emblems of his primary power. The authority of other kings is derivative, and their use of the insignia gains its authority from the imperial use. In short, the Emperor is *princeps mundi et dominus* (Hürbin, XIII, 182–86).

Although we shall touch on the *Imperium* repeatedly, we have with the three major learned texts thus far surveyed—those of Cusanus, Aeneas Sylvius, and now Hermann Peter—the basic picture of the

---

[39] Hürbin, XIII, 174. The text reads that the Iron Crown is conferred in Cologne. This must be an error in the transmission. The fame of the Iron Crown and its connection with the kingdom of Lombardy was too well known to permit Hermann Peter to have made such an error himself; but cf. James Bryce, *The Holy Roman Empire* (1904; reprinted New York, 1961), p. 194. For the history of the Iron Crown in Hermann Peter's time, cf. Reinhard Elze, "Die 'Eiserne Krone' in Monza," in *Herrschaftszeichen und Staatssymbolik*, Percy Ernst Schramm, ed., 3 vols., Schriften der MGH, XIII (Stuttgart, 1954–56), II, 477.

[40] In theory, Burgundy or the Arlate was also an imperial possession, and a coronation at Arles was occasionally held in addition to the others. The famous Duke of Burgundy, Charles the Bold, lusted after this crown. The feeble Frederick III decided to do nothing and thus eventually gain everything, thereby initiating a great Hapsburg tradition: cf. Sidney Painter, *A History of the Middle Ages* (London, 1965), p. 394.

myth of the *Imperium* in the Renaissance in Germany. All the other implications could be extracted from the statements of these authors. Let it not be believed, however, that these authors had more than one original idea each, if that, about the question of the Empire. Their opinions have full traditions, some as old as the Empire itself, some not older than two hundred or so years. Yet for the period, my suggested pattern—the Empire is Roman, German, sacred, and supreme— may be seen to represent with fair accuracy the picture these men had of the imperial myth.

The myth of the Empire could be a very delicate matter for the Italians with widespread political involvements. The most sophisticated of them had more than a mild contempt for the impotent political institution. The myth was, however, far from impotent and could not be wholly rejected or ignored. In 1471, Aeneas Sylvius sent his poet laureate ANTONIO CAMPANO to Germany to raise an army against the Turks. Elements of the imperial myth crept into his attempts at persuasion. His broadest effectiveness in Germany, however, had little to do with his mission. Campano suffered the fate of many a homesick European abroad: he was found out. His praise for Germany was unbounded when he was trying to win the German princes for the Turkish war; his disdain was unbounded when he was writing private letters home—and these soon found their way into German hands. The Germans are known to be barbarians, drunkards, enemies of learning, and what is more, they smell vile: "Taedia Germanica infinita sunt."[41] This was hardly calculated to make friends among the Germans. Some maintain that Campano was the source of the defensiveness that frequently marred German national self-consciousness among the humanists (Paul, *Studien*, p. 65).

Campano's praise, however, found in Germany at least as many eager ears as his criticism found angry ones. Other than Campano's few remarks on the Empire, all his comments seem to be directed toward the myth of ancient German warlike valor. This is quite understandable under the circumstances. Even the *Imperium* is used to move the Germans to take up the crusade. The Empire has always been in German hands, and the fate of Christendom has always been the fate of the Empire (Paul, *Studien*, pp. 60–61). Campano told his audience of German princes that the ancient Germans had never been

---

[41] Freher/Struve, II, 294; also Hans Tiedemann, *Tacitus und das National-bewusstsein der deutschen Humanisten . . .* (Berlin, 1913), p. 2.

conquered, that they never suffered foreign rulers, and that they became the noble families of all European nations. In ancient times their inborn martial quality was readily visible in their terrifying appearance. Even the women shared this—the inborn martial quality, of course. Alexander the Great himself admitted the invincibility of the Germans. The saying is well known: Let him who wishes to make an unfortunate war make it with Germans.[42] In the old Empire, the greatest victories were won with German armies, and the Emperors themselves kept German bodyguards. The very name "Germanicus" became a title of honor among generals and Emperors (Paul, *Studien*, pp. 60–65). It is a considerable irony that Campano, who was terribly unhappy during his German sojourn and who detested everything north of the Alps, gave several German patriotic slogans the formulation in which they were to become common usage.

Up to this point, Alexander the Great has been seen only as an antecedent of Germans, that is, Saxons, and hardly as one who had either to deal or to avoid dealing with Germans. The mythical connections happen to become much closer than mere avoidance. Alexander as ancestor and as antagonist of Germans appears with numerous other myths of German antiquities in WERNER ROLEVINCK's book in praise of Westphalia (ed. princ. 1472).[43] I return to the pattern of origins, heroes, religion, virtue and vice, and the *Imperium* for a systematic review of Rolevinck's book.

All the people of Germany seem to stem from Japhet, over Magog. This includes Poles, Austrians, Bohemians, Prussians, Thuringians, Hessians, Swabians, Franconians, Saxons, and Westphalians. Of all Germans, the oldest are the Goths. Their first ruler was Tan of the line of Japhet. Tan is the father of the Hungarians and their neighbors the Danes (*De laude*, pp. 22–23). Even Alexander the Great feared the Goths, saying, "let him who desires to be victor, abstain from Goths" (pp. 20–21). The Saxons originate more proximately from Alexander's Macedonian army. Rolevinck perhaps forgets that he already has the Saxons stemming from Japhet, over Magog. Perhaps he meant to imply that Alexander was a Saxon to begin with. Actually

---

[42] Much the same sequence of persuasive tactics appears in Paulus Riccius's speech exhorting to a Turkish war in 1544, see Freher/Struve, III, 455.

[43] Hermann Bücker, ed., *Werner Rolevinck (1425–1502): Ein Buch zum Lobe Westfalens des alten Sachsenlands* [*De laude antiquae Saxoniae nunc Westphaliae dictae*] (Münster, 1953), p. vi [hereafter cited as *De laude*]. Cf. Potthast, pp. 982–83. Rolevinck's *Fasciculus Temporum* was a greater success; cf. Borst, III.i, 1038–39.

Japhet is traditionally considered the father of the European peoples, which would include Macedonians. Magog, however, is normally reserved for the Goths or Scythians, so that a real, if slight, confusion prevails in the account.

Rolevinck takes his readers back to the Golden Age, the *Saturnia tempora*, to explain the aboriginal conditions of Westphalia which, like Italy before the arrival of Aeneas, was simple but free. Westphalia, like Italy, was invaded. The invaders were members of Alexander's army who had been left behind at the Caspian Sea to guard the rear when Alexander attacked Porus of India. When Alexander returned to Babylon and died of poisoning, they were stranded at the *Saxum Marpesiae*. They crossed the sea, and twenty-four of their ships eventually reached the mouth of the Elbe. When asked whence they came, they replied, "de saxo," which is why they are called Saxons. Some withdrew to the woody marshes and so named Holstein, which is derived from "Holtsassen,"—"wood-Saxons." They faced and defeated the Thuringians, whom they drove into the Harz (*De laude*, pp. 28–31). Their lands include Westphalia whose original inhabitants are said to have been giants (pp. 12–14).

In the time of Theodosius II some of the Saxons moved to the court of the British king to ask if they might settle his lands. They had been selected by lot to emigrate from their overpopulated homeland. In Britain, they aided the King against his rebellious subjects and married him off to a Saxon maiden, Engela, daughter of the Duke of Engern, whence England later received its name. The island had been called Albion in the time of David the Psalmist, and after Brutus of Troy conquered it, Britain (*De laude*, pp. 38–43). The Saxons are thought also to have fathered the Turkish menace: some pagan Saxons fled Charlemagne into Sarmatia and to this day wage war against the Christians (pp. 114–15).

Certainly the greatest hero of the German past for Rolevinck was Charlemagne, despite Charles's difficulties with the Saxons. He was an heir of the noblest Roman, Greek, Frankish, and Alemannic lines (*De laude*, pp. 72–73). Charles's victories were universal. He was the only conqueror, since the Macedonian Saxons, to subdue Westphalia, and the first since Julius Caesar to subdue the Saxons. For Caesar and Drusus, these successes had been at the cost of tremendous losses (pp. 12–13, 28ff., 32–38). Of course, things did not always go smoothly with Charles. Once he had to flee an exceptionally large host which outnumbered his own forces. He crossed the river Main and thus named Frankfurt. Fleeing, he said, "it is better to say that Charles fled his enemies than to say that he was killed" (pp. 70–71). In his outraged sense of justice, Charles established secret courts to deal with marauding Saxons. They were called "veme" out of "we my," that is, "woe is me" (pp. 92–95).

The ancient religion of the Saxons seems to have included worship of the sun. Upon their first entry into Britain and their appearance at the royal court, they confessed this to be their cult and that of their ancestors (*De laude*, pp. 40–41). They seem also to have worshipped Hermes, as witness the "Hermeseul" which was destroyed by Charlemagne. In its vicinity, there stood statues of Mars, Mercury, Hercules, and Apollo. The most important of these was Mars, and it was the first one that Charles destroyed (pp. 74–75). Rolevinck strongly implies that the ancient Westphalians are among those pagans, or rather pre-Christians, who had been granted extraordinary favor as regards their salvation, if they had been just (pp. 26–77). Rolevinck does not, however, go into the theological details of this justice.

A strong sense of human justice had always been among the first virtues of the Westphalians. For example, a ten-year-old boy had been told by his father to hold a man by the coat while the father killed the man. The father was executed. The boy was held until he was fourteen, and then he, too, was executed (*De laude*, pp. 50–51). Among the Saxons, crimes against marriage were severely punished. Adulterers were hanged over the graves of the adulteresses who were punished with suffocation and burning. Adulteresses might also be punished by being driven from village to village by the honorable women, who struck them with whips and knives until they died (pp. 46–47). Humility is also a virtue of the Westphalians. Whereas the Romans performed great deeds and complained of having no one to immortalize them, the Greeks did next to nothing but had loquacious authors to preserve their meaningless history. The Westphalians, in apparent analogy to the Romans, had to wait until Rolevinck, so he modestly assures us, for their modest silence to be broken (pp. 10–11).

Slanderers say that Westphalia comes from the word "fallo," "I deceive," and that the Westphalians are robbers, but that is untrue (*De laude*, pp. 202–3). The Westphalians were peace-loving, but nonetheless valorous in war. Let him who doubts that the Westphalians are the descendents of a peace-loving people read the old histories. Nowhere will they find a mention of the Westphalians in accounts of all the gruesome wars (pp. 28–29). On the other hand, only Macedonians and much later Franks were able to conquer Westphalia. An extension of Westphalia's peaceful virtue is the present flourishing of scholarship: there are Westphalians at every university in the world (pp. 130–31).

The warlike valor of the Germans at large takes an important part of Rolevinck's eulogy of Westphalia. Alexander the Great knew enough to fear the Goths. Caesar was able to defeat the Goths en route to his battle with Pompey only because fortune had turned her back on them, as Caesar was the first one to admit. The Goths in their various branches conquered not only Rome herself, but all of Italy, Africa, Lombardy, Gaul, and Spain. But the great realm of the Goths could not become one of the principal nations because they were too barbaric (*De laude*, pp. 22–23). (This is one of those historical observations that makes a student wonder just how unsophisticated the unsophisticated historical writing of the fifteenth century was.) Barbaric or not, the German nations caused their enemies considerable grief. The costly wars of the Romans against the Germans, where, for example, Quintilius Varus lost so many men, were thought to be the worst since the Punic wars (pp. 14–15). The Saxons, too, were virtually unconquered, falling only to Caesar and Charlemagne (pp. 30–33). They won the whole island of Britain in two hundred years of battle (pp. 42–43). Their ferocity had emblematic representation in the banners which they carried into battle. These were covered with images of lions, dragons, and eagles (pp. 76–77). They were so insistently independent that they never enjoyed a king, but had satraps, individual warlords, until the time of Charlemagne (pp. 44–45, 58–59).

All of Rolevinck's myths of the *Imperium* are interwoven with the great Charles. The supremacy of the Empire over other monarchies has no explicit defense in Rolevinck, although it may be assumed or implied in the sanctity of the Empire. The identity of the Roman and German Empires is clear to the chronicler: Charlemagne's wars in behalf of his own state were waged for the glory of the Roman people (*De laude*, pp. 74–75). The Romans cried out at Charles's imperial coronation: "*felicior Octaviano, melior Traiano!*" (pp. 110–11). The German character of the Empire or, perhaps better, the unity of German and Roman is well demonstrated in Charles's ancestry, a neat balance of Germanic and Mediterranean (pp. 72–73).

Charles was called by God to win the Saxons to Christianity by the sword (*De laude*, pp. 66–67). His destruction of pagan idols is but one example of his labor in behalf of the freedom of Christianity. Only fitting to his apostolic dignity—the words are Rolevinck's—were his efforts for the expansion of the true faith (pp. 74–75). He came into possession of the Empire when Pope Leo, eyes and tongue cut out, fled to Saxony and sought Charles's aid (pp. 106–7). He rendered a greater service to the Church by the foundation of various bishoprics, churches, and missions, for example, in Osnabrück, Halberstadt, Min-

den, Bremen, Paderborn, Magdeburg, Hildesheim, and Hamburg.[44]
Perhaps the most vivid reminder of the sanctity of the Empire is to be
found in the elevation to sainthood of the renewer of the Empire:
Charlemagne was eventually canonized.[45]

It is a pity that Werner Rolevinck's praise of Westphalia has escaped the attention of so much past research; his work is quite charming and contains many fine stories which would be of interest to folk-
lorists, jurists, and cultural historians, not to mention students of
literature. Its value does not always lie in its originality; originality is
not necessarily a virtue in the writing of history, particularly so in the
Renaissance. The work of Rolevinck's is, however, hardly an imitation
of the older traditions of historical writing. On the contrary, it is
written partly in the most up-to-date style of the fresh-look-at-history
in the fifteenth century: he surely had a Gobelinus manuscript before
him while composing his eulogy.[46] Alongside the tales of origin, stories
of the few heroes of German-Germanic antiquity, and significant comments on the Empire, Rolevinck's most notable addition to the picture
is his description of the virtue of his people. It gives a good insight
into what a Renaissance man, who happened not to be a humanist,
thought important: piety, modesty, learning, justice, peace, and valor.
This may be accepted as a further indication of the gradual burgher
domination of cultural values. These very values set the tone for much
of the historical writing of the period. The burghers wished their
origins praised, their homelands honored, and their values glorified.
One might venture to suggest that burgher interests contributed es-
sentially to the new attention given national and provincial history.
Dynastic ambitions still prevailed and still enforced their control of
most cultural expressions. But historical writing became progressively
more indebted to the wealth and curiosity of the new social force.

---

[44] *De laude*, pp. 98–105. While Charles founded many religious institutions,
several of those attributed to him were the work of the Ottos. The fact that most
of them were intented for the germanization as much as for the christianization of
the trans-Elbe Slavs made little difference to Rolevinck, although he may have been
aware of it; see pp. 86–87.

[45] *De laude*, pp. 112–13. Rolevinck places it correctly at the time of Frederick I,
but mistakenly names one Pope Zachary as the promulgator of the new saint. In
fact, Barbarossa's anti-pope Pascal III canonized Charlemagne. The canonization
was never ratified, but Charlemagne may be revered as "beatus" in the diocese of
Aachen; cf. Bücker's note 68, *De laude*, p. 253, and comp. Hermann Bücker,
Werner Rolevinck: Leben und Persönlichkeit, Geschichte und Kultur, IV (Münster,
1953), p. 52.

[46] Cf. Bücker, *Leben und Persönlichkeit*, p. 49; Rolevinck's debt is greater than
a mere perusal ("einsehen") of the *Cosmodromium* would suggest.

A further sign of these developments is the burgher support of the Empire, implying the classic alliance of city and central government against a divisive aristocracy. Nürnberg, for example, housed both the imperial regalia and some of the most articulate burghers of the Renaissance. One of these was the Meistersinger HANS FOLZ. In a graphic and rather difficult poem of 1480, the reformer of the Meistersang puts the imperial myth in a literary costume.[47] I pass over the abstruse musical and emblematic preface and begin where a traveler tells the poet of the origins of the Empire. After the flood, the world was divided among Noah's sons, and the four Empires stem from them: from Cham, the Babylonians; from Sem, the Medes and Persians, followed by the Greeks; and from Japhet, the Romans (ll. 243–70); (Keller, p. 1308). The Empire moved from one to the other of these until it settled with the Romans (ll. 299–406). The poet then hears the history of Rome from the Kingdom, through the Republic, to the Empire (ll. 407–78). The Roman Empire then came to the Germans in the person of Pippin when he helped the pope. Helping the pope in like manner, Charlemagne defeated the Lombards and was crowned Emperor. He fathered an empire and a knighthood that thirsted for justice (ll. 564–97). The traveler then goes on to describe the organization of the Empire and thus to name the various Electors (ll. 610–22):

> Nun die nacion euch zu bedewten
> Sag ich römischen kanczler an
> Von meyncz pischoff auf deutsch nation
> Als schwaben peyern francken östreich
> Winden vngern peheim vnd der gleich
>
> Vnd über die welschen der von köln
> Zu des nacion mus hörn vnd söln
> Kalabria vnd portigall
> Aragon cecilg die vier lant all
>
> Der gallischen ist der von trir
> Der selb hat vnter seinr rifir
> Yberniam vnd auch norweden
> Engellant schotten vnd auch sweden.

[Now, to explain the nations to you,/ I list the Roman chancellors:/ the Bishop of Mainz is for the German nation,/ including Swabia, Bavaria, Franconia, Austria,/ Slavonia, Hungary, Bohemia, and the like.

---

[47] "Ystori vom Römischen Reich," in Adalbert von Keller, ed. *Fastnachtspiele aus dem fünfzehnten Jahrhundert*, BLVS, XXX (1853; reprinted Darmstadt, 1965), III, 1301–24. Also edited by Hanns Fischer, *Hans Folz: Die Reimpaarsprüche*, Münchener Texte und Untersuchungen zur deutschen Literatur des Mittelalters, I (Munich, 1961), pp. 331–57.

And for the Italians, the Bishop of Cologne./ To his nation must submit Calabria and Portugal,/ Aragon and Sicily, those countries four./

The Gallic chancellor is the Bishop of Trier./ The same has in his territory, Hibernia and Norway,/ England, Scotland, and Sweden.]

The traveler concludes by picturing the Empire as a well-built house with four columns who are the four dukes, followed by sets of four margraves, landgraves, burgraves, barons, counts, and knights, and then the commons, cities, towns, and villages (ll. 638–677).[48] The poet then takes up the narrative and tells of the terrible cost of internecine strife (ll. 692–754). He declares that the secular head of the world is ill, deceived by all (ll. 773–75):

> Nye süsser drost im geben wart
> Dan von reichart gebhardt clinghart
> Die ye der heyden apt göt warn

[Never was sweet consolation given him/ other than by Reichart, Gebhardt, and Clinghart,/ ever idols of the heathens.]

Folz concludes with a prayer for liberation from all tyrants, particularly the Turks (ll. 781–874).

Folz's poem manifestly accepts the imperial myth in its four elements. Although the entry of Pippin may seem somewhat troublesome, it is an acceptable variant. The historical and mythical traditions behind it are formidable. The mention of the three pagan gods is a serious curiosity, only partially explained by widespread dissatisfaction with Frederick III and the equally widespread knowledge of Frederick III's occult activities. Despite its simple verse form, naive tone, and seemingly transparent conceits, Folz's is a most sophisticated poem, rather like a Breughel engraving. Firm knowledge of the imperial myth in the Renaissance would be only a preliminary step toward interpreting the poem successfully. But that task must be reserved for another time and place.

Folz and Rolevinck are members of a popular, non-humanist tradition in Germany. The great progress of historical writing in the Italian *quattrocento* was accompanied by real counterparts who did not share the innovations. One such is the chronicler JACOBUS PHILIPPUS FORESTA of Bergamo. His compilation, however old-fashioned and non-humanistic, proved to be one of the most influential historical works

---

[48] The entire picture Folz describes, from the electors through the "pauren" appears in the great Nürnberg chronicle of Hartmann Schedel (Nürnberg, 1493), fols. CLXXXIII[v] to CLXXXV[r].

of the Renaissance.[49] Nine editions were published between its first appearance in 1483 and the author's death in 1520, and twenty-one Latin and vernacular editions had appeared, one in Spanish, by the end of the sixteenth century (Potthast, pp. 454–55). Although not a German, Foresta has a great many comments about things German, both fabulous and, in this case more importantly, real. He says little concerning the ancient religion of the Germans, and nothing of their ancient virtue and vice except for comments on their habitual victory in war. He deplores the immorality of the moderns, calling Vienna whore-ridden (*Supplementum*, p. 200[r]). Foresta deals extensively with the origins and heroic figures of many nations, even though we shall dwell only on the Germans.

While Meisterlin rejected Trojan origins for the Swabians, he tolerated such origins for the Franks and named the Trojan Franco as their ancestor. Foresta selects the same tradition for Frankish origins.[50] Francius, one of the sons of Hector, fled fallen Troy with Anthenor over the Maeotian Swamps, the Don, and the Danube. Later the Franks, named after Francius, came into contact with the Roman world. Emperor Valentinian confirmed the privilege of their using the name Frank as reward for their aid to the cause of Rome against the Alani (*Supplementum*, pp. 51[v]–52[r]). Trojan origins are also to be seen for the Sicambri, a people of Germany who settled in Flanders and are named after Sicambria, a sister of Priam (pp. 88[r] and 199[v]). Cologne, a city in lower Germany, also takes its origin from Troy. It was founded at the time of Aeneas and is named after Colonus of Troy.[51]

After Troy, the most popular place of origin for German people seems to be Scandinavia. Although the Burgundians initially came from Scythia, the home of the Huns, their more proximate origins are to be sought in "Scantania," an island in the Northern Ocean between Germany and Gothia. They took their name from their own word for castle, "Burg." In 39 A.D., this nation invaded Gaul (*Supplementum*, pp. 124[r]–124[v] and 169[r]). The Lombards, too, stem from that northern island, or to be more precise, from "Codanus" near Cymbria (p. 178[r]).

Foresta devotes much attention to the wars between Romans and

---

49 *Supplementum Supplementi Chronicarum.* I use the Venice edition of 1513, cited simply as *Supplementum*.

50 German authors of the period insist on the distinction between French and Frank, but persist in ignoring it nonetheless. Foresta seems to use the term "Franci" to indicate the tribe represented in Franconia and settled in France, in other words, correctly. When he wishes to contrast French and German he uses "Galli" and "Germani": *Supplementum*, p. 195r.

51 *Supplementum*, p. 92r. The context fails to reveal whether "Colonus" indicated a proper name or merely meant "colonist" or "farmer." Since it was taken up as a proper name in Germany, I chose that interpretation.

Germanic invaders and thereby betrays a sense of the history of the great migrations. Rome's early attempts to ward off the Germans met with dubious success, for Augustus is known to have lost three legions in Germany (*Supplementum*, p. 199ʳ). In the time of Valerian, the Germans burst upon Italy itself (p. 144ᵛ). The Vandals, whose home, Vandalia, is in northern Poland, had difficulties with the Goths under Geberich back in the time of Emperor Constantine. The Goths seem to have been the prime moving force of the Germanic migrations. The Gothic king, Theodoric, who was a contemporary of Attila ("rex superbia inflatus"), had a brother called Henry who ruled over the Spaniards, in Aquitaine, and over the Suecii (p. 156ʳ).⁵² It was at the hands of the Goths that the Empire was eventually destroyed (p. 160ᵛ). Perhaps Foresta uttered a sigh when he wrote that the last triumph of the Romans over the Germans took place under Probus in 278 A.D. (p. 147ᵛ). Despite all of this, Foresta was able to praise the fortitude and chastity of the German women during and after the battle of the Cimbri and Teutones against the Romans (p. 109ᵛ). It may have been a consolation to Jacobus that the Romans won.

Significant of a shifted emphasis in Renaissance historical writing is a growing tradition of attention to men of learning. We have thus far seen only isolated examples, such as Cusanus's mention of Hugh of St. Victor or Kiburger's probable invention of Alphonsus of Frisia. Foresta lists, as a regular and important item in his chronicle, a brief biography and bibliography of the scholars of any given age. He begins at least as early as Tacitus (*Supplementum*, p. 147ᵛ) and mentions among many others Merlin (p. 169ʳ), Paul the Deacon (p. 190ʳ), Hrabanus Maurus (p. 192ᵛ–193ʳ), Hildegard of Bingen (p. 220ᵛ), and Dante (p. 244ᵛ–245ʳ). Otto III also appears as a man of learning, with the additional title "mirabilia mundi" (p. 203ᵛ). To be noted in passing is Foresta's entry on Johannes, the German Benedictine, Abbot of Sponheim, whose life-long fame and posthumous notoriety help make him one of the most intriguing figures of the Renaissance; Foresta writes also of a man called "Faustus," who taught many the German art of printing books (pp. 332ʳ and 229ʳ resp.).

Foresta's myth of the *Imperium* rests on a tradition similar to that of Andreas of Regensburg, that is, the Ottonian succession to the Empire. Foresta tells us, like Folz, that the pope transferred the authority from the Greeks to the Franks with Pippin, and the Empire itself with Charles (*Supplementum*, pp. 188ʳ–190ʳ). The Empire was then held

---

⁵² The contemporaneity of Theodoric and Attila is an old fiction, represented in the popular tales of Theodoric as reflected in the last adventures of the *Nibelungenlied*. I mention the rule over the Suecii, because it seems to be an early and influential reference to possible connections between the Swiss and the Goths.

by the Gauls and the Lombards, until it came to Otto, and then for the first time it reached Germany where it remains to this day: "Imperium titulique imperiales a Romanis Gallisque ac Longobardis nostris ablati et Othone nunc translati: hic primum in germaniam transierunt: ubi et nunc usque conservant" (p. 198ᵛ). Despite the fact that the Goths destroyed the Empire, it seems to have survived long enough to move from the Romans to the Germans. Thus the Roman and the German aspects of the myth remain intact. Jacobus says little about the suzerainty of the Empire. Perhaps the Gaul–Italy–Germany pattern we saw in Andreas might prevail for Jacobus, but he does not give a clear statement on the extent of imperial authority. As a North Italian, Foresta could not view the Empire's actual authority with total equanimity, since the mere proximity of Lombardy constantly invited German intervention.

The Empire's religious function, on the other hand, is clearly demonstrated. Foresta tells of many pious acts by the Emperors, such as the transfer to Aachen of the robe of the Virgin by Charlemagne (*Supplementum*, p. 191ʳ). Charles, when he received the imperial crown, was thrice acclaimed by the Roman people, who wished life and victory to Charles, the great and peaceful Emperor of the Romans, who was crowned by God (p. 190ʳ). The poet Dante, Foresta tells us, asserted that the Empire depended from God alone (p. 244ᵛ–245ʳ).

Foresta's chronicle is a sign that major intellectual reforms like those of the Italian humanist historians were slow in permeating all instances of learned historical expression—even in Italy, and all the more so in Germany. Germany was particularly receptive to Foresta's manner of writing and his conception of history. Within a few years, his chronicle would become one of the basic constituents of the bibliophile world's most renowned historical work, Hartmann Schedel's *Nürnberger Chronik*. Foresta's importance lies, first, in his encyclopedic knowledge and, second, in his ability to give it comprehensible shape. This alone could guarantee his chronicle considerable influence. In addition, his innovations are relatively few and are wholly absorbed by the traditional form of the cosmography or universal chronicle. Thus, an imitation would represent a familiar historical genre to a non-Italian audience. This gradual introduction of innovations was precisely what the study of history was able to absorb in the North. Schedel's chronicle is the best example of the painfully slow but nonetheless certain diffusion of a new historical awareness.

Before turning to Schedel, however, we return to Schedel's friend SIGISMUND MEISTERLIN and Meisterlin's own Nürnberg chronicle (1488), produced some thirty years after his work on Augsburg.[53] If these thirty years increased Meisterlin's erudition—of the many sources credited to his preparations for the Nürnberg chronicle, over half are classical—they did nothing to dull his imagination.

Meisterlin is the first author of this group to trace the origins of the Swiss back to the Huns. In the year 470 A.D. Switter and Senner were the leaders of a tribe of Huns who were stranded in the Alps upon the death of Attila. The one took to the mountains, the other to the valleys. They grew to be enemies, and the one died at the hands of his brother. Switzerland takes its name from Switter (Kerler, p. 104). The Saxons, Meisterlin tells us, came from Britain in the time of Charlemagne (p. 69), and the Sicambri are a German tribe that migrated to Flanders (p. 36). He, of course, feels called upon to explain at least the origins of the name of his new city. One explanation is that it means "only one hill," "nur ein berg." Yet another says the name refers to nourishment, "Nährung-berg," as it were. Meisterlin seems to prefer the rendering "Nero-nberg," for the city was founded by Tiberius, called Nero (pp. 42–45). As for ancient worship, Meisterlin adds to his preoccupation with Zisa the East Frankish worship of Mars and Diana, also called Vesta, to whom a temple was supposed to have been dedicated in Würzburg (p. 54). Of ancient virtue and vice, the most important issue for Meisterlin seems to be that the ancient Germans failed to write their own history (p. 99): "das doch schentlich und kleglich ist,"—"which is, after all, disgraceful and lamentable." His sincere and angry denunciations of this omission appear repeatedly (e. g., pp. 55 and 167). Most movingly does Meisterlin the humanist mourn the loss of Pliny's thirty-two books on Germany (p. 55): "o daß die in unser hant weren komen!"—"Oh, that they were come into our hands!" One cannot help but concur.

The *Imperium* appears in most of its conventional aspects in this work of Meisterlin. Before he introduces Charlemagne, he proceeds through a list of emperors from Constantine the Great (Kerler, pp. 56–58). This is, of course, done not in order to demonstrate Charlemagne's valid succession, but because it was assumed. Charlemagne and the Empire were both German; Charles was an East Frank, and when the Empire came to him, it came to Germany (p. 195). Curiously, Meisterlin writes "in Germaniam" in the German text (p. 58). Latin phrases are in themselves not extraordinary, but this case assumes certain difficulties. Possibly Meisterlin wished to avoid a duplication of

---

[53] Dietrich Kerler, ed., *Sigismund Meisterlin's Chronik der Reichsstadt Nürnberg 1488*, Chroniken der deutschen Städte, III (Leipzig, 1864), pp. 5–6 and 9 [henceforth "Kerler"].

the transference of the Empire to Germany, for he says that Otto was the first Emperor in "hoch teutschen landen" (p. 67)—this in spite of the fact that Otto was anything but High German. The religious aspect of the Empire is suggested by the title "aller cristenlichster keiser," which Meisterlin gave Otto (p. 67). This is almost certainly an unobtrusive complaint against French monopoly of the title "christianissimus." Later humanists were to consider this a most controversial issue (cf. Bebel, below).

In many ways, Meisterlin combines the worst virtues of old-fashioned and new humanistic writing in the Renaissance. He is firmly ecclesiastical and quite credulous when it comes to miracles and the like. On the other hand, he attempts to be critical and thereby excises some of the most charming materials from his sources. He lost the sense of naivety that characterized most of his German predecessors and he failed, on the other hand, to acquire either the critical acuity of a Bruni or the anecdotal talents of an Aeneas Sylvius. Meisterlin's importance to German historical writing is that of a pioneer. The cultivation and reaping of the idea was to be the work of other hands.

The disparity between humanist historiographic standards and popular tastes remained great in the fifteenth century. Meisterlin's works were not printed until well into the next century, and much more fantastic works proved to be incunabula best-sellers. One of the most fantastic and popular was THOMAS LIRER's chronicle of lies.[54] What appears to be a twelfth-century document was expanded, amended, and linguistically revised for the fifteenth-century audience, so we may fairly consider it in the company of other documents of this period. There is in fact no other place for it.

In the year 104, Emperor Kurio and his Empress Docka were converted to Christianity by Theonestus who was preaching in Rome (*Chronik*, fol. a, iiii^r). The imperial family was subsequently driven out by an infidel Senate and fled to the north (fol. [a v]^r). Kurio performed many good deeds there, christianizing far and wide, and defeating in battle many pagans. Through him, Rumulus became the first Christian Duke of Swabia (fol. [b i]^v). The exiled Emperor died in the year 172 and was buried in the monastery at Fischingen (fol. [b ii]^v).

---

[54] Ernst Voulliéme, ed., *Thomas Lirer: Schwäbische Chronik ... 1486* (Potsdam, n.d.), postscript, p. 4; comp. Eugen Thurnher, ed., *Thomas Lirer: Schwäbische Chronik*, Vorarlberger Schrifttum, VIII (Bregenz, n.d.), p. XIIf., who maintains that it is a fifteenth-century document in its entirety.

Rumulus followed him into a Christian death in A.D. 222 (fol. [b iii]^v). The family of Rumulus included Ernst and Ludwig of Bavaria who met Emperor Constantine while attacking the Huns. In the night before the attack, Constantine was told to make a banner with a red cross on the one side and the Virgin with Child before a sun on the other. With it he defeated the enemy, although outnumbered by thirty times (fol. [b viii]^r). Many Germans helped Constantine in his victory, and for their service, he granted them the privilege of native judges (fol. [c i]^v). His mother, Helena, found in Jerusalem the true cross and many sacred relics, of which she sent a great part to Germany (fol. [c v]^r f.).

Somewhat later in the chronicle, the author tells us of the first Roman Emperor fol. [f ii]^v): "der hieß Julius, der was ain teütscher man und was von Trier bürtig." [His name was Julius. He was a German born in Trier.] Julius was sent from Rome to Swabia in order to collect tribute, but the Swabians and Julius got along very well (fol. f iii^r f.). He built them the city of Vienna (fol. f iii^v), and for their aid to him against the Romans he gave them special privileges fol. [f iv]^v). The chronicle which is appended to Lirer's work begins with the fall of Troy and the founding of Rome (fol. i ii^r), and continues over Julius Caesar and Charlemagne to Charles IV, concluding with the history of several German cities up to the year 1462.

Lirer's chronicle is so imaginative that one wonders whether it has any place at all in the historiography of the period. Its relationship to recognizable historical writing is approximately that of the Tristan Chapbook to Gottfried von Strassburg's epic. Lirer's fantasies would make no sense at all without the categories of historical thought we have seen expressed in these texts. The German-ness of the Empire and the sanctity of its work are so important to Lirer that Caesar becomes German, and Germany the home of christianization. In the woodcuts accompanying the text, the Emperor—be he Kurio, Constantine, or whoever (fols. [a iii]^v and [b viii]^v)—appears with the same imperial crown as worn by Frederick III. A German, a Byzantine, and a confabulated Roman Emperor were all one and the same for the artist. Lirer would certainly have agreed.

Lirer's chronicle, in delightful and straightforward German prose, possesses no small quality as pure story-telling. It is uncritical and naive, but a good fairy-tale also has these characteristics. Neither can ignore the strict requirements of narrative literature. This curious chronicle calls for interpretation as a Chapbook, that is, as literature of a popular vein. That call is a reminder that "story" and "history" have more than etymological similarities in early modern literature.

The great humanist and *magus*, Agrippa of Nettesheim, makes no distinction between the historians of Arthur, Lancelot, and Tristan, and those of Hannibal, Pompey, and Caesar. They are all equally liars according to Agrippa.[55] Poor Lirer was similarly abused by the chroniclers of the Zimmern family, who themselves were no Leopold von Rankes.[56] It is, however, quite unfair to accuse Lirer or his kind of lying. They were writing "Geschichte," whether "story" or "history." Lirer is perhaps too free. But one must think of Jean Paul's Schulmeisterlein Wuz, who was too poor to purchase or otherwise acquire the famous books—so he sat at home and wrote them out, imagining what they ought to contain. Lirer's history is the product of a similarly deprived and imaginative author.

Wide distribution was not limited only to the most fantastic works. Those which spoke to the interests of the fifteenth century could include attempts at major synthesis. Of these the most popular was the work of one of the busiest and friendliest humanists of the fifteenth century, HARTMANN SCHEDEL. He is a household word among bibliophiles, but for others he remains a somewhat two-dimensional figure. There seems to be a vague recollection that he copied a great many manuscripts, some of which are the unique copies of the works they contain. Others may remember his name in association with one or another renowned scholar or poet, for he seems to have known all his contemporaries. But his abiding fame lies with the great *Liber Cronicarum* of 1493. Schedel's chronicle contains a wealth of material which is just short of opulent, if almost entirely unoriginal. The volume itself is a handsome thing and a pleasure to work with. A bibliophile description is available in Henry Lewis Bullen's *The Nurenberg Chronicle* (San Francisco, 1930), so I shall forego further rhapsodizing.

The map of Europe in Schedel's chronicle was little changed from the time of Gobelinus Persona. Germany still was bounded by the Danube, the Rhine, and Ocean, and was still so named because of the number and great size of its people and the fertility of its increasing land. In antiquity, Germany was famous for its export of crystal gems (fol. XIII^v). Japhet, son of Noah, is known as father of Europe. Gomer, the eldest grandson, is father of the Gauls; Magog, the next in age, father of the Goths (fol. XVI^r). The Swabians stem directly

---

[55] *De incertitudine et vanitate scientium et artium*, ch. V; cf. Fritz Mauthner, ed., *Agrippa von Nettesheim: Die Eitelkeit und Unsicherheit der Wissenschaften*, 2 vols., Bibliothek der Philosophen, V and VIII (Munich, 1913), I, 42–48.

[56] Hansmartin Decker-Hauff, ed., *Die Chronik der Grafen von Zimmern*, 6 vols. in progress (Darmstadt, 1964, 1967——), II, 365.

from Japhet, and their city Augsburg, fortified by Drusus, is said to be older than Troy (fol. XCI^v). Nürnberg seems to have younger origins, since it is named after Tiberius or Drusus Nero (fol. C^v). The Franks stem from Franco who left Troy and founded Sicambria; Mainz also took its origins from Troy, as did the whole nation of the Turks (fol. XXXVII^r and XXXIX^v). Cologne is said to have been built by Colonus of Troy (fol. XC^v). The Lombards come from Scandinavia, a German island, and their original leaders were Aio and Thato. The next generations under Agelmundus and Godooth consolidated Lombard power (fol. CXLVII^r).

Regrettably we must pass over Tubal, father of Spain; Czechius, father of Bohemia; Aeneas Sylvius, ancient King of Rome; Joachim, the apocalyptic prophet; Sophia and her three daughters, Faith, Hope, and Charity; Merlin, Arthur, Dante, Petrarch, Pope Joan, and a host of other mythical figures, who would be of great interest. Alas, they are not German. Schedel does, however, mention a good many German-Germanic figures. His portrayal of them is, by and large, so simple that only the briefest mention need be made to indicate his awareness of their importance. Alaric the Goth is known to have been buried in the river Busentus, which had been diverted by his men so that no one could desecrate the grave (fol. CXXXV^v). Hermigildus of the Visigoths converted Spain to orthodoxy (fol. CXLIX^v). Hrabanus Maurus and Walahfrid Strabo are learned men who flourished in the time of the Carolingians (fol. CLXIX^r). Hildegard of Bingen, a woman of great learning and, some say, prophetess, flourished in the time of Frederick I (fol. CC^v). And so it goes on. With Foresta and Schedel, it is possible to see the gradual establishment of the convention of including the learned in works of history. This is a rather significant practice, since it implies a power and influence of the man of learning comparable to that of the man of politics, and implies at least equal importance as a constituent of a culture.

Of ancient religion, Hartmann tells us that Ziza had been worshiped at Augsburg (fol. XCIV). There are indications that the ancient Germans included Venus in the pantheon, for Magdeburg was once called Parthenopolis after "Venus Parthenis" (fol. CLXXIX^v). Hartmann passes on a description of a curious custom, the conjuring of the Rhine. Every year on the vigil of the feast of John the Baptist, the women of Cologne go out and wade into the river, strewing herbs on the water so that the Rhine may bring them good fortune in the coming year (fol. XCI^r).

Valor is, as usual, the great virtue of the ancient Germans, even in the defeat of the Cimbri and Teutones by Marius (fol. LXXXV^v). It is illustrated in their battles with Caesar, the defeat of Varus, German penetration into Spain, and the need of Rome to make peace with them (fols. XCIᵛ, CXXIʳ, CXXXVIIʳ). Perhaps learning may be added, in view of the biographies of German scholars among the other historical figures. Piety is most certainly an ancient virtue of the Germans, as represented for example by Clovis, with his abandonment of idolatry and his revival of the *respublica christiana* (fol. CXLIIIʳ).

This of course brings us to Clovis's successor Charlemagne and to the *Imperium*. The propriety of Charles's eventual succession to the Empire is shown by his virtue as ideal ruler. He brought peace and justice to Italy (fol. LVIIIᵛ), defeated the impious Milanese (fol. LXXIIʳ), and brought the robe of the Virgin to Cologne. He is called "the Great" because of the multitude of merits he won and because of his efforts for the liberty of Christians (fol. CLXVIIIʳ). Charles was King of the Franks and by nation a German. After his death, the Empire moved to Gaul and Lombardy, and was rescued from obscurity by Otto (fol. CLXXVIIIʳ). Thus did Schedel reconcile his source, Foresta, with his own budding nationalism. Charlemagne and the Empire are German. The Empire and the Emperors are Roman as well. The handful of woodcuts that had to be used for hundreds of illustrations often repeated themselves. Julius Caesar and Ludwig II are, as it happens, identical (fols. XCIIIʳ and CLXXIʳ). What is more, they both carry the imperial insignia and crown of Frederick III. The stability and continuity of the Empire are further confirmed in Schedel's use of Foresta's migration of the Roman Empire from Gauls to Lombards to Germans. The sanctity of the Empire is shown by Charlemagne's divine coronation (fol. CLXVIIᵛ), his above mentioned services to Christendom, and by a curious occurrence at Mantua: the blood of Christ appeared miraculously and Pope Leo, seeing it, thought it proper to send it to Charles in Germany (LXXXIVʳ). The Emperor holds the supreme *potestas* in temporal matters (CLXXVIIIʳ). The reputation of one Emperor, Frederick II, was such that many years after his death a man appeared pretending to be the dead Emperor. He and his followers were burned (fol. CCXXᵛ).

Hartmann Schedel, as well as Andreas von Regensburg, Aeneas Sylvius, and Jacobus Foresta, appear among the sources of the Bavarian chronicler Veit Arnpeck (fl. 1493).[57] Despite the fact that these important sources of Arnpeck's work have been investigated here, enough new material appears to warrant a brief consideration. The Swabians

---

[57] Georg Leidinger, ed., *Veit Arnpeck: Sämtliche Chroniken*, Quellen und Erörterungen zur bayerischen und deutschen Geschichte, N.F. III (Munich, 1915), pp. xxv, xxixff. [henceforth "*Arnpeck*"].

here also originate from Japhet. They encountered the Amazons and worshipped Zisa (*Arnpeck*, pp. 26–27). We have seen these frequently. It might, however, be worthwhile to mention that a Varus Day was still celebrated in Augsburg in Arnpeck's time, as he reports. It was to commemorate the Swabian victory over the Romans near Augsburg, as they thought, that led Augustus to cry out (p. 449): "Quintili Var du wirdest widergeben die erschlagen legion!"

Veit Arnpeck gives a minor variant on the tale of the origins of the Bavarians. Baioarius led his people out of Armenia with his sons, Boemund and Ingeraman. Their great city, Nürnberg, was founded by Noricus, son of Hercules, around 1200 B.C. (*Arnpeck*, p. 447; cf. p. 22). Among the younger rulers and heroes of the Bavarians are another Boemundus, who was Duke at the time of Caesar (p. 25), Theodo, who fled Tiberius alongside the Ostrogoths (p. 28), Adalger, son of Theodo, who battled Emperor Severus (p. 453f.; cf. p. 38), Udo, Theobald, Tassilo, and Garibaldus, King of Bavaria, who married into the Lombards (p. 43). The vitality of these traditions is demonstrated in a *Chronik der Pfalzgrafen bei Rhein und Herzogen in Bayern* of 1501 in which a family tree quite literally sprouts Bavarus, Ingram, Boemund, Adelger, and Norix, among others.[58]

Of their ancient religion it is known that they worshipped Mercury, Hercules, and Mars (*Arnpeck*, p. 4). Mercury, we read in a contemporary and related document, had been given a temple near Trier by Caesar.[59] Charlemagne is supposed to have destroyed such a temple at Regensburg. Of ancient virtue it is enough to know that the Germans were strong and generous (p. 4), and their piety is well represented by the sainted Empress Kunigunde (pp. 147ff.).

If Arnpeck's contributions to the myth of the Empire are negligible, SEBASTIAN BRANT is a good complement, since his contributions to the other myths of the German past seem to be negligible. In Brant's famous *Narrenschiff* (1494) the continuity of the Roman Empire into his own times is assumed. In the chapter "von end des gewalttes"—of the end of power—Brant speaks of the vanity of power. He begins speaking of Julius Caesar and ends (*Brant* LVI, ll. 83–94):[60]

---

[58] Vol. II, plates, unpaginated, edited by Georg Leidinger (Strassburg, 1902).

[59] Dietrich Kerler, ed., "Eine deutsche Weltchronik," *Chroniken der deutschen Städte, III* (Leipzig, 1864), p. 270.

[60] Friedrich Zarncke, ed., *Sebastian Brant: Narrenschiff* (1854; reprinted Darmstadt 1964), p. 57 [henceforth "*Brant*"]. The reference in l. 93. is to the Hapsburg motto AEIOU, "alles Erdreich ist Österreich Untertan." The translations from the *Narrenschiff* here and below were taken from Sebastian Brant, *The Ship of Fools*, Edwin H. Zeydel, trans. (1944; New York, n.d.), pp. 193 and 320.

Groß narrheyt ist vmb grossen gwalt
Dann man jn seltten langzyt bhalt
So ich durch such all rich do hår
Assyrien, Meden, Persyer,
Macedonum vnd kriechen landt
Carthago, vnd der Römer standt
So hatt es als gehan sin zyl
Das römsch rich blibt so lang got will,
Got hat jm gsetzt syn zytt vnd moß
Der geb, das es noch werd so groß
Das jm all erd sy vnderthon
Als es von recht, vnd gsatz solt han.

[Great folly 'tis to have great might,/ It often lives one day or night./ When all the states on earth I scan,/ Th' Assyrian, Persian, Median,/ And Macedon, the states of Greece,/ Or Carthage, Rome, they found their peace,/ They all now slumber under sod./ Our Roman Empire trusts in God,/ He's granted it a time and fate,/ May He still fashion it so great/ That all the world its cause may serve/ To such extent as it deserve.]

Emperor Maximilian is addressed by Brant "Traiano melior,"— "better than Trajan" (*Brant*, p. 197). Throughout his work, Brant insists upon the German character of the Empire. In the poem he prepared for Jacob Locher's (called Philomusus) Latin translation of the *Narrenschiff* (1497 and 1498), we read that Charlemagne was born in Germany, near Mainz. He was an East Frank, from which nation the France of the Gauls is named, and he brought the holy sceptre of the Empire to Germany, where it resides to this day (p. 125). In the *Narrenschiff* itself Brant says (XCIX, ll.140–42, p. 95):

Der tütschen lob was hochgeert
Vnd hatt erworben durch solch rům
Das man jnn gab das keyserthům

[The Germans once were highly praised/ And so illustrious was their fame,/ The Reich was theirs and took their name.]

The holiness of the Empire comes to the fore in the poet's confidence that Maximilian will reconquer the Holy Land, a task intimately connected with his worthiness to wear the Roman crown (XCIX, ll.159ff., p. 95). A special duty of the defender of Christianity is to assault the pagan. The primacy of the Empire is clearly in Brant's mind when he writes that right and law make the whole world subject to the Roman Empire, as we have just seen in Brant's chapter on the end of power.

With Brant there enters a new generation of Renaissance men in Germany. Other authors mentioned here lived most of their productive lives in the reign of Frederick III. Brant and his contemporaries are much more closely associated with Maximilian I, among the most interesting of Renaissance princes. In their generation the influence of humanism grows visibly more pervasive. Although many traditions and some genres remain untouched, the greater part of scholarly life is determined to some extent by Italian (and anti-Italian) humanism.

Aeneas Sylvius, Antonio Campano, and Jacobus Foresta are by no means the only Italians to have left their mark on Renaissance myths of the German past. At least as influential as Aeneas Sylvius is the deservedly unremembered ANNIUS of VITERBO, a librarian and censor in the service of the Borgia pope Alexander VI. Annius died in 1502, some say poisoned by the emnity of Cesare.[61] Like any self-respecting humanist, Annius felt a compulsion to discover and publish the texts of antiquity. He brought to light, by his industry and ingenuity, the long-lost books of Berosus of Babylon, Manetho, Metasthenes of Persia, and others. The discoveries were greeted with instant gratitude, as can be seen, for example, in their immediate and extensive reception in Germany.[62] In introducing his work to Ferdinand and Isabella, Annius explained his special duties to the truth, particularly due to his profession as theologian.[63] His discoveries were fabrications.

Annius of Viterbo's *Commentaria . . . super opera diversorum auctorum de Antiquitatibus* was published in Rome in 1498. In the same year, the texts alone without commentary were published in Venice, under the title *Auctores Vetustissimi nuper in lucem editi.* The heading of the first book of the antiquities of Berosus in the latter edition is (fol. f ii^v): *Berosi Babylonici dignitate Chaldei ad emendandos antiquitatum errores.* That errors about antiquity were to be emended by Annius's Berosus is a particularly tasty example of the topos of critical rejection.

Berosus, who flourished long before the reign of Alexander the Great, relates that Noah, also known as Janus and Caelum, fathered among many sons, Tuyscon Gygas, who was born to him after the flood. Tuyscon in turn fathered the Germans and Sarmatians. He was King in Europe from the Don to the Rhine. The Sarmatians include

---

[61] Cf. J. A. Farrar, *Literary Forgeries* (London, 1907), pp. 67–68.

[62] Cf. D. C. Allen, *The Legend of Noah* (Urbana, Ill., 1963), pp. 114–15 and Paul, *Studien*, p. 122.

[63] Cf. Farrar, *Literary Forgeries*, p. 69.

those who were to become Poles, Goths, Russians, Prussians, and Daci. The immediate ancestor of the Prussians is Prutus, son of Scytha, who gave his name to Prutia, now Prussia.[64]

Tuyscon's children include Mannus who, together with his father, was celebrated in song by the ancient Germans. Mannus's three sons named the Ingaevones who lived near Ocean, the Hermiones who lived in the midlands, and the Istevones who populated the rest of Germany. While Ingevon ruled among the Tuyscones, Osiris was teaching agriculture in Egypt. Tuyscon's posterity included Marsus, Gambrivus, Suevus, Vandalus, Hunnus, Hercules, and Teutates, all of whom fathered nations. While Herion, a man of ferocity in arms, ruled in Germany, Bardus ruled among the Celts. Gambrivus, who also ruled among the Tuyscones, was a man renowned for his fierce spirit. Later Sevus (or Suevus) ruled the Tuyscones. From Vandalus stem not only the Vandals, but also the Burgundians. Certainly among the most famous descendents of Tuyscon is Hercules Alemannus, who was also king among the Tuyscones, and who was sung by the Germans. Manethon, whose supposed works complement Pseudo-Berosus, informs us that while Aeneas Sylvius was King of the Latins, Francus, a son of Hector, ruled among the Celts.[65]

These myths will be viewed again in connection with a number of subsequent authors, for Annius's influence in Germany in this time was quite widespread. Despite the fact that the fraud was exposed early and often, it continued to find believers, even among the most distinguished humanists in Germany. It must indeed have been difficult for them to reject such fine origins, which happened to be corroborated by the unimpeachable Tacitus.[66] Annius's work went beyond mere pretense at fact. It was, in part, programmatic and prejudiced. The program included the establishment of independent origins and ancestries for all the known peoples of the West. Its prejudice included violently anti-Greek feelings. Both of these had warm receptions among the German humanists. The whole phenomenon is such a scholarly outrage that one wonders about Annius's intentions. It is conceivable that his works were misread in his time, and continue to be, insofar as they are read at all. A certain uneasiness accompanies

---

[64] *Commentaria*, fols. [N vii]r, P [i]v, P iir, [P iv]r. *Auctores*, fols. f iiiv, g iir.

[65] *Commentaria*, fols. [P iv]r, [Q v]r, [X iv]r, [Z viii]r. *Auctores*, fols. [h ii]rf., [h iii]vff., and i iiiv.

[66] Even the Italians were not immune. Farrar, *Literary Forgeries*, p. 78, gives one example of the survival of Annius's work into the 16th century: "Poor Leandro Alberti, who in 1568 published a *Description of Italy*, is said to have died of annoyance when he became aware of the worthlessness of some of the statements he had borrowed from Annius."

the facile dismissal of Berosus as a fraud. Undoubtedly, it was not what it pretended to be, but it may have been considerably more.

On one level, it would be interesting to discover what sources Annius plundered in addition to Tacitus. Some might be rare, still unknown, forgotten, or lost. As papal librarian, he may have had access to unusual materials. On another level, his confabulations beg for historical interpretation. The principles of his theft, of its organization, and of his bias may reveal a great deal about the history and historical imagination of his time. The possibility that it may be a *histoire à clef* cannot be excluded. Berosus is far from unique in the Renaissance. Fictitious authorities appear quite regularly, from Alfonsus of Frisia and "Pliny" to Hunibald, Schreitwein, and Freithylph. The tradition of forgery and fictitious authority is, to the best of my knowledge, almost wholly ignored by respectable scholarship. I cannot see why this tradition should be less informative than any other conventional way of describing the universe. Unfortunately, this is not the place to support these speculations, or even to continue them. The problem itself, however, calls attention to a great treasury of documents that awaits daring and creative exploitation. In 1605, Francis Bacon called for a history of monsters and exceptions. For historiography, it has yet to be written.

The tradition in which Annius wrote is still uncertain and obscure, and thus leaves room for much original work. The same is, alas, true of traditions that are more familiar. In the year after the publication of Annius's inventions, an anonymous chronicle appeared "van der hilliger stat van Coellen, 1499."[67] It is known as the *Koelhoffische Chronik* after the Cologne printer who published it. The Anonymous read Gobelinus Persona, Werner Rolevinck, Jacobus Foresta, and Hartmann Schedel, among others (Cardauns, p. 257), and is firmly in the tradition for which they stand. He nonetheless puts some myths into a new light.

The *Koelhoffische Chronik* touches none too lightly on myths of origin. It rejects most of the tales of the pre-Roman foundation of German cities, particularly the one making Colonus of Troy founder of Cologne (Cardauns, p. 278). The origin of Cologne is clear and known (p. 284):

---

[67] H. Cardauns, ed., in *Chroniken der deutschen Städte*, XIII (Leipzig, 1876), pp. 204–638; and all of *Chroniken . . . XIV* (Leipzig, 1877), pages numbered consecutively [henceforth "Cardauns"].

> Der herliche Marcus Agrippa ein heidensch man
> Vur gotz geburt Aggripinam nu Coelne began.

[The magnificent Marcus Agrippa, a heathen man/ before God's birth Agrippina, now called Cologne began.]

The Trojan origin of the Franks, however, seems perfectly acceptable. The chronicle selects the version that has Priam and Anthenor lead the Sicambri to Europe. From them originate both the French and the Franks, and the two nations are of equal distinction (pp. 364–65). The Anonymous's rejection of pre-Roman origins in no way influences the myths of Roman origins. Cologne, Trier, Regensburg, and Metz were all Roman fortifications. Augsburg was named in honor of Augustus, and Aachen (*Aquisgranum* or *Aquae Grani*) after Nero's brother Granus (pp. 276 and 412). This sharply skeptical and no less credulous approach to the myths of origin falls generally under the topos of critical rejection, *anasceua*. Although the Anonymous does not normally reject the one myth specifically in order to support the other, his iconoclastic view of origins lies well within the common Renaissance practice of selective criticism. His standards for accurate history come before his submission to written authority. Where the authority fails to meet his standards, the Anonymous is critical. Where there is no conflict between the two, the Anonymous submits to the authority. As far as the learned Latin tradition of the Middle Ages is concerned, such selective criticism is wholly unthinkable.

Among the figures larger than life that are mentioned in the chronicle are Attila, whom the Anonymous makes King of the Goths, Hildegard of Bingen, and Rainald, Archbishop of Cologne and Barbarossa's chancellor for Italy, who brought the remains of the Three Magi to Cologne (Cardauns, pp. 374, 508, 512ff.). This last event is a source of local pride to the Anonymous. He goes so far as to vary an almost invariable formula in honor of the Three Magi. He adds their names, "Jaspar, Balthasar, Melchior," to the traditional appeal to the Trinity at the outset of his work (p. 253). Local pride arises again when the Anonymous pointedly identifies Albertus Magnus and Duns Scotus with Cologne (p. 289). He denies indignantly all credibility in the stories that connect Judas the Betrayer and Pontius Pilate with German lands (pp. 311–12). Emperor Trajan, while himself not a German, did grant the city of Cologne a number of privileges, including a Golden Bull that excused them from tribute (p. 319). Of ancient religion the Anonymous knows only that Jupiter had once been worshipped at Trier (p. 278).

Of the hero Charlemagne the Anonymous relates one story little indebted to the *Imperium,* but of interest nonetheless. It has most distinguished Renaissance credentials, a connection with Petrarch. The story must originally have been in the mouth of the people. It came into learned tradition in a letter of Petrarch's, remained in the form he established, and is generally associated with his name. The Great Charles is said to have been so attached to his beloved that, when she died, he refused to let her body be taken away. A pious cleric, suspecting magic, discovered a ring under the tongue of the corpse. When he removed the ring, Charles was completely disgusted at the sight of the corpse. The priest saw the influence of the ring and, fearing that it might fall into the wrong hands, cast it into the waters near Aachen. From that time on, Charles preferred nothing to lingering near those waters (Cardauns, p. 412).[68]

The warlike valor of the Germans is supported by reports of the victory of the Cimbri and "Duitschen" (Teutones) over Manlius in 89 B.C. As though in complement, the Anonymous describes the defeat of the Franks, Saxons, Bavarians, Swabians, and Poles by Caesar (Cardauns, pp. 268–69). Caesar was, incidentally, a man of great learning, an astrologist, and the discoverer of the *aureum numerum.* The Anonymous also gives us Caesar's epitaph (p. 270):

> Julius bin ich, van roemschen rich
> der eirste keiser geweldichlich
> ich hain gewonnen met der hant
> Franken, Swaven, Schotten, Engelant,
> Flanderen, Frieslant, Brabant, Duitschlant, Nederlant,
> hoe ind neder Alemanien,
> Egipten, Africken, alle Hispanien,
> darzo vil ander koninkriche ind baroin
> zwank ich al an die roemsche kroin.
> nochtant weigernden si mir dat roemsche rich.
> dat gewan ich doch wederumb menlich
> ind regierde in groisser eren
> ind blief up erden here boven alle heren.
> zwei ind viertzich jair zovoren
> starf ich ee Christus wart geboren.

[Julius I am, of the Roman realm/ the first Caesar, powerful./ I won by arms/ Franconia, Swabia, Scotland, England,/ Flanders, Frisia, Brabant, Germany, the Netherlands,/ high and low Alemannia,/ Egypt, Africa, all Spain,/ and in addition, many kingdoms and principalities/ I forced to submit to the Roman crown./ But yet they denied me the Roman power./

---

[68] See Grimm, *Deutsche Sagen,* item 458, pp. 426–27.

I won it nonetheless, bravely,/ and reigned with great honor/ and remained on earth, lord over many lords./ Two and forty years before/
Christ was born I died.]

The Anonymous was evidently undisturbed by the Renaissance's discovery of the principle of anachronism.

The next generation of Roman conquerors included Drusus who
was poisoned at Mainz and buried outside the walls. A great monument marked the spot (Cardauns, pp. 274–75). The Anonymous has a
tolerably good sense of the succession of the great invasions, enumera-
ting the Goths, Huns, and Lombards, in that order, as enemies of
Italy—which is basically accurate. For the north he describes the invasions of Germany by the Hungarians (by which he means the succession of Huns, Avars, and Magyars), the Saxon invasion of Britain
(p. 276), and the Vandal invasion of Spain (p. 375).

The Anonymous of the *Koelhoffische Chronik* is thoroughly involved with the myth of the *Imperium*. He understood enough of the
implications of the legend of Saint Maternus to reject all connections
with Saint Peter (Cardauns, pp. 314ff.). The legend appears primarily
as an illustration of the early christianization of Germany. The connections with Saint Peter imply the dependence of the Empire in
northern possession on the See of Peter, which an imperially minded
historian would wish to avoid at all costs. A simple example shows
that the Anonymous conceives of the Empire as Roman and German
simultaneously: when he introduces Henry V, he identifies him as the
eighty-fifth Emperor since Julius and the eighth German Emperor
(p. 502). Counting backwards through the Salian and Saxon lines, one
reaches only Otto I. Yet the Anonymous makes it quite clear that
Charlemagne was German, had been born in Germany, and accepted
the Empire for Germany in his person (pp. 412 and 415). A certain
attempt at reconciliation of the traditions comes through in the Anonymous's denunciation of the Greeks, saying that they had no power in
the West since the Empire came to the French and the Germans—"an
die Franzosen is kommen ind an die Duitschen" (p. 415). The reconciliation becomes clearer when the Anonymous deeply regrets that
there are now two entities where, under Charlemagne, there had been
only one (p. 425). Thus, when Otto took the Empire, he became emperor only in Italy and Germany (pp. 429–30). In no case, however,
does the Anonymous tolerate the slightest interruption in the transmission of the Empire: "So is it clairlich zo mirken, dat sich dat regi-
ment Constantinus des V ind sinre moder verstreckt hait bis zo der zit

dat Karolus Magnus keiser wart" (p. 411)—"let it be clearly noted that the reign of Constantine V and his mother extended only to the time when Charlemagne became emperor."

The Anonymous is largely unconcerned with the sanctity of the Empire. He does, however, mention that God chose the time of Emperor Octavian to become man (Cardauns, p. 280). He also chooses to dwell on one of the personages inseparably bound to the sacred function of the Empire, Frederick II. The Emperor is supposed to have spoken Latin, German, Greek, Lombardic, and Turkish (p. 534). He died so mysteriously that some people say that he never died at all. In the time of Rudolf of Hapsburg, a man did appear who claimed to be Frederick (p. 539). The Anonymous's mention of Frederick adds to his myth only the one element of prodigious learning, evident in his linguistic abilities. We may assume that, even in the Age of Humanism, excessive knowledge was suspect, and that this suspicion colored the memory of Frederick.

Despite his exclusion of France from the Empire, the Anonymous maintains the concept of the broad suzerainty of the Empire. He names the electors with their titles, including those of the Archbishops of Mainz, Trier, and Cologne, as imperial chancellors for Germany, Gaul, and Italy (Cardauns, pp. 446–47). These, however, he limits realistically to those lands which were in truth vaguely under imperial jurisdiction. The Anonymous is among those critics and patriots who acknowledge the decline of the Empire from the time when it had included all of Gaul, Italy, and Germany (p. 641). Regardless of the decline, Germany was in great debt to the Empire. Germany grew better and stronger under its emperors (p. 277). Awareness of the immanence of ancient Roman culture varied in Germany from time to time and from place to place. Nowhere was it stronger than in Cologne, which had architectural reminders of the Roman presence. This feeling of harmony with Roman antiquity became very much a Renaissance preoccupation in the North, when the humanists began to scour the old *limes* for Roman monuments.

This last conception represents an entirely new outlook in Germany. In the past, the Italian humanists had tried to impress the Germans with their debt to Rome. Now some northern thinkers began to picture Germany as a separate entity from Rome and as its sole valid heir. The Germans thus considered the Italians insubordinate and treacherous, since the Roman Empire of antiquity and the Middle Ages seemed indistinguishable to them. They could not understand why the Italians protested imperial overlordship. By distinguishing between Germany and the Empire, however slightly, the Anonymous showed a first dim glimmer of a national self-consciousness apart from the imperial myth. By making Germany indebted to Rome and not simply its political outgrowth, he assumed a separateness that most earlier writers could not fully imagine. As humanism took over the reins of historical writing in the next decades, this conception arose again. It was, however, doomed by the overpowering imperial myth which suppressed the idea of a German state unrelated to the Empire.

The *Koelhoffische Chronik* was thoroughly a product of fifteenth-century Germany. Like in most of the histories before it, compilation was its author's prime task. This he does very well. Unlike most of his predecessors in Germany, he is deeply concerned with seeking the truth in the morass of conflicting authorities, but here he is perhaps less successful. He is no humanist, and his tone is completely popular. He writes with the intention of informing the intelligent layman, who may be ignorant of Latin, but who nonetheless may wish or even need to know what the chronicles contain (Cardauns, p. 256). Seen in the light of Luther's vernacular policies, the Anonymous becomes a notable precedent for the demand that the layman be granted access to the sources. The trend is, of course, much older than either Luther or the Anonymous.

The spirit of popular erudition signaled by the *Koelhoffische Chronik* was not to prevail in the Renaissance, although it did not perish altogether. One might conjecture that its energies went over, in part, into the Reformation. In any case, the investigation of the German past wandered from the purview of popular tradition. Henceforth, the contributions of a Küchlin or Kiburger retreated behind the wild and erudite speculations of the German humanists. In the fifteenth century, the humanist tradition of Cusanus, Aeneas Sylvius, Campano, and—to a lesser extent—Meisterlin, Schedel, and Brant represented only one of several equally important manifestations of Renaissance curiosity about the past. The popular tradition, vernacular as well as Latin, predominated. In the sixteenth century, the humanist tradition predominates and becomes the prime manifestation of Renaissance curiosity about the past. Popular interests dissipate in countless directions which only occasionally coincide with the interests of the learned. Much later, toward the second half of the sixteenth century, this development seems to reverse itself or to take a new turn that resembles fifteenth-century manner and style. This stage is, however, well beyond the scope of this study. In short, the *Koelhoffische Chronik* is typical of the fifteenth century. But, while its conventions do not disappear entirely, another style and set of conventions become typical. Both old and new styles have one essential character in common: curiosity about the past as formative of the present.[69]

---

[69] This suggests a somewhat earlier disruption of the medieval view of history than Adalbert Klempt describes in *Die Säkularisierung der universalhistorischen Auffassung*, Göttinger Bausteine zur Geschichtswissenschaft, XXXI (Göttingen, 1960). He is, however, concerned with the whole new genre of Reformation and Counter-Reformation historiography, which is beyond the time limitations of this book, and which in truth restored the other world and tomorrow to the center of the historical focus.

III

The renaissance myths of the german past under the ægis of northern humanism

It is largely coincidental but most appropriate that we begin the new century with JACOB WIMPHELING (1450–1528), a bona fide humanist and one of the most highly respected men of his time. Of the humanists appearing in the following pages virtually all are somehow associated with the great Alsatian teacher. His lifetime encompassed some of the most important events in human history, the invention of printing with movable types, the discovery of America, and the Protestant Reformation, and with it, the dawn of German national self-consciousness. He was an avid critic of Church abuse, but remained a steadfast adherent of Christian unity like his fellow-humanist Erasmus. The Reformer Jacob Sturm was a student of Wimpheling; when the scandalized master called Sturm a heretic, the student gave a reply which any good teacher should be honored to hear: "If I am a heretic, it is you who have made me one."[1] Wimpheling's patriotism brought him to produce a series of documents studded with myths of the German past. He repeats many myths we have already noted, but conceals them in humanistic trappings, characterized by the exploitation of Tacitus.

The beginning of the sixteenth century is marked by a conspicuous friendship between German and French men of learning. This har-

---

[1] Charles Schmidt, *Histoire littéraire de l'Alsace à la fin du XVe et au commencement du XVIe siècle*, 2 vols. (Paris, 1879), I, 96.

mony, however, in no way intruded upon the debate over the national identity of Alsatia. Wimpheling contributed to this dispute an annoyed and learned treatise, *Germania* (1501).[2] His heated defense of the German character of Strassburg is of interest here only insofar as it depends upon one or two myths of the German past. Strassburg and the other cities on the west side of the Rhine have always belonged to the Roman and never to the French realms, and this from the time of Julius and Octavian (Borries, pp. 94–95). With the German geography of Alsatia established, Wimpheling goes on to say that the Roman Empire, Alsatia included, has never been under French rule, from the time of Julius through to the present reign of Maximilian (pp. 96ff.). The perfect identity of Germany and the Roman Empire implied by this position is a logical conclusion of the myth of the Empire. The identity illustrates yet again how completely the myth was a part of the Renaissance universe, at least for Germans, humanists not excepted. Having assumed this identity, Wimpheling goes about proving it. The Romans, seeing the great similarity between themselves and the residents of the Rhine land, called them brothers —"Germani" (pp. 106–7). This particular derivation is scorned by Wimpheling's rival, Thomas Murner. The witty Franciscan proposed two alternatives in his refutation of Wimpheling, the *Germania Nova* (1502). The first is that the two peoples on either side of the Rhine who were to become the French and the Germans noticed their fraternal similarity and thus called one another "Germani" (Borries, pp. 202–3). The other is that the Strassburgers originally came from Troy, and thus were brothers of the Romans. In any case, Murner assures us, Wimpheling's explanation is asinine (pp. 212–13). More *anasceua.*

The abiding German-ness of the Empire after Charlemagne sets the theme for a large part of Wimpheling's essay, particularly in reference to Charlemagne himself. He seeks to prove beyond question that Charles was German. A good number of works already examined here make similar assertions, others contend that Charles was French, and yet others betray some confusion. The latter traditions were strong even in Germany and gave good occasion to the patriotic humanist for the defense of Charles's German nationality. Neither Wimpheling, nor his time, nor the antecedent and subsequent traditions can be blamed or accused of chauvinism. The issue is quite as sensitive today, despite the fact that modern scholars know enough to realize that at-

---

[2] I use the edition with Wimpheling's own translation in Emil v. Borries, *Wimpheling und Murner im Kampf um die ältere Geschichte des Elsasses,* Schriften des Wissenschaftlichen Instituts der Elsass-Lothringer im Reich (Heidelberg, 1926), pp. 90–175 [henceforth "Borries"].

tribution of "German" or "French" to Charlemagne, and even to his immediate successors, is completely anachronistic. The descendents of Charles as far as his grandchildren were surely bilingual. If they had any loyalties to an object other than themselves, it was no doubt to the Frankish interests at large, whether Romance or German speaking and, most probably, their loyalties did not extend beyond the immediate family.

Wimpheling, like most of our contemporaries, was unable to imagine Charlemagne without an anachronistic "nationality." Murner's attack on Wimpheling rests upon a more balanced opinion, wondering why Charlemagne cannot be both German and Gallic (Borries, pp. 208–9). This is out of the question for Wimpheling. All the best authors and even canon law attest to Charles's German-ness (pp. 102–5). Pippin and Charles were most certainly born in Germany, be it at Ingelheim, Jülich, or Lüttich. Charlemagne is also known to have named the winds and months in his own language, German (pp. 100–101). This stress on the German puts the Roman somewhat into the background of the myth of the *Imperium*, and this was not Wimpheling's purpose. A *Declaratio*, which Wimpheling wrote to accompany the *Germania* and to attack Murner's *Germania Nova*, concludes as follows: in Alsatia, may there flourish and increase *Romana libertas et Germanica virtus!* (pp. 184–85).

Wimpheling goes beyond the myth of the Empire in his *Epitoma Germanicarum rerum* of 1505.[3] German antiquities extend for Wimpheling at least as far back as the beginnings of the city of Trier. Ammianus Marcellinus, so Wimpheling's text asserts, dated the founding of Trier at some 2,000 years before Christ, whereas Rome was founded only in 752 B.C. (*Schardius Redivivus*, p. 199). The ancient name "German" is known to come from the phrase, *Germania . . . a germine dicitur, est enim germen Nobilitas*—from the seed that is nobility (p. 198). This is supported by Campano's suggestion that the Germans are the source for the noble families of all Europe. Consider the Visigothic rule of Spain, that "Cathelania" in Spain is named after the Goths and German Alani, *Gothialania*. Consider the Manfredi and Vicecomites (Visconti) in Italy (pp. 173 and 198–99). Wimpheling mentions many more such actual and imagined aristocratic origins.

Retreating farther back into Germanic mythical history, Wimpheling describes the ancient division of the people into five nations: the Vindelici, who are represented today by the Burgundians; the In-

---

[3] In *Schardius Redivivus*, 4 vols. (Giessen, 1673), I, 170–99. Vol. I of this essential collection will be cited henceforth simply as "*Schardius Redivivus*."

gaevones, to whom the Cimbri and Teutonici belonged; the Istaevones, who resided along the Rhine and included the midland Cimbri; the Hermiones, to whom the Swabians belonged; and finally, the Peucini, who are represented by the Dacians. The Cimbri, who are also called the Teutonici, conquered the Scythians around the time of Homer, and were the habitual victors over the Romans until they were themselves defeated by the Roman Consul Marius (*Schardius Redivivus,* p. 171).

Wimpheling's heroes are all either emperors or scholars. Charlemagne will appear again more closely connected with the myth of the *Imperium.* The first two Fredericks made a considerable claim on Wimpheling's interest. The first, called Barbarossa, was a most glorious Emperor of the Romans, not inferior to Charlemagne. During his reign, the relics of the three Magi were taken to Cologne. Frederick made war on Saladin, a man of humanity and fidelity, but one who oppressed Jerusalem. Frederick succeeded in bringing Lesser Armenia under his sway. The East, however, cost Frederick his life. There he perished by drowning, and the Empire has been much troubled ever since (*Schardius Redivivus,* pp. 179–81). Frederick II was a most magnificent Emperor who made war on Asia in order to win forgiveness of the pope. Not since Charlemagne had there been a more powerful Emperor. Frederick II held the crowns of Italy, Sicily, Jerusalem, and Swabia, as well as of the Empire. His work in Asia has made him immortal there (pp. 182–84). The complementary tradition of learning was naturally important to Wimpheling the humanist. He mentions with pride Albertus Magnus, the Canonist Johannes Teutonicus, and a large number of his own predecessors and contemporaries such as Cusanus, Agricola, Gutenberg, and Dürer (pp. 186–87, 193, 197–98).

Of at least equal importance for Wimpheling is the warlike valor of the ancient Germans. This is perhaps the proper place to cast the extraordinary humanist emphasis on warlike valor into some kind of historical perspective. Polemical as Wimpheling was in moral and learned matters, he was a humanist and, like the Erasmus of the *Querela Pacis,* an irenicist in matters military. Why then so much attention to bravery and military success? A glance at the history of Germany before 1870 is sufficient to explain Wimpheling's seeming inconsistency. Germany's martial disasters extend in an uninterrupted succession from Barbarossa's battles with the Lombard League through Maximilian I's hostilities with France, Venice, the Papacy, the Turks, and every other available enemy. The dawning of German national self-consciousness in a period of political and military impotence called for some model to support the national pride, a model corresponding to the values proclaimed by the age. Pacificism, despite Erasmus and other men of foresight and good will, was not one of them. Cultural, social, and religious virtues could satisfy patriotic emotion no more fully in Wimpheling's time than they can today.

Wimpheling tells us that, in contrast to his own time, the Germans of antiquity were the victors of the world. Although Alexander the Great had conquered so many nations, the reputation of the Germans kept him from engaging them, whence the famous saying: *Male qui velit pugnare cum Germanis pugnet.* Germans, it will be remembered, helped Caesar defeat Pompey. The bodyguard Caesar chose for himself was German, and even the women and children of these people bore arms. On account of German valor, the Romans took the title *Germanicus* as a special honor. In spite of this title, the Romans were defeated by the Germans, as in the cases of Varus and Drusus. The great defeat of Varus caused Augustus to cry out, *Quintili Vare legiones redde!* Not only Augustus, but Vespasian also had to proceed cautiously with the Germans. It is unnecessary to dwell on the destruction of Italy all the way up to Ravenna or on the battles of the Goths and Vandals among whom the Swabians also fought. But the greatest of virtues, and one associated with their valor, was the freedom which the Germans have always preserved for themselves (*Schardius Redivivus,* pp. 172–73).

The Empire is again a sensitive issue to Wimpheling in the *Epitoma.* He explains that the Empire had not actually been transferred to the Germans, but had been returned to them, since Diocletian, Decius, Probus, Jovian, and Valentinian had all been German. Not warlike valor rewon them the Empire, but rather the Germans' piety. Maximilian's ancestor, Charlemagne, came to the aid of Pope Leo III who fled, blinded and mutilated, to Charles. Charles conquered Lombardy and took its king, Desiderius, away into exile. For such services Charles was crowned in Rome, to the cry of the Roman people, *Carolo Augusto a Deo coronato, Magno et Pacifico Imperatori, vita et victoria!* The Emperor at Constantinople lacked similar piety, and therefore the Empire was taken away from the Greeks and given permanently to the Germans. Charles's recognized piety is preserved in the honorific inscribed on his tomb in Aachen: *Magni Caroli Regis Christianissimi Romanorum Imperatoris Corpus Hoc Sepulchro conditum jacet.* Among Charles's other virtues was love of learning, for he founded the academy at Paris (*Schardius Redivivus,* pp. 173–74). What Wimpheling repeats here, presumably in case someone had not read his *Germania,* is a proof for Charlemagne's German nationality, in six points. They include Charlemagne's parentage, birth, language, and burial (p. 177).

The sanctity of the Empire continued to be demonstrated by the activities of Charlemagne's imperial successors, such as Otto II's defeat of the Saracens and Greeks in Apulia and Calabria (in truth, Otto was vanquished), Otto III's renunciation of the right to name the pope, and by the sanctity of the imperial pair, Henry and Kunigunde (*Schardius Redivivus*, pp. 175–77). It is curious that Wimpheling, like his friend Brant, does not bother to present special data for the supremacy of the Empire.

Jacob Wimpheling was the intellectual father of a whole generation of humanists, and he remained until his death the respected elder of the German humanist community. His view of history, while far from original, determined the aspect from which the German past was to be regarded by many of his followers. There is very little in Wimpheling that has not appeared before, in authors without his humanist disposition. The difference is the costume. The prime means of expression is the new humanist Latin. Wimpheling prepared a German translation of his *Germania*, but never bothered to publish it. His reference to Ammianus Marcellinus is a typical humanist tactic. The story of the founding of Trier is medieval in origin, and no ancient source could conceivably verify it. Wimpheling merely "interpreted" a respected ancient author to support the younger myth. In similar fashion, a thoroughly medieval explanation of the name of the Germans—one invented by the glossators of canon law—is, as it were, verified by appeal to a distinguished humanist, Antonio Campano. The pathetic appeal of the Augsburg Anonymous of 1467 to Horace and Ovid is a degeneration of medieval practice and may be summoned to represent the half-understanding of humanist historiographic conventions in the popular history writing of the fifteenth century. It suggests also the obscure tradition of forgery and fictitious authority. The appeals of the Anonymous contrast sharply with the practice of Wimpheling which is vastly more subtle, has a prima facie likelihood of correctness, and is rarely employed. Wimpheling's erudition spared him frequent resort to such transparent devices, but his history can hardly be called much more sophisticated. In substance Wimpheling is rooted wholly in the past; in form he is a sign of the present and of the future.

Much the reverse is true of Wimpheling's less long-lived contemporary, the traveler FELIX FABRI (ob. 1502). The Dominican monk's history of the city of Ulm, *Tractatus de civitate Ulmensi*,[4] is written

---

[4] Gustav Veesenmeyer, ed., BLVS, CLXXXVI (Tübingen, 1889), henceforth "Fabri."

in unreformed ecclesiastical Latin. It moralizes occasionally and faithfully cites the Church Fathers as unimpeachable authorities. On the other hand, his investigations into the past of the city and its families is almost wholly original. Fabri's work is patriotic and secular, glorying in the achievements and ancestry of a contemporary political entity. Although Fabri uses a few humanist embellishments, and although he had clearly read Tacitus, his chronicle appears medieval; by language and convention, it is. In contrast to the form, the substance shows that Fabri is among the first in Germany to take historical writing far from the history of salvation and to dedicate his findings entirely to the glory of the secular past. His history is neither as objective and disinterested as those written by his medieval predecessors whenever they were able to disengage themselves from theology, nor as bound to the didactic as most medieval histories were. When Fabri describes the past of his city it is for a reason, its fame. When he describes the past of its inhabitants, it is to tell a story and not, usually, to make a moral.

Felix Fabri's *Tractatus de civitate Ulmensi* remained unprinted until long after his death, but manuscripts circulated among his friends and contemporaries, such as Hartmann Schedel, and perhaps Conrad Celtis and Willibald Pirckheimer.[5] Practically all of Fabri's myths are myths of origin. Although no ancient documents survive on the history of Ulm, one can deduce some information from the very name of the city, as for example, that it received its name from the marshy, "uliginosus" quality of the soil (Fabri, pp. 6 and 8). The name also implies the presence of the Amazons, since elms "ulmae" were their sacred trees among which they worshipped Diana. These women held power from before the time of Abraham to the time of Alexander the Great. They penetrated as far as Rhaetia and Swabia in the course of their wars. They brought their religion with them, and thus Ulm might be named after the elms sacred to the Amazons. Ulm may also be named after the Ulmerigi, who were driven from their lands by the Scandinavian Goths. After their flight, the Ulmerigi founded Ulm or Hulm, since they were actually called Hulmerigi after Hul, son of Sem, grandson of Noah (pp. 9–12, 216–17). Some say that the city was founded in the year 1055, and that Ulm was named as an anagram of the Roman numeral MLV. They are, however, not at all certain whether it was 1055 B.C., which would place the founding of the city in the time of Solomon, or 1055 A.D. which Fabri reckoned to be the

5 Erich Schmidt, *Deutsche Volkskunde im Zeitalter des Humanismus und der Reformation*, Historische Studien, XLVII (Berlin, 1904), p. 45.

time of Henry II (pp. 14–15). Others say that the Romans founded Ulm, and that it received its name as a pious acrostic: "Ulma" with "u" for "unity," "l" for "law," "m" for "'moderation," and "a" for "ad," indicating direction, inclination toward the prince or Lord (p. 15).

While defending his etymological method in preparation for its application to the name of Ulm, Fabri reveals the names of other German cities in their true origins. Strassburg, for example, is called "Argentina" because of the large amount of silver collected at the ancient Roman treasury there (probably correct). Basel is so called after the Greek word for "royal," signifying the basis of things (also probably correct). Zürich comes out of "zwirich" because the city was between the two realms, Germany and Gaul (certainly incorrect). Fabri suggests elsewhere that Germany itself was named after the hero Tuisco mentioned by Tacitus. The origins of the Germans seem to reside in Troy, although the Swabians stem directly from Japhet by way of the Macedonians. Brennus who conquered Rome was, by the way, Swabian (Fabri, pp. 6–7, 214–16).

Ulm's families, too, have honorable origins. The Neithart family comes from old Norica and ultimately stems from Armenia with the Bavarians (Fabri, p. 93). The Vetter family has its origins in Troy, Rome, and Carthage, from which cities they migrated to Ulm (p. 96). Remus, brother of Romulus, is ancestor of the Rem family (p. 99). The Renzen family's ancestry is to be sought in Frederick II's son, "Renz" and "Rentius," Enzio and Cola di Rienzo respectively (pp. 117–18). Among the heroic figures besides Brennus and the various forefathers may be mentioned Charlemagne, who gave Ulm a charter, and Albertus Magnus or preferably "Magus" or "nigromanticus" (pp. 22–23, 104, and 126–27).

The accuracy and traditional-ness of Fabri's chronicle is of no particular concern here, although there is unquestionably much accurate and traditional in it—much more than these extracts indicate. What is striking and important here is the obvious freedom Fabri felt with his subject. His speculations, however wild and inaccurate, are expressions of the same demand for historical knowledge that moved the coterie of German humanists to search out and publish Germanica wherever they could find it—and where they could not find it, to invent it. Fabri's intentions in writing the history of Ulm make him a brother to the humanists. As manifested in his concentration on families and similar local history, these intentions display the monk's most unmonkish abandonment of traditional medieval history, an abandonment of the ecclesiastical, the universal, and the dynastic in favor of the secular, the national or provincial, and the bourgeois. In everything but his language, the roughness of which he himself regrets in an admittedly traditional humility formula, Fabri is a notably "modern" historian.

The step to fully humanistic history in Germany is taken, appropriately, by the German arch-humanist, Conrad Celtis (1459–1508), who combines in his patriotic writings the free speculation and secular character of Fabri's work with Wimpheling's commitment to the new form. In a poem written to preface an extensive description of Germany (a description which was never to appear), Celtis sang the praises of the ultimate origins of the Germans. The bringer of order to primeval chaos, the *Demogorgon,* fathered an arctic nation which became known as the Germans, those who lived as brothers among themselves (*Schardius Redivivus,* pp. 226–27). The nation is named, in its own language, after the one divinity the people worshipped, Tuisco. This hero is ancestor of the Charleses, Conrads, Ludwigs, and now of Maximilian, who directed and direct the Roman Empire.[6]

It is perhaps regrettable that Celtis never completed his projected Latin epic on Theodoric the Great.[7] Among the learned men of the Renaissance in Germany, the pursuit of the heroic national past rarely left the restrictions of historical writing. Popular literary tradition remained largely untapped by the humanists. The historical tradition is, from a twentieth-century point of view, hardly more reliable than the literary, but the humanists seemed to sense a distinction. If not that, they were simply at a loss when confronted with vernacular documents. This is the crucial distinction between them and the closely analogous revival of the past which occupied early baroque poets and scholars. The humanists may have praised the vernacular tradition, but not one vernacular document was revived by their efforts. I specify "humanist," because other Renaissance forces did preserve and revive medieval vernacular traditions. The baroque counterparts of the humanists, however, scoured the literary tradition with the same zeal their predecessors had applied to the historical tradition.

If Celtis as a Renaissance humanist was unable to redeem the popu-

---

6 Hedwig Riess, *Motive des patriotischen Stolzes bei den deutschen Humanisten* (Berlin, 1934), p. 45, text item 11, and cf. p. 3 [henceforth "Riess, *Motive*"].

7 Lewis Spitz, *Conrad Celtis, the German Arch-Humanist* (Cambridge, Mass., 1957), p. 104.

lar literary hero Theodoric for the learned world of his time, he more than made up for it with his discovery of the works of Hrotswitha, the extraordinary tenth-century nun of Gandersheim in Saxony. For the humanist, she was a Sappho, deserving to rank with the fabled Veleda and Aurinia, ancient German poet-priestesses.[8] Hrotswitha's fame spread with remarkable speed across the Alps. She was mentioned and praised as early as 1509 by Battista Fregoso, the Doge of Genoa, in a book of memorabilia composed for the guidance of his son.[9] For the arch-humanist, the history of learning was of prime importance, and he proudly counted Albertus Magnus among the Germans.[10] The greatest of Celtis's learned heroes are unnamed: they are the pious Greek-speaking Druids of German antiquity.

In the reign of Tiberius, the Druids were driven out of Gaul. They moved across the Rhine and established themselves in Germany, where they were well received. They brought with them their pristine worship of one god, Tuisco, who did not demand material sacrifice. They worshiped in simple groves, not in temples, and brought the whole of Greek learning with them. Eventually, the Druids became Christians and, in the time of Charlemagne and the Ottos, they converted Germany.[11]

Ancient virtue usually interests Celtis when it gives him the opportunity to praise such learning as embodied in Hrotswitha. He is much distressed at the ancient reputation of the Germans as drunkards and savages, and is equally distressed at the survival of such vices into his own time. He could, however, always commend the severity of ancient law.[12] Defiant of Italian opinion, Celtis recommends for the Germans of his own time a return to the ferocity of their predecessors who had caused the world to tremble.[13]

---

[8] Karl Hartfelder, ed., *Fünf Bücher Epigramme von Konrad Celtis* (1881; reprinted Hildesheim, 1963), book II, item 69, p. 38. Celtis's praise of learned women, where Veleda and Aurinia are mentioned, appears in the introduction to his Hrotswitha edition: cf. Ludwig Sponagel, *Konrad Celtis und das deutsche Nationalbewusstsein*, Bausteine zur Volkskunde und Religionswissenschaft, XVIII (Bühl/ Baden, 1939), p. 42.

[9] I use the edition by J. Gaillard, *Bap. Fulgosii Factorum Dictorumque Memorabilium Libri IX* (Paris, 1588), p. 277ᵛ.

[10] Hartfelder, *Fünf Bücher Epigramme*, book II, item 81, pp. 41–42.

[11] *Schardius Redivivus*, p. 228. Albert Werminghoff, ed., *Conrad Celtis und sein Buch über Nürnberg* (Freiburg/Br., 1921), pp. 122–26. Cf. Riess, *Motive*, pp. 3, 45; and Hans Tiedemann, *Tacitus und das Nationalbewusstsein der deutschen Humanisten am Ende des 15. und Anfang des 16. Jahrhunderts* (Berlin, 1913), pp. 84–85.

[12] Hartfelder, *Epigramme*, book II, item 15, pp. 24–25; Werminghoff, *Conrad Celtis*, pp. 192–99; Leonard Forster, *Selections from Conrad Celtis* (Cambridge, 1948), pp. 42–45, 103.

[13] Forster, *Selections*, pp. 38–41, 105.

German possession of the ancient Empire is a major constitutent of Celtis's proud picture of the nation's history.[14] He finds it silly, for example, that students go to Italy to learn the Roman law, when the very incarnation of the law, the Roman Emperor, is in Germany.[15] The full significance of this extraordinary declaration emerges only from the background of Germany's legal history. Roman law was quite foreign to all Germanic peoples. In Germany itself, customary law had until very recently prevailed without a serious rival in the secular courts. Nonetheless, insofar as the Emperor in Germany was a legal figure, he was not considered German at all, but entirely Roman. This was suggested earlier, when Cusanus associated the modern Emperor with Justinian. The complete identity of German Emperor and Roman law was an opinion, curiously enough, not limited to Renaissance Germany. As we shall see in a subsequent chapter, medieval France also accepted it. A purely symbolic function, in this case one completely divorced from reality, could and did command practical juridical consideration.

Celtis's conception of the German past is so thoroughly a Renaissance phenomenon that it requires no intricate interpretation to fix its place in the tradition. His harkening back to the simplicity of the Druids recalls Italian infatuation with the Roman Republic and primordial "virtú." His emphasis on the learned past recalls the cult of Cicero. His recovery of Hrotswitha and other important literary documents of the Latin Middle Ages in Germany recalls the limitless collector's zeal of the *quattrocento* humanists. The main difference is that Celtis's sentimental journey took him only as far as the Middle Ages, whereas the Italians traveled back to classical antiquity. The German, of course, had little choice but to study the Middle Ages. The complex of assertions connected with the Druids is of classical provenance, but the remainder is medieval. Even the *Demogorgon*, who seems ostentatiously classical, is unhappily a medieval invention: the father of a whole race of gods, according to Boccaccio,[16] and of the Germans, according to Celtis, is a medieval scribe's mistake, "a grammatical error, become god."[17]

---

[14] Ibid., pp. 56–57; Hartfelder, *Epigramme*, book III, item 25, p. 53.

[15] Hartfelder, *Epigramme*, book I, item 87, p. 20; book II, item 2, p. 23. Cf. also Karl Hartfelder, "Konrad Celtis und Sixtus Tucher," *Zeitschrift für vergleichende Literaturgeschichte und Renaissance-Literatur*, N.F. III (1890), 336.

[16] Vincenzo Romano, ed., *Genealogie deorum Gentilium*, 2 vols., Scrittori d'Italia, no. 200–201, Boccaccio Opere, X–XI (Bari, 1951), I, 14.

[17] Jean Seznec, *The Survival of the Pagan Gods*, trans. Barbara F. Sessions, Bollingen Series XXXVIII (New York, 1953), p. 222 (and bibliography, n. 12).

Celtis was, next to Reuchlin perhaps, the best known pre-Reformation humanist in Germany. A substantial body of scholarly work has grown up about him, much of which deals with Celtis's conjectures about the German past. His opinions, discoveries, and inventions survive in their influence on contemporaries and disciples as much as in their own right. His friend Johannes Trithemius, Abbot of Sponheim (Foresta's German Benedictine), brought many of Celtis's ideas to their logical or illogical conclusions. Aventinus, a student of Celtis, took many of his teacher's themes and developed them in his own historical writing. Although these paragraphs hardly do Celtis justice, his seminal ideas will recur, harvested in the works of others.

A name as renowned in its time as that of Celtis—however dimly it is remembered today—belongs to the humanist, geographer, farceur, and folklorist HEINRICH BEBEL (1472–1518). It is perhaps well to point out that Bebel's reputation extended from Cracau, where he and the young Copernicus were fellow students, to the court of Henry VIII.[18] His fame seems to have arisen equally from all his learned endeavors, which included manuals of cosmography, poetry, and letter-writing, several patriotic works, a collection of *Facetiae* in the tradition of Poggio, and a collection of proverbs gathered from the mouth of the people. In the latter, he is among the first of the unequivocally Renaissance men in Germany actually to leave the confines of the study in order to overhear and preserve popular vernacular utterance. His only real predecessor, at least in these pages, is Gobelinus Persona. Like Celtis, however, Bebel failed to bridge learned history and popular literature. Gobelinus could read the past in the vernacular usages of the present. For Bebel, they were unhistorical, although they and Bebel's interest in them reveal a good deal about the Renaissance in Germany. These proverbs are only of secondary interest here, but it might be worthwhile to see the place that the idea of history—as distinguished from real historical perspective—had taken in the popular mind. It had become the necessary accoutrement of a wise man. The Latin is Bebel's version of the proverb, the early New High German his translation of the Latin:[19]

---

[18] See for example the dedication to Henry by an English translator, Palsgrave, in James L. McConaughy, *The School Drama*, Columbia University Contributions to Education, LVII (New York, 1913), p. 109.

[19] Gustav Bebermeyer, *Tübinger Dichterhumanisten: Bebel, Frischlin, Flayder* (1927; reprinted Hildesheim, 1967), p. 38.

Der Weise

Haec tria faciunt sapientem virum—
Haec sunt prudentis, faciunt haec iure sagacem:
Copia librorum cui sit pervisa frequenter,
Qui mores hominum multas et vederit urbes,
Calleat historias regumque heroica gesta.

Den schrybend die alte wyß und clug,
der vil biecher gelesen hat und lender gnug
erfaren, darzu menchen man,
der vil alte geschichten weist und kan.

[The Wiseman: him the ancients describe as wise and witty,/ who has read many books, and ample lands/ has seen, and many men,/ and knows much ancient history.]

It is reminiscent of Wagner in Goethe's *Faust*, even though Wagner would probably avoid countries and peoples in favor of books and histories. Bebel took his history and heroic deeds seriously, despite his disdain for what popular tradition had to say about them. Like Celtis, he sensed a distinction between history and popular memory. In the first years of the sixteenth century, Bebel produced a series of works strongly patriotic in tenor, deeply involved with mythical history, and wholly devoid of vernacular contributions, indeed hostile to them. The earliest of these is an *Oratio ad Maximilianum* (1504), delivered before the Emperor in honor of Bebel's coronation as poet laureate.[20]

Far outshining Bebel's other contributions to the myths of the German past is his statement of the thesis that the Germans were autochthonic. The thesis results in the greatest incidence of the topos of critical rejection. The corpus of carefully evolved myths of origin falls victim. Bebel must, for example, reject the Trojan origins of the Franks, whether in the version with the younger Priam or that with the Trojan Francus. In the same breath, he accepts the Greek pseudo-etymology which gave Francus the meaning of "free" in Attic and confirms the story that Valentinian used this word of the Germans. But heroes named Francus, Sycambrus, or the like, never appeared in the works of the true ancients. Similarly, the stories of Saxon origins from

---

[20] The Oratio is in *Schardius Redivivus*, pp. 95–104. The other texts are: "Germani sunt indigenae," *ibid.*, pp. 105–107, "Apologia pro defensione imperatorum," pp. 108–15, "Quod Imperator Romanorum jure sit Christianissimus dicendus," pp. 116–17, "De Laude, antiquitate, imperio, victoriis rebus gestisque Veterum Germanorum," pp. 117–34, "Epitome laudum Suevorum," pp. 137–42. Since I am concerned only with Bebel's myths and not with the structure of his individual works, I shall pass freely from one text to the other, citing only the page numbers in *Schardius Redivivus*.

Alexander the Great have no foundation (*Schardius Redivivus*, pp. 106, 131). In another document of later date (1508), Bebel rejects with great annoyance the myths promulgated by Petermann Etterlin to the effect that the Swiss stem from the Swedes, Goths, and Huns (p. 132). Petermann Etterlin's chronicle had been published posthumously in 1507 and clearly represented for Bebel an unworthy popular expression of historical consciousness. The chronicle specified that the Swiss in Canton Uri stemmed from the Huns and Goths. The same theory espoused even earlier by his fellow humanist, Willibald Pirckheimer, elicited no such annoyance from Bebel.[21] The source and not necessarily the content was evidently Bebel's criterion for judgement.

Bebel accepts Tuisco as ancestor of the Teutones, believes that Mannus and Hercules Alemannus ruled among the Tuiscones—Teutones or Germans—and that all three heroes were venerated and sung in battle cries. Bebel cites Tacitus and Berosus as his authorities. They were obviously more reliable than Petermann Etterlin's, whoever they may have been. Original speculation on Bebel's part supports the reliability of Tacitus and Berosus. A figure on the island of Reichenau was known as the *Idolum Alemannum aureum*, which could have meant the golden German, Alemannic, or Swiss idol. Bebel identifies the idol with Hercules Alemannus, and believes that he has thus proven the accuracy of Tacitus's and Berosus's reports about the worship of Hercules in Germany (*Schardius Redivivus*, pp. 101–2, 138). The humanist shows that he has some of the genuinely historical sense to which he pretends when he agrees to the Scandinavian origins of Goths and Lombards. Of course, the Middle Ages anticipated Bebel in this particular insight. In his numbering of some sixteen tribes and nations among the Germans, Bebel includes not only Franks, Burgundians, and Goths, but also Picts and Scots, who were by no stretch of the imagination either German or Germanic. Bebel advises his readers to ignore those who would deny German nationality to all these tribes (pp. 130–31). Several of the known etymologies of German appear in Bebel without much distinction: some say they were named after the word for growth, others that they were named for their

---

[21] On Etterlin, see Baechtold, *Die Stretlinger Chronik*, Bibliothek älterer Schriftwerke der deutschen Schweiz, I (Frauenfeld, 1877), p. LXXIf. Petermann Etterlin's most distinguished contribution is the tale of Wilhelm Tell, which Etterlin is the first to preserve in writing: cf. Brothers Grimm, *Deutsche Sagen*, 3rd ed. (Darmstadt, 1960), item 518, pp. 490ff. and note on p. 628. Pirckheimer's mention of the Hun and Goth theory appears in his *Belli Helvetici Historica* (1499), in Marquard Freher and Burkhard G. Struve, eds., *Rerum Germanicarum Scriptores*, 3 vols. (Strassburg, 1717), III, 58. We have seen above the Hunnish origins theory in Meisterlin, and implications of Gothic connections in Foresta.

brotherhood with the Gauls, or for their brotherhood among themselves (p. 97).

The invention of a new body of texts was not a necessity for Bebel; that had been done for him by Annius of Viterbo. But Bebel articulated a principle which was at least as effective as an imaginative but believable forgery: when Celts are mentioned by ancient authors, Germans as well as Gauls are being spoken of (*Schardius Redivivus*, pp. 128–29). With this, the whole contact between Celts and classical antiquity was placed at the service of the humanists and their patriotic urges. Before Bebel's articulation, Celtis had implicitly accepted the principle with his Druids, and Pseudo-Berosus had so confused Celtic and Germanic elements as to assume the principle's validity. Bebel was, no doubt, encouraged by Celtis and found inspiration and corroboration in Berosus, but the principle itself is his own. Several important humanist successors were to make use of it. A practical utilization of the principle might have been the story that Brennus was a Swabian (p. 101). Since Bebel himself was one, however, he would have had no reason to reject the story, regardless of the principle of Celtic-Germanic identity.

Heinrich Bebel's heroic figures include not only Tuisco, Hercules, and Brennus but, in typical humanist fashion, Hrotswitha, Walahfrid Strabo, and Otto von Freising as well (*Schardius Redivivus*, pp. 107 and 137). Charlemagne, the Ottos, and the Fredericks remain larger than life and retain their traditional importance in the myth of the *Imperium*. Of ancient religion we have already noted the veneration of Tuisco, Hercules, and Mannus. Of ancient virtue, warlike valor and freedom are again the most significant recollections. Alexander the Great declared that the Germans were to be avoided. Pyrrhus shuddered at the thought of confronting them. Caesar withdrew altogether, whence the proverb: let him battle with the Germans who wishes to do battle and lose (p. 123: cf. Campano, Rolevinck, and Wimpheling, *supra*). While the Germans have always been the terror of the Romans, they did aid Caesar in his victory over Pompey (pp. 100, 120, 122). Later the Germans caused another Caesar, Augustus, to cry out, *Quintile Vare legiones redde* (p. 101). The valorous Swabians took Spain, *Nostra est Brittania, Nostra est Prussia.*[22] The Germans and only the Germans are undefeated (p. 105), and today enjoy the freedom they have always had (p. 127). His appropriation of Prussia for the Germans makes immediate historical sense. That of Britain refers presumably to Anglo-Saxon, hence Germanic suzerainty. That of Spain

---

[22] *Schardius Redivivus*, p. 99. Cf. Riess, *Motive*, p. 52.

for the Swabians refers presumably to the still inadequately explained Suevic kingdom of northwest Iberia in the fifth and sixth centuries A.D.

The *Imperium* appears in fully elaborated mythical form in Bebel's works. In the course of defending the dignity of the imperial title in his own time, Bebel puts forth three closely printed folio pages of proofs, all from Roman antiquity *(Schardius Redivivus,* pp. 109–11), and thereby clearly indicates the identity in his mind of the Roman Empire of antiquity and that of the sixteenth century. This Empire came to Charlemagne, who was a German Frank and not French. Its sanctity is revealed in part by Charlemagne's title, "Christianissimus," which properly belongs to the German Emperor and not to the French King. This is so not only because Charles was German, but also because the Roman King is a sacred defender of the Church in a degree greater than all other monarchs. The divine liturgy itself affirmed this sanctity (pp. 116–17). In the *Oratio,* Bebel addresses Maximilian as "sacratissime Rex . . . Imperator . . . Caesar" (p. 95). The Emperors have consistently fought for the faith and defended the Christian religion (p. 97). Charles conquered Saxony, Frisia, and Spain for Christ. Otto won the Slavic East for Christ and Empire (pp. 102–3). Frederick I subdued Armenia and Greater Asia for the Church. Frederick II, whose name was terrible among the Gentiles, drove the Sultan to flight, and then was acclaimed and crowned King of Jerusalem (pp. 102, 140). The supremacy of the Empire is implied in its superior duties to religion. Bebel goes beyond this to maintain that the Empire of his day holds the same authority over other kingdoms as it held in Charlemagne's day. The triple coronation—Aachen, Milan, and Rome —presumably stands as an outward sign of the primacy (pp. 112–13).

Despite the humanist attempt at critical use of materials and the very occasional success at this attempt, Bebel remains well within the realm of imaginative and scientifically unacceptable history, the subject of this book. He shares the realm with Wimpheling and Celtis and indeed all the other historians considered here, even those whom he disliked or rejected. Like most of his peers, he made several important contributions to mythical history. He is among the first to exploit fully the texts of Pseudo-Berosus, and with them to promulgate a grand new body of myths at the cost of older ones. His thesis of the autochthonic origins of the Germans combines with Berosus to give the strongest possible impression of critical stance toward the traditional historiography of the ancient Germans. That all of this criticism did absolutely nothing to advance the cause of truly accurate history would certainly have been a serious disappointment to Bebel. He was a confident scholar and saw in his ratiocinations the possibility of new and important truths. The only major handicap he felt—and it was an extremely troublesome one for a Renaissance man and humanist—was that classical antiquity, particularly the Greeks, had been hostile to Germany and had suppressed so much ancient German history (*Schardius Redivivus*, p. 137).[23] Bebel nonetheless succeeded in describing with fair detail a certain picture of German antiquity. The whole-hearted rejection of medieval fable to support a Renaissance chimera of history only makes his efforts somewhat poignant.

The rediscovery of Tacitus, the publication of Berosus, and the medieval fables of origins are woven into an internally consistent whole by another renowned humanist, inscription gatherer, and map owner, CONRAD PEUTINGER. His *Sermones Convivales* (1505) perceive no contradiction in multiple German origins, from Tuisco (thus Tacitus), who was a son of Noah (thus Berosus), and from Troy (thus medieval tradition).[24] However, following the practice of selective critical rejection, Peutinger does object to the notion that Emperor Valentinian gave the Franks their name: more *anasceua* (*Schardius Redivivus*, p. 209). Other myths of origin in Peutinger include the story that Aachen, Aquis Granae, was named after Nero's brother Granus (pp. 210–11). Peutinger's heroes contain the name of Henry II, who brought the remains of Saint Dionysius the Areopagite to Regensburg —this proves of course that they were not at St. Denis near Paris (p. 201).[25] Peutinger could not have known that there was no St. Denis either as he or the French imagined him. Of ancient religion Peutinger reports only that Isis and Hercules were worshipped among the Germans (pp. 204–5). Of ancient virtue he mentions primarily warlikeness (p. 206).

Of the myth of the *Imperium*, Peutinger affirms the identity of Roman and German. He suggests a vague explanation for the conflicting traditions concerning Charlemagne and Otto and the arrival of the Empire in German hands: Otto I's father, Henry, was called *primus Rex Theutonicorum*, not because he was in truth the first German king, but because he was the first king of the Germans who was not a Carolingian and hence not a Frank. If this explanation

---

[23] Cf. Gerald Strauss, *Sixteenth-Century Germany* (Madison, Wis., 1959), pp. 8–9.
[24] *Schardius Redivivus*, pp. 200–213; comp. pp. 204 and 209.
[25] A similar tale appears in Otto von Freising's *Chronik oder die Geschichte der zwei Staaten*, ed. and trans. by Walther Lammers and Adolf Schmidt (Darmstadt, 1961), VI.11, pp. 448–49. In Otto, however, it is King Arnulf who transferred the relics, and they were transferred from Gaul.

seems tenuous as it stands, it becomes even more tenuous in the light of Peutinger's assertion that Charlemagne was German and that the France of the Gauls took its name from the German Franks (Brant is given due credit: *Schardius Redivivus*, pp. 210–11). Peutinger's reasoning seems mildly defective, but must have satisfied him. Actually, his argument is not so impenetrable. It rests on a distinction analogous to that of Germanic and German. Charlemagne represents the broader concept, and Otto the narrower. The dispute arises only in cases of equivocation, which are frequent enough.

The whole issue of the *Imperium* was a matter of grave concern to the patriotic humanists of Germany. Some, who ignored other myths of the German past, made it a point to comment on and reinforce the myth of the Empire. A student of Wimpheling and prolific translator MATTHIAS RINGMAN PHILESIUS is one of these. His Caesar translation of 1507 concludes with a listing of the Emperors, and naturally proceeds from Julius Caesar through Maximilian I.[26] Ringman's publisher, Grüninger, placed on the title page of the translation an illustration representing Julius Caesar on horseback; decorating the saddle cloth was Emperor Maximilian's coat of arms.[27] In the previous year, 1506, Ringman Philesius published a tract by MICHAEL COCCINIUS (KÖCHLIN), a student of Bebel: *De imperii a Graecis ad Germanos translatione*.[28] Coccinius, as his title immediately suggests, affirms both the Roman and German character of the Empire. He adds the thought that Charles was already Emperor of the Germans when the *Imperium* was transferred to him from the Greeks. The existence of a German Empire parallel to the Roman Empire and prior to the coming of the *Imperium* to the Germans is a significant expression of rising national self-consciousness among the humanists. Coccinius no doubt took the idea from his teacher, Bebel (cf. *Schardius Redivivus*, p. 117). This German *Imperium* existed implicitly in the various realms of the Trojan and Macedonian refugees. Within a decade after Coccinius's tract, this Empire was to receive an ample and imaginative evaluation in the chronicle of the Abbot Trithemius. The notion of an independ-

---

26 Richard Newald, *Probleme und Gestalten des deutschen Humanismus* (Berlin, 1963), pp. 449–50.

27 Charles Schmidt, *Histoire littéraire de l'Alsace*, II, 108.

28 *Ibid.*, p. 398; see Index Bibliographique, No. 223. Edition in Simon Schard, *De iurisdictione autoritate et preeminentia imperiali* (Basel, 1566), pp. 717–27. Cf. also Newald, *Probleme und Gestalten . . .*, pp. 449–50, and Theobald Bieder, *Geschichte der Germanenforschung, Erster Teil, 1500–1806* (Leipzig and Berlin, 1921), p. 8.

ent German Empire remained somewhat daring for the early sixteenth century (indeed, for the subsequent several centuries as well), and in Coccinius the prestige of the Roman Empire prevailed. He varies only slightly the acclamation given Charlemagne by the Roman people: *Carolus rex iustus et fortis Romanorum Imperator semper Augusto a Deo coronatus*, preserving the divine stamp of the Emperor's coronation and adding the mythically charged epithet, "rex iustus," with its liturgical, eschatological, and humanist overtones (Schard, *De iurisdictione*, p. 720).

The new and strong conventions of historical writing had, by the end of the first decade of the sixteenth century, taken over almost entirely from the antecedent learned tradition. The language and historical ideas of humanism had achieved such currency that new works of the character of Gobelinus Persona's, Werner Rolevinck's, and Hartmann Schedel's were most improbable. Although humanism's conquest of learned historical writing was complete, its influence on the survivals of popular history was partial at best. At its peak, the popular tradition had produced the Swiss myths of the mid-fifteenth century, Hans Folz's poetic history, and the publication of Lirer's chronicle. In the sixteenth century, popular history made a strategic withdrawal behind its humanist counterpart. Insofar as it maintained any identity at all, popular history proceeded at its own pace and on its own course, only occasionally borrowing some interest, bias, or convention from humanism. Much later in the century, when local, provincial history again came to the fore, did the popular historical tradition demand attention equal to other forms of historical writing. In the period under scrutiny in this chapter, 1500–1529, one fanatic and several minor publications, one major imperial tradition, and one forgotten chronicle represent popular historical writing. All the rest is humanist. Its weakness does not, however, make the popular tradition any less interesting. On the contrary, few texts are as revealing as the extraordinary polemic produced by an anonymous Alsatian around the year 1509.[29]

The ALSATIAN ANONYMOUS, whoever he was, seems to have been on

---

[29] Hermann Haupt, "Ein Oberrheinischer Revolutionär aus dem Zeitalter Kaiser Maximilians I.," *Westdeutsche Zeitschrift*, Ergänzungheft VIII (Trier, 1893), 79–228 [henceforth "Haupt"]. Cf. p. 102 for the problem of the dating and comp. Annelore Franke and Gerhard Zschäbitz, eds., *Das Buch der Hundert Kapitel und der vierzig Statuten des sogenannten oberrheinischen Revolutionärs*, Leipziger Übersetzungen und Abhandlungen zum Mittelalter, Reihe A, Band 4 (Berlin, 1967), p. 34.

the crusade to Belgrade in 1456 and to have seen Aeneas Sylvius with his own eyes (Haupt, pp. 92–93). The Anonymous prepares the way for his views on German antiquity by casting out all previous speculations and insisting "Adam ist ein tuscher man gewesen." His is the most extreme instance of *anasceua* in the whole of the Renaissance. Adam's and Noah's language was "all man's," that is, Alemannic. Seth, a "tuscher kůner man," and Jobal were the first German scholars and law-givers. The people of Japhet left Babylon before the confusion, so that when they came to Germany and settled Alsatia, their primordial language was preserved; all other languages are a result of the Babylonian confusion. Japhet himself lies buried at Istein in Breisgau (pp. 141–43). The city of Basel was built originally by Japhet and his sons (p. 90). The Germans are also known to have built Jerusalem (p. 145).[30] Trebeta, son of Semiramis (one is surprised to find a familiar, positively conventional lie) is said to have founded Trier (p. 143). The Amazons were Saxons, and the ducal family Zimmern descend from the Cimbri (pp. 143, 145).

Among the heroic figures populating the anonymous tract is Alexander the Great, who was born in the west of the Rhineland-Palatinate and was German viceroy in Macedon (Haupt, pp. 90, 144). Tamerlain the Great was a German king. Prester John was King of the Germans in Asia and Africa (p. 145). We need hardly to mention Wilhelm Tell (pp. 91, 151). The successors of Trebeta at Trier—Hero, Catholdus, and Belgio—created an ideal state in that city (pp. 111, 143). Emperors Henry IV and Frederick II are also among the Anonymous's favorites (pp. 151–52), which reveals something of his feelings about the papacy. Of the ancient religion, he reports only that Japhet built a temple to *Jupiter Christus* at Istein, and it is that temple which protects Japhet's tomb (pp. 143, 188). The Germans, needless to say, had the first scholars and jurists, and were the ones who taught the Greeks their philosophy (p. 149). But not only learning, valor too characterized the ancient Germans: the Germans of Trier, for example, helped Caesar defeat Pompey (p. 147).

Our Anonymous seems to find it unnecessary to elaborate any part of the imperial myth other than the apocalyptic mission of the Empire. He does, however, touch lightly on its German character and supremacy. He repeatedly announces Charlemagne's German or rather Alsatian birth (Haupt, pp. 90, 147, 150). The Empire which is to rule the whole world was given by God to the Germans alone.[31] An

---

[30] Cf. Joachim Wagner, *Nationale Strömungen in Deutschland am Ausgang des Mittelalters* (Weida in Thüringen, 1929), pp. 70–71.

[31] *Ibid.*

Emperor named Frederick will come, born in Alsatia, who will reform the Church (p. 90). He will begin by exterminating the clergy (p. 198). In his time, the Brotherhood of the Yellow Cross will bring to light again the laws and the ideal state established by Trebeta and his descendents at Trier (p. 112). The Brotherhood of the Yellow Cross was founded when St. Michael the Archangel, under the sign of such a cross, destroyed thousands of Turks before the walls of Belgrade in the year 1456. Each brother is to be initiated under the same sign, the Yellow Cross (pp. 193–94). Frederick's rule will last a thousand years and will grow into the Golden Age (pp. 203–4).

To see in the fanatic Alsatian Anonymous the chilling anticipations of a later fanaticism is tempting but unhistoric. His excesses cloud the attempt to place him correctly in the tradition, although the perspective of German historical writing in the Renaissance places him squarely in the mainstream. In certain ways, he is ahead of his time, but only by a century or so. His Brotherhood of the Yellow Cross, dedicated to universal reform and the establishment of a universal state, anticipates not the horrors of the twentieth century but the humanism of the Baroque. The coincidental rise of the Rosicrucians, the Brotherhood of the Rosy Cross, and the theories of international law in Althusius, Grotius, and Pufendorf are closely analogous to the program underlying the ravings of the Anonymous. The eschatological mentality was widespread in the sixteenth century, and generally connected with the imperial myth. In the seventeenth century, the breach between this popular mentality and learned expression was closed. The Anonymous's sense of the millennium is hardly new. Even the notion of a secret society probably has antecedents in the Joachimites of the thirteenth century and similarly unorthodox groups. He is nonetheless an important milestone between the chiliasts of the Middle Ages and those of the seventeenth century, whose sense of history helped to form modern learning, to establish the principles of internationalism, and, incidentally, to populate the New World.

To avoid anachronistic interpretation and to calculate his position in the whole topography of Renaissance history, three coordinates, as it were, help. Two are temporal, one geographic. The geographic coordinate locates the Anonymous in a border territory. Like many members of frontier populations who feel threatened by a militant neighbor or simply by the proximity of a foreign culture, the Alsatian Anonymous went to considerable extremes in his patriotism. One of the time coordinates moves, so to speak, vertically from the Middle Ages to the Baroque. It fixes the Anonymous in a part of the tradition that extends from the Pauline Epistles to the Fifth-Monarchy men and beyond. It has been discussed above. The other time coordinate is, as it were, lateral, and fixes the Anonymous in the contemporary practice of history. I have suggested that he was in the mainstream and, apart from his ire, it is relatively clear that he was. While it is difficult to distinguish between imagination and gall in his outrageous assertions, they do have a great deal in common with the older and similarly preposterous historical writing for popular consumption. The differences between story and history, as we have seen at length, were not quite fully developed in the popular tradition. Even northern humanism left something to be desired in this regard, and the Anonymous is not all that remote from his humanist equivalents. He shares with Annius of Viterbo the wholesale rejection of previous fable; he shares with Bebel and Peutinger the pseudo-critical urge reflected in this rejection. The interest in origins, the *Imperium*, and German antiquities altogether is also a humanist occupation. The Alsatian Anonymous was blessed, however, with an ignorance of which the humanists were deprived. No matter how vivid their imaginations, humanists could never speculate quite so freely as he, although some did come close. The most basic historical problems bind the Anonymous to his contemporaries. His obsession with German, as in the identification of Adam and Seth, points to an inchoate sense of separate German nationhood, particularly in the just state of ancient Trier and the Empire to come. This dissipates, however, precisely in the dilemma of province and Empire. It is this inchoate sense of nation that the Anonymous shares with Bebel and Coccinius, but the provincial-imperial dilemma he shares with many, most comparably with Wimpheling.

The problem of national *vs.* provincial and imperial history does not abate in the reign of humanism. A small and very elite tradition falteringly attempts to construct a strictly national history. It includes Celtis and Bebel, whom we have seen, and several others, who are to come. Most historians gripped either one or both horns of the provincial–imperial dilemma. The development of secular historiography was to witness a further separation of the alternatives, with provincial history making the greatest advances and imperial history assuming the ill-fated burden of national self-consciousness. The most readable, informative, and still usable historians of the period are those who tended toward local history (e.g., Albertus Krantz and Johannes Aventinus). The nationalists (e.g., Celtis and Bebel) are ultimately a kind of anachronism and are interesting primarily for their foresight.

The imperial or universal historians (e.g., Johannes Naucler and Sebastian Münster) are usable today only as illustrations of their time. However, as their time is the subject of this book, such limitation can be faced with equanimity.

The humanists dabbled in all variations of historical writing, so it is difficult to isolate one form as characteristically theirs. They did make very much their own the medieval convention of the world chronicle, so much so that it perished with the demise of Renaissance humanism. The convention has been represented in these pages by Gobelinus Persona, Jacobus Foresta, and Hartmann Schedel. A humanist extension of this tradition is the *Chronicon* of JOHANNES NAUCLER. Like all humanist historians, Naucler was much concerned with the recovery of antiquity. As with the German historians of all persuasions, the antiquity at issue was German. Even without the advantages of the Alsatian Anonymous's ignorance, the humanists found in their body of learning ample evidence of past glories. Naucler could do no less. He died in 1510, leaving his *Chronicon* in the drawer. It was published six years later, under the supervision of Erasmus and Reuchlin.[32] Naucler generally passes as one of the earliest critical humanist historians in Germany, one who had the insight to reject most medieval fables but who could not resist accepting virtually without question Pseudo-Berosus.

In imitation of Berosus, Naucler begins the genealogy of the Germans with Noah, whom he identifies syncretistically with Janus and Caelum. Under the name of Caelum, Noah fathered Saturn, who was in turn father of the Golden Age. Japhet's son Magog fathered the Goths, as Gomer did the Scythians (*Chronicon*, I, 10–11, 14). Tuisco, son of Noah, was the first King of the Germans and was the primordial law-giver (I, 24). Suevus, a descendent of Tuisco, fathered the Swabians (II, 325). Trebata fleeing Semiramis founded Trier many years before the founding of Rome (I, 32). A certain Francus did once exist, a son of Hector, who fled into Gaul, and he might be the father of the Franks. But in no case were they first named Franks in the time of Valentinian (I, 625ff.). Thus also Peutinger. It must also be clear that those who live near the Seine are not "Franci" but "Francigenae" (I, 628). The Burgundians are supposed to come from Scandia, an island in Scythia (I, 657), and are called after their word for fortification, "burgi" (II, 32). The Lombards, a German nation, came from Scandinavia under Ibor and Aio (I, 729).

---

[32] August Potthast, *Bibliotheca Historica Medii Aevi*, 2 vols. consecutively paginated, 2nd ed. (Berlin, 1896), II, 806; Schmidt, *Deutsche Volkskunde*, p. 44. I use the Cologne edition of 1584 in two volumes, cited as "*Chronicon*."

Naucler preserves most of the fabulous tales of origin at great length, even if he declines to accept them, sometimes in whole, sometimes in part. To be found are the origins of the Franks (*Chronicon*, I, 265), the Bavarians (I, 73 and II, 100), the Saxons (II, 76), and the Swiss (II, 363–64). In the last case, Naucler quotes fully Eulogius Kiburger's explanation of the origins of the Swiss from Sweden, only changing the name of Remus to Rhenus. He acknowledges Eulogius as his source, but casts doubt on the truth of the theory. He seems to prefer Hemmerlin's version with the Saxons at the Alpine passes in Charlemagne's service. "Schwitten" became in Alemannic "Switzer" or "Schwitzer," he explains, that is, sweat-ers.

The heroic figures in Naucler's work are many. Of primary importance are Tuisco, who gave his name to the "Tuitschen," and Teuto, who gave his name to Teutonia (*Chronicon*, II, 22). There are also the innumerable offspring of Tuisco in the line of Hercules Alemannus (I, 14). Naucler adds to the common herd of heroes Zoroaster, who practiced in lands near the Baltic Sea (I, 28–29). Brennus is thought by some to have been British. He was Swabian (I, 166–67 and II, 28, 333). Immortal is the Duke Arminius, who destroyed the proud and vicious Quintilius Varus. This is the very defeat which caused Augustus to cry out, *Quintili Vare redde legiones* (I, 494–95). Naucler's identification of Arminius is one of the earliest, preceding by some years the extensive glorification of Arminius as a national hero. Prester John ("Priester Johan" in the Latin text of the chronicle) is thought to have converted the Frisians to Christianity (II, 53). Usogast, Losogast, Visogast, and Salagast are supposed to have compiled an elaborate and just law which King Pharamundus of the Franks promulgated (I, 663). It is called the "lex Salica" after Salagast (I, 625). Alaric, King of the Goths, died suddenly during his Italian adventure, and his men buried him in the bed of the River Busentus. They had diverted the river for this purpose and returned it to its course, so that the grave never be discovered (I, 660). Tetricus—Dietrich or Theodoric—is said to have defeated the last remainders of the Amazons (I, 589). Theodoric, a contemporary of Arthur of Britain, was a peaceful king. To protect the Church and preserve order in Rome, he summoned a council (I, 695 and 697ff.) Naucler seems to take some pride in the deeds of Frederick I's chancellor, Rainald (II, 221), and in those of his master, Barbarossa. I might add that the glossator of the 1584 edition of Naucler's *Chronicon* (II, 103) uses "Ahenobarbus," Nero's cognomen, to translate the "Barbarossa" of Frederick I.

Among the men of learning Naucler mentions Hrabanus, his student "Godescal," Hermannus Contractus, Hildegard of Bingen, Otto of Freising, and Albertus Magnus (*Chronicon*, II, 65, 125, 229, 352).

The entry on Gottschalk leads one to wonder whether Naucler was merely reflecting a model or actually knew the work of this tragic and gifted medieval poet. Any evidence of first-hand knowledge of Gottschalk's poems would be a great step forward in the study of the Renaissance revival of the Middle Ages. It may be noted in passing that Naucler devotes an extraordinarily long section to Nicolaus, Knight of the Holy Spirit, the severe and clement Liberator of the City, Zealot of Italy, and August Tribune, and to his flight to Emperor Charles IV (II, 391–94). This is Cola di Rienzo, of whom more later.

By way of ancient religion, Naucler reports the Germans' practice of worshipping Nertha, who was equivalent to Magna Mater. They seem also to have worshipped Sol, Luna, Vulcan, Mercury, Mars, Hercules, and Isis. Hercules and Teutates were especially venerated. Teutates was the last direct descendent of Tuisco, and his name is equivalent to Mercury. The Saxons are supposed to have worshipped Mercury at Irmensul, at a place called Eresburg, which Charlemagne destroyed (*Chronicon*, I, 62, II, 14, 21, 37–38, 76). Eresburg was located among the Wesphalians, and their brothers, the Saxons, are known to have engaged in human sacrifice (II, 14, 38). The major virtues of the ancient Germans were chastity, justice, and valor. All three are well illustrated in the conduct of ancient German women, who were famed for their modesty, who were severely punished for any infraction of it, and who spurred their men on to brave deeds (II, 36, 41). German valor was exemplified by Caesar's high regard for their armies and his supposed use of German cavalry against Pompey. Arminius's defeat of Quintilius Varus also shows this German virtue (II, 30). The valor of the Germans won them England by the Angles, France by the Franks, and Lombardy by the Lombards (II, 32–33). Even Naucler could not distinguish between these tribes and Germans.

The 1584 Cologne edition of Naucler's *Chronicon* I use opens (sig. *a* ii^r) with a dedication to the Archbishop of Trier, *S. Romani Imperij per Galliam Archicancellario*. The myth of the Empire was no less alive when Naucler's work was originally produced. Even though Naucler firmly attests that the monarchy which had begun with Augustus ended in 477 [sic] with Augustulus (*Chronicon*, I, 684), he nonetheless wholly accepts the continuity of Roman and German Empires. Naucler begins the "Sixth Age" of his chronicle—after the birth of Christ—with a catalogue of Emperors from Octavian to Maximilian I (I, 501–2). A certain appropriateness is attached to the report that Henry III is supposed to have found the monstrous body of Pallas. Pallas was an ally of Aeneas and hence of the Roman Empire at its very source. He was killed by Turnus, enemy of Aeneas and of the founding of Rome (II, 124).

As for the German character of the Empire, Naucler casts out the problem of the Ottonian succession altogether and takes the most direct course with the German nationality of Charlemagne: the Empire came to the Germans in the person of Charlemagne and not of Otto. Charles was born at Ingelheim near Mainz and named the twelve months in his own Teutonic language (II, 26–27).[33] It is unclear whether Naucler saw Theodoric so much a German prince as to let him prefigure the Empire in its German possessions. Theodoric's jurisdiction over ecclesiastical matters (I, 695) becomes an important precedent for the relationship of Church and Empire. The Church was restored to its grandeur by the German Emperors, who have always been dedicated to religion and the universal faith (II, 33–34). This seems to have a symbolic precedent in the death and resurrection of St. Maternus in Alsatia by the staff of St. Peter, the upper half of which resides in Cologne, the lower half in Trier (I, 517–18). The Empire's sanctity is also attested to by the lives of Emperor Henry II, the Saint, and his sainted wife, Empress Kunigunde, both of whose deaths were attended by miracles (II, 113).

The supremacy of the Empire is shown by the titles of the ecclesiastical electors as established by Otto III (*Chronicon*, 96–97). It is no ordinary monarch whose coronation calls forth the participation of other monarchs to give obeisance. But consider Conrad II, whose crowning (1027) was witnessed by Canute the Great of England and Rudolf III of Burgundy, distinguished kings (II, 115). When the Germans received the Empire, they received with it the monarchy of the world.[34] Despite the silence of Brant and Wimpheling, there is no question but that the supremacy of the *Imperium* remained among the humanists a stable element in the imperial myth.

Naucler's chronicle is a major monument of Renaissance historiography in Germany. It has been recognized as such in the past, even though it is now little read by anyone but specialists. Its importance has been seen by recent historiographers in Naucler's progress beyond "scholastic" history writing, a vice as it were of Schedel and Foresta.[35] This view has held that the progress was toward more critical and accurate history. Perhaps it was. But perhaps the category, "accurate," misses the main contribution of Naucler's labors. His chronicle is so thorough and economical a compilation that it becomes a common-

---

[33] Cf. Riess, *Motive*, pp. 11 and 49–50, and the basic survey, Paul Joachimsen, *Geschichtsauffassung und Geschichtschreibung in Deutschland unter dem Einfluß des Humanismus*, Beiträge zur Kulturgeschichte des Mittelalters und der Renaissance, VI (Berlin and Leipzig, 1910), p. 94.

[34] Riess, *Motive*, p. 12.

[35] Joachimsen, *Geschichtsauffassung*, pp. 91–104.

place book of the notions conventional among German humanists with patriotic leanings. That some of these notions coincide better than previous speculations with the conclusions of modern historical thought is to see Naucler's *Chronicon* fragmentarily and anachronistically. The brief description above of his myths of the German past is also fragmentary. It can, however, encompass a greater portion of Naucler's contributions, that is, it permits more or even the whole of Naucler's history to be considered on its own terms. The "accurate" and the imaginative were not separated in the minds of the humanists (or, for that matter, in the minds of their popular counterparts), and there is no reason for them to be separated by the modern investigator.

Naucler's name would be forgotten altogether, were it not for his ample contribution to historical writing. We turn now to three humanists of equal or greater fame, who in more typical humanist fashion spread their interests and effectiveness over greater areas of activity. Two helped make history, and all three dabbled in its written preservation. The first is JOHANNES COCHLAEUS, who was to achieve a certain notoriety as Luther's adversary, "Dr. Köchel." In 1512, Cochlaeus published an edition of the *Cosmographia* of Pomponius Mela, and attached to it a description of Germany.[36] Tacitus appears as the starting point of this description, and so, like Bebel before him, Cochlaeus has reason to believe the indigenous origins of the Germans at the cost of the traditional myths of origin. Cochlaeus accepts the etymology of German that rests on the presumed brotherhood of German and Gaul (Langosch, p. 41–42). He depends heavily on Wimpheling's *Epitoma*, and borrows from it such items as the age of Trier (pp. 48–49, 158–59), the antiquity of the Cimbri (pp. 42–43), the defeat of Varus (pp. 44ff.), the invincibility of the Germans (pp. 46–47), and more. Significantly, the work which purports to describe Germany devotes considerable energies to the activities of the Goths, Vandals, Lombards, and Huns (pp. 50ff.). Cochlaeus considers German the first three; the last, the Huns, are Scythians, but could not have achieved their great successes without the aid and direction of Germans (pp. 56ff.). A description of Germany, presumably geographic in purpose, finds need to mention the transference of the Empire. Cochlaeus, however, specifically states that he passes over the deeds of the Emperors up to Maximilian for reasons of brevity; it is enough to deal with

---

[36] Karl Langosch, ed. and trans., *Johannes Cochlaeus: Brevis Germanie Descriptio (1512)* (Darmstadt, 1960), p. 7 [henceforth "Langosch"].

the history of the Germans up to the time of the transference of the Empire from the Greeks (pp. 58ff.). We may borrow his suggestion and, for reasons of brevity, pass over the remainder of the *Descriptio* with the comment that it stresses alike the warlike valor of the Germans and the peaceful, specifically artistic accomplishments of many cities and regions in the author's own time. The humanists may have been an intellectual aristocracy, but socially they were almost all burghers, and the interests of their social class were much advanced by their brilliance and scholarship.

A long-time friend of Cochlaeus was the less controversial Swiss scholar, HENRICUS GLAREANUS (1488–1563). His humanistic credentials are quite unimpeachable. In his many productive years he composed an influential geography and one of the most popular works on the theory of geography, not to mention numerous editions and commentaries including the works of Livy, Ovid, Caesar, Terence, Cicero, Lucan, Boethius, Valerius Maximus, Eutropius, and Solinus.[37] Glareanus's humanist activity casts particularly interesting light on his conjectures concerning the origins of the Swiss. Like Celtis and others, Glareanus did not let his erudition interfere with his imagination. In 1514, the humanist, also a poet laureate, produced a description of his Swiss homeland that, like Cochlaeus's of Germany, goes well beyond simple geographic observation.[38] Having praised the warlike valor of the Germans in general and the Helveti in particular, and having praised the excellence of Rhaetic wine, Glareanus turns to the origins of the various Swiss peoples (Näf, pp. [20–23]). Those from the Canton Schwyz stem from the Scandinavian Goths, whose name is equivalent to "guoten," that is, the good. Those from Canton Uri stem from the Huns who had been driven from Scythia.[39] Those from Unterwalden stem directly from Rome (pp. [56–57]). Solothurn is as old as Rome or older, for it is a sister city of Trier. It was founded by Thebans who fled their city with Ursus; and they are brave like (an) Ursus in the conduct of war (p. [90–91]). In a poem attached to these works and

---

[37] Otto F. Fritsche, *Glarean: Sein Leben und seine Schriften* (Frauenfeld, 1890), pp. 5, 91–126.

[38] Werner Näf, ed. and trans., *Henricus Glareanus: Helvetiae Descriptio, Panegyricum* [*Heinrich Glarean: Beschreibung der Schweiz, Lob der dreizehn Orte*] (St. Gall, 1948), pp. 7 and 103, note 1 [henceforth "Näf"].

[39] Näf, pp. [28–29] and [48–49] and note to l. 146. Cf. *Schardius Redivivus*, p. 329 and Ulrich Paul, *Studien zur Geschichte des Nationalbewusstseins im Zeitalter des Humanismus und der Reformation*, Historische Studien, CCXCVIII (Berlin, 1936), p. 96.

addressed to Glareanus, his friend and fellow-laureate, Vadianus concurs with the bravery of the Swiss: Mars has his home in their land
(pp. [90–91]). Bebel's furious rejection of Petermann Etterlin and thus
implicitly of Meisterlin and Pirckheimer clearly left little impression
on his time, and less on Glareanus.

JOACHIM VADIANUS became the avid reformer of St. Gall; his zeal
and moderation represent the Reformation at its best. In 1515, several
years before his conversion and in fact before the formal beginnings
of the movement, Vadianus delivered an *Oratio* before Emperor Maximilian.[40] It illustrates well the vitality of the imperial myth in these
critical years. Vadianus addresses Maximilian as "divus, pater patriae,
fidei protector" (Gabathuler, p. 48). The first two titles are transparently of Roman provenance, even though the special notion of
Germany may have been attached to "patria" by this time. Vadianus
does incline to see Germany as an entity with a political past distinct
from the Empire's. The Germany which defeated Quintilius Varus
(pp. 68–69), the unconquered Germany which out of love of freedom
never submitted to the Empire, is now the state which selects the
Emperor from among its own people (pp. 64–65). Had it not been for
unconquered Germany, the heritage of Romulus and the *Imperium* of
Rome might have come to naught (pp. 60–61).

The title "fidei protector" may seem so conventional as to be worth
passing over altogether. However, when considered in the company of
the countless statements on the sanctity of the Empire, the title becomes a pointed and concise expression of the great symbolic importance of the antiquated political institution. A fully adequate evaluation of the part played by the imperial myth in the hard politics of
subsequent years is, to the best of my knowledge, still wanting. Occasionally, it seems that the only political force dedicated to the crush-
ing of the Reformation was the Empire. Certainly not the Papacy or
the Catholic Kingdom of France could claim that distinction when it
came to the homeland of the Reform. When the Emperor had wars
on the west with the French, on the south with the Italians, on the
east with the Turks, nothing could have been more sensible than to
abandon the Roman Church and thus to win the full support of a
largely reformed population and their Protestant Princes, rather than

---

[40] Matthäus Gabathuler, ed. and trans., *Joachim Vadian: Lateinische Reden,*
Vadian Studien, III (St. Gall, 1953), pp. 47–81 [henceforth "Gabathuler"]. Vadianus
produced several major historical works later in life, as resident Reformer of St. Gall.
They are most interesting, but fall outside the period under discussion here.

having to make war with them on the north as well. I suggest that the sacramental stamp of the Emperor's office, in addition to his personal piety, may have outweighed political advantage in the case of the Reformation. The Emperor could not abandon the papacy, despite the fact that it was financing wars against him, that it was encouraging the Emperor's most Christian adversary in France to join with the Turk in alliance against the Empire. I suggest that a force transcending hard politics kept the Empire Roman. In all logic it should have declared its independence. The illogic surely resides in the symbolic importance of the Emperor as "fidei protector." Vadianus understood this charismatic stamp when he applied the title to the office of Emperor, even though he may not have imagined or liked the idea that imperial forces were soon to be used against what he was to become.

A reformer of another kind and an earlier generation, JOHANNES TRITHEMIUS, published in the year before his death a remarkable *Compendium* (1515) of Frankish history out of the works of one Hunibald.[41] Trithemius, Abbot of Sponheim and later of Würzburg, was one of the most learned and distinguished men of his age. He has in the meantime become one of the most misunderstood. Partly because of public distrust of his work on cryptography, this pious and gentle man was considered a black magician.[42] Trithemius is one of the few witnesses to the existence and activity of the historical prototype of Faust. The good monk might indeed have wished to be a magician, and may have been one in the uniquely Renaissance sense of that profession, but he was a monastic reformer first, then a humanist, and only in the last place a "magus"—and in no case as necromantic as later eras have made him.

Trithemius was a good friend of Conrad Celtis, and some of Celtis's most exciting manuscript discoveries were made in collaboration with him. Perhaps as a consequence of his association with Celtis, he reflects several of the arch-humanist's most inventive myths of the German past. For example, he calls himself a Druid, and his monastery a home of Druids.[43] It must have been an abiding disappointment to Trithemius, himself no less a humanist than Celtis, that he could nowhere

---

[41] I use the edition in *Schardius Redivivus*, pp. 143–69.

[42] P. Paulus Volk, "Abt Johannes Trithemius," *Rheinische Vierteljahrsblätter*, XXVII (1962), 41–42, 45. Father Volk's article contains an excellent bibliography of recent work on Trithemius and valuable suggestions for further work.

[43] Paul, *Studien*, p. 89 and cf. pp. 91–108 on other matters concerning Trithemius.

find the texts to support this kind of myth. Like Annius of Viterbo before him, Trithemius did the next best thing. He invented them. The great Hunibald existed, as far as modern scholarship can determine, only in Trithemius's imagination, thence in his work, and thence in the work of others. Due primarily to this invention and to an earlier, less certainly fictitious authority, Trithemius has acquired the reputation of an inveterate liar. His remarkably accurate bio-bibliography, *Catalogus Scriptorum Ecclesiasticorum* (ed. princ. 1494), the first such work in modern times, is widely attacked as untrustworthy. When a modern bibliographer fails to find a title or incipit entered by Trithemius, he assumes that it is a fabrication, not that the document in question may be known in another form or may have passed from sight. Perhaps Trithemius is himself to blame, but his reputation as trickster and fraud is hardly deserved. We shall, alas, do nothing to dispel these erroneous notions, for it is precisely his fabrication and his imaginative work that are of interest here.

Rather than separate Trithemius's many myths from one another and subject them to my categories of origins, heroes, religion, virtue, and Empire, I shall summarize the larger part of the *Compendium*. It is the closest to an ordered, unified mythology of the German past that the Renaissance produced. Had Trithemius restricted himself only to known myths, his fiction would probably have become a standard reference work. As it is, it found productive readers, went through four Latin editions, at least two, possibly three, or more translations in the sixteenth century, and was published on into the eighteenth century.[44]

In 439 B.C., at the time of Cyrus, 750 years after the fall of Troy, the Goths left the island Scandia, now called *Gothia Septentrionalis*. These Goths confronted and killed many Sicambri in the course of their travels. The Sicambri initially came from Troy. At the time of the Gothic oppression, Marcomir, son of Anthenor, ruled the Sicambri. He appealed to the Saxons for aid. They too had come from Troy; hence the Sicambri and Saxons were brothers. The Saxons invited the Sicambri to Germany. In 433 B.C., Marcomir and his brother Suimo migrated to the fertile lands between Saxony and the Rhine, primarily in order to escape further contact with the Goths. The Sicambri eventually crossed the Rhine and made war on the Gauls. Marcomir died in 410 B.C., and in his time, Wasthaldus produced his twelve

---

[44] Potthast, p. 1072. The Newberry Library in Chicago houses two separate translations, one of which was unknown to Potthast. This one is prefaced with a foreword by Sebastian Franck, but is undated.

books on the origins of the Sicambri from the fall of Troy. In continuance of this work, Hunibald wrote his book, the history of the Franks up to his own time and the reign of Clovis the Great.

Marcomir's son Anthenor succeeded him and ruled for thirty years. Together with the Saxons, the Sicambri waged war on the Gauls and Romans. They also invaded Frisia, which takes its name from the Sicambrian general Phriso. In the twelfth year of Anthenor's reign, his uncle Suimo died, leaving two sons, another Marcomir and Hector. The former perished in the Rhine. The latter ruled in his father's stead the lands west of the Rhine (*Schardius Redivivus*, p. 143).

Anthenor died in 380 B.C. leaving one son, Priam, who reigned for twenty-four years. In this time, the Sicambri and the Saxons began to forget their Greek language, and little by little used only German. In the sixth year of Priam's reign, Theocalus died. Theocalus, a descendent of Suimo, had founded the priesthood of Jupiter. Until then the Sicambri had worshipped only in simple oak groves. King Priam built a great city on the Rhine called Neopagus—Nimwegen, Neumagen?—where for many years the Sicambrian kings held court.

In 356 B.C., Priam died suddenly and was succeeded by his son Helenus, who venerated Pallas and established human sacrifice with the sons of captives as his victims. Diocles succeeded Helenus. In his reign, a people from Scandiana (now called Gothia) devastated Saxon lands. While Diocles was away avenging his brother Saxons, the Gauls at home rebelled. Their rebellion was put down, and a number of Gallic children were sacrificed to Jupiter and Venus.

Diocles died in 297 B.C. and was succeeded by his son Helenus, who was a lascivious man. After fourteen years of misrule, he was deposed, and his brother Basanus was placed on the throne. He was called *Magnus Basan* or, in the vernacular, "der grosse Basan." He was very highly regarded because he brought law that applied to all alike. Basanus had, for example, an adulterous son, Sedanus, on whom he pronounced judgement. When accused by the woman's husband, Sedanus was condemned to death. Appeals were made, but Basanus replied that it would be easier to keep the wind from blowing than to retract a law which he had made (*Schardius Redivivus*, p. 144). He turned to his son and said that it was not he who killed the son, but the law which the son knowingly tried to circumvent.

Sedanus's mother raged to the King, claiming that a cruel tyrant is not a king when he murders in the name of law. Basanus replied that it was not the woman's role to reproach her husband, but rather to obey him. Instead of having her killed, he sent her back to her father, the King of the Orchadares. From that time on, the Sicambrian King was known as the "dickaeo Basan," that is, Basan the Just. He is the one known in the famous saying, "Kennet ihr den grossen Basan nicht?" Because of the repudiation of his daughter, the King of the Orchadares launched, with the aid of the King of Britain, an attack on the Sicambri. When the two saw the strength of their adversary, they did not even complete the assault, but simply turned back. In these years, Basanus built a great palace in a city he had recently founded on the banks of the Mosel.

In the twenty-sixth year of his reign, Basanus re-established the worship of Jupiter. He imported men learned both in Greek and German for prophecies, dream interpretation, astrology, ethics, physics, and metaphysics, in order to conduct proper worship. The King was at this time *Summus Pontifex*, but this practice changed. In the absence of the king, the priests had the highest jurisdiction and in general were empowered to pass judgement on everyone except the person of the King. The worship of Pallas and Venus was fostered, and their temples were attended by virgins. Basanus also captured all the lands between the North Sea and the Main, so that the Saxons rejoiced at having on the South and West such defenses against the Romans and the ferocious Gauls.

In 240 B.C., on his birthday, Basanus ordered seven days of prayer to the gods, and on the eighth day named Clodomerus his successor. Amerodacus relates that Basanus was most desirous of divinity, that he cultivated justice, loved the oppressed, despised the evil, and rewarded the good. During the convocation summoned to name his successor, Basanus disappeared. He was placed among the gods, and for many years the Sicambri praised their "Basangott" in sacred song.

During the reign of Clodomer, the Gauls rebelled, thinking that the disappearance of Basanus meant his death (*Schardius Redivivus*, p. 145). Clodomer utterly defeated them. At his death, he was succeeded by Nicanor who defeated the King of the Archades—Orchadares? Orkneys?—in behalf of the King of Britain. Nicanor had the British Princess Constantia to wife. Marcomer succeeded Nicanor and reigned for twenty-eight years. He was a modest prince, severe in war and kind to the oppressed. From the priests of Jupiter he learned the secrets of dreams, prophecies, predictions, and auguries, the like of which had never before been known in Germany. He died in 158 B.C. and was succeeded by Clodeus, then Anthenor, Clodomer, and Merodach.

Merodach made war on the Romans and in alliance with the Saxons conquered Italy as far as Ravenna. The Romans set the Goths and Slavs on the Saxons, so that they could not come to the aid of their brother Sicambri. Merodaeus (the Schard text varies Latin and "German" forms), that is, Merodach, took the aid of the Cimbri instead and with them attacked the Romans. His and the Cimbrian forces were defeated by Marius. After this defeat, Merodach reorganized his armies and invaded Gaul, for the Gauls had been allied to Marius and the Romans. Merodach died in 93 B.C.

After Merodach, Cassander ruled (*Schardius Redivivus*, p. 146). He was succeeded by Antharius. Antharius's son, Franck, succeeded him. It is after this Franck that the Franks are named. Salagastald related that in battle, for example, against the Goths and Scandian peoples, the enemy cried "hie Franck! hie Franck!" The council of the Sicambrian nation resolved that their name be changed to Frank, that is, free, noble, warlike, to be feared by all nations. The name Sicambri, however, only gradually receded to oblivion. Francus died in 9 B.C., and his deeds are preserved in the songs of the *Pontifex Maximus* Clodomer and in the prose of Hunibald.

Clogio, an admirable man, succeeded his father Francus. Clogio's mother, Lothildis, became high priestess in the temple of Pallas. His son Phrisus, became King of Frisia (*Schardius Redivivus*, p. 147). During the reign of Clogio, Christ was born. Clogio died in 20 A.D. For the remainder of his deeds, see Hunibald. Either Trithemius's imagination failed him, or he assumed the device would lend verisimilitude to his fabrication, or indeed he had a manuscript before him—an extremely unlikely but tempting possibility.

The kings preceding Richimer, crowned in 89 A.D., seem relatively uninteresting. Richimer defeated the Goths at Frankfurt on the Oder and thus named that city, since he was leading, of course, an army of Franks. One of his sons, Suimo, gave his name to a place on the river Spree called Suimonia—Stralsund (which is, however, far from the Spree). A contemporary named Brand gave his name to Brandenburg (*Schardius Redivivus*, p. 148). After Richimer's son Odemarus passed on, another Marcomir ruled the Franks. He married Athilde, daughter of the King of Britain, who gave him seven sons. Among them were Marcomer, who founded Marburg; Frank, Duke of Koblenz, who named Frankfurt on Main; and Odomer, who was made high priest. Odomer was a man of counsel, a philosopher, and learned in all the sciences of the world. He wrote poetry and annals.

Several generations later, in the reign of Hildericus, the great philosopher Hildegast flourished. He taught the Franks to sing in their own German language. In his time, an important prophecy was made concerning Frankish greatness: the eagle would collide with the lion and serpent. Incidentally, lions and serpents populate the Saxon coat of arms in the fifteenth century as Rolevinck describes it (Bücker, pp.

76–77). There were many prophecies, Trithemius tells us, but he could not decipher them, because they were written in an irregular combination of German, Greek, and Roman, which he could not understand. Precisely what the learned Abbot had in mind here is uncertain. He had, however, seen Old High German texts and might have been inspired by a frustrating inability to read them. A further curiosity appears when Trithemius's other activities are considered. As the author of a stenography and a cryptography, such secret writing would certainly fascinate him. He could conceivably have seen ancient inscriptions or perhaps even runes, and have decided to memorialize the experience in his chronicle. However that may be, the great philosopher Hildegast died in 253 A.D., and Trithemius again refers the reader to Hunibald for further information (*Schardius Redivivus*, p. 149).

We pass over some two hundred years of Trithemius's history to the year 405 A.D., when Pharamundus was elected King as reported by Salagast Philippus. During his reign, a Frankish duke founded Sunnenberg—Sonnenberg in the Mark Brandenburg—and Suntheim. These years also saw Christianity reach the Saxons, whose first Christian duke was called Helenus (*Schardius Redivivus*, p. 155). Clodius Crinitus succeeded Pharamund in 431. In his reign, Salagastus flourished. He was the wise philosopher of the Franks who gave written form to Frankish law, which is known as Salic in his honor. Salagastus also built up a city which became known as Selgenstat, by corruption of the name. In this time, all of Gaul was under the rule of the Franks. Those who were in Gaul took Gallic wives, gave up their own tongue, and assumed Gallic customs, all of which prevails to this day (p. 158). Clodovaeus was the first King of the Franks to accept Christianity. In the eleventh year of Clodovaeus's reign, Theodoric, King of the Goths, was sent by Emperor Zeno to do away with Odoacer, Tyrant of Saxony, who ruled Rome. Theodoric killed Odoacer, seized the *Imperium Romanum*, and ruled it for thirty-one years (p. 159).

Thus far Hunibald. After him, Trithemius tells us, the sources are Haduard, Richer, and Hermanfrid (*Schardius Redivivus*, p. 160). Lothar, King of the Franks (ob. 564), had a son named Granus after whom Aachen—Aquis Granae—is named (contrast Peutinger). This same Lothar is the ancestor of the Hapsburgs. In this time, Brunhilde, murderess of kings, was cruelly but justly put to death. Not long after Lothar's death, the Lombards left Scandia and invaded Italy (p. 161). There is little sense in continuing Trithemius's fiction beyond prehistoric times. It continues with the history of the Merovingians through the assumption of power by the majordomos.

It is no mean achievement to invent a thousand years of history. But Trithemius succeeded and, I think, with a modicum of style, with a certain command of the story-teller's craft, and with a good deal of historical imagination. All appearances to the contrary, the good Abbot was not at liberty to invent as his Muse dictated. He had assumed the task of writing in one of the most restricted and demanding of literary genres, forgery. His fiction had to look like a chronicle, and indeed it does, with its occasionally tedious listing of reigns and *gesta*. Periodically, however, as in the case of Basan, he begins to create a living personality. It is not the purpose of this study to give a literary evaluation of such a text. Considering its imaginativeness, its popularity in the vernacular translations of the sixteenth century, and the relative fame or infamy of its author, the absence of extensive critical investigation is most troublesome. The oversight of literary scholars must be ascribed to Trithemius's attempt to pass the work off as history. The historians and historiographers feel free to ignore the work since it is a fabrication. But just as this study is not the place for a literary evaluation of Trithemius's text, it is not the place for a political evaluation. Nonetheless, there can be no doubt that a strong propagandistic program underlies Trithemius's *Compendium*. It is patriotic in the extreme. But there is a refinement nowhere else so clearly articulated. We shall touch on it below, in discussing Trithemius and the myth of the *Imperium*. His fabrication is a work of many ramifications and is fully undeserving of the condescension with which it is generally greeted.

Within the limits imposed by the character of the forgery, Trithemius contained a historical mythology of the German past that was, in many ways, quite traditional. He accepts the Trojan origins of the Franks and invents the same for the Saxons. Elsewhere he transmits the analogous fable for the Bavarians, their exodus from Armenia and their heroic ancestors, Boioarus, Norix, son of Hercules, and the like.[45] Trithemius preserves the Scandinavian origins of the Goths and Lombards, and identifies the Vandals with the same geography. He counts among his heroes first the politicians such as Hector, Francus, Helenus, Basanus the Great, Brand, Theodoric the Goth, and then the scholars such as Wasthaldus, Theocalus, Amerodacus, Salagastald, Clodomer, the high priestess Lothildis, Hildegast, and of course Hunibald and his successors. Of ancient religion, we have seen the veneration of Venus, Pallas, and Jupiter, simple worship in groves and in temples attended by virgins, and an occasional human sacrifice. Of

---

[45] *Opera Historica*, Marquard Freher, ed., I (Frankfurt, 1601), 100.

ancient virtue, we have seen warlike valor and the development of legal justice. And of the *Imperium*, we have seen almost nothing.

In these works, Trithemius makes specific reference to the imperial myth only twice: first with the statement that Theodoric ruled the *Imperium Romanum*, and then with the prophecy that the lion and serpent would confront (and destroy) the eagle. The first creates no complications if *Imperium* is translated as "realm" or "authority, power." If, on the other hand, Trithemius meant "Empire," then his statement is another example of patriotic historical "interpretation." It seems not to have disturbed Trithemius and his peers that such interpretation might be contrary or contradictory to tradition, or even to their own interpretation elsewhere. Theodoric would then be a type of the lasting rule over the *Imperium Romanum* by the German line. Emperor Maximilian seems to have considered himself a descendent of Theodoric, and Trithemius devoted much energy to tracing his fabulous genealogy.[46] Trithemius, however, concluded that the Hapsburgs sprout from the Merovingians, in direct succession from Basanus, as it were. In the context of the myth of the Empire in the Renaissance, Theodoric's "historical" position is clear. In the context of Trithemius's works themselves, it is altogether another matter.

The eagle in Hildegast's somewhat iconographic prophecy is plainly the Roman Empire. The lion and the serpent represent, as they do on various coats of arms, Germany or, more properly, the Franks and the Saxons. Hildegast's prophecy could be made to concur with the standard implications of the imperial myth: the Germans win the Roman Empire to themselves, first through the Franks and then through the Saxons. This, I suggest, may be unsatisfactory. Trithemius's *Compendium* rests on a single assumption and attempts to demonstrate a single political proposition. The assumption is that an independent German Empire existed parallel to the Roman, indeed from the same source—Troy—as the Roman Empire. The political proposition is that the German realm and the Roman Empire are not co-extensive, that the Emperor bears the Roman *Imperium* as a responsibility in addition to his duties as monarch of Germany. Hildegast's prophecy seems very much to mean that German forces have confronted and overwhelmed the forces of the Roman Empire, as with Theodoric.

---

[46] Maximilian's real and supposed ancestors surround what was to have been his tomb in Innsbruck. The statues, designed by Dürer and Peter Vischer the Elder, among others, included Theodoric and King Arthur. Cf. illustrations in E. Heyck, *Kaiser Maximilian I.*, Monographien zur Weltgeschichte, V (Bielefeld and Leipzig, 1898), pp. 8–9. Cf. Isidor Silbernagel, *Johannes Trithemius, eine Monographie* (Landshut, 1868), p. 197.

Trithemius's fabrication gives the distinct impression of having almost nineteenth-century nationalistic implications. In the Renaissance, they have analogues in Bebel's and Köchlin's independent glory of a specifically German antiquity. Trithemius may or may not have meant to reject the old *Imperium*. But more than any German author of the period, he does distinguish national interest from that of the Roman Empire. Concealed in the wraps of ancient history—a fictitious ancient history at that—lies a political document, an articulation of a "historical," political nationality as, presumably, existed nowhere else in sixteenth-century Germany. Trithemius was a remarkable man, and there is no reason that a monastic reformer, witch-hunter, bibliographer, genealogist, historian, and white magician might not also have been a prophetic political commentator.

A friend and student of Trithemius, Paulus Langius, returns the myth of the Empire to more conventional lines in his *Chronicon Citizense* (ca. 1515–20).[47] He tells of Otto I's journey to Rome, for the purpose of reforming the villainous Pope John XII. Entering the city, Otto was received honorably by the clergy and the people, and crowned Emperor. Some say that Otto was the first German to receive the Empire, but they are in error. Long before, Charles the Great, a Teutonic Frank, had received the power. Those positively stumble, "hallucinantur," who maintain that the Empire was ever in the hands of the Gauls or the French: not one Emperor was ever in origin a Gaul (Pistorius, p. 757). Langius also relates the story of the recovery of the body of Pallas in the reign of Henry III. By some miracle, the body of the son of Evander was preserved, uncorrupted. It was Turnus, enemy of the origins of Roman power, who had killed Pallas, but the remains of the victim reappeared intact now, thousands of years later (Pistorius, p. 773). I presume that this was interpreted as a sign of the supernatural favor enjoyed by the Empire since time immemorial; that the miraculous preservation of Pallas suggested the longevity of the Empire; and that the mythical content of the ninth and tenth books of the *Aeneid* (those in which Pallas plays a part) was being applied to the medieval Empire.

Langius's chronicle contains a great many fables of Slavic history

---

47 Johannes Pistorius, *Illustrium veterum scriptorum ... tomus unus* (Frankfurt, 1583), 755–907. Langius repeatedly acknowledges his debt to Trithemius, e.g., pp. 787, 802, 905. Cf. also Paul Lehmann, *Merkwürdigkeiten des Abtes Johannes Trithemius*, SB Bavarian Academy, philos.-hist. Kl., vol. 1961, no. 2 (Munich, 1961), p. 50.

from the east-central section of Germany he knew. They are peripheral to the subject at hand. The chronicle itself is an interesting Renaissance document, nevertheless. The closer it comes to modern times, the more it becomes a history of scholarship. The author begins seriously with Albertus Magnus (Pistorius, p. 807) and continues with brief notices and lengthy paragraphs on the distinguished minds of the time: Thomas Aquinus (p. 811), Dante (p. 829), Occam (p. 833), Boccaccio (p. 841), Gert Groet and the Italian humanists at the Council of Constance (p. 851), Cusanus (p. 867), Ficino (p. 885), Celtis (p. 881), Pico and Reuchlin (p. 885), Wimpheling (p. 886), Brant (p. 894), and Luther (p. 899). I mention these, even though they are apart from the matter of this study, because they signify clearly a Renaissance awareness in Germany. Such awareness can be found in the most peculiar places.

Langius makes few contributions to the legendary pre-history of German lands. The master perhaps went so far that the student could not even begin. Langius restores the traditional picture somewhat through his conventional treatment of the imperial myth, down to the topos of critical rejection. The larger part of his history is serious, scholarly, rooted in tradition, and colored by the humanist ambitions of its author and his friends.

One of the most critical historians of the age was the north German chronicler ALBERTUS KRANTZ. He was far from a programmatic mythmaker and should pale by comparison to an historian quite as creative as Trithemius. Somehow, this is not the case. Krantz died in 1517, before any of his works were printed, although they were undoubtedly distributed in manuscript. He had been the Rector of the University of Rostock, and his fame spread quickly late in his lifetime and after his death. His works are among the most popular histories of the sixteenth century, having enjoyed no less than eighteen editions and translations by 1601.[48] I discuss three of his major works, the *Saxonia*, the *Dania*, and the *Metropolis*, and return to the pattern of origins, heroes, religion, virtue, and the Empire.[49]

Krantz's critical inclinations demonstrate themselves early in his

---

[48] Paul Schaerffenberg, *Die Saxonia des Albert Krantz* (Meiningen, 1893), pp. 7–8. Cf. Potthast, pp. 700–701.

[49] I use the German translation of the *Saxonia* by Basilius Faber (Leipzig, 1563), the text of the *Metropolis* published in Frankfurt in 1576, and the 1546 Strassburg edition of the *Chronica regnorum Aquilonarium Daniae, Svetiae, Norvagiae*, normally called the *Dania*, and so cited here.

Saxonia, where he rejects many familiar theories of origins. The Saxons do not come from Britain (thus Meisterlin); on the contrary, the Saxons invaded Britain. Nor do the Saxons stem from Macedon. What could Alexander's men conceivably have to fear? And needless to say, the geographic situation would have prevented the Macedonians from reaching Saxony as the myth describes. It would be exceedingly difficult to sail from the Caspian Sea to the mouth of the Elbe. That only twenty-four out of three hundred ships are supposed to have arrived is more than understandable. It is furthermore nonsense to say that the Saxons migrated to Germany when Theodoric was King of the Franks. All these theories, Krantz assures us, must be wrong, because the Saxons are known to have been where they are now, quarreling with the Danes ever since 1000 B.C. (*Saxonia,* sig. A [i]ʳf.). There were, of course, in 1000 B.C. no such things as Saxons and Danes, at least not as Krantz imagines them. Serious historians of the Renaissance could not avoid *anasceua.* Krantz is nonetheless a truly critical and discriminate historian, despite the fanciful conclusions this inclination leads him to.

With the certainty that the first historical appearance of the Saxons comes about 1000 B.C., Krantz feels free to reject and propose other theories. What one reads of the Boi, he feels, cannot be applied to the Saxons, for the Boi (Bohemians for Krantz) were Vandals (*Saxonia,* sig. A iiᵛ). The Cimbri were also Vandals (*Saxonia,* fol. VIᵛ), as were the Winuli (*Metropolis,* p. 95), and the Venetians (*Dania,* p. 435). The Vandals are the same as the Sorabi or Slavs (*Saxonia,* fol. XXXIᵛ). This illustrates the extent which the confusion between Vandals and Wends could reach. Sorb or Sorab is another word for Wend, as applied to the remaining Slavs in present-day Lausitz. The Vandals, according to Krantz, have their origins in Scythia (*Saxonia,* sig. A iiᵛ). He seems uncertain as to whether "Hassens" (Hessians) were originally Saxons, but one could be led to believe so, since the Greeks often converted "s" to "h". Those whom Tacitus calls "Chatti" seem certainly to have been Saxons (*Saxonia,* sig. A iiiʳf.).

Krantz also rejects the theory that Saxon lineage derives from Japhet, Gomer, and "Assenez." Actually, they stem from Noah over Tuisco, as Berosus proves all Germans do (*Saxonia,* sig. A iiiᵛ). More *anasceua.* Krantz accepts the theory of Scandinavian origins for the Goths (*Dania,* p. 370), but does not, on that account, reject the origins from Scythia (*Saxonia,* sig. A iiᵛ). The Bavarians originate among the Huns and are named after the Hunnish general Avarius (*Dania,* p. 97). The Scots take their name from Duke Scoto (*Dania,* p. 14), and Krantz, like Bebel, seems to consider them German.

For the first time among our Renaissance authors, the naming of the Lombards is related in greater detail by Krantz, although the tale is by no means original with him. There was a nation in Scandan that was ready to make war with its enemies. The warriors sent prayers to their goddess Frigg, who advised them to have their women tie their hair about their chins. Frigg's husband, Wodan, favored the enemy, and promised the victory to the army he would see first upon arising the next morning. He assumed, of course, that it would be his favorites. When he awoke he saw what Frigg had arranged and was so startled that he asked, "who are those long beards?" Frigg said, "you have given them a name, now give them the victory." Thus they became known as Langobards. The bards of antiquity who sang poetry were really the Langobards (*Dania*, p. 72).

The meaning of England's name is also reported by Krantz, who accepts Gobelinus's derivation from the Saxon duke "Angul," adding that this particular explanation is widely attested (*Dania*, p. 5). Angaria, that is, Engern in Saxony, had been called Anglia, but the name was changed to avoid confusion with the magnificent island that now bears it (*Saxonia*, fol. XV^r). The change is clear in view of the fact that the Angli and Angri of Saxony were one and the same tribe (*Metropolis*, p. 74).

The practice of eponymy, finding in national and place names a hero after whom they were named, was well established in historical tradition. Although Krantz does his best to discriminate, he cannot escape the seductive ease of such explanations.[50] Many ages before the coming of Christ, well before Rome was founded, Dan became the first King of the Danes, to whom he gave his name (*Dania*, p. 5). Humblus and Lothar, sons of Dan, succeeded him. Lothar did away with Humblus, just as Romulus had done away with Remus (*Dania*, p. 6), and incidentally, as Schwyter had done away with Schweyg in the founding of canton Schwyz.[51] It is necessary for Krantz to disabuse those misguided enough to think that Caesar built seven fortresses in Germany to honor seven pagan gods, Sol, Luna, Mars, Mercury, Jupiter, Venus, and Saturn. These seven happen to be those who gave their names to the days of the week, but Krantz is unmoved by the coincidence. The glossator explains what the seven places were: Soltwedel after Sol, Lüneburg after Luna, Merseburg after Mars, Eilenburg ("eilen"—to rush, as with a message) after Mercury, Hamburg

---

[50] See my "Etymology in Tradition and in the Northern Renaissance," *Journal of the History of Ideas*, XXIX (1968), 415–29.

[51] Baechtold, *Stretlinger Chronik*, p. LXXIV.

after Jupiter "Hamon" (Ammon of Egypt), Magdeburg after Venus, and Saturburg or Hartzburg (more 's' and 'h' variation) after Saturn (*Saxonia*, fol. XVIᵛ). Krantz's rejection of this explanation is repeated specifically for Hamburg (*Metropolis*, p. 11). The city cannot be named after "Hammon" since that deity was Libyan. Actually Hamburg is named after Hama, a Saxon warrior defeated by a Dane (cf. *Saxonia*, fols. VIIIᵛ and XXXIIIᵛ). Minden means "min" and "din," "meum et teum," and that seems to be where the city receives its name (*Metropolis*, p. 9). One explanation for the name Thietmarsi is that it comes from Titus Marcius (*Metropolis*, p. 144). The son of Ninus of Babylon is believed to have built and named Trier (*Metropolis*, p. 203).

As in other works, the myths of heroes here coincide at least in part with the myths of origin. The ancient Germans, he reports, praised their heroes in song (*Saxonia*, sig. A iiiᵛ). Among those sung might have been Roe, who founded Roschildia (*Dania*, p. 17) or his contemporary Hunding, son of Siegfried, King of the Saxons (*Saxonia*, fol. IIᵛ). Krantz tells the stories of the Gothic women left behind by their men who went off to fight Vexor of Egypt. Lampedo and Marpesia organized an army and had great victories. Orithia, also called Sinope, followed Marpesia as leader (*Dania*, pp. 372–77). This is perhaps the fitting place for such figures as Froto I, who was King of the Danes when Christ was born, Suibdgerus, first King of the Normans, and Aquinus, first King of Norway (*Dania*, pp. 15, 594, 597).

Among the few really fine tales out of dim "antiquity" told by German Renaissance chroniclers (one, again, not original with Krantz) is the story of the aged Wermundt, King of the Danes, and his idiot son, Uffo Gigas. The Saxons and Danes are traditional enemies, and the Saxons upon one occasion believed that they could subdue the Danes without bloodshed. They must only persuade Wermundt to name a Saxon prince his heir, since his idiot son Uffo could not rule. The next step would be to persuade Wermundt to give up the throne on account of his age. Wermundt flatly refuses their suggestions, furious that they abuse him with his useless son, whom he loves and whose idiocy was sent by God. The Saxons then suggest a duel between the Saxon prince and Uffo. Wermundt grows more furious that they insist upon bringing his idiot son into the discussion. When Wermundt is informed that his son wishes to speak, he thinks the abuse will take no end. But it is no joke. Uffo, in articulate, nay, eloquent response, accepts the challenge. He says that he will fight the Saxon prince and his whole retinue, with the victor taking both the Saxon and the Danish crown.

When everyone has left, Wermundt asks his son how it could be that after all these years he was no longer an idiot. Uffo replies that when his father was strong he had no need of a strong son; but now that he is old and weak, he needs the strength of his son. The duel takes place on an island in the river Eydor on the border between Denmark and Saxony. Wermundt is blind, but attends the battle nonetheless, so that he may drown himself immediately if his son should lose. By the sound of the weapons, Wermundt knows that his son has decapitated the Saxon prince and his men, one by one. Thus, by their own arrogance, the Saxons are forced to submit to the power of the Danes (*Saxonia*, fols. IV ʳ–V ʳ, comp. *Dania*, pp. 23ff.). Krantz's work is written from a so blatantly pro-Saxon bias that the above stories seem to have little place in his history. As a matter of fact, the tale points clearly to Krantz's valiant attempt at objectivity.

Krantz not only populates fabulous or uncertain pre-history with heroes. Without serious interruption, he passes to the dawn of historical time as it applies to the Germanic north. Ariovistus is made King of the Saxons (*Saxonia*, sig. A [i] ᵛ). Wiho seems to have been their first Christian bishop (*Metropolis*, p. 2). The well-known story of Alaric's burial in the Busento is preserved (*Dania*, p. 456). Theodoric's memory is also preserved with both the good and the bad. He was protector of the Church and of the City (*Dania*, p. 474), but he is supposed to have perished in a flaming volcano for his later crimes against religion (*Dania*, p. 492). Emperor Frederick II was known as a terrifying man who fully deserved the title of *malleus orbis* (*Metropolis*, p. 190). His deeds, great and infamous, were such that his reputation flourished even after his death, and men came forth claiming to be the deceased Emperor. In the reign of Rudolf, a false Frederick appeared who, upon questioning, turned out to be merely a survivor of Frederick II's court (*Saxonia*, fol. CLXXXVIII ᵛ).

Of ancient religion Krantz knows and surmises a great deal more than any of his contemporaries. He is familiar with such divinities as Wodan and Frigg (Fricka), whom he also calls Fricco. He names Thor and declares that the Swedes once worshipped him in a great temple. Freia is correctly identified with love and Thor with thunder. Jupiter is seen as Thor's Roman identity and Mars as Wodan's. Human sacrifice prevailed (*Dania*, p. 368). Even though Krantz rejected the theory that Caesar founded Magdeburg in honor of Venus, he believed that a statue of Venus in that city was destroyed by Charlemagne in a battle against the Saxons. The Romans under Drusus are supposed to have left it there. Krantz describes the statue at some length, including such details of the decoration as the presence of swans, graces, and doves (*Saxonia*, fol. XXXI ʳ). It would perhaps be an interesting challenge to reconstruct the statue on Krantz's description, or better yet, to find the illustration he probably had before him when writing that part of his chronicle. Krantz also mentions the Irmenseul on the Eresburg in Merseburg and its destruction. This holy place of the Saxons was thought to be dedicated to Hera, Hermes, or Mars. According to some, the name meant "anybody's column," since it was a place of public refuge (*Saxonia*, fol. XXXIX ᵛ).[52] Pagan ritual appears in Krantz in his description of the funeral of the Saxon King Gelder, given him by his Swedish enemies because of his nobility. A great ship was supplied with stores and a crew, and was burned with great ceremony (*Saxonia*, fol. IV ʳ).

Krantz succeeds in adding some variety to the brief list of ancient German virtues by stressing rhetorical achievements. Warlords were in the habit of delivering moving and elegant speeches before battle (*Saxonia*, fol. II ᵛ). The Saxons must have been at some advantage in this, for theirs was the purest language (*Saxonia*, fol. I ʳ).[53] These ancients, although pagans, were known to have been very strict in their morals and, among their other restraints, kept only one wife (*Saxonia*, fol. II ʳ). The ancient Saxons' love of freedom is shown by their rebellion against the successor of Uffo the idiot, Dan III, and the restoration of their liberty (*Saxonia*, fol. V ʳ). This same love of liberty moved them to abandon Italy, which they had attacked with the Lombards, and again to seek their own lands (*Saxonia*, fol. XIX ᵛ).

The warlike valor of the ancient Germans can be shown in the Goths whom Alexander, Pyrrhus, and Caesar made it a point to avoid (*Dania*, p. 370). The Goths were supposed to have pursued a very cultivated existence in the period after Alexander the Great's death but later they reverted to superstition (*Dania*, pp. 400–401). The valorous Germans repeatedly defeated the Roman Emperors. One of them, Augustus, cried out at the defeat of Varus, *Redde Germaniam Quintili Vare, redde Germaniam* (*Saxonia*, fol. IX ᵛ). The extent of their conquests is revealed in the very name of France (*Saxonia*, fol. XXIV ʳ). The Franks, including those in Gaul, were of German origin. This is shown by the fact that "Franck" is a German word meaning "free." Some claim that the Franks came from Troy, but that is a Gallic fable

---

[52] Heinrich Meibom wrote a learned essay gathering together most available references to the Irmensul, and venturing even to picture it: *Rerum Germanicarum Tomi III*, (Helmstedt, 1688), III, 3–32; illustration inserted between pp. 30 and 31. On the assumption that the illustration is authentic, the dates of the German Baroque may safely retreat from the seventeenth or eighteenth century back to the eighth century.

[53] Cf. Gobelinus Persona, sup., and Paul, *Studien*, p. 111.

(*Metropolis*, p. 96), which may indeed be the case if the Arverni were Gauls and if the Franks stole the myth from them—but more of that below.

There are special reasons for Krantz's rejection of the Troy myth of the Franks. Not long before Krantz's death, French ambitions on Alsace-Lorraine, or—perhaps more appropriately—Alsatia and Lotharingia, were reaching one of their early peaks. One of the arguments used to support French claims went as follows: the French were Franks, independent of and co-eval to Rome and the (Holy) Roman Empire. Since the Alsatians and Lotharingians were Franks, regardless of the language they spoke, they and their lands belonged to France and not to the Roman Empire.[54]

Krantz does nothing to tamper with the conventional form of the myth of the *Imperium*. The typical history of the Emperors begins with Julius Caesar and continues over Charlemagne without interruption (*Saxonia*, fol. XLVII^v ff.), which fully confirms the Roman character of the Empire and its unbroken continuity from Claudio-Julian times. With Charles, a born German, the Empire was transferred from the Greeks to the Germans (*Saxonia*, fols. XXIX^r, LXIV^v; cf. *Metropolis*, p. 59), which asserts the German character of the Empire. Krantz also prefigures German possession of the Empire by identifying Emperor Maximus as a Goth (*Dania*, p. 423). While Krantz passes over the legend of St. Maternus with suspicion (*Metropolis*, p. 3), he maintains the sanctity of the Empire again and again. One of the titles of the Emperor is "defensor ecclesiae" (*Metropolis*, p. 73). The Carolingians and Ottonians demonstrated their service to the Church in numerous generous deeds. Charles's very coronation called upon divine intervention, for he was crowned by God (*Saxonia*, fol. XXXIV^v). Frederick I Barbarossa used the same honorific, "a Deo coronato," of himself in a letter to the Emperor at Constantinople, whom he called "Graecorum Moderator" and not Emperor (*Metropolis*, p. 173). As for the supremacy of the Empire, be it known that the Emperor has been placed at the head of the world (*Saxonia*, fol. CXXXIX^v).

Renaissance chronicles, such as Krantz's, are interpretive works, no matter how objective they may have attempted to be. The question

---

[54] Maria Klippel, *Die Darstellung der fränkischen Trojanersage in Geschichtsschreibung und Dichtung vom Mittelalter bis zur Renaissance in Frankreich* (Marburg, 1936), p. 51. The dissertation contains an extensive collection of texts pertinent to the Troy myth in Germany as well as France.

may arise whether these apparently naive interpretations of history had any life at all outside the scholar's study. They did, even those politically, "realistically," most untenable. The myth of the Empire is everywhere affirmed. The documents from which written history today is taken were no exception. The title page of a broadside of the year 1518 reads in part, "Iupiter in coelis Caesar regit omnia terris."[55] The supremacy of the Empire could have no more explicit support. Broadsides were the forerunners of modern newspapers and are excellent keys to the issues of the time. Another broadside, one from the late fifteenth century, mingles the imperial myth with other mythical historical material. The German Hercules, as purported by Berosus, for example, is superimposed on the figure of the Emperor; a motto clearly identifies Hercules as Maximilian.[56]

Hercules is included among Maximilian's ancestors in a public oration addressed to the Emperor by Ulrich Zasius.[57] Maximilian's notorious genealogical efforts resulted in a most distinguished ancestry. Jacob Mennel, one of the Emperor's genealogists, had such figures as Hector, Aeneas, and Clovis sprouting from various branches of the Hapsburg family tree. In addition to their obvious ancestors, the Hapsburgs seem to have had a Greek line which Hector began, and a Roman line begun by Aeneas.[58] Priam, father of the Franks, and the Frankish kings, Marcomir and Faramundus, are given important places in Maximilian's lineage by the Italian humanist Riccardo Bartholini in his Latin epic, *Austriados Libri XII.*[59] To return to the initial question, Renaissance chroniclers do not represent an isolated scholarly phenomenon. Their interpretations of history had considerable currency in everything from the newspapers of the day to learned epic poems. German Renaissance chroniclers may be safely thought to have invented relatively little. The mythical aura attached to history is not the result of their inspiration alone; in fact, when it appears in these chronicles, we may be fairly certain that they were acting as mirror and not as lamp.

---

[55] Julius von Pflugk-Harttung, *Im Morgenrot der Reformation*, 5th ed. (Basel, 1924), p. 398.

[56] Franz Unterkircher, ed., *Maximilian I. 1459–1519*, Biblos-Schriften, XXIII (Vienna, 1959), p. 133, catalogue no. 431, illustrated on plate 62.

[57] Not to mention Priam: Freher/Struve, II, 466; also see above, note 46 of this chapter.

[58] Unterkircher, *Maximilian I.*, p. 57, catalogue nos. 183–88.

[59] Justus Reuber, *Veterum Scriptorum ... Tomus Unus* (Frankfurt, 1584), p. 712, with exhaustive commentary by Jacob Spiegel. The poem was first published in 1519, and Joachim Vadianus was the editor: cf. Potthast, p. 134.

One of the most accurate mirrors was made known in 1518, when FRANCISCUS IRENICUS published his *Exegesis,* one of the fullest Renaissance descriptions of Germany.[60] Unlike Annius of Viterbo or Trithemius, Irenicus is a man of limited imagination. He resembles more Albertus Krantz, a compiler who had to use great scholarly ingenuity to make any sense out of his sources. This is not to say that Irenicus did not invent a few notions of his own.

On the question of German origins, there are massive difficulties in method, Irenicus assures us, for the Germans were constantly changing their names. For example, the Galatae, who were descendents of Galates, son of Hercules, made their homes between the Rhine and the Danube and thus were obviously Germans (*Exegesis,* p. 11). Also the Celts were German (p. 12), as were the Belgi (p. 18), the Norici (p. 18, *recte* 20), the Goths, and the Getae (p. 28), not to mention the Avari, the Slavs, the Huns, and the Alani, who stem from the Goths, the Bruteni, the Bohemi (p. 37), the Lombards (p. 42), the Cimbri, and the above Galatae (p. 211).[61]

Irenicus accepts the principle of the indigenousness of the Germans (*Exegesis,* p. 48), but is loath to give up the medieval tales of origin. On the one hand, there is no question but that the Germans stem from Tuisco (p. 13). On the other hand, as ancient and reliable an author as Hunibald asserts that they stem from Troy (p. 145). The solution is simple. The Trojans who became Franks were Germans before they became Trojans (p. 51). This is shown by the fact that there were Cimbri in Troy before its fall (p. 50). Thus the Germans, although associated with Trojans and Romans, stem from neither Troy nor Rome (p. 105).

From the Germans stem the Danes, who are named after their prince, Dan; the Normans and Norwegians also stem from the Germans, as do the Swedes (*Exegesis,* pp. 30, 33). The Lombards and the Goths stem from Scandinavia (pp. 42, 145). The Bavarians are said to be named after their king, Bavarus, or after the tribe of the Boi. There are those who say that the Bavarians stem from Troy (p. 146). The English stem from the oldest duchy in Saxony, Engern. The word "Engelschen" was developed in order to distinguish the West Saxons

---

[60] I use the 1570 Frankfurt edition, whose title reads: *Totius Germaniae Descriptio.* The standard fashion, however, of citing this work is "*Exegesis,*" which appears at the head of each page of the above edition. On Irenicus and his work, see Walter Steinhauer, "Eine deutsche Altertumskunde aus dem Anfang des 16. Jahrhunderts," *ZfdA,* LXVI (1929), 25–30.

[61] On the issue of Goths as Germans, see Joachimsen, *Geschichtsauffassung,* p. 175, and on Irenicus in general, there pp. 169–81.

in Britain from the "Engerschen," the Saxons back home on the continent (p. 140). The Swiss supposedly derive from the Swedes or the Swabians (p. 415). The Saxons are variously reported to stem from the lands of the Normans and Danes, or from the host of Alexander the Great. Regardless of their origins, their deeds were always notable (p. 417). The cities too enjoy origins of the greatest antiquity. Trier, for example, was founded by Trebata, son of Ninus of Babylon, and Augsburg was named after Emperor Augustus by his loyal retainer, Drusus (p. 369).

Irenicus repeats much of the conventional understanding of heroic antiquity, adds several notions, and canonizes, as it were, several mythical-historical neologisms. The Argonauts are made to have sojourned in Germany, and Osiris to have ruled there (*Exegesis*, p. 6). Brennus was one of the so-called Gauls who were German, in fact Swabian (pp. 36, 147). Hector and Alexander the Great find a place in the ancestry of Charlemagne (p. 133). The heroic antiquity of the Germans was peopled by the great kings whom Hunibald describes, Priam, Helenus, Diocles, Basanus, Francus who named the Franks, and more (p. 145). Alongside them stand the forefathers of the Bavarians, Boamundus, Ingramus, Adelgerus, and Gundoaldus (p. 146). Immortal is Arminius who defeated the Romans (pp. 108, 228–29), and no less is the great Theodoric (p. 110). The poets and scholars are far from ignored. The memory of Heligastus—Hildegast—and Doracus—Amerodacus—is preserved by Hunibald, and equally reliable authorities tell of the priestess Veleda (p. 53) and of Hrabanus, Hrotswitha, and Otto von Freising, to name only a few.

The ancient religion of the Germans appears to have been complex almost beyond belief. Ulysses and Hercules were sung among the people (*Exegesis*, p. 5), and they worshipped Mercury, whom the Egyptians called "Thier."[62] Neptune was worshipped in Etlingen and Alemannus (Hercules Alemannus) on the Reichenau. Mars, as well as Hercules, received animal sacrifice from the Germans.[63] The Germanic Pantheon contained also the Sun, the Moon, Vulcan, Castor and Pollux, and Mother Earth under the name of Nertha (p. 52). Diana seems to have accepted human sacrifice, but otherwise the Germans restricted themselves to the ritual slaughter of animals (pp. 54–55). The priests were most expert in the art of augury (p. 53), and their

---

[62] The supposed worship of Mercury is well documented, although Irenicus seems to be the only one to call the divinity "Thier." Normally he is seen as the Egyptian "Thot" or "Teutatis," god of death: see Bartolini's *Austriados Libri XII* in Reuber, *Veterum Scriptorum*, pp. 479–80, and the gloss there by Jacob Spiegel

[63] Erich Schmidt, *Deutsche Volkskunde*, p. 58.

number included the Druids who had been expelled from Gaul in the time of Emperor Claudius. Later they introduced Christianity to Germany (p. 55).

Irenicus enumerates a great many of the Germans' virtues and for spice adds a vice. The ancients were known for their humane and friendly treatment of strangers (*Exegesis*, p. 59), for their chastity (pp. 70–71), their loyalty, and the reliability of their word (p. 61).[64] The Germans were learned and taught the Greeks philosophy (pp. 90ff.)[65] Leisure was avoided, and the new filled them with curiosity (p. 207). Their women were brave and industrious (pp. 194ff.). Altogether, the nation suffered under one major vice, rashness and short temper (p. 198), which grew worse the farther north the people lived: the most violent were the Low Germans (p. 64).

The German language becomes the object of extensive praise in the work of Irenicus, despite his choice of Latin for the chronicle. German is an almost perfect language, because of the preponderance of monosyllables, such as "brot" (*Exegesis*, p. 73). Irenicus explains the meanings of German personal names, no doubt to illustrate that they were reducible to perfect monosyllables: "Heinrich" meant "hân rich," "Genzerich" means "gantz rich," and "Dietrich" seems to be explained as "rich in wealth," as Irenicus assumes "dieth" to mean "wealth" (pp. 73–74). The excellence of the German language is further demonstrated by its obvious consanguinity to Greek. The fact that both languages use the article and that many words are common to both (German "thyr," "tier," and "lallen," corresponding to Greek "thúra," "thér," and lal(l)eîn") prove the relation (p. 68, *recte* 72). This is not the first defense of the German language seen in these pages, and there are many more that will not find room here.[66]

Probably because of Luther and the success of the Bible translation, the whole attitude of the German humanists toward their native language is a neglected issue. The great reforms justly attributed to the language societies of the Baroque have a concrete precedent in these patriotic writings of an earlier generation. But curiously, this native tradition behind the Baroque societies is nowhere as clearly delineated

---

[64] Tiedemann, *Tacitus*, pp. 62 and 66f.

[65] H. Dannenbauer, *Germanisches Altertum und deutsche Geschichtswissenschaft*, Philosophie und Geschichte, LII (Tübingen, 1935), p. 10.

[66] For example, Wolfgang Lazius, in D. C. Allen, *The Legend of Noah* (Urbana, Ill., 1963), p. 117–18. Irenicus's daring associations of Greek and German are not all as fantastic as they may seem. The examples chosen here are valid cognates, albeit over Indo-European.

as the influences and models from abroad, mainly the Pléïade and the sixteenth-century Florentine Academy. The Romance precedents were certainly normative for the Baroque poets, who, however, were as infatuated with the national past as the humanists were. And they read the humanists. Consequently, they were exposed to the learned theorizing about the German language that preceded their own speculations and accompanied the corresponding work on the vernacular in Italy and France. Humanist thought about the German language had to have been a constituent of the baroque reforms, more or less as weighty as the Romance models. As I suggested above, Luther is probably the prime reason for the present obscurity of humanist contributions to the vernacular and its theory, but the humanists themselves are in part at fault. Their consistent affection for Latin seems to give German a low status among their preoccupations. Further, their widespread (but not universal) disinterest in vernacular literature seems to imply a similar disinterest in the language. The latter was by no means the case. But their interest in the language was historical and publicistic and not literary. In this, they differ from the baroque poets, whose interests were both historical and literary. Irenicus's speculations are typical of the humanist form of linguistic concern with the vernacular, and are mildly indicative of the intensity of the concern. The baroque poets who avidly read their German history in Renaissance chronicles cannot have missed the philological excurses. The continuity of the tradition from Renaissance in Germany to German Baroque stands in need of closer investigation.

Any Renaissance list of ancient German virtue is incomplete without the seemingly omnipresent praise of warlike valor. Irenicus joins in with his reports that the ancient Germans were physically huge (*Exegesis*, pp. 178–79). Their bravery was the cause of Alexander the Great's failure ever to conquer Germany (pp. 181, 253), although he did deal with German emissaries (p. 211). If the ancient Germans were defeated from time to time, it was always by other Germans. Roman armies employed German troops if it was at all possible (p. 208), and "Germanicus" became an honored title among the Roman Emperors even, as in the case of Caligula, if they did not deserve it (p. 226). By their valor, the Germans conquered and named France and peopled Italy, Spain, and England (p. 106).

The valor of the Germans is matched by their piety, and the two virtues are united in the Teutonic Knights, who win pagans for Christianity by their bravery (*Exegesis*, p. 247). No nation in the world is more Christian than Germany, and Germany alone deserves the appelation "most Christian" (pp. 56–57). The piety of the Germans was from time immemorial a part of their right to political power. Piety and piety alone led them to reject the privilege of interference in papal elections, even though this right was held by the Carolingians and Ottonians (p. 106). Ever since the arrival of Saints Maternus, Eucharius, and Valerius, and the transference of Saint Peter's staff to German lands, the Germans have been engaged in the conversion of heretics (pp. 57–58). The antiquity of German orthodoxy is the bridge to the worthiness of the Germans to bear the burden of Rome. Irenicus uses all of Wimpheling's examples—Diocletian, Decius, Probus, Jovian, and Valentinian—to show that the Empire had been in German hands even while the Romans still held the power. Irenicus adds the example of Maximinus, whom Krantz identified as Maximus the Goth. The sainted Helena, who combines piety and Empire as the mother of Constantine the Great, was German born (pp. 122–23). Charlemagne is unequivocally German, and the Empire he received made the living Emperor the lord of the world (p. 116ff.). The sanctity and the supremacy of the German Roman Empire come together in the *Exegesis* as yet another example of the fully elaborated myth of the *Imperium*.

Despite the massive erudition of the *Exegesis* and the not very irenic patriotism of Irenicus, his work maintains a peculiarly objective and impersonal tone. One rarely senses the presence of the historian. By certain standards, this would seem to be a great advance in historical writing. In the context of the times, it is not. The language is basically humanistic; the discoveries and rediscoveries are most up to date; the preoccupation with Germany and its antiquities is very much a sign of the Renaissance in the North. Yet the *Exegesis* conveys a distinctly "medieval" impression, that is, in the structure and style of its historical conception, it is more reminiscent of the major chronicle compilations of the Middle Ages than of the creative and erratic historical speculation of the Renaissance in the North. This is not to imply that Irenicus necessarily regarded secular and national history as subordinate to the history of salvation. On the contrary, such an organizing principle would hardly have admitted this kind of glorification of a worldly and quasi-political entity like the German nation. His manner coincides with the medieval chronicles more superficially in his faithful adherence to authority and his disposition to harmonize disharmonious sources as opposed to the Renaissance practice of selecting and rejecting at whim. Perhaps for this reason, Irenicus's work was coolly received by his learned contemporaries. The first edition was succeeded by only one other, and that was more than fifty years later.

With the exception of the Alsatian Anonymous and the broadsides connected with Emperor Maximilian, all the works we have examined in the first part of the sixteenth century have been humanist in coloring. Irenicus, along with Naucler, Trithemius, and Krantz, represents the status of learned historical writing in the second decade of the century. The method fixed by them, such as it is, prevails until the reforms of Beatus Rhenanus in 1531. I have suggested that the humanists' interest in history was so intense as to suppress the normal development popular history might have taken. It seems as though humanist historical writing absorbed and exhausted a large part of the popular tradition with all its fancies, biases, and inaccuracies. Only those popular themes which the humanists ignored had the opportunity to proceed unhindered by learned investigation. This last statement is easily verifiable as far as most Chapbooks and "Heldenbücher" are concerned. They continued to lead an independent existence until well into the eighteenth century, and many dealt somehow with historical figures such as Theodoric and Pope Gregory. I hazard to make the conjecture that the distinction between "history" and "story" began to evolve precisely in the difference between the materials taken up by the humanists and those ignored by them. There is only one major exception to all of this, and it is the LEGEND OF EMPEROR FREDERICK. Here "story" and "history" remain perfectly undifferentiated. The legend seems to have developed in popular forms, only occasionally influenced by the learned tradition, but nonetheless faithfully reported by it. It may be more than coincidence that popular and learned "Geschichte" in Renaissance Germany touch specifically where the myth of the *Imperium* is at issue.[67]

In 1519, a Chapbook was published under the title,

Ein wahrhafftige historii von dem Kaiser Friderich der erst seines names, mit ainem langen roten bart, den die Walchen nenten Barbarossa. . . .[68]

[A true history of Emperor Frederick, the first of his name, with a long red beard, whom the Italians called Barbarossa. . . .]

---

[67] Several points at which the traditions touch are discussed by Will-Erich Peuckert, *Die Grosse Wende*, 2 vols., (1948; reprinted Darmstadt, 1966), I, 227–34; II, 606–13.

[68] Franz Pfeiffer, ed., "Volksbüchlein vom Kaiser Friedrich," *ZfdA*, V (1845), 253. The Humanists happened to be interested in the same material at the same time. Johannes Adelphus Muling published another history of Frederick, in German, the following year (1520): Paul Heitz and Fr. Ritter, *Versuch einer Zusammenstellung der Deutschen Volksbücher des 15. und 16. Jahrhunderts* (Strassburg, 1924), p. 10, note 1; also Herman Grauert, "Zur deutschen Kaisersage," *Historisches Jahrbuch*, XIII (1892), 141.

The text of the Chapbook in truth deals largely with the adventures of Frederick I Barbarossa. It concludes, however, as follows (Pfeiffer, p. 267):

> [Friderich] ist zuoletst verlorn worden, das niemandt waist, wo er hin ist komen noch begraben. Die pawrn und schwartzen künstner sagen, er sey noch lebendig in ainem holen perg, soll noch herwider komen und die gaistlichen straffen und sein schilt noch an den dürren paum hengken, welchs paums all Soldan no fleissig hüeten lassen. Das ist war das des paums gehüet wirt, und sein hüeter darzy gestifft: wölcher Kaiser aber seinen schildt sol daran hengken, das waiss got.

> [At the end, Frederick was lost, and no one knows where he came to or where he lies buried. The peasants (heretics) and black magicians say he is still alive in a hollow mountain, that he is supposed to return again, punish the clergy, and hang his shield on a bare tree, which tree all the Sultans carefully keep guarded. It is true that such a tree is carefully guarded, and that a guard is determined for it; but which Emperor is supposed to hang his shield on it, that God alone knows.]

Here then is the canonized confusion of the two Fredericks. Barbarossa, the first Frederick, died in the Crusades, and his grave is unknown. His own contemporaries, however, had no doubt that he was dead and lay buried in Palestine.[69] Then there are the stories that Frederick II never died, supported by the appearance of a false Frederick, that the real Frederick was not always a friend of the Church, and that he would be "Endkaiser" (cf. Rothe's Thuringian chronicle, the anonymous Augsburg chronicler of 1469, and the Alsatian Anonymous of about 1509). In the Chapbook, the traumatic memory of Frederick II is attached to the beloved memory of Frederick I. In the immediately preceding popular tradition, a third Frederick, an abstraction of the first two as it were, assumes the eschatological responsibilities of the Empire. A folksong of 1474 contains the substance of the above prophecy in the larger context of the end of the world and the antecedent winning of the Holy Land:[70]

---

[69] Paul Scheffer-Boichorst, "Barbarossas Grab," in E. Schaus and F. Güterbock, eds., *Gesammelte Schriften von Paul Scheffer-Boichorst*, II, Historische Studien, XLIII (Berlin, 1905), 156ff.

[70] Rochus von Liliencron, *Die historischen Volkslieder der Deutschen vom 13. bis 16. Jahrhundert*, II (Leipzig, 1866), 26, no. 129. Cf. Wagner, *Nationale Strömungen*, pp. 51ff. The hanging of a shield on a tree is supposed to be the ancient Germanic symbol for the opening of a legal action: Franz Guntram Schultheiss, *Die deutsche Volkssage vom Fortleben und der Wiederkehr Kaiser Friedrichs II.*, Historische Studien, XCIV (Berlin, 1911), pp. 60–61, and also Peuckert, *Grosse Wende*, I, 173–77, for the history of the symbol.

> Das glück sich alls zů senket
> Sibilla redt nit uß troum,
> bis kaiser Fridrich henket
> sin schild an türren boum;
> denn wirt erfullt die prophezi
> in himel und uf erden. . . .

[Fortune affects everything—/ The Sibyl speaks not out of a false dream:/ when Emperor Frederick hangs/ his shield on a bare tree,/ then the prophecy will be fulfilled/ in heaven and earth. . . .]

When these prophecies are brought into the company of the learned views on the finality of the Empire, as in Aeneas Sylvius and Hermann Peter of Andlau, then the highly charged significance of the Emperor Frederick grows clear and unequivocal. Such a connection has already been made for us by the Alsatian Anonymous, although it is not original with him.[71]

Not long before the Barbarossa Chapbook, around the year 1513, another Chapbook of extraordinary character made its first appearance in print, the *Zwölff Sibyllen Weissagungen.*[72] After assuring us that there is no credible evidence for the existence of a ninth, the European Sibyl (fol. A ii[v]), the anonymous author lists the Sibyls and their prophecies (more *anasceua*). One of the Sibyls was the Queen of Sheba. She announced that the Roman Empire would grow weak and that no one would wish to rule it (fol. C v[v]), and then both Church and Empire would become corrupt to be followed by a new order (fol. [C viii][r]). Before that occurs, another prophecy relates, the Eagle—the Empire—will crush the Church, and a ruler will arise, who will reign from the Southern to the Western Seas; the city of Rome and its bishop will mourn (fol. D iv[v]).

The Alsatian Anonymous had already noted with glee the future oppression of the clergy by the final Emperor Frederick. The prophecy at the close of the Barbarossa Chapbook includes the punishment of the priests as a basic element, "die gaistlichen straffen." Depending then on pro- or anti-clerical leanings, the last Frederick would be considered heroic, as by the Alsatian Anonymous, or villainous, as by the Sibylline Chapbook.

The stories of national heroes not dead but asleep in a hollow hill, as Frederick is in the Chapbook report, or of heroes destined to return to lead their people, as with the Alsatian Anonymous, are a part of

---

[71] F. Vogt, "Über Sibyllen-weissagung," *PBB*, IV (1877), 68.
[72] *Ibid.*, pp. 51–52. The Sibylline Chapbook appeared frequently in this period. I use the Leipzig printing of 1592.

international folklore. Stith Thompson finds examples in the Irish, Welsh, Norse, Aztec, Jewish, Persian, Lithuanian, and American folk heritage.[73] The same is to be found in Bantu and Czech. In the Armenian version (twelfth century), the hero waits in a hill called the "Rock of the Raven," until the second coming of Christ, which brings this version very close to the Frederick myth in its modern trappings, where ravens guard the hill in which Frederick sleeps. It would be far-fetched to associate the Armenian version too closely with the German, although the chronological and geographic coordinates do not exclude consanguinity. Barbarossa himself visited and ruled a country called Armenia in the twelfth century. A century later, Frederick II's cosmopolitan court in Sicily surely contained Armenians who knew or possibly even sang their national epic. Definite proof of such a connection is probably out of the question, but the possibility is intriguing.

Other connections, more confined to Western tradition, also suggest themselves as intriguing possibilities. The following lines attempt to be a fair description of the simple form, the basic outlines of the villainous side of the Frederick myth: A Roman Emperor with a red beard, an enemy of the Church, is supposed never to have died; he is supposed to return one day, again to oppress the Church and take the role of Antichrist; within the living memory of his demise, a man appeared claiming to be the dead Emperor. Aventinus, to whom we shall return at greater length, tells the identical story of Nero: The Roman Emperor called Ahenobarbus—red beard or Barbarossa—and enemy of the Church is supposed never to have died; he is supposed to return one day again to oppress the Church and take the role of Antichrist; within the living memory of his demise, a man appeared claiming to be the dead Emperor.[74] This is a more than remarkable coincidence, however, one that Aventinus did not recognize. Aventinus did not even invent the story, for it has weighty written tradition that we shall touch on in the next chapters.

One or several false Fredericks did actually appear, and the tales about them and their namesake grew up in popular tradition.[75] The written tradition did little more than report the oral development of the story in its various stages. There is little reason to believe that the

---

[73] *Motif Index of Folk-Literature*, 6 vols. (Bloomington, Ind., 1955–58), A 570ff., D 1960.2.

[74] *Johannes Turmair's genannt Aventinus Sämtliche Werke*, II.i, 182, and IV.ii, 802 [see also n. 92 below]. Lion Feuchtwanger refers to the same legend in his novel, *Der Falsche Nero*, Gesammelte Werke, IX (Amsterdam, 1936).

[75] Cf. supra ch. 2, note 34.

myth was fostered by learned speculation. In its ramifications, it was ultimately heretical, and this was recognized early in the history of the myth. The dominant orthodoxy of the Middle Ages surely discouraged learned contributions to it. On the other hand, the similarities between the Nero and the Frederick tales are so startling that one is reluctant to attribute them entirely to chance. Although an exact time cannot be fixed—it must have been very soon after Frederick II's death and following the appearance of the impostors—the analogues may have been brought together by someone who knew the popular rumors and had read Suetonius and Saint Augustine. The leap between the notorious Frederick and the no less notorious Nero is, after all, not difficult, since both were honored with the title of Antichrist. It would be a matter of learned form and popular content, hardly a rarity in the late Middle Ages. This must, however, remain pure conjecture.

The confusion of the two Fredericks and of the heroic and villainous interpretations began to be apparent here in the anonymous Augsburg chronicle of 1469, but the beginnings of the confusion are even older. It progressed to the form preserved in the 1519 Chapbook and in that form lives to this day in Germany:

> Der alte Barbarossa
> Der Kaiser Friederich
> Im unterird'schen Schlosse
> Hält er verzaubert sich. . . .[76]

[Old Barbarossa/ Emperor Frederick/ in a castle underneath the earth/ he hides, enchanted. . . .]

We turn now to a series of minor texts by major authors or major texts by minor authors. These incline to fill in the gaps left by the more extensive histories, such as those by Naucler and Irenicus, and contrast generally with the more historical, imaginative, and cohesive work of Aventinus, with whom we shall conclude this survey of the Renaissance myths of the German past. In these texts I have been more than usually selective and point out only those items that seem quite new or that otherwise help complete the Renaissance picture of German mythical antiquity. Some myths, such as the defeat of Varus now correctly coupled with the newly discovered Arminius, simply continue

---

[76] The poem by Rückert (1788–1866) is just short of folk-poetry today; cf. Schultheiss, *Die deutsche Volkssage*, p. 110.

their development in this period and need not be discussed here since scholarship has evaluated their importance.[77]

The Alsatian humanist HIERONYMUS GEBWILER (1473–1545) published a patriotic tract, *Libertas Germaniae*, in 1519 and, sometime later, a chronicle of Strassburg which has survived only in fragments.[78] Most of the conventional myths are accepted by Gebwiler, despite the critical rejections characteristic of his fellow humanists. He nonetheless demonstrates his intellectual harmony with them by the introduction of new critical rejections and even more outrageous interpretations. The Trojan origins of the Franks appear in his work in the version that takes them over the Maeotian Swamps and the founding of Sicambria. He dislikes the explanation of the name from Franco, Hector's or Priam's son (*Schardius Redivivus*, p. 219). But he has no objection to the belief that Hector was venerated in ancient Germany (p. 223). Gebwiler, like Peutinger, accepts both the Troy myths and the Berosus myths, without feeling troubled by the contradictions. The Trojans who married Teutonic women are the same Teutones of whom Tuisco was the first king. Tuischburg (i.e., Duisburg) is named after the same hero. He is also ancestor of the Hapsburgs, who stem as well from Troy by way of the younger Priam (p. 220).[79]

Gebwiler assures us that it is nonsense to believe that Strassburg is named after the four "Strassen" Attila is supposed to have put through after he destroyed the city. Actually, Strassburg was founded before Romulus founded Rome. A group of men from Trier under one Tyras founded the city and named it Tyrasburg after their leader. By lapse of the 'i' sound and addition of initial 's' it became known as Strassburg (Stenzel, p. 48). Gebwiler is no exception to the rule that serious historians of the Renaissance in Germany could hardly avoid *anasceua*. His explanation of the name sounds not unlike Gobelinus Persona's curious philological vocabulary but makes much less sense. In his zeal to recover the German past, Gebwiler extends the questionable principles invented by his predecessors. He outdoes Bebel, and comes close to Irenicus by redefining all versions of Celt and Gaul in

---

[77] As for example, Richard Kuehnemund, *Arminius or the Rise of a National Symbol in Literature*, University of North Carolina Studies in Germanic Languages and Literatures, VIII (Chapel Hill, 1953).

[78] *Libertas Germaniae*, in *Schardius Redivivus*, pp. 219–26. Karl Stenzel, ed., *Die Strassburger Chronik des elsässischen Humanisten Hieronymus Gebwiler*, Schriften des wissenschaftlichen Instituts der Elsaß-Lothringer im Reich (Berlin and Leipzig, 1926), pp. 1 and 15 [hereafter cited as "Stenzel"].

[79] See also Riess, *Motive*, p. 55.

the ancients to mean what the moderns understand as German (*Schardius Redivivus*, p. 226).

Added to the heroes named in the origins of peoples and cities are the mythical and historical figures whose fame is meant to establish beyond doubt the grandeur of German antiquity. As though Hercules were not sufficiently occupied by his other labors, Gebwiler makes him lend his presence and distinction to the German cause. Hercules was, after all, a descendent of Tuisco, and hence as German as Gebwiler himself. The dawn of medieval history contributes to the assemblage of heroes the first constituted king of the Franks, Pharamundus (*Schardius Redivivus*, pp. 220–23). The veneration of Hector and Hercules joins the heroic to the ritual without implying an overly offensive pagan cult. Later, however, idols were worshipped in Alsatia, the first of whom was Cham, succeeded by Mercury and Diana, in whose honor temples were built in Ebersheim (Stenzel, pp. 54–55).

The most important strictly historical hero is Charlemagne, and he is completely identified with the *Imperium*. The Empire is Roman, for it was not the Greek but the Roman power which was transferred to the Germans. It is German, for Charlemagne was German, and he received the Empire when it was removed from the Greeks. It is sacred, because it was a reward for a pious act (Charles's aid to Leo), and because Charles was crowned by God. It transcends other realms by the precedent of Charlemagne's power over many kingdoms (*Schardius Redivivus*, pp. 220–24).

Gebwiler's vastly more talented student, BEATUS RHENANUS (1485–1547), had an incisive critical hand which eventually led him to reject most of the myths we have seen here. In 1519, however, he was still learning his skill, and seems to be only one of many searching historians. In this year, he published a commentary on the *Germania* of Tacitus, and it is basically a conventional tract.[80] He applies the traditional category of etymology to the name of the Germans and seems to prefer an explanation that makes the word cognate to the Greek for "genuine"—"gnesion." He does not elucidate the mysterious sound-shifts as Gebwiler had for the shift of "Tyrasburg" to "Strassburg," and that is perhaps to his credit. Beatus derives the name of the Alemanni much the same way as the Alsatian Anonymous, that is, from meaning "all kinds of men" (*Schardius Redivivus*, p. 71). The

---

[80] In *Schardius Redivivus*, pp. 70–76, there wrongly attributed to Glareanus: cf. Strauss, *Sixteenth-Century Germany*, p. 169, note 65.

Hercynian Forest of antiquity is the same as the Harz, according to Beatus. In 1519, he still accepted Berosus and could trace the Germans' vernacular name from "Tuisto" (p. 72). It is a sign of his developing acuity that Beatus prefered the form "Tuisto" to the more popular "Tuisco," thus agreeing with modern Tacitus scholarship. The Gotthones of Tacitus, he tells us, became the Pruteni, the Prussians of later times (p. 75). A later work of Beatus, his renowned biography of Erasmus (1538), contains one curiosity that demands attention. Referring to Charles V's coronation at Aachen, Beatus states that Theodoric the Goth had preserved the Roman Empire.[81] It points to an extraordinary sense of the German–Germanic character of the Empire and is all the more extraordinary in the pen of one of the most reputable of Renaissance scholars, one known for his critical acuity and not his free imagination. This fleeting glance at Beatus Rhenanus is almost insulting in its brevity, considering his importance to German historiography. It is, however, precisely this importance, this progress, this critical sense which makes him relatively unimportant here.[82]

Beatus Rhenanus and several other authors seen here touched briefly on the origins of the Prussians. This people was not properly German, except in the peculiar perspective of Renaissance historiography. For some decades, the Prussians had been growing in influence, although no one could have imagined the role their lands were to play in the world history of the next centuries. The place of myth in this history seems to me unchallengeable. Yet the myth of Prussia in modern times is somehow disconnected from its sources in the Renaissance. These pages are not the proper place for the description of the whole myth in its historical evolution. But the ideas of supra-national *vs.* colonial state, of a holy Protestant kingdom outside the Roman Empire, of a new polarity of German power in the North, all these preceded the policies of the Great Elector and had their roots in Renaissance historical myth. Here we are only digging at the roots.[83]

ERASMUS STELLA was a teacher of Greek at Zwickau, where he died

---

[81] John C. Olin, ed., *Desiderius Erasmus: Selected Writings* (New York, 1965), p. 43.

[82] Evaluations of Beatus Rhenanus can be found in Joachimsen, *Geschichtsauffassung*, pp. 125–46, and Strauss, *Sixteenth-Century Germany*, pp. 42–44.

[83] Theodor Hirsch, ed., "Erasmi Stellae Libnothani De Borussiae Antiquitatibus Libri Duo," in *Scriptores rerum Prussicarum* (Leipzig, 1870), IV, 275–98 [henceforth "Hirsch"]. M. Perlbach *et al.*, eds., *Simon Grunaus Preussische Chronik*, 3 vols., Die Preussischen Geschichtsschreiber des XVI. und XVII. Jahrhunderts, I–III (Leipzig, 1876), henceforth "Perlbach."

in 1521 (Hirsch, p. 275). He held basically the same theory as Beatus Rhenanus on the origins of the Prussians, that is, that their ancestors were the Gotthones, one of the nations of the Vindelici (p. 286). The Goths and the Prussians were one and the same nation (p. 292), and hence, the Prussians were always German (p. 285). Their heroic ancestor was Hercules, which is proved by a tomb inscription found by Stella. It contained the genealogy of a princess that was traced back to that hero (pp. 277, 285). The remainder of Stella's myths are, by and large, borrowings from Gothic "history," and we have met them elsewhere.

SIMON GRUNAU was a Dominician monk who flourished in the third decade of the sixteenth century. He seems to be almost wholly forgotten, is found in none of the standard bibliographies, and when he does appear in works on the Old Prussian language or Prussian history and historiography, he receives abuse. I have studied the first chapters of Grunau's Prussian chronicle to seek his fables of origin and have only perused the rest which is overwhelming in its length and rich variety of subject.[84] The reading reveals that Grunau's chronicle is among the wittiest, most imaginative, and most informative works of Early New High German prose literature.

Grunau's imagination was not confined to an escape as primitive as borrowing the myths of another nation. He accepts that device as one of many alternatives. The difficulties of tracing the origins of the Prussians, he assures us, are very great, because the Prussians are so mixed with Saxons, Meisseners, Thuringians, Hessians, Rhinelanders, Franks, Swabians, Bavarians, and Austrians (Perlbach, p. 2). One of his definitions of "Prussian" emerges from this mixture. He clearly means the inhabitants of the northeastern German-speaking territories of his time, and not necessarily the members of one linguistic or ethnic group. Grunau does, however, distinguish between old and new Prussians. The old ones he identifies with the Goths and Bruteni—Pruteni —in the following fashion.

Around A.D. 500, the Goths were forced the leave Italy by Emperor Justinian. Under their King Witthigi, they left for Westphalia and, in the course of their wanderings, named Göttingen. They were driven away, however, and moved on to Denmark. Theudott, King of Denmark, allowed them to settle the island of Cymbria. Wisboo, the Gothic leader, made himself tributary to Theudott. Wisboo drove the Scandiani to Ulmiganea—Ulmigeria: cf. Fabri supra—and changed

---

[84] See Sallie Jo Strouss, "A German Renaissance Encyclopedia: Folklore and Literature in the Prussian Chronicle of Simon Grunau" (unpublished diss., Northwestern University, Evanston, Ill., 1968), for a survey and sampling of the contents.

the name of Cymbria to Gothland (Perlbach, pp. 59–60). In 521, the Goths conquered Ulmiganea as well, and named it Bruthenia after their current leader, Brutenus (p. 62). The Prussians also have the name "Bruten," that is, "Bruteni," which carries the meaning of brutal (p. 9). The older Prussians thus were in at least remote origin Goths, and all spoke Gothic (p. 53). The linguistics make all the difference for Grunau who distinguishes between the new settlers in Prussia, Christian and German-speaking, and the old settlers, heathen and Prussian-speaking, which he thought to be Gothic.

Among the heroic figures we find Maso, a famous prince of the Prussians, who made the people submit to the "Kyrwaiten" or high priests and their idols. A descendent of Maso built the castle "Fogilge-sang" in Prussia. The early "Kyrwaiten" may also be considered heroic in stature, and Grunau mentions a great many specific names, of which we need see only a few typical examples: Bruteno, Thywaito, Jaygello, and Alleps, the last "Kurwait" before the coming of the Christians (Perlbach, pp. 11–13). Grunau also praises the great chroniclers of the Prussians from whom he claims to have his information: Jaroslaus, Christian, and Diwoynis (pp. 5 and 55f.). Although chroniclers of such or similar names seem in truth to have existed, no known texts in the historiographic tradition preserve the kind of information which Grunau credits to his authorities. He either knew sources lost since then or, like several of his monastic predecessors, invented them. Known sources were also generously tapped, but they are largely outside the historical literature, primarily in the category of folk tale, novella, and legend, such as the *Miracula Virginis*.

Grunau expends considerable energies describing the religion of the Prussians. Originally, they worshipped only the sun, but the Cimbri introduced them to the worship of multiple gods (Perlbach, pp. 94–95). This particular convention seems to permeate German Renaissance historiography, that is, that the barbaric peoples began with a simple and often monotheistic religion and only later were corrupted. The new gods included Patollo, chief of the gods and god of death and vengeance; Potrimpo, god of good fortune, who received the sacrifice of slaughtered children; and Perkuno, god of weather (pp. 94–95). In addition, the Prussians worshipped Wurschayto, also called Borss-kayto, who received fish in sacrifice, Szwaybrotto, who received poultry and piglets in sacrifice, and Churcho, god of the crops, in whose honor wheat, flour, honey, and milk were burned.[85] The latter three gods

---

[85] According to Perlbach's notes (pp. 3, 62, and 79), the pagan Prussians did worship a Patolla and a Churcho. The other divinities are apparently inventions or misunderstandings on Grunau's part, primarily of Lithuanian phenomena.

could be worshipped anywhere, but the former three could be worshipped only among certain sacred oaks (pp. 95–96). The priest appointed by the Kyrwait was called the Rickoyto (p. 62).

Evergreening oaks were supposed to be the homes of the gods. A fire was burned night and day for Perkuno. For Potrimko, a snake was put into a pot and covered with milk and grain. Heads of a man, a horse, and a cow were suspended in honor of Patollo (Perlbach, p. 78). The reason that the worship of the major gods was reserved to a special sanctuary is as follows: The Kyrwait, Bruteno, and his brother King Widowuto, chose to immolate themselves in a great fire before the assembly of the nobles. Thunder and lightning accompanied the event, and the place was marked as a special sanctuary (p. 79). The law of the Prussians required that everyone worship the gods, and those who refused were burned to death with live coals. Those who were so pious as to immolate themselves for the glory of the gods were certain of joy with them in the afterlife. Bruteno formulated in 523 A.D. a simple credo for the Prussians, which included belief in the afterlife, the reward of the good, and the punishment of the evil. The rewards of the good were numerous in the afterlife, and happened to include that they "werden sloffen auf grossen weichen betten" (pp. 63–64)—that they would sleep on great soft beds.

Grunau also lists a series of beliefs and superstitions that survived out of the antiquity of the Prussians. They believed fire to be a god, and that gods dwelled throughout the trees of the forest and particularly in juniper (Holunder) bushes. The leaves of oak trees were believed to hold the images of the three primary gods. Superstitions are properly the material of folklore and perhaps have little place here in the mythical antiquity of the Germans. Nonetheless, one or two should be mentioned in passing, to indicate the comprehensiveness of Grunau's interests and observations. He explains, for example, why storks have to be protected and why hens cackle at certain times—storks are not ordinary animals but rather epiphanies of distant human beings; and hens cackle when the ghosts of the dead walk among them—implying an elaborate system of etiological explanations for everyday events.

A Dominican monk and orthodox Catholic, Simon Grunau tells of a ceremony he claims to have witnessed. On the open road, he met a Prussian, descendent of the old settlers, for he spoke Prussian. At first, the monk was in danger of his life, but when he demonstrated that he could speak a little Prussian, he was welcomed to the man's house. There a pagan priest recited ten commandments—which ones is quite unclear—and slaughtered a goat in honor of Perkuno. The participants in the ceremony attacked then the holy man and pulled his hair. The loudness of his screams showed the degree to which the gods had forgiven their sins. Then everyone drank, and no one was allowed to go home sober (Perlbach, p. 91). It seems authentic, although the conclusion of the event might have dulled Grunau's memory.

Of the four virtues which distinguish great nations—orthodoxy, wisdom, valor, and freedom—the Prussians were noted only for the fourth, their love of freedom, for they bear no tyranny (Perlbach, pp. 2ff.). The Cimbri taught them the art of writing, and the Prussians found it a good thing (p. 66). The Prussians of ancient days were also quite temperate and drank only milk. King Widowuto, however, discovered the art of mixing honey and water into a beverage that makes the drinker drunk (p. 65). In summer, the Prussians normally drank "Gerstenbir," the best of which came from Danzig and Elbing (p. 34). They also drank wine, which used to be grown natively. Later, however, the grapes froze, and then wine was imported from the Rhine, Hungary, and Pomerania (pp. 33–34). The air is quite good in Prussia, and if the Prussians did not drink so much, they would live a very long time.

Grunau's chronicle is a great reservoir of folklore, fact, and fiction. His reports about his own time are detailed, fascinating, and, as far as I can tell, not altogether invented. The undisguised hostility with which Germans have greeted the chronicle—and this includes even the editors of the only proper edition—may be due to Grunau's pro-Polish point of view. I have avoided mentioning it, since it plays no important part in myths of the German past. Grunau's assumption of this point of view is, however, quite reasonable. Grunau was an orthodox Catholic and a monk, isolated in Protestant and pagan lands in the first years of the Reformation. He would have every reason to prefer the Catholic crown of Poland to the reformed Teutonic Knights and the various North German princes—all already Protestant—with claims on Prussia. The hostility to the old faith was great, and the effect of this in Prussia was devastatingly thorough. Grunau reciprocated these feeling with political antagonism to German hegemony. This annoyance nevertheless failed to move Grunau to write his chronicle in Polish, or Latin, or Old Prussian. He wrote it in German, and in witty German at that. Nineteenth-century concepts of nationality and nationalism were, of course, quite as foreign to Grunau as they were natural to his critics of the last century. Grunau's provincial patriotism in lieu of nationalism was typical of his time, and simultaneously it had presaged an important part of the myth of Prussia as it was to develop in later times.

The cold North is abandoned for the time being in favor of the cold South in a description of Alpine Rhaetia, produced by the Swiss humanist, AEGIDIUS TSCHUDI in 1528.[86] Tschudi was much disturbed by all the unreliable tales he heard about ancient German history, such as those about Hildebrand of the old and new *Hildebrandslied*. What happened, Tschudi asks, that the fine tradition of German erudition died out, that texts, once produced, were then left to rot away (*Schardius Redivivus*, p. 270)? Tschudi had reason for his complaint. He had seen ancient manuscripts of the Gospels in German at St. Gall (p. 298). He might have meant the Tatian translation which St. Gall possessed in a ninth-century transcription.

Since the written tradition was defective, antiquities had to be discovered elsewhere. Like many others, Tschudi searched in etymology and onomastics. He explains that the derivation of German is "garman," that is, "totius vir"—"the man of the whole of accomplishment." In addition to this etymology, he preserved many others which had by his time become completely conventional. He continues to explain that the concept of German included those who seem to be Gallic in Julius Caesar's works. When Caesar wrote "x," he in truth meant Greek "chi." Hence Orgetorix is equivalent to Horderich, Ambiorix to Emberich or Heimrich, etc. (*Schardius Redivivus*, pp. 299–301). By the wildest coincidence, Tschudi does succeed in touching upon an important linguistic difficulty and its barely satisfactory historical solution.

Tschudi's philological flights are not all so fantastic or unfortunate. To prove that the Gauls—the French here and less so the Celts—once spoke German, Tschudi gives at least fairly accurate examples of vocabulary indebtedness, such as "bourgois" from "burger" (p. 298). He adds, however, that both Germans and Gauls used to write Greek (p. 297). This is not to imply that all Germans stem from Greeks. Several renowned Swiss families have obvious Roman origins, as the names reveal: the Metsch family's name comes from Latin "amasius" —"lover"; the Saz name from "saccus"—Middle Latin for "sack-cloth"; the Emps from "amisius"—the river Ems, and hence perhaps not an incorrect derivation; and finally, the Flumbs family name from "de flumine" (p. 271). The consistence of the reasoning leaves a great deal to be desired since, for example, "Emps" and "Ems" seem much more closely related than "Emps" and "amisius." This seems to have not at all disturbed Tschudi, who perhaps saw "amisius" as the common

---

[86] *De prisca ac vera Alpina Rhaetia ... Descriptio* in *Schardius Redivivus*, pp. 269–314. This work was written in 1528 but not published until later: Strauss, *Sixteenth-Century Germany*, pp. 92 and 172, note 27.

ancestor of both names. His derivations are based on the premise that Latin is the older language and, hence, that geographical names with Latin and vernacular alternatives had to have been originally Latin. The logical extension is understandable, however erroneous or only very partially correct it is by modern standards. It reflects the authority which the sacred languages bore in the Renaissance, and highlights the humanists' will to distribute their distinction to the popular language, its speakers, and their homeland.

Tschudi's use of language in lieu of documents is a common device in this period and one we have often met. It characterizes not only the work of Tschudi but also that of ANDREAS ALTHAMER who, in 1529, first published an influential commentary on Tacitus's *Germania*.[87] As in the paragraphs on Tschudi and the following section on Münster, I mention Althamer's contributions to the myths of the German past only insofar as they are new or concur with familiar trends. To give a complete evaluation would be to repeat even more than has already been repeated.

Althamer was one of the Germans-are-indigenous school of historians, and this assumes a certain critical stance over the tradition. He rejects Macedonian origins for Saxons and Swabians and, similarly, Trojan origins for Sicambri and Franks. All those tales are nonsense: a good part of the German nobility does, however, stem directly from Rome. Althamer is in perfect agreement with Tschudi on this myth, but maintains that ultimately all the Germans stem from Tuisco who gave them their name (more *anasceua*). Tuisco himself enjoyed honorable parentage, Janus and Vesta, whom the Germans believed to be equivalent to Caelum and Terra (*Schardius Redivivus*, pp. 4–5). Precisely what place German–Germanic interpolations had in the syncretistic mythology of the Renaissance is, to the best of my knowledge, unknown and a sufficiently curious problem to warrant fuller study.

The high regard in which Tuisco's son, Mannus, was held by the ancient Germans reveals itself, according to Althamer, in the names of the Germans, e.g., Ger*man*, Marco*man*, Nord*man*, Bider*man*, Edel*man*, Zimmer*man*, etc. Among the other heirs of Tuisco is Hermion, who fathered not only the Hermiones, but the Lusatians (Lausitzer) as well. Suevus, yet another example of Tuisco's prodigious progeny, fathered the Swabians and through them the Lombards. He also named the river Suevus, now called "Sprevus," which runs through "Perolinum"

---

[87] *Schardius Redivivus*, pp. 1–37, contains an emended edition.

and "Colonia" (*Schardius Redivivus*, pp. 5 and 30). The geography refers to the river Spree and the unimportant fishing villages Berlin and its neighbor Kölln through which it ran.

While Mancaleus, fourteenth King of the Assyrians, was ruling among his people, Hercules ruled among the Germans. His son Cygno, named Zwickau (*Schardius Redivivus*, p. 6). Hercules himself founded many cities along the Rhine. This is shown by the many Greek inscriptions there and the many Greek words active in German (p. 7). Ulysses also appeared in Germany and built an altar to his father, Laertes, at Aschenburg (p. 7). Althamer repeats several of Irenicus's suggestions to prove the Greek influence, adding "pfeil"—"bélos," "küssen"—"kuseĩn," and others, occasionally of startling accuracy from a modern comparative linguistic viewpoint (p. 33–34). His etymology of "German," an explanation similar to Tschudi's, reads: "gar" means ready, robust, strong, to which "man" is added in honor of Mannus (p. 6). The Hercynian Forest of antiquity seems to be today's Harz, or possibly Schwarzwald (p. 20).

Teuto, Isis, and Hertha were divinities worshipped by the Germans, not to mention Mercury, Hercules, and Mars, among others (*Schardius Redivivus*, p. 10). An idol of Mars was still to be found at Ehl in Alsatia in Althamer's time, according to his report. Ehl is, incidentally, the town in which St. Maternus is supposed to have died the first time around. His first grave there was believed still to be standing in the sixteenth century, according to the reports of Beatus Rhenanus.[88] The worship of Isis explains the survival of her name in Zizenberg, which is equivalent to "z' Isen-berg" (p. 11). One wonders what relationship could be conjectured with the "Zise" of the Swabians, but that is perhaps falling victim to the Renaissance's dubious historical method. In any case, Althamer assures us that Isis came to Germany with her brother Osiris in the reign of Gambrivus (p. 18).

Althamer's commentary on Tacitus contains one curiosity in reference to the myth of the *Imperium*. Perhaps due to the piqued vanity common among German humanists, Althamer found it necessary to define "barbarian" in a manner contrary to the Italians' abuse of the Germans. In ancient times, "barbaric" applied to something or someone not Greek, Latin, or Hebrew. In modern times, it refers to something or someone not in accord with the Christian faith or not subject to the Roman Emperor (*Schardius Redivivus*, p. 16). For Althamer then, the Empire legitimized to no less an extent than the Church. I

---

[88] Herbert Grundmann and Hermann Heimpel, eds., *Alexander von Roes: Schriften*, MGH Staatsschriften des späteren Mittelalters, I.i (Stuttgart, 1958), p. 143.

suspect that Althamer's notion relies heavily on legal thought and interpretation of Roman Law in favor of the German Emperor. In the very years surrounding the publication of his commentary, the Holy Roman Empire was briefly realizing an apparent glory befitting its mythical status. In 1530, Charles V chose the opportunity for a spectacular demonstration of this glory when he had himself crowned King of the Lombards and Roman Emperor in Bologna. The renowned Agrippa of Nettesheim, presumably a historical cynic, witnessed the coronation and wrote a description. His description documents the enthusiastic and unconditional acceptance of the imperial myth among even the most critical of German humanists.[89] Althamer cannot be excepted. His legalistic conception of "barbarian" was, after all, not employed to praise the dignity of the Empire; the dignity of the Empire was rather a given, from which the conception of "barbarian" could be turned upon the Italians for their hostility to the Germans and their Roman Empire.

For all his erudition and influence, Althamer was not an original historian. He was an encyclopedist, like most of his humanist colleagues. For our purposes, the virtue of his work lies in the fact that it was typical. It could be used to summarize the myths of the German past in this period, had we not chosen a more engaging author to fill that task.

As for the making of a synthesis, much the same could be said of SEBASTIAN MÜNSTER, only more emphatically so. He personally produced a distinct tradition of cosmographic study that lasted for generations. I mention only enough of his speculations to show that his tradition in turn was rooted in the familiar historical mode which the Renaissance produced in Germany. His extensive historical work includes a description of Germany which was published in 1530.[90] In it Münster expresses his great displeasure at the paucity of reliable information about ancient Germany. He considers it a disgrace that the ancients, the Romans in particular, were not driven by curiosity to write down the manners and deeds of such inaccessible nations as Gemany. Münster was not quite as bilious as the other German humanists, who lamented the absence of sources and used their lament to attack the ancestors of the Italians. He was, on the contrary, a gentle man and a balanced historian—which led him to admit, in phrasing from Tacitus, that the ancients were prevented partly by fear and

---

[89] *Schardius Redivivus*, II, 266–78.
[90] *Schardius Redivivus*, I, 238–58.

partly by geography from doing justice to the subject of Germany (*Schardius Redivivus*, p. 239).

The dearth of sources drives Münster, like many before him, to the questionable comforts of etymology and onomastics. Tuisco's descendent Marsus is seen to be a real, not fictitious figure by the evidence of such place-names as "Thie*mar*" and "Wil*mar*." Similar evidence connects Vandalus with a variety of peoples: the "Wini," who are the Pomeranians, and the "Winuli," who are the Pruteni—Prussians— from whom also the Lombards stem (*Schardius Redivivus*, p. 241). Brunswick, he tells us, is named after Bruno, Henry I's uncle. The neighboring lands are known as Westphalia from those Saxons who accompanied the Lombards to Italy: when these Saxons returned home, they were called "Walen" (Welsch), the German name for Italians. The relative location of their settlement explains the rest, "Westwalen" (p. 244). Brandenburg and Frankfurt on the Oder were both named after Brando, a Frankish duke. As Felix Fabri and Simon Grunau stated or implied, Prussia was known in ancient times as Hulmerigeria, and the name meant fertile land (p. 245).

This glance at Münster's work might suggest that he was as defective a historian as the worst we have seen. That would be incorrect and most unfair to Münster; however, as with the other authors, Münster's valid contributions to modern historiography and geography are not as important to this study as his inaccuracies and imaginative interpretations.[91]

The last Renaissance author whom we shall consider in these pages, JOHANNES AVENTINUS,[92] was described by a distinguished scholar as a

---

[91] Among Münster's many interesting incidental reports is the full title of Attila the Hun: "filius Bendeucum, nepos magni Nimbroth, educatus in Engaddi, gratia Dei [sic!] Rex Hunorum, Medorum, Gothorum, atque Dacorum, pavor orbis et Flagellum Dei" (*Schardius Redivivus*, I, 247). A more satisfactory evaluation of Münster can be found in Strauss, *Sixteenth-Century Germany*, pp. 111–13, and more recently in his "A Sixteenth-Century Encyclopedia: Sebastian Münster's *Cosmography* and its Editions," in *From the Renaissance to the Counter-Reformation: Essays in Honor of Garrett Mattingly*, Charles Carter, ed., (New York, 1965), pp. 144–59.

[92] I use the Bavarian Academy edition, *Johannes Turmair's genannt Aventinus Sämtliche Werke*, 6 vols. in 7 (Munich, 1881–1908) [hereafter *Aventinus*], cited here by volume, sub-volume, and page numbers only, since I shall be moving freely from one work to another. On these texts, see Paul, *Studien*, pp. 30 and 114; Friedrich Gotthelf, *Das deutsche Altertum in den Anschauungen des sechzehnten und siebzehnten Jahrhunderts*, Forschungen zur neueren Litteraturgeschichte, XIII (Berlin, 1900), pp. 11–13; Dannenbauer, *Germanisches Altertum*, p. 24; and to correct Dannenbauer on the subject of "Askenas," Arno Borst, *Der Turmbau von Babel*, 6 vols. in 7 (Stuttgart, 1957–63), III.i, 1057, who shows that Krantz promulgated the "Askenas" theory well before Althamer or Aventinus; also cf. Riess, *Motive*, pp. 4–9, and 46–47.

historian who did not "flinch from an occasional departure into pure fantasy."[93] For our purposes, he is an author who did not flinch from an occasional departure into pure fact. Aventinus died in 1534, having refused to be drawn into the religious strife of his time. He also remained uninfluenced by the new turn Beatus Rhenanus had taken in the investigation of the German past. Aventinus kept the imagination of his teacher Celtis, but surpassed him in industry. While refraining from the excesses of a Trithemius, he managed to discover connections which only a fertile and uninhibited mind could see.

The Germans at large stem directly from Noah, who was known as Janus and after whom January is named (*Aventinus* IV.i, 75). Noah was also called "Himmel" by the Germans. With his wife, variously called Vesta or Nertha, Noah is ancestor of all heroes (I, 364; IV.i, 92). Noah settled in Armenia after the flood (IV.i, 51), but it is complete nonsense to say that Bavarus led the Bavarians out of Armenia. Bavarus is a name wholly destitute of German or Latin credentials. True, one King Baius once led the Bavarians as far as Armenia in war, but he is not the same man (IV.i, 145ff.). Actually Tuisco, son of Noah, conducted the Germans out of Armenia, all the Germans, including the Bavarians. He departed Armenia with a number of heroes 131 years after the flood (I, 112–13). The topos of critical rejection so pervades Aventinus's work that it requires little further comment. As uncritical as the topos may seem today, it was the necessary first critical step of any historian as manifestly serious, yet burdened with legend, pseudo-history, and pure fiction as Aventinus was.

The company of heroes who left Armenia with Tuisco included Gomer, father of Italy and grandfather of Spain through his son Tagus. Asch, also called Askenest or Ascanius, was a prince who left with Tuisco and settled Prussia. Albion, also one of the original *émigrés*, won and named the island that was to become England and Scotland (*Aventinus* IV.i, 65). Tuisco, called "Gigant," is the father of the Germans and Wends and, just like Emperor Charles IV, could probably speak both German and Wendish (I, 330). In the earliest times, before German unity gave way to various nations, the Phrygians flourished. The Phrygians, whose name means "free," were the ancient Franks and Bavarians before the two nations existed as separate entities (I, 342; II.i, 426).

Tuisco's companions represent one source for the various nations. His own children represent another. Panno was one, who gave his name to Pannonia; Penno another, who did the same for the Apen-

---

[93] Gerald Strauss in the only major biography, *Historian in an Age of Crisis: the Life and Work of Johannes Aventinus* (Cambridge, Mass., 1963), p. 100.

nines (*Aventinus* I, 34). Mannus, the German Jupiter, a son of Tuisco, was one king of the Germans. His son Trevir founded Trier while Semiramis was Queen of Babylon and Abraham flourished among the Jews (I, 113; II.i, 24; IV.i, 89). Those who say that Trevir, or Treiber, was son of Ninus cannot read. They misunderstand "Nini" for "Mani" (IV.i, 97). Trevir built a great palace at Trier, and after it the Palat-inate is named. Colonies seem to have radiated from Trevir's Trier, including Mainz, Metz, Basel, Strassburg, Speyer, and Worms (IV.i, 96). The same great family encompasses Scythes, who is ancestor of the Prussians through his son Pruto (I, 333). Marsus is a near descendent of Tuisco, and after him Merseburg is named (II.i, 59). The eleventh ruler of Germany and direct heir of Tuisco was Hercules Alemannus, in German, Alman Ärgle, and from him the Boi, that, is the Bavarians, stem (II.i, 41; IV.i, 43). Some say that the Bavarians had been called "avari," avaricious, and had bought an initial "B" to avoid the shame (IV.i, 34). Actually, the Bavarians take their name from Hercules's son, called variously Boius, Baigr, Boiger, Baioarius, or even Bavarus (I, 113–14).

Hercules Alemannus also sired Noricus, called Norein in German. This son named the province Noricum and the city "Noreinburg," that is, Nürnberg (*Aventinus* I, 34 and 38). Theodo, called Diet in German, is a descendent of Hercules and ancestor of the Diet who fought Emperor Severus and founded Dietfurth (I, 50). The elder Theodo's wife, Reginopyrga named Regensburg (II.i, 29). The Bava-rian hero Brennus had a son named Hector and called Hiccar in German, who in turn had a son Franco, who in his turn fathered the Frankish nation (II.i, 68). This shows that the Franks find their origins in an old Bavarian royal family (II.i, 425). It is nonsense to say that the Franks stem from Troy since they flourished long before that city. King Frank the Bavarian reigned at the same time as the German Queen Amär, who destroyed Ephesus (IV.i, 197). Frank has nothing to do with Troy despite the similarity of the name of Hector in both stories. Frank's grandchildren, Kels and Gal gave names to the Celts and the Gauls—which shows that those nations are also at least in origin German (I, 370; IV.i, 205).

Of the other German nations, the Danes stem from Dan, and the Goths from Gott (*Aventinus* IV.i, 67). The Goths, whose name means "the good," founded the Catalan nation, Gothia-Alania (IV.i, 34; IV.ii, 1077; thus also Wimpheling and Glareanus). King Switz is the immedi-ate ancestor of the Swiss (IV.ii, 1163). Switz is also known under the names of Sido and Sito. He fled to Helvetia, which is named after Hercules's son Helvos (II.i, 31; IV.i, 142).

The Sicambri are the ancient nation that became the Westphalians

(*Aventinus* II.i, 30). The Saxons are Sicambri who were expelled from Cymbria by the Danes (III.i, 8). The various names by which Germans have gone in history are Sarmatae, Scythae, Galli, Galatae, Celtae, Traci, and Teutoni (IV.i, 206ff.). The various nations to which the Germans in turn have given their names, other than those already mentioned, like France (IV.ii, 1155), are Belgium, Burgundy, Normandy (II.i, 25), and Macedon, named after Wolf, son of Osiris called Oryz, to whom we shall return in another context (IV.i, 120). England is named after King Ängel, who also named Ingolstadt, and who ruled about the time that Joab held Jerusalem (IV.i, 246).

The above are some of the myths of origin in Aventinus's works. There are several I have knowingly passed over as unimportant, and no doubt a number which simply escaped me. It is difficult to accuse Aventinus of open invention, and yet many of the myths seem quite new. The explanation lies in Aventinus's talent of combining, which we shall continue to see in his myths of heroes, religion, virtue, and the Empire. He succeeds, merely by the extent of his historical speculation, in representing the status of the mythical German past as we have defined it and as it existed on the threshold of modern historical writing in the North.

The heroic figures in Aventinus seem mostly to be related to Tuisco, at least those from dimmest antiquity. Among his descendents or their contemporaries are Inwoner, called Eingeb or Ingen (Ingevon), Eistwoner (Istevon), and Hermon (Hermion), probably the oldest heroes, followed closely by Mers (Marsus), Kemper (Gambrivus), Wandler (Vandalus), Teutscho (Teuto), and of course Almon, called Altmon, Ergle, Ercle, etc., who was Hercules Alemannus (*Aventinus* I, 113; IV.i, 99). Hercules used to bear a lion on his shield, as many German Princes do today (I, 359; II.i, 61).

In the reign of Marsus, Osiris came from Egypt to Germany with his sister-wife Isis. The two taught the Germans agriculture and the medicinal use of herbs (*Aventinus* I, 113; II.i, 59). Osiris, called Oriz in German, was also known under the names Apis, Serapis, and Mizrain. Isis, called Frau Eisen in German, was known under the names Ceres, Juno, Io, Hera, and Demeter (IV.i, 93 and 118–31). Isis was the mother of Libys, the Hispanic Hercules who visited Germany in the reign of Gambrivus (I, 309; II.i, 59).

There were a great many old German songs which celebrated Seyphyl and Mopser, who defeated Myrein and her Amazons (*Aventinus* IV.i, 101). Brigus had been sent by Ingevon to defeat the Amazons. While Ingevon was also abroad making war, Bardus was selected to rule at home. King Bardus invented music, song, and dance.

That is why Gallic poets were called Bards (I, 369; IV.i, 118 and 176–77). King Drud named the Druids, who were to religion and philosophy what the Bards were to art (IV.i, 104–5) . King Theodo began the line of German rulers which extends directly to Charlemagne and Maximilian (I, 49; V.i, 117). King Ylsing and his father Larein also seem to have dwelled in Germany. Ylsing is Ulysses, and Larein is Laertes (VI.i, 173 and 176–77).

Contemporary with Mithridates was the German and Bavarian king, variously called Scierer, Scheier, and Schorio. He gave his name to the tribe of the Schiri, who occupied Vindelicum with the Boi under King Theodo (*Aventinus* I, 3; IV.i, 519). Other famous rulers of the Germans were Myela, Penno, Venno, and Helto, who gave his name to the German word for hero, "Held" (IV.i, 263). Sigweis, Walweis, and Zecco seem to be contemporaries of Helto. All of them were great and successful warriors (I, 112). Old German histories and heroic songs told of King Mader, called Meder, Mäer, or Meer (IV.i, 267).

At the time of Julius Caesar, Voccio was King in Germany. He is the one who aided Caesar against Pompey (*Aventinus* I, 34). There seem to be several heroes named Brennus (Brenner, Prienner), but in any case, they are all German (I, 114; IV.i, 22 and 278). Among the German monarchs who reigned after the birth of Christ are Kotz, Ermon (Arminius), Suitzer, Bother, and Erbor (I, 119). Arminius dealt the Romans a terrible defeat which caused Emperor Augustus to cry out, *Quintili Vare, legiones redde* (II.i, 127). Marcomer, Sunno, and Merweg were German kings who also defeated Rome (I, 119). Of these were descended Hydericus and Litavicus, who first ruled as kings among the Franks (II.i, 129). Other German rulers stood in conflict with Rome, and they included Alaric (Adelreich), who was buried in the diverted Busentus; Theodoric the Great, who became King of Rome; Attila, who married Grimylda, daughter of King of the Tuogi, Gunther, (I, 118–19; II.i, 19 and 302; IV.i, 26; IV.ii, 1122). These last confusions refer to the mythical-historical complex at the roots of the *Nibelungenlied.*

The great learning of the ancient Germans is shown by the above-mentioned origins of the Druids and Bards. But the tradition is even older. Tuisco invented all the basic letters of the alphabet. Those added later were mere combinations of earlier letters. This tradition of learning was preserved, for example, among the German Goths. Wolphilas invented an alphabet for them. The Prussians, some people say, are learned enough to have developed their own alphabet and language, but German is beginning to displace it (*Aventinus* I, 352).

The "Drudden" and "Bärding," Druids and Bards, the philosophers and poets of Gaul, were driven from their homeland by Tiberius; they returned to greater Germany, bringing their learning with them (II.i, 72; IV.ii, 741). Their tradition was revived by Altwein (Alcuin), who was Charlemagne's tutor (IV.i, 22). Charlemagne himself served learning well, preserving ancient German works, so that some have survived the ravages (I, 259 and 331). Aventinus attributes a portion of his information to the historians Schreitwein and Freithylph, and they may be considered distinguished antecedents of German learning (I, 114; II.ii, 561–62; IV.i, 140).

No agreement has been reached on the authenticity of these last figures. It is possible that they belong in the company of Berosus, Hunibald, and Diwonys, and thus in the convention of fictitious authority. They may, however, represent real authors whose texts have been lost or have changed identity. Considering Aventinus's outrageous license with the forms of names, Schreitwein and Freithylph could stand for any number of known medieval chroniclers.

The religion of the ancient Germans seems rarely to have included churches or idols, but centered upon heroic ancestors venerated in groves. Near Regensburg there is a wood called Hergle, which indicates that the Germans not only chose groves for their worship but specifically honored Hercules in such places (*Aventinus* I, 345). Ingevon was the equivalent to Mercury. His wife, Phrea, was the German Venus, whence "frein," which still means to marry, as Gobelinus had observed a century earlier. Ingevon taught the Germans philosophy (now we know whom to blame). He venerated his father Tuisco and Tuisco's mother Nertha. It was Tuisco's *mother* who was worshipped at the winter festival. On this occasion the teetotaling Germans were allowed to drink *wine*. For these reasons Christmas, which was celebrated at the same time of year, had its festival at "Mutternacht" and was called "Weinnachten." Aventinus continues, saying that Manno and his wife Sunna were also venerated, whence the confusion that the Germans worshipped the moon, "der mon," and the sun, "die son" (I, 365; IV.i, 86). Herman (Hermion) developed a cult of himself and built a temple called Hermansal which was not destroyed until the time of Charlemagne (I, 371; II.i, 59; IV.i, 117). Frau Eisen, that is, Isis, spent her sojourn in Germany at the court of King Schwab, that is, Suevus; this is the reason that the Swabians had a special cult for her, under the name of Ceres (II.i, 60; IV.i, 131).

The Druids were the ancient German equivalent of monks. Their name survives commonly in such proper names as Ger*traud*. These pious men worshipped in groves and knew the Greek language and all Greek learning. We have seen that the Romans drove these Druids into Germany (*Aventinus* I, 366–67; IV.i, 106). Their teachings included the immortality of the soul (I, 366–67; IV.i, 77).

Aventinus chronicles a variety of virtues for the Germans, but warlike valor is as important to him as it is to the other historians of his age. The Roman provinces suffered under the attacks of the Boi and Suevi under King Theodo (*Aventinus* I, 35). The younger Theodo fought Emperor Severus (I, 50). The valor of the Germans, specifically of the Bavarians, made Julius Caesar delighted to accept their oath of eternal allegiance. Yet the Bavarians' military might won them Roman lands in their many conquests. Bologna was once capital of Bavaria (I, 112). The rulers of many lands come originally from Germany, for example, the rulers of Italy, France, Spain, England, and Scotland (I, 313; IV.ii, 1130 and 1155). The Persians were in time past defeated by the Bavarians, who also made war on Philip of Macedon. His son, Alexander, conquered the whole world except Bavaria (IV.i, 306 and 365–66). When Alexander and Aristotle asked some Germans why they did not fear Alexander, the Germans replied that their whole capacity for fear was exhausted by their greatest worry: that one day, quite by accident, something might fall down on them from heaven. In other words, they feared nothing (IV.i, 340ff.). Their women were of similar stamp (IV.i, 111). An indication of the general valor of the Germans, indeed of their ferocity, resides in the name of Hercules Alemannus. In the vernacular the name is Ergle, meaning "ein arger löw"—a fierce lion (I, 359).

The learning of the Germans has been demonstrated adequately by the great deeds of Tuisco, Ingevon, Bardus, Wolfilas, and the Druids. Tuisco not only invented the alphabet, but also promulgated exemplary laws (*Aventinus* I, 343ff.; IV.i, 76ff.). We have also touched on the moderation of the ancient Germans, shown by their usual abstinence from wine (IV.i, 116). One might see from the emphasis on religion in general and the good influence of the Druids in particular that the Bavarians were a simple and pious folk (II.i, 40).

Aventinus's assumption of the myth of the *Imperium* is unreserved. In describing the mores of ancient, let us say Augustan, Rome, Aventinus uses the term "des *heiligen* römischen Reichs Landen" and recognizes no anachronism or anachorism in the attribution of "holy" to the ancient Empire (IV.ii, 631). In a certain respect, Aventinus implies an even older continuity. The second and third empires, that is, Persian and Macedonian, were defeated by the Germans who thus long ago justified their claim to the Empire (IV.i, 290).

The German possession is prefigured elsewhere as well, for example, in the Bavarians' oath of perpetual allegiance to Caesar (*Aventinus* I, 112). After Augustulus fell in the West, Odoacer and Theodoric successively held the kingship of Rome (I, 118–19). The kingship was presumably short of the imperial title, but remains a satisfactory mythical anticipation of the German possession. Charlemagne in whom the Empire finally came to the Germans, was of course German, in fact, Bavarian. He was born in Karlsberg near Munich, and then raised at Ingelheim (I, 125 and 259; V.i, 117). Charles stems from an old Bavarian royal family, as we have seen. Remotely he descends from Hector and his son Francus, who were Bavarians, and more nearly from Theodo the Great of the Bavarians and Utilo (II.i, 68 and 423–25; V.i, 117). Charles's very name is German. "Karl" means "a brave man" in German. In Slavic it means "king" (I, 360). In Dutch it means "strong" or "chosen" (cf. Andreas of Regensburg supra, a source known to Aventinus). It is a very old German name (IV.i, 22).

The sanctity of the Empire from its earliest times has been seen in Aventinus's application of "holy" to the old Empire. The title of the Emperor reaffirms this, since "Augustus" means "holy, chosen, and consecrated by God," and has been worn by the Emperor ever since Octavian (*Aventinus* I, 261). In connection with the legend of Emperor Frederick, we have seen the associations of Antichrist and the story of Nero, the false Nero, and the special functions of the Empire in the eschatology of history accepted by Aventinus—all of which helps to constitute the sanctity of the Empire (II.i, 182; IV.ii, 802). Charlemagne's activities in behalf of religion are shown to some extent by his destruction of the Hermansal (I, 371–72; II.i, 58; IV.i, 117).

The supremacy of the Empire reveals itself in such concrete authority as that held by the Elector of Trier, whose power extends from the Rhine to the mountains separating Gaul from Spain (*Aventinus* IV.i, 98). Aventinus makes one of the simplest and strongest statements in all the present texts dealing with the myth of the Empire (III.i, 439):

> Sacrosanctum Imperium summa in terris potestas, caeleste donum est. Imperator enim primus ante omnes, secundus post deum est et tam grande nomen a solo deo traditur. . . .

> [The sacred Empire, the highest power on earth, is a divine gift. The Emperor, indeed, is the first before all others, following only after God, and so great a name is granted by God alone. . . .]

The preceding survey of Aventinus's contributions to the myths of the German past by necessity excluded his sound and objective historical writing. But even his wildest fancies are not without logic or occasionally significant insight. Aventinus was a Northerner, a Christian, writing national history in the Renaissance. He suffers no less than other Northern historians from a sense of inferiority to the Italian models. He declines to degrade the Italians, but does upgrade the Germans quite considerably, first by tracing the origins of both to heroes of equal antiquity and distinction, Tuisco and Gomer. Similarly, the tradition of learning is given native as well as classical credentials; and to a certain degree this nationalistic view is not wholly defiant of historical fact. We should, after all, have little of classical antiquity, were it not for the monks of Carolingian and Ottonian Europe.

Aventinus's rosy picture of ancient Germanic worship, veneration of ancestors rather than pagan gods, is a typical "soft primitivistic" view, one quite common in the reform-minded Renaissance. This position is, however, also dictated by contrast to the Italians. They were in the habit of telling the Germans that Roman Christianity civilized Germany. By distinguishing German-pagan from Roman-pagan worship—the only context in which his description makes sense—Aventinus at one blow succeeds in cancelling one of Germany's debts to Italy and in positing the superiority of German religious antiquity. Parts of this fiction point to a further insight: Aventinus does not complain of the ancient Germans' dearth of historical writing; rather, he introduces repeatedly the "liturgical" aspect of the ancient German religion—heroic song celebrating the venerated ancestors. Aventinus seems to imply that religion among the ancient Germans was what we call history: the memory of the past preserved for the ages.

Nor is Aventinus's historical sense as clouded as his gullibility or patriotism might indicate. The explanation of the winter festival is, of course, ludicrous; but he is surely among the first modern scholars to connect Christmas celebrations with their pagan antecedents. Nationalistic pride or, conversely, sensitivity to Germany's political impotence in the Renaissance no doubt led Aventinus to his notions about the naming and ruling of European countries. The substance of the observation is, however, quite correct. It required no small historical acuity in Aventinus's age to identify the Germanic invaders with the knightly caste of medieval Europe. Aventinus must be forgiven his confusion of "German" and "Germanic," since modern propagandistic scholars who should know better preserve the same confusion, either to the aggrandizement or condemnation of the Germans.

With Aventinus then, we conclude our survey of the Renaissance myths of the German past, in the full knowledge that much has been oversimplified or omitted. The omissions include the whole of the incipient Reformation and its attendant historiography, with such important figures as Sebastian Franck, Hans Carion, and Philipp Melanchthon. To evaluate Reformation historiography even cursorily would require another monograph. Happily, the texts we have examined are sufficiently important to stand on their own, and we may with a clear conscience comment on them without particular reference to the religious cataclysm.

Having read these pages, a critical reader is justified in asking many questions, the first of which might be methodological. Have the texts been fairly dealt with? Are they not more reliable and as wholes far more balanced than one might infer from the presentation? The answer to the second question is yes; to the first, a qualified no. The fairest and soundest method would have been to take each text as a unit, to examine its basic premises, to weigh the relative reliability and imaginativeness of its contents, and to attempt an evaluation of its implicit world-view. Ignoring the enormity of such a task for the historiography of any period, we may point out another reason for taking an admittedly particularistic approach. Previous scholarship has chosen to regard these texts as either reliable or unreliable, historic or unhistoric.[94] Here the unreliable and imaginative have been identified with the historic as the reliable and critical have previously been. Although Jacob Burckhardt condemned the German chroniclers of this period, specifically their tales of origin, calling them "fantastic rubbish," he admitted that the Italians indulged no less fantastic whimsies.[95] What could be more natural to a Renaissance mind than a return to origins, to the golden, distant past that was, as it were, being revived? Burckhardt stressed the growing critical stance of historical writing in Italy, and this point of view has overwhelmed modern historiographic scholarship, even when it challenges Burckhardt elsewhere. The imbalance, then, in the present study seeks to restore balance.

The "revival" of the aboriginal past in the Renaissance at large is a sign of an active historical consciousness, one that expressed itself differently in the different phases and homes of the Renaissance. The fifteenth and sixteenth centuries in the North developed a view of the past that was in part what we term history and in part what we term, at best, folklore. Such distinctions are, however, anachronistic. No

---

[94] See the bibliographic appendix.

[95] Jacob Burckhardt, *The Civilization of the Renaissance in Italy*, trans. by S. G. C. Middlemore (New York, 1958), pp. 250 and 188ff., where Pius II traces his family to Aeneas and Sylvius, and other Italians to ancient Roman and even Ostrogothic origins.

Renaissance historians in the North simply contrasted fact and fable: even though certain fables might be considered objectionable, they were no more objectionable than certain facts. Historical verity was interpreted more broadly, to include much of what today is fiction. The extent and significance of the problem has been recognized for the whole range of Western tradition from the time of the ancients. No less eminent a thinker than C. S. Lewis observed—and seemed disturbed by—Robert Burton's (d. 1640) indiscriminate appeal to fable "as if Romance were history."[96] The problem has been restated for the medieval epic and modern historiography in the challenging works of F. P. Pickering,[97] and is touched upon by Rosalie L. Colie from the viewpoint of the history of ideas.[98] In each case, the broad coincidence of history and fiction is recognized. But the problem remains unsolved by a mere statement of it. Let it suffice to say that historical writing extended deep into the realm of the imagination.

Any successful evocation of the past will, to some extent, be the work of the imagination. It was the distance of that extent that was not yet strictly defined in the Northern Renaissance. Chapbooks, legends, outright forgeries were sometimes considered as reliable as chronicles or annals. Any written text that purported to be about the past, and explicitly eschewed the label of poetry was history. In the years just covered by this study, the tradition of written history in Germany runs so close to that of narrative fiction, that the two are often indistinguishable. Emperor Maximilian's *Weisskunig* and *Theuerdank* are indeed nothing but history handsomely clad as fiction. Just so was Trithemius's *Compendium* probably nothing more than fiction reduced to history. The repercussions of this virtual fusion grow in importance only later in the Renaissance and in the Baroque, when prose fiction evolves as an identifiable genre. In these later periods, the relations between historical and novelistic writing are close, complex, and in great need of thorough investigation. This study does not, however, propose to take the problems of Renaissance historiography forward in time to the literature of the Baroque and beyond. I leave this task to more able hands or for another occasion.[99]

---

[96] C. S. Lewis, *The Discarded Image* (Cambridge, 1967), pp. 31–32 and 177–78.

[97] F. P. Pickering, *Literature und darstellende Kunst im Mittelalter*, Grundlagen der Germanistik, IV (Berlin, 1966), pp. 113–15, 163–66; *idem, Augustinus oder Boethius: Geschichtsschreibung und epische Dichtung im Mittelalter und in der Neuzeit*, Philologische Studien und Quellen, XXXIX (Berlin, 1967), I, pp. 46–61.

[98] Rosalie L. Colie, "Literature and History," in *Relations of Literary Study*, James Thorpe, ed. (New York, 1967), pp. 1–26.

[99] Important work on this issue has been published by Lieselotte E. Kurth, "Historiographie und historischer Roman: Kritik und Theorie im 18. Jahrhundert," *MLN*, LXXIX (October, 1964), 337–62.

We have dealt and shall continue to deal primarily with the mythical, the legendary, and the imaginative in the history of history. In the subsequent chapters I shall outline the not surprising fact that imaginative historical writing in the Renaissance in Germany is deeply in debt to the Middle Ages. There is every reason to believe that these texts as wholes are as indebted as their imaginative parts. However deep the debt, on the other hand, a distinctly new tradition had developed, one that in little more than a century fully absorbed the more than thousand years of historical writing that preceded it.

IV

The renaissance myths of the german past: the sources in antiquity and the middle ages

Like the images seen through a kaleidoscope, the Renaissance myths of the German past gave only a fleeting appearance of unity and deliberate composition before another author rearranged the order and presented a different picture—a sight at once familiar and novel. One picture in this sequence of kaleidoscopic images could look very like the other or very unlike it. The differences were basically arbitrary, depending upon the stance of the author. The similarities rested on a common collection of ideas and common categories of thought. In the manner of a child tinkering with a Christmas toy, we are going to expose the insides of this kaleidoscope to investigate the constituent parts and the principles of organization; unlike him, however, we should not be disappointed by the color and variety of stones or the relative simplicity of the mechanism.

As befits our subject, this investigation takes the shape of a select historiography, a story of the historical writing that treated German antiquity. The beginning of this story is provided by TACITUS, who—by all standards—is the father of ancient Germanic studies. The recovery of his works in the Renaissance, particularly the *Germania*, has been called "a romance."[1] Boccaccio, Poggio, Bessarion, and

---

[1] William Peterson, ed. and trans., *Tacitus: Dialogus, Agricola, Germania*, Loeb Classical Library (London, 1958), p. 3.

Cusanus were all somehow involved in it.[2] Annius of Viterbo, Conrad Celtis, Beatus Rhenanus, and Johannes Aventinus were among the many who were mightily in debt to it. The influence of Tacitus on German humanism was profound, but since it is well known, I shall offer only a brief review of the *Germania* and several collateral texts, insofar as they bear directly on the Renaissance myths of the German past.[3]

The larger part of the fables of origin after Annius of Viterbo had their ultimate roots in Tacitus. Tacitus believed that the Germans were indigenous because no one would willingly leave pleasant surroundings and risk a dangerous ocean voyage in order to enter a land with a bad climate and a sorry landscape, where no one would choose to dwell—unless it were home. The notion that the Germans were indigenous pleased the humanists since it gave them a primordial right to their country, but they were less enthusiastic about Tacitus's explanation, which they attacked (what does one expect from Italians?), ignored, or did their best to refute.[4]

The Germans, Tacitus tells us, praised their earth-born god Tuisto in ancient song. Beatus Rhenanus was the first to use the now accepted manuscript reading that prefers "Tuisto" to "Tuisco." The son of Tuisto, Mannus, was considered the father of the nation. Andreas Althamer's assumption that the veneration of Mannus was shown by names with "man" is remotely correct. Sanscrit, as it seems, contains a cognate which also means "father of the nation." The Germanic word itself was used apparently to indicate gods as well as men (*Germania*, c. 2; Much, pp. 17–23).

Mannus's three sons fathered the three main tribal divisions of the Germans, the Ingaevones, the Hermiones (Herminones), and the Istaevones. Among the Ingaevones, Pliny (Much, p. 24) numbers the Cimbri, Teutones, and Chauci; to the Hermiones he adds (Much, p. 25) the Suebi, Hermunduri, Chatti, and Cherusci; to the Istaevones (Much, p. 26), the remainder of the tribes, those not on the sea or midland. Other sons of Mannus fathered the Marsi, Gambrivi, Suebi, and

---

[2] Ludwig Pralle, *Die Wiederentdeckung des Tacitus* (Fulda, 1952), pp. 13 and 70.

[3] Hans Tiedemann, *Tacitus und das Nationalbewusstsein der deutschen Humanisten* ... (Berlin, 1913) and Paul Joachimsen, "Tacitus im deutschen Humanismus," *Neue Jahrbücher für das klassische Altertum*, XIV [XXVII] (1911), 695–717, discuss Tacitus's influence quite thoroughly. Texts and translations are numerous and excellent. The *Germania* is cited by chapter; edition and commentary by Rudolf Much, *Die Germania des Tacitus*, 2nd ed. by Richard Kienast (Heidelberg, 1959), which is also the source of the cross-references to other classical authors.

[4] On German reaction to such negative views of the homeland see Gerald Strauss, *Sixteenth-Century Germany* (Madison, Wis., 1959), pp. 9–10.

Vandilii. Pliny counts (Much, p. 29) among the Vandilii the tribes of the Burgoniones, Varinnae, Charini, and Gutones. Tacitus and, collaterally, Pliny seem clearly to be the sources from which Wimpheling derived his description of the primitive tribes.

The heroes of whom Tacitus writes (*Germania*, c. 3; Much, pp. 46ff.) are Hercules and Ulysses. Hercules was supposed to have visited Germany personally, and his memory was preserved in the songs used to encourage warriors at the start of battle. The kind of song was known as "barditus" or "barritus." The debate about the correct choice of these two forms is far from settled (cf. Much, pp. 49–53). For our purposes, "barditus" is preferable. Although the form probably has nothing to do with the Celtic bards, it does appear to support such Renaissance inventions as Aventinus's King Bard.

The extensive travels of Ulysses seem to have taken him to Germany where he dedicated an altar to his father Laertes at Asciburgium on the Rhine. Andreas Althamer's "Aschenburg," apparently today's Asberg (Much, p. 58), seems to be the same place and is connected with classical antiquity at least insofar as it was a Roman military station. We might include among the heroic figures Veleda and Aurinia, famed prophetesses who were highly regarded by the Germans. Both names seem to mean "seer," "knower of secrets" (Much, pp. 118–19). Celtis's Hrotswitha was called a spiritual descendent of these ladies. I shall also mention Arminius, although he does not appear in the *Germania* (but see Much, p. 288).[5] It is first through Tacitus's *Annals* that the German Renaissance discovered the identity of the man who caused Suetonius's Augustus (XXIII.2) to cry out, *Quintili Vare, legiones redde!*[6]

Of religion Tacitus reports (*Germania*, c. 9; Much, pp. 122ff.) that the Germans worshipped Mercury, who accepted human sacrifice, and Hercules, and Mars, both of whom accepted animal sacrifice. Isis was worshipped among the Suevi. It might be a consolation to the reader of Aventinus, who gave Isis at least six identities, that Isis is known elsewhere (cf. Much, p. 126) as the "thousand-named." Peculiarly, Much fails to mention the reports of Zisa (Ciza, Cycza, Zisaris), which often accompanied descriptions of the Swabians' religion. Aventinus had made the connection between Isis and Ceres, and the connection

---

[5] Richard Kuehnemund, *Arminius or the Rise of a National Symbol in Literature*, University of North Carolina Studies in the Germanic Languages and Literatures, VIII (Chapel Hill, 1953) gives a complete description of the sources and course of the Arminius myth.

[6] J. C. Rolfe, ed. and trans., *Suetonius*, 2 vols., Loeb Classical Library (London, 1960), I, 154–55.

between Ceres and Zisa appeared at least as early as Meisterlin. The Germans, Tacitus continues, also worshipped Mother Earth under the name of "Nerthus" (*Germania*, c. 40; Much, pp. 344ff.). Much insists that "Hertha" is an unjustified reading and not to be sought in "Nertha" (p. 351). Althamer would have been disappointed. The Germans also included a version of Castor and Pollux among their gods (*Germania* c. 43; Much, pp. 373ff.).

Worship among the ancient Germans, as Tacitus describes it (*Germania*, c. 9; Much pp. 122ff.), was simple, housed in groves and not requiring great temples. This found echo in Celtis and Trithemius among others. The Germans were also experts in augury (c. 10; Much, pp. 129ff.). Germanic augury seems to have left a notable impression on Roman antiquity. Suetonius's Domitian (XVI.1) had a Germanic soothsayer killed for prophesying a change in the leadership of the state.[7] Tacitus relates (c. 27; Much, pp. 247ff.) that German funerals were unpretentious, by cremation, with a shield or horse perhaps added to the fire. Krantz's funeral of King Gelder was more elaborate, but Krantz was not indirectly chiding a luxurious civilization as was Tacitus.

Tacitus gives a full list of virtues and vices for the ancient Germans. Valor is of prime importance and is a fitting accoutrement of their huge bodies (*Germania*, c. 4; Much, pp. 65ff.). They detested rest, preferring battle with its spoils (c. 14; Much, pp. 159ff.). The Germans were also most chaste, normally taking only one wife and punishing adultery severely (c. 18; Much, pp. 190ff.). They also exacted terrible penalties for cowardice and other vice (c. 12; Much, pp. 146ff.). Among their greatest virtues was hospitality (c. 21; Much, pp. 207ff.). Franciscus Irenicus was clearly under the influence of Tacitus and his rather favorable picture of ancient Germanic behavior. Tacitus was impressed that the primitive nation he described could command and respect eloquence (c. 11; Much, pp. 139ff.). Albertus Krantz was no less favorably impressed with the same faculty a millennium and a half later. The women of the Germans shared these virtues (*Germania*, c. 7–8; Much, pp. 112ff.), and by their valor and eloquence they had been known to turn the tide of battles.

Tacitus, unlike most of his Renaissance readers, enumerates vices along with virtues for the Germans. When not engaged in making war, they slept and over-ate (*Germania*, c. 15; Much, pp. 166ff.). Although the Germans were frank and simple, they were wont to drink and quarrel (c. 22–23; Much, pp. 213ff.). Their short tempers were a matter

---

[7] *Ibid.*, II, 374–75.

of some interest to the ancients, specifically Seneca (cf. Much, p. 287), whose comments are reflected by Irenicus. Considered as a vice by the ancients, not so by Meisterlin and Celtis, was the *furor Teutonicus*, meaning generally the plague of Germanic military invasion. Its first appearance in letters seems to be in Lucan's *Pharsalia* (Book I, ll. 255–56).[8] There the words were used in the genitive and split between two lines, hardly a likely candidate for an inflammatory slogan.

In the *Germania*, Tacitus does not touch on the charged associations of the idea of the *Imperium Romanum*. The Empire had nonetheless by his time acquired mythical stature. Wilamowitz-Moellendorff tells of the almost immediate deification of Julius Caesar after his death, and of the sacred aura surrounding Augustus, the *pater patriae*, even before his death. These notions were apparently foreign to the sober Romans, but they developed a formal cult of the Emperors to unify the most disparate elements of the Empire. Exploiting this cult, one or several false Neros appeared and won acceptance among certain nations.[9] Suetonius reports ("Nero," LVII.2, in Rolfe, II, 186–87) the appearance of a young man twenty years after the death of Nero; he pretended to be the dead Emperor and was well received among the Parthians. At least two other false Neros seem to have appeared, one of whom Tacitus describes in the *Histories* (II.8–9). Suetonius's report is very probably one of the sources for Aventinus's myth of Nero. Aventinus, in imitation of his source, chose to note the popular success of the false Emperor. This very characteristic marks the surprisingly similar career of the dead Frederick II. Unlike Tacitus, Suetonius was not forgotten in the Middle Ages, but remained a relatively influential author. His report could well have been known among those who constructed the myth of Emperor Frederick.[10]

Among the texts of late antiquity, most important for the Middle Ages was a *Breviarium* of Roman history produced by EUTROPIUS upon the order of Emperor Valens (364–78 A.D.), whose *magister memoriae* he was. The popularity of this work in the Renaissance is shown by

---

[8] J. D. Duff, ed. and trans., *Lucan*, Loeb Classical Library (London, 1962), p. 22–23.

[9] Ulrich von Wilamowitz-Moellendorf, *Der Glaube der Hellenen*, 3rd ed., 2 vols. (Darmstadt, 1959), II, 422–23 and 440.

[10] On Suetonius's survival in the Middle Ages see Paul Joachimsohn [sic], *Die humanistische Geschichtschreibung in Deutschland: Die Anfänge—Sigismund Meisterlin* (Bonn, 1895), p. 41, and Martin Schanz, Carl Hosius, et al., *Geschichte der Römischen Literatur*, 2nd to 4th eds., 4 vols. in 5, Handbuch der Altertumswissenschaft, VIII (Munich, 1959), III, 65–66 [henceforth "Schanz-Hosius"].

the thirteen editions it enjoyed between 1471 and 1532, among which several were the product of Erasmus and the press of Aldus Manutius.[11] The Renaissance editions contained emendations and continuations by Paul the Deacon and a later Anonymous, sometimes known as Landulfus Sagax. Both Paul and the so-called Landulfus will be considered in their chronological place.

Eutropius's concern with the Germans was limited largely to their incursions on the Empire, and thus his influence on the later recreation of the German past is restricted. Due to his popularity, however, this little influence is quite permanent. Eutropius preserves the story of the alliance of Gallic and Germanic tribes against Rome (Eutropius V.1, in Droysen, p. 84). The alliance of Cimbri, Teutones, Tuguri, and Ambrones suffered a disastrous defeat at the hands of Marius (V.2, in Droysen, p. 84). The opposite turn of events is represented in the reign of Valerian (A.D. 253–59) when such tribes invaded Italy and reached as far as Ravenna (IX.7, in Droysen, p. 152). This detail seemed of sufficient importance to Renaissance historians to be given frequent mention by them: e.g., Wimpheling and Trithemius. Eutropius is also a source for information about the Alemannic invasions of Gaul and Italy (IX.8, in Droysen, p. 154). A Greek translation of the *Breviarium* illustrates that the Renaissance confusion of ancient Germanic and other clearly non-Germanic tribes was not unprecedented and probably not made in bad faith. A contemporary of Eutropius, one Paianios, made the translation and rendered Eutropius's word for "Goth" with the Greek word for "Scythian" (Droysen, pp. 174–75).

Eutropius begins his work with the statement that the Roman *Imperium* had been founded by Romulus (I.1, in Droysen, p. 8). The use of *Imperium* here of course implies "power," "authority," or "the state." In the Northern Renaissance, the Roman *Imperium* generally implied the state of the Emperor. A Renaissance German reading Eutropius's text would very likely apply the connotations of "imperial" to the very founding of Rome. It is this combination, the *Imperium* as the heritage of Romulus and as the Empire of the Caesars, that Vadianus employed in his *Oratio* to Maximilian. The Middle Ages and most of the Northern Renaissance considered the Roman Empire the creation of Julius or Augustus Caesar. For Eutropius, the Roman *Imperium* in Valens's time was indistinguishable from the political entity legendarily founded by Romulus. Vadianus then has his usage

---

[11] Cf. Schanz-Hosius, IV.i, 77–78 and note 5. I use the edition by H. Droysen, MGH auct. antiq., II (Berlin, 1879). See also August Potthast, *Bibliotheca Historica Medii Aevi*, 2nd ed., 2 vols. consecutively paginated (Berlin, 1896), p. 902–3 [henceforth simply "Potthast"].

of the word coincide with the ancient usage, expressing the continuity of the Roman state. It is, incidentally, not improbable that Eutropius served Vadianus as a model for the connotations attached to *Imperium*.

At the end of the fourth century, within a few years of the work of Eutropius, the West enjoyed its flowering period of CHURCH FATHERS. Amongst many of their greater contributions to learning, they left an indelible mark on the tradition of the mythical past of the Germans. SAINT JEROME, for example, preserved for posterity the identification of the Goths with the Getae, and so gave the Germans a claim to an antiquity that they would have been hard put to find elsewhere. Jerome suggests the identity of the two tribes in his genealogy of the barbarians: of the sons of Japhet, Gomer is father of the Galatae, Magog of the Scythae, and Gog and Magog together of the Getae or Goths.[12] The tradition is traced back to the anti-pope Hippolytus (d. 235), and became a matter of some importance in the thought of Saint Ambrose (d. 397), who saw in the Goths the Gog and Magog of eschatological prophecy.[13] Jewish tradition in late antiquity similarly traced the Goths to Magog, eventually identifying all Teutons with the biblical forebear.[14] In Jerome's translation of Eusebius's ecclesiastical chronicle, another origin is suggested for the Goths: "Aschonez," son of Gomer, is their ancestor.[15] The Babylonian Talmud preserves, as it seems, the same tradition.[16] Aschkenaz, or Askenest, or Assenez is the suppositious ancestor of the Germans in the discussions of Krantz and Aventinus.

Hermann Peter of Andlau in the fifteenth century cited SAINT AUGUSTINE's *City of God* as his authority for the sanctity of the Empire. Augustine wrote in interpretation of Saint Paul's eschatological warnings (II Thess. ii.7):

> By "mystery of iniquity" they say he meant Nero, whose deeds greatly resembled those of Antichrist, so that some think that he shall rise again

---

12 P. de Lagarde, ed., *Hebraicae questiones in libro Geneseos*, Corpus Christianorum, Series Latina, LXXII: S. Hieronymi Presbyteri Opera, I.1 (Turnhout, 1959), p. 11, to Gen. X.21.

13 Arno Borst, *Der Turmbau von Babel*, 6 vols. in 7 (Stuttgart, 1957–63), II.i, 384.

14 *Ibid.*, I, 193–95.

15 Eusebius-Jerome was often printed in the Renaissance, e.g., 1475, 1483, 1512, 1518, 1529 (Potthast, p. 595). I use the edition by Johannes Sichard, *En damus Chronicon . . .* (Basel, 1529), p. 5 on the issue of "Aschonez." The chronicle was similarly influential in the Middle Ages: Schanz-Hosius, IV.i, 445.

16 Borst, I, 255.

and be the true Antichrist. Others think he never died, but vanished, and that he lives (in that age and vigour wherein he was supposed to be slain) until the time comes that he shall be revealed and restored to his kingdom.[17]

Between this statement and Suetonius's report of the false Nero, we have the sources of Aventinus's version of the Nero myth and, simultaneously, the oldest analogue in the West and one of the prototypes of the myth of Emperor Frederick. Augustine more or less rejects these fables as soon as he relates them. He does, however, identify "him who is now holding" (also II Thess. ii.7) with the Roman Empire. The identification of Rome with the "holder" enters tradition in Augustine's formulation, and although he may not have originated the interpretation, it is he who transmitted it to Aeneas Sylvius and Hermann Peter directly and indirectly by way of later medieval authors.

Augustine was still writing the *City of God* and Jerome was working in Bethlehem when a young Spaniard, PAULUS OROSIUS, visited Hippo. He made a favorable impression on Augustine, and in 415 he delivered correspondence from Augustine to Jerome at Bethlehem. Perhaps as an additional favor, Augustine asked Orosius to write a history demonstrating the African Father's premise that Christianity had brought relative peace into the world. This was intended to refute the pagan conviction that the fall from the old gods had brought on the barbaric invasions.[18] The result of Augustine's request was Orosius's *Historiarum adversum paganos libri VII*, published about 418.[19] It became a most influential work in the Middle Ages, enjoying even a translation into Old English. In the Renaissance, Orosius became immensely popular. By the end of the sixteenth century, he was available in some twenty-five Latin editions and translations into German, French, and Italian (Potthast, pp. 882–83). The Renaissance plundered Orosius for mythical material, some of it original with him, some a transmission of older thought, some the raw stuff of later fabrications.

---

[17] *City of God*, XX.19, in John Healy, trans., and R. V. G. Trasker, ed., Everyman's Library 983, 2 vols. (London, 1962), II, 296; cf. J. P. Migne, *PL*, XLI (Paris, 1900), 686.

[18] Schanz-Hosius, IV.ii, 484 and 486.

[19] Paulus Orosius, *Historiarum Adversum Paganos Libri VII*, Carolus Zangemeister, ed., Corpus Scriptorum Ecclesiaticorum Latinorum, V (Vienna, 1882) and trans. by Irving Woodworth Raymond, *Seven Books of History against the Pagans: The Apology of Paulus Orosius*, Columbia University Records of Civilization, XXVI (New York, 1936) [henceforth "Zangemeister"].

An example of the latter lies in Orosius's description of the Amazon queens, Marpesia and Lampeto, who are, however, not yet connected with the Goths (I.15.1–4, in Zangemeister, pp. 65–66). Orosius does connect them with the Scythians, so that the leap to the Goths in later authors is short indeed. The complex of Amazon stories includes the adventures of Plynos and Scolopetius, who found their way into the anonymous Augsburg chronicle of 1469 in tongue-twisting vernacular translation. The Goths appear somewhat farther on in Orosius's chronicle (I.16.2, in Zangemeister, p. 68), where they are made the later equivalents of the Getae. This mention is the authority for the widespread Renaissance notion (e.g. Rolevinck, Campano, Wimpheling), that the great military leaders of antiquity feared the Goths and thought that they should be avoided. Orosius names Alexander, Pyrrhus, and Caesar as three who shared such caution. The etymology of the name of the Burgundians—derived from "burgi," their word for "outpost"—is also given by Orosius (VII.32.12, in Zangemeister, p. 514), who is effectively the ultimate written source of this information for the historiography of the following thousand years or so.

Those historians who had no Suetonius at their side could report the Germanic victory over the forces of Augustus in the version preserved by Orosius, including the Emperor's cry, *Quintili Vare, redde legiones* (VI.21.27, in Zangemeister, p. 426). Those who quote Augustus's words in an inversion of Suetonius's *legiones redde* are probably following Orosius. The confrontation of Barbarian and Roman worlds appears often in Orosius's work. He describes the defeat of Manlius by an alliance of Germanic and Gallic tribes, and the subsequent defeat of the Cimbri and Teutones by Marius (V.16.7 and 12–14, in Zangemeister, pp. 314–16). The leader of the barbarian alliance Teutobodus died in the battle. The women of the defeated forces asked that their honor be preserved and that they be allowed to become vestal virgins. When Marius refused this request, the women killed their children and took their own lives rather than face dishonor.

A sixteenth-century German translation of Orosius by one Hieronymus Boner reveals what these various events meant to popular understanding at the time. The Cimbri and Teutones of Orosius's report are rendered in German as "Zimbrischen und Teutschen."[20] The Renaissance entertained no doubt that the Teutones were anything but identical to their apparent namesakes in modern times. That the tribe was annihilated seems to have left no impression. Elsewhere (fol. XXXIV^v),

---

20 Hieronymus Boner, *Chronica vnd beschreibung so er gethon in Latin* ... (Colmar, 1539), fol. LXXI^r.

Boner translates "virgo vestalis" as "ein Westvalisch Klosterfraw," a Westphalian nun. The name of the Westphalians in sixteenth-century Latin could appear as *Vuestuali*,[21] so that the logical distance between "vestal" and "Westphalian" was by no means as unbridgeable as it might seem today. Boner and his readers may well have believed that Westphalian nuns could be represented in the sacred college. No explanation is offered for the unreasonable refusal to admit the wives of the "Zimbrischen und Teutschen," other than perhaps that as wives they were not likely to be virgins, Westphalian or any other kind.

The myth of the Empire as it found expression in later historical writing owes several of its major features to Orosius. His formulation of the theory of the four Empires exerted considerable influence as a geographic and epochal pattern. The four Empires were in sequence of time, Babylon in the East, Carthage in the South, Macedon in the North, and finally Rome in the West. Carthage and Macedon were, however mere caretaker Empires (Orosius II.1.4–6, in Zangemeister, p. 82). As the fortunes of Babylon sank, those of Rome rose, with Empire shifting unremittingly from East to West (V.2.1–2, in Zangemeister, p. 434). The westward move of Empire is traceable as a traditional historical notion to Orosius, although, again, he did not necessarily invent the idea. He is clearly a source for such speculation in Hermann Peter of Andlau. The identity of this conception of universal Empire with the Holy Roman Empire of the Renaissance is betrayed by a gloss in Boner's Orosius translation: the present glory of Empire is named, and the name is Charles V (fol. XIX ʳ).

Orosius, like Eutropius, applies the term *Imperium Romanum* to the period before the end of the Republic (e.g., V.17.1, in Zangemeister, p. 319). His idea of the continuity of the Roman state is, however, far from that of Eutropius. It is first of all thoroughly christianized. The divine establishment of the state is maintained, but it is the true and Christian God who ordained it and supervised its progress to the time of Augustus (VI.1.1–6, in Zangemeister pp. 349–50). In the reign of Augustus, when one peace prevailed over the world, when all nations were joined together under the Roman census, Christ was born (VII.2.13–15, in Zangemeister, pp. 436–37). For Orosius, the continuity of the *Imperium* had little to do with the heritage of Romulus. On the contrary, the *Imperium* as such had passed through several hands. The continuity of the *Imperium* and the particular significance of the *Imperium Romanum* resided in God's purpose. The central event of history was the Incarnation, and the Roman Empire was its preparation, setting, and aftermath. Orosius's personal evaluation of Rome

---

[21] E.g., Johannes Naucler, *Chronicon*, II (Cologne, 1584), 38.

is equivocal. On the one hand, the City is implicitly the New Babylon; on the other hand, the divine purpose seems to single Rome out for special favor. Although the historical writing of the Middle Ages and Renaissance relied heavily on Orosius, few historians before the Reformation wholeheartedly identified the Rome of the popes and medieval emperors with the whore of Babylon. The idea of the New Babylon was most often transferred to the spiritual, minimized, or suppressed altogether, and the vacuum filled with an emphasis on the sacred function of the Empire.

Orosius lays the groundwork for other traits of the myth of the Empire in his description of the Gothic King Athaulfus (VII.43.2–6, in Zangemeister, pp. 559–60). The King, as it seems, did not consider the Gothic incursions on the Empire the destruction of one order and the rise of another. The Goths had no intention of overthrowing the Empire; rather, they were destined to restore it. As extraordinary as this opinion may be to us, it was not at all uncommon and had analogues in the whole tradition of historical writing from Orosius to Trithemius. The Goths as restorers of the Empire—a nightmare of illogic to the modern—must have been an important element of thought in the fifth century. A return to the old Empire was not only impossible, but also less than desirable for the Christian. Most Roman pagans believed that a return to the old religion would mean a return to Roman grandeur. A Christian who agreed with this logic would certainly have preferred no return to Roman grandeur. The alternatives were few, and one was to make the best of a bad situation. The Germanic invaders, although Arian, were at least Christian, and they could bear the sceptre abandoned by imperial Rome. Athaulfus believed that *Gothia* was to become heir to *Romania*, that the *Imperium Romanum* was to be restored by its apparent destroyers. From a certain point of view, precisely this occurred in history. Athaulfus's suggestion anticipates the synthesis of classical and barbaric, Roman and Germanic, that was to become medieval and subsequently modern civilization.

The mutual assimilation of Gothic and Roman was of prime importance to a later Gothic king, Theodoric the Great. In implementing this policy, Theodoric engaged the services of several distinguished Romans, not the least of whom was the Senator and Consul, FLAVIUS MARCUS AURELIUS CASSIODORUS.[22] Cassiodorus, like his Gothic patron,

---

[22] About whom cf. Schanz-Hosius, IV.ii, 93–96, and Max Manitius, *Geschichte der lateinischen Literatur des Mittelalters*, 3 vols., Handbuch der Altertumswissenschaft, IX.ii (Munich, 1911–31), I, 36ff. [henceforth "Manitius"].

was much concerned with giving the Romans reason to accept their conquerors. To this end, Cassiodorus produced historical works with an openly pro-Gothic bias. His chronicle of 519 describes the history of Rome up to his own time, the consulship of Theodoric.[23] Theodoric, Gothic king and Roman citizen, bore the title legally. It represents both the idea of continuity and the attempt at assimilation. One of the standard ecclesiastical histories of the Middle Ages, the *Historia Tripartita*, was compiled at the order of Cassiodorus. It contains the important tidbit of information that Bishop Vulphilas invented Gothic letters and rendered scripture into the language of the Goths.[24] The greatest of Cassiodorus's historical works, the Gothic history in twelve books, was intended to prove the Goths worthy successors to power in Italy and worthy compatriots of the Romans. Among other proofs of Gothic worth, Cassiodorus employed the supposed co-eval antiquity of the Goths and the Romans. Unfortunately, this work is lost, and only the extract made by Jordanes survives.

JORDANES, a Goth, was Bishop of Crotona, and wrote his summary of Cassiodorus's Gothic history in 551 A.D.[25] After Tacitus, Jordanes is one of the earliest historians to be exploited widely in the Renaissance for "German" content. From Gobelinus Persona through the humanists, the debt—direct and indirect—is extensive.

Among the many nations that originated from the isle of Scandza, including the Dani, are the Goths. They stem from Magog, and long ago under their King Berig, they left Scandza by ship and landed at that place that even today is called Gothscanza. There they drove the Ulmerugi out of the land and subdued the Vandals. With their King Filimer, they continued on to Scythia (Jordanes III.23–IV.29, in Mommsen, pp. 59–61). The Gepidae were those slow ones who re-

---

23 J. P. Migne, *PL*, LXIX (Paris, 1848), 1248. The ed. princ. was produced by Cochlaeus, in Sichard's *En damus Chronicon.* Cf. Migne, col. 540 and Potthast, p. 197.

24 Migne, *PL*, LXIX, 118. Early printed editions of the *Historia Tripartita* abound. Potthast (p. 197) lists three up to 1472 and nine more in the sixteenth century, these based on Beatus Rhenanus's 1523 Basel edition. It also enjoyed a sixteenth-century translation into Czech and a translation by Caspar Hedio into German, which was printed seven times after 1530.

25 Cf. Schanz-Hosius, IV.ii, 117–20, and Manitius, I, 210–15. Edition by Theodor Mommsen, *Iordanis Romana et Getica*, MGH auct. antiq., V.i (Berlin, 1882); translation by C. C. Mierow, *The Gothic History of Jordanes*, 2nd ed. (1915; rpt. Cambridge and New York, 1960). The work was first printed in Augsburg in 1515, edited by Peutinger, and again in 1531, edited by Beatus Rhenanus, and six times again in the sixteenth century (Potthast, p. 682). MSS were in the possession of Cuspinianus, as well as Peutinger and Beatus (Mommsen, pp. li–liv).

mained behind (XVII.95, in Mommsen, p. 82). We find an early isolated example of the topos of critical rejection when Jordanes denies
the stories that the Goths were a subject people in Britain and had
been redeemed at the price of a single horse (V.38, in Mommsen, pp.
63–64).

Jordanes takes the raw material of the Amazon fable from Orosius,
giving due credit; connects the Amazons with the Goths by making
them their wives; and so creates a new myth of the German past. It
is based on the identity of Goths and Scythians, since tradition maintained that the Amazons were originally the women of the Scythians.
Vesosis, King of the Egyptians made war on this people, Goths or
Scythians. The nation under its King Tanausis defeated Vesosis and
pursued him even to his own kingdom. After the death of Tanausis,
enemies attacked the women at home who had banded together to
protect themselves. They elected Lampeto to protect the homeland
and Marpesia to lead an army. Marpesia went off on conquests as far
as Asia and en route delayed long enough on the Caucasus to name
the *Saxum Marpesiae* (Jordanes V.44–VI.50, in Mommsen, pp. 65–67).

Strangely, the large numbers of heroes, warriors, and learned men
of the Goths found little or no directly identifiable echo in the Renaissance. The Renaissance passed over, as far as I can tell, Zalmoxes,
Zeuta, and Dicineus, philosophers and historians of the ancient Goths,
and Eterpamara, Hanala, Fritigern, and Vidigoia, whose great deeds
were preserved in song (Jordanes V.39–44, Mommsen, pp. 65–66).
Seemingly forgotten by the Renaissance is also the Gothic King Tele-
fus, who was a son of Hercules and a husband to a sister of Priam
(IX.59, in Mommsen, pp. 70–71). The connections of Hercules and
Troy to Germanic antiquity, the preservation of the memory of learned
men, the insistence on a historical tradition—if only an oral one—are
all commonplace in the Renaissance re-creation of the German past.
Their relationship to Jordanes seems, however, to be oblique, probably
because the Renaissance depended too heavily on medieval intermediaries. Jordanes was available complete to the Renaissance as well as
truncated in a series of authoritative medieval chronicles. In blithe
disregard of their war-cry, *ad fontes,* most Renaissance historians probably knew Jordanes only through chrestomathies that carefully sifted
out what the Middle Ages thought irrelevant.

The account of the ancient religion of the Goths is almost entirely
fused with Jordanes's views on their virtue. Mars is said to have been
born among the Goths (consider Vadianus and Glareanus on the subject of Mars's birth among the Swiss, who stem from the Goths). The
Gothic priests offered to Mars human sacrifice of captives. In honor of

Mars, the armaments of defeated enemies were hung in trees—an act reminiscent of Emperor Frederick's last deeds and surely related to the juridical symbol of hanging a shield in a tree.[26] Jordanes seems to have thought all of this a sign of piety (Jordanes V.40–41, in Mommsen, p. 64). The funeral of Alaric may also be considered a religious ceremony, although it is hardly probable that rivers were often diverted to bury Gothic heroes. The river in question is the Busentus which was temporarily turned from its course to hide the body of Alaric, and the great treasures buried with him (XXX.157, in Mommsen, p. 99). In the time of the dictator Sulla, King Burista invited the priest Dicineus to come to the Goths, whom he taught theology, philosophy, ethics, physics, logic, astronomy, and the written law. Dicineus became priest-king and was succeeded by Comosicus, also priest and king (XI.67–73, in Mommsen, pp. 73ff.). One thinks of Trithemius's Druid priests and just, learned kings. A definite connection cannot be stated with certainty, even though Trithemius unquestionably knew the work of Jordanes.[27] It is, however, along such lines that a closer investigation of Trithemius's fabrication should be pursued.

Jordanes preserves and advances the tendentious strains of Orosius and Cassiodorus. Gothic invincibility is used to demonstrate the dignity of the rivals and conquerors of Rome. Even Julius Caesar, first Emperor and victor over most of the world, was obliged to leave the Goths in peace (Jordanes XI.68, in Mommsen, p. 73). In combination with the ancient tradition of learning, valor made the Goths worthy successors to the Romans. Their worthiness had at least once been concretely tested, in that Emperor Maximinus was a Goth: thus also Krantz and Irenicus. Jordanes specifies that his words on Maximinus are written to show that Goths could achieve the highest honor of the Empire (XV.83–88, in Mommsen, pp. 78ff.). The founding of Constantinople involved the assistance of the Goths, and Jordanes uses the second Rome to cement the association of Goths and Empire (XXI.112, in Mommsen, p. 87). The Gothic Kingdom of Italy becomes in Jordanes's work the successor of the Empire in the West: when Augustulus ended what Augustus had begun, the power came to the hands of the Gothic kings (XLVI.242–43, in Mommsen, p. 120).[28]

---

[26] Cf. ch. 3 supra, n. 70; and cf. Jacob Grimm, *Deutsche Rechtsaltertümer*, 4th ed., 2 vols. (1899; reprinted Darmstadt, 1965), II, 484.

[27] Johannes Trithemius, *Catalogus scriptorum ecclesiasticorum* (Cologne, 1531), fol. XLIVʳ, where the learned abbot claims autopsy.

[28] The report was taken directly from the chronicle of Marcellinus Comes (d. 534), in Theodor Mommsen, ed., *Marcellinus Comes: Chronicon*, MGH auct. antiq., XI, chron. min., II. 37–108 (Berlin, 1844), p. 91; comp. Mierow, trans., *The Gothic History of Jordanes*, p. 177.

Jordanes is believed to have been himself a Goth, and this would explain his affectionate propaganda in behalf of his people. He does not, however, consistently pursue the issue of Gothic rights to the Empire. His is the time of Justinian, Belisarius, the end of the Gothic Kingdom in Italy, the short-lived restoration of the old grandeur of the Empire, and the disintegration of urban Rome.

Jordanes's Gothic history is the earliest extant construct of a German-Germanic empire prior and parallel to the Roman Empire. The importance of this precedent is clear in the light of Renaissance imagination. We have repeatedly confronted German empires, without publicistic intent as with Gobelinus, and with emphatic publicistic intent as with Bebel, Köchlin, Celtis, and Trithemius. The basic patterns of Jordanes's construct appear in remarkably similar form in the Renaissance: that is, the antiquity of the origins, the bravery and learning of the heroic figures, the character of the ancient worship, the warlike valor of the people at large, all are summoned to support the German-Germanic nation's worthiness to be heir of the Roman *Imperium*. The antiquity may be Trojan, Macedonian, antediluvian, or of the progeny of Noah, the learning may come from the hands of law-givers or priestesses, the warlike valor may be directed against Rome or against other enemies—in any case, the nation is made an equal of Rome.

The Goths were not to live up to the expectations of Orosius or his Athaulfus, nor to the hopes of Theodoric and Cassiodorus, nor to the dignity constructed by Jordanes. Another tribe would assume the mission to revive, or perhaps better, to preserve the symbolic continuity of the Roman Empire, with its political, religious, and cultural tasks, its sacred function, and its supreme position.

The reversal of Gothic fortunes proceeded with unrelenting disaster until the disappearance of the last vestiges of the Goths, a pastoral people on the Crimea, sometime in the seventeenth or eighteenth century. Symbolic of this reversal is a new myth attached to the person of Theodoric. Pope GREGORY I, also regarded as "the Great" (ca. 540–604), was in the matter of Germanic-Romanic assimilation not in the most conciliatory tradition. With Gregory a third force emerged in the West: Germanic invader and vestigial Empire would now both have to learn to deal with the papacy. Gregory, like Cassiodorus, had been in imperial service and became Praetor of the City before he retired, like Cassiodorus, to the monastery. After his election to the Chair of Peter he wrote (ca. 600 A.D.) his four books of dialogues. They seem to be the ultimate Latin source for the tale of Theodoric's death. In a vision, the Gothic king is seen hurled into the mouth of a volcano, while Pope John and the patrician Symmachus, both of whom he had ill-treated, look on.[29] Publication of such a fable would, needless to say, have been unthinkable at the height of Gothic power in Italy.

The Germanic tribe that was mythically to preserve the Roman power was the Franks. GREGORY, BISHOP OF TOURS (538–594) produced a lengthy description of their deeds up to his own time.[30] This early historical work, filled with miracles and legends, is peculiarly lacking in influence on the myths of the German past. Gregory mentions nothing of the Trojan origins of the Franks, but does supply some of the names of their primitive history, including Genobaud, Marcomer, and Sunno, leaders of the invasion of Gaul (Gregory I.9, in Buchner, I, 82–83).

These invasions make up much of Gregory's chronicle, as they did the history of his time. If any period of the Middle Ages deserves to be called the "Dark Ages," it is surely his lifetime. The relative equilibrium of medieval political power was still in the making, and major invasions were still vivid memories. He reports, for example, the alliance of Franks and Suebi (also called Alemanni) that overran Gaul and Spain (Gregory II.2 and 9, in Buchner, I, 60–61, 88–89), and recalls the alliance of Goths and Franks against the Huns (II.7, in Buchner, I, 78–79). His work is virtually destitute of the mythical understanding of the Roman Empire, which helps explain the absence of otherwise predictable interpretations. Imperially minded historians would surely have associated the Germanic alliance against the Huns with a defense of the Roman Empire and an anticipation of Germanic rights to it. Gregory, however, could not conceivably have had the historical perspective to see that the Franks were in the process of establishing a center of power and political stability that was in truth the successor of Rome and a basis of medieval Europe.

Gregory's history does contain one legend that hovers on the periphery of the imperial myth. The tyrant Nero sent into exile Saint John the Evangelist, who, after the death of the Emperor, returned from exile and, in his old age, retired to a sepulchre where, not tasting

---

[29] *Dialogorum Libri IV*, IV.30, in J. P. Migne, *PL*, LXXVII (Paris, 1849), 368–69. Cf. Schanz-Hosius, IV.ii, 605ff. and Manitius, I, 92ff.

[30] Ed. and trans. Rudolf Buchner, *Gregor von Tours: Zehn Bücher Geschichten*, 2 vols. (Darmstadt, 1959) [henceforth "Buchner"]. Cf. Manitius, I, 216ff. The history was first published by Badius in 1512 (Potthast, p. 542), and was before that known to Trithemius (*Catalogus*, fol. XLIVrf., *recte* XLVIIrf.).

death, he awaits the coming of the Last Judgement (Gregory I.27, in Buchner, I, 32–33). The exasperating similarity to the legends of Nero and Frederick allows only impressionistic conjecture. The motifs of return and deathlessness seem to have attached themselves permanently to the situation of political or religious oppression. Christian theology added the eschatological element, and with it the simple form of an important legend was fixed.

The stories surrounding Brunihilde of Spain, who survived Gregory by a few years, may have a remote or collateral source in his chronicle. It is, however, more likely that this terrible woman and her reputation survived in popular memory, substantially unaided by written tradition. A "Bisin," King of Thuringia also appears in the Frankish history (Gregory II.12, in Buchner, I, 94–95), and his name may conceivably have found its way into Trithemius's Basan. These seem to be the lot of Gregory's rather tenuous connections with the Renaissance myths of the German past. However credulous his history may seem today, it must have been simply too historical to fire the imagination of his Renaissance successors.

A younger contemporary of both the previous Gregorys, Isidore of Seville (570–636 A.D.), did not suffer from an overwhelmingly modern sense of history and could find echo among imaginative Renaissance historians where the fact-filled account by Gregory of Tours proved uninteresting. Isidore is in the tradition of Cassiodorus, a Roman by birth, a (Visi-) Gothic subject, who fully supported the Germanic suzerainty. The matter is somewhat different in Isidore's case, since the assimilation of the Visigoths in Spain moved swiftly after their acceptance of orthodoxy in Isidore's youth. He nonetheless represents, like Cassiodorus, an accommodation of Roman to barbaric; in the very accommodation he represents as well the first flowering of the Middle Ages.[31]

The region of the world after Asia, Isidore tells us, is Europe, and the second region of Europe after Lower Scythia is Germany. Germany is the home of many peoples, and on account of the fertility of its growing population it has its name.[32] Isidore also suggests that the nations called Germanic receive their name from the immense bodies

---

[31] Cf. Manitius, I, 52ff. Isidore's works went through numerous editions before 1600 (see Potthast, pp. 687–89) and remained influential throughout the Renaissance. His importance to the Middle Ages is too well known to require comment.

[32] W. M. Lindsay, ed., *Isidori Hispalensis Episcopi Etymologiarum sive Originum Libri XX*, 2 vols. (Oxford, 1957), unpaginated: XIV.4.1–4.

of their people (Isidore IX.2.97). The Goths, who are the same as the Getae of antiquity, stem from Magog, son of Japhet, and are a fierce nation (IX.2.27 and 89).[33] Aschanaz, son of Gomer, is father of the Sarmatians (IX.2.32). Another son of Gomer was father of the Phrygians (IX.2.33). The Scythians, like the Goths, stem from Magog, and their first king was called Tanus (IX.2.27; XIII.21.24). In the Renaissance, Aventinus for example considered the Sarmatians, Phrygians, and Scythians all Germans, and Rolevinck considered Tan a Gothic king and ancestor of the Danes. The Burgundians, Isidore tells us after Orosius, take their name from their word for outposts or camps, "burgi" (IX.2.99 and 4.28).

A major figure of national importance but not identified with the origins of peoples is the bishop who translated scripture into the language of the Goths. Isidore spells his name "Gulfilas."[34] His knowledge of the translation undoubtedly came out of Cassiodorus or the *Historia Tripartita*. In the unlikely event that Isidore ever saw a copy of the translation, he could perhaps not even have read it. Despite that, and despite Wulfilas's Arian religion, Isidore seems proud indeed of the achievement.

Isidore mentions nothing of the ancient religion of the Germans that was to find its way into the Renaissance. Of vice and virtue, Isidore preserves Orosius on the subject of Alexander's, Pyrrhus's, and Caesar's respect for Gothic valor.[35] The Saxons were renowned for their hardiness and bravery, which is reflected in their very name (Isidore IX.2.100). Gobelinus Persona's eulogy of the Saxon language relies on Isidore's classification of gutteral (Oriental or Hebrew), palatal (Mediterranean or Greek), and dental (Western or Latin) languages (IX.1.8). The supremacy of the palatal and the identification of Saxon and Greek is Gobelinus's own fancy, however.

The etymologies of Isidore contain little in support of the myth of the *Imperium*. He does point out that in the old days, the king was *sacerdos vel pontifex* [priest or pontiff, with distinct liturgical implications], and that the emperors were regularly known as *pontifices* (VII. 12.14): thus also Cusanus. Byzantine power in Spain was negligible, and yet at Isidore's death in 636, the conventional manner of dating

---

[33] Comp. Theodor Mommsen, ed., *Isidori ... Historia Gothorum Wandalorum Sveborum ...*, MGH auct. antiq. XI, chron. min. II.241–390 (Berlin, 1894), p. 268; Gordon, B. Ford, Jr., and Guido Donini, trans., *Isidore of Seville's History of the Kings of the Goths, Vandals, and Suevi* (Leiden, 1966), pp. 3 and 30–31.

[34] Mommsen, *Historia Gothorum*, p. 270; Ford-Donini, pp. 5–6. Comp. Theodor Mommsen, ed., *Isidori ... Chronica minora ... Chronicorum Epitome*, MGH auct. antiq. XI, chron. min. II.391–506 (Berlin, 1894), p. 469.

[35] Mommsen, *Historia Gothorum*, p. 268; Ford–Donini, p. 3.

included the name of the Emperor in Constantinople, as well as that of the Visigothic King in Spain: [*Isidorus*] *obiit temporibus Heraclii imperatoris et christianissimi Chintilani regis* [Isidore died in the time of Emperor Heraclius and the most Christian King Chintilanus].[36] A residue of the imperial myth obviously survived in far-away Spain. Later, in the ninth century, Isidore was to make vicarious contributions to the legal history of the Middle Ages and hence to the imperial myth, when he lent his name to a series of influential forgeries. Though more or less mythical to begin with, they became critical in the struggle between Church and State, and thus all too historical.

A generation after the death of Isidore, around 660 A.D., several anonymous compilers who go under the name of FREDEGARIUS began to assemble a chronicle out of the works of Jerome, Gregory of Tours, Isidore, and others.[37] This chronicle, its continuators and successors culminating about the year 739 established for written tradition the earliest forms of several important Renaissance myths of the German past.

The Langobards, Fredegarius tells us, come from Schatanavia. When they left their homeland they confronted the Huns, who demanded war. The people of Schatanavia had their women tie their hair about the face, so that the women too would look like bearded warriors and thus deceive the enemy. A great voice, supposedly Wotan's, is thought to have shouted, "These are the Long-beards."[38]

Another, undoubtedly older, version of the origin of the Lombards was transcribed a few years later, ca. 670 A.D., in the reign of Rothar.[39] An island in the north, Scandanan, housed the tribe of the Winniles. Ybor and Agio were the brothers who ruled. Their mother, Gambara, was a very wise woman. The tribe came face to face with the Wandals

[36] Manitius, I, 53.

[37] Manitius, I, 224–25; Potthast, pp. 468–69. Cf. Siegmund Hellmann, "Das Fredegar-Problem," in his *Ausgewählte Abhandlungen zur Historiographie und Geistesgeschichte des Mittelalters*, Helmut Beumann, ed. (Darmstadt, 1961), pp. 101–57, esp. pp. 101–103, 151–53.

[38] Wilhelm von Giesebrecht, trans., "Sagen aus Fredegar und der Chronik der Frankenkönige," in *Zehn Bücher Fränkischer Geschichten vom Bischoff Gregorius von Tours*, 2nd ed., 2 vols., Geschichtsschreiber der deutschen Vorzeit, 2. Gesamtausgabe, 6. Jahrhundert V (Leipzig, n.d. [1879]), II, 279. What the Grimms called the *Epitome* of Gregory in *Deutsche Sagen*, 3rd ed., 2 vols in 1 (Darmstadt, 1960), p. 618, is in fact Fredegarius; see Potthast, p. 543.

[39] *Origo gentis Langobardorum*, in MGH SS rerum langobardicarum et italicarum saec. VI–IX, ed. by L. Bethmann and Georg Waitz (Hannover, 1878), pp. 1–6. Cf. Potthast, p. 881.

in its wanderings, who through their leaders Ambri and Assi asked the Winniles for tribute or war. War was declared. The god Godan had been asked to give the Wandals victory. He replied that he would give the victory to those whom he should first see at sunrise. Gambara prayed to Godan's wife, Frea, for the victory of the Winniles. Frea told Gambara to have the women tie their hair about their chins. The goddess then turned Godan's bed about after he went to sleep, so that at sunrise he would see the Winniles first instead of the Wandals. At sunrise Godan awoke, saw the spectacle, and exclaimed, "who are these long-beards?" Frea said to Godan, "you have given them a name, give them also victory." From that time on, the Winniles were called Longobards. These reports have been proven to be a translation into Latin of a lost Germanic stave-rhyme poem.[40]

Foundations were laid for another myth of origin at this time. The Fredegarius chronicle reports that, after the fall of Troy, the younger Priam, first king of the Franks, fled to Macedon. Later Friga left for Ocean with a part of the nation, as did Francio, who went to the Rhine and founded New Troy. Among the descendents of Francio are Richimer, Theudemer, Clodeo, and Merowech, who gave his name to the Merovingians.[41]

A history of the Frankish kings dated in the first half of the eighth century expands on the Fredegarius invention. It was not only Priam, but Anthenor with him who fled Troy after its fall. While Aeneas proceeded to Italy, the others sailed to the river Don, continuing on to the Maeotian Swamps, where they founded the city of Sicambria. After some years, the Romans required assistance in their wars with the Alani (later called Alemanni) and promised ten years' freedom from tribute to whoever should defeat the Alani. The founders of Sicambria did just that. Emperor Valentinian called them for their valor "Franci," which in Attic means "fierce." After the ten years had passed, the Romans began demanding tribute again. The Franks refused and were driven from their lands to the Rhine. Priam's son Marcomir and Anthenor's son Sunno led them thither. Faramund,

---

[40] William D. Foulke, *History of the Lombards by Paul the Deacon* (Philadelphia and New York, 1907), pp. 346–48.

[41] Giesebrecht, "Sagen aus Fredegar . . . ," pp. 268–69. Cf. Maria Klippel, *Die Darstellung der fränkischen Trojanersage in Geschichtsschreibung und Dichtung vom Mittelalter bis zur Renaissance in Frankreich* (Marburg, 1936), pp. 7ff. and ix–x for texts and bibliography. To the latter: K. L. Roth, "Die Trojasage der Franken," [Pfeiffer's] *Germania*, I (1856), 34–52, and F. Zarncke, "Über die s.g. Trojanersage der Franken," *SB Sächsische Gesellschaft der Wissenschaften*, philol.-hist. Classe, XVIII (1866), 257–86; and [Wilhelm] Wattenbach and Wilhelm Levison, *Deutschlands Geschichtsquellen im Mittelalter: Vorzeit und Karolinger*, 4 vols. and Beiheft (Weimar, 1952–63), I, p. 111, n. 247.

Marcomir's son, was elected king. Later, laws were promulgated by Wisovast, Wisogast, Arogast, and Salegast. Chlodic later became king, and then Merovech, from whom the Merovingians take their name. This work is, incidentally, also the source for the descriptions of the Visigothic Brunihilde's brutal execution. She was torn apart by wild horses—an event which her contemporaries regarded with more than perfect equanimity, indeed, considerable pleasure.[42]

Another text out of the first half of the eighth century, self-credited to Aethicus Hyster or Cosmographicus, adds the last variants to the early Troy myth of the Franks. Francus and Vassus, Trojans, fought with Romulus, were defeated, and fled to Germany. A contemporary "Pseudo-Dares" makes Frigio father of Francus and Vassus.[43]

"Fredegarius," the *Liber Historiae Francorum,* "Aethicus Hyster," and "Pseudo-Dares"—all anonymous or pseudoepigraphal—seem to be the ultimate written sources for the Frankish Troy myth. The whole affair is a historical curiosity, but nonetheless an influential one. The Germanic invaders from the fifth through the eighth centuries had Italy or, more specifically, Rome as the major goal of their influence. In the fifth and sixth centuries it was the Goths; in the sixth and seventh, the Lombards; in the seventh and eighth, the Franks. Contact with Rome in each case brought forth a legendary ancient history. For the Goths, it was the descent from Gog and Magog, the tradition of learning and warlike valor from the time of Hercules to that of Alexander the Great and then Caesar. For the Lombards, it was the divine name-giving and victory in war. Now the Franks begin their long hegemony over western Europe, and they also require an ancient history. A pseudonymous chronicler conveniently grants them the boon with which they acquire an instant antiquity equal to that of the Romans.

The contact with Rome was not necessarily the cause of the creation of origins myths. The Germanic peoples, if we may believe Tacitus, were quite independently inclined to preserve the memory of their ancestors. Rather, the contact with Rome gave the occasion and the model for the appearance of these myths in learned historical writing. The Goths chose or were given a biblical lineage; the Lombards maintained a native tradition; and the Franks borrowed classical anteced-

---

[42] Giesebrecht, "Sagen aus Fredegar . . . ," pp. 282–85, 299; Cf. K. L. Roth, "Die Trojasageder Franken," p. 37. Cf. Manitius, I, 227ff. and Potthast, p. 736, who judges the *Liber historiae Francorum* "dürftig aber zuverlässig."

[43] Cf. K. L. Roth, "Die Trojasage," p. 36; Klippel, *Die Darstellung,* pp. 12–14. Pseudo-Dares should be called Pseudo-pseudo-Dares, since the narrator of the original Troy novel is himself a fake and the Frankish interpolation doubly so. Hartmann Schedel had an Aethicus MS: see Manitius, I, 229–33.

ents. We may assume that all were older than their first preserved appearance in Latin historiography. The equating of Goths and Getae must have been a learned confusion on the part of educated Greeks and Romans who sought to place this unknown and all too present force somewhere in known history. The extension to biblical sources by way of the Getae surely reaches back to the oldest scriptural commentaries. The origins of the Lombards must also be sought in what is for the Germanic tribes dimmest antiquity. Their name was reported at least as early as Tacitus. On the assumption that the etiological myth antedated Christian contact and had its roots in the natural calamities which may have initiated the Great Migrations from Scandinavia around the change of the eras, the Lombard song could be dated tentatively in the first century B.C. Shortly, I shall suggest a similarly ancient precedent for the Frankish Troy myth. The point is that the myths most probably circulated as a part of the general historical consciousness of the times well before they were grafted onto the regular learned historical tradition. Rome provided the occasion by demanding an adequate explanation for the Germanic proximity and its uncomfortable success; Rome provided the model in its own historical writing which demanded an explanation for origins even if they were historically unknowable.

The authority of the Roman model may explain why a warrior people like the Franks would choose a defeated nation like the Trojans for its ancestors.[44] Strong arguments favor this interpretation, to which I might add an important and generally ignored precedent. Lucan (A.D. 39–65) tells us that a tribe in south-central Gaul, the Arverni (whence "Auvergne") who produced Vercingetorix, claimed descent from Troy and thus brotherhood with the Romans.[45] Memory of this claim may have survived until Frankish conquest of Gaul and been simply transferred to the conquerors. The precedent of the *Aeneid* certainly contributed to the choice, particularly since the Franks incorporated previously Roman territory into their realms and saw themselves on occasion as successors rather than usurpers. In this light, the Roman coronation of Charlemagne becomes the culmination of a growing sense of identity, between barbarian intruder and Roman substrate in the West. The objections to Charlemagne's title came, after all, not from Italy but from Byzantium.[46]

---

[44] Cf. Robert W. Hanning, *The Vision of History in Early Britain* (New York and London, 1966), p. 214 n. 47.

[45] Lucan, *Pharsalia* I.427–28, in Duff, pp. 34–35.

[46] Alois Dempf, *Sacrum Imperium*, 3rd ed. (Darmstadt, 1962), p. 145.

The notion of Frankish-Roman assimilation does not, however, explain certain parts of the new Trojan origins fable. The details of the conflict with Rome and the defeat of the Franks do not seem consistent with the upsurge of Frankish power, which is supposed to have given rise to the myth in the first place.[47] Even if the broad outlines were limited by the precedent of the Arverni or some similar, normative tradition, the elaboration in detail must have been the product of free improvisation by the historians. Flight and defeat have a peculiar place in the psychology of the Middle Ages. Normally the signs of dishonor, they characterize countless heroes under the guise of exile. The *Aeneid* may conceivably have determined the pattern with its history of tribulations preceding the founding of the Roman *Imperium*. Perhaps also a more basic psychological pattern prevails, underlying the appearance of this motif in biblical, classical, and northern myths of origin. The details of the Frankish myth remain troublesome nonetheless, and I can find no fully satisfactory interpretation of them.

Once the Frankish myth was established, as it had been by the mid-eighth century, repetitions, additions, and variations did not cease to appear.[48] We shall touch the consequences of the myth as we proceed through the Middle Ages. Toward the end of the thirteenth century, yet another version of the Troy myth entered the tradition, a significant variant since it was to receive widest currency in the German Renaissance. The thirteenth-century version was openly tendentious. Publicistic intent seems suppressed, however, in the original sources of the myth. It begins to emerge openly only when the Franks assume the authority to which their distinguished origins presumably gave them the right, that is, in the time of Charlemagne.

Before turning to the Troy myth at the height of Carolingian power, we shall hastily consider two major medieval historians. The first is the VENERABLE BEDE (ca. 672–735). Like Gregory of Tours, Bede fills his chronicles with Christian miracles, but contributes little to the secular mythology of the German-Germanic past. In the Renaissance, Werner Rolevinck depended on Bede for the reports of Saxon entrance into Britain under Hengist and Horsa, and for the information that the continental Saxons had many satraps rather than one

---

[47] Klippel, p. 9.
[48] Cf. K. L. Roth, pp. 36–37 and Klippel, pp. 15–21 for several later versions.

king.[49] The name of the Germans in the form "Garman" is also preserved in Bede's history, but he is not necessarily Tschudi's source for his etymology of the Germans' name.[50]

Succeeding Bede as chronicler of a new European nation is PAUL THE DEACON (ca. 720–ca. 797). The relationship between Charlemagne, conqueror of the Lombards, and Paul, the patriotic Lombard who once rebelled against the Franks, is an extraordinary one. The pleasure with which Charlemagne received him into his service is one of the historical indications that Charlemagne deserved the personal esteem later ages awarded him.[51]

Paul's history of the Lombards—his own people—preserves several important conventions regarding Germanic antiquity. Isidore of Seville's explanation of the name of the Germans, from the great number of peoples, appears in Paul, as does the traditional story of the origin of the Lombards.[52] The Lombards were originally called Winnili and came from Scandinavia. On account of a great famine they had in part to abandon their homeland. The nation was divided into thirds, and by lot one third was selected to seek out new lands. The chosen third left under its leaders, Ibor and Aio. In the new territory they confronted the Vandals who demanded tribute. Rather than pay, Ibor and Aio, with the approval of their mother Gambara, decided to make war on the Vandals. Paul continues with the obviously pagan story of the naming of the Lombards but rejects it out of hand because of its unchristian connotations. Actually, Paul tells us, the name came simply from the length of the beards. Paul also touches upon the Trojan origins of the Carolingian house, when he explains that the majordomo Anschis (Ansegisal, fl. 635 A.D.) was named after Aeneas's father Anchises (Paul V.23, in Bethmann-Waitz, p. 172).

This explanation of Charlemagne's ancestry was preserved and with it various tales of the Trojan Franks. An anonymous poem on the origin of the Franks (ca. 844 A.D.) changes, without further apology,

---

[49] Bede, *The Ecclesiastical History*, I.15 and V.10, in J. E. King, ed. and trans., *Bedae Opera Historica*, 2 vols., Loeb Classical Library (London, 1954), I, 72–73 and II, 242–43. Cf. Manitius, I, 70ff. Bede's history enjoyed nine printings by 1514, all but one of which were made in Germany (Potthast, p. 139). Badius printed one edition in Paris: P. Renouard, *Bibliographie des impressions et des oeuvres de Josse Badius Ascensius...1462–1535*, 3 vols. (Paris, 1908), II, 147ff. [henceforth "Renouard"].

[50] Bede V.9, in King, II, 234–35.

[51] Manitius, I, 257–58.

[52] Paul I.1–3, 7–9, in L. Bethmann and G. Waitz, eds., *Pauli Historia Langobardorum*, MGH SS rerum langobardicarum et italicarum saec. VI–IX.12–219 (Hannover, 1878), pp. 47–49, 52–53.

the spelling of the majordomo's name to "Anchises."[53] A little later in the ninth century (ca. 867–96), a perfectly conventional genealogy of Frankish kings begins with Priam and Anthenor, proceeds through Marcomir, Suno, Faramund, Clodius, Merovec, Hilderic, and thence into fully historic times.[54] In the Latin poem *Waltharius*, the hero Hagen, whose model in history was presumably Burgundian, becomes a Frank of the seed of Troy.[55] The ancient dignity of the Franks entered OTFRIED VON WEISSENBURG's defense of their language in these years. Otfried (fl. 865) determined to write his Gospel harmony in Frankish, that is, Old High German, rather than in Latin, for he considered the Franks no worse than the Greeks or Romans, Medes or Persians. His choice of these nations for comparison to the Franks makes it clear that in his mind the Franks had taken their place in history alongside the other imperial powers. He gives the Franks Macedonian origins from the race of Alexander the Great and wishes their deserving language to be glorified by a sacred text.[56] Otfried claims to have found these stories of Macedonian descent in a written source.

With the exception of the suppositious source, Otfried is the first to make the connection between Troy and Macedon. The Troy myth allows for this connection, in that the Franks are related to the Phrygians and made to pass through Macedon. The Phrygians, Franks, and Macedonians, all of the same Trojan seed, thus become one nation which can boast Alexander the Great as a member. Although Alexander was occasionally considered German in the Renaissance, and although Otfried was known as early as the 1480s or 1490s, he is not the likely source for that Renaissance notion. The preposterous Alsatian Anonymous, for example, could hardly have read Otfried's Old High German, even if he had had access to a text. In any case, Otfried's remarks represent a notable precedent. He also anticipates typical Renaissance patriotic utterances by his defensive stance, his attacks on the ancients for ignoring or suppressing Frankish history, and the gran-

---

[53] G. H. Pertz, ed., *Regum Francorum Genealogiae*, MGH SS, II.304–14 (Hannover, 1829), p. 313. Cf. Ernst Dümmler, ed., *Poetae Latini Aevi Carolini*, MGH Poetae Latini medii aevi, II (Berlin, 1884), 143.

[54] Pertz, *Regum Francorum*, pp. 310–11.

[55] *Waltharius*, Karl Strecker, ed., in MGH Poetarum Latinorum ... Tomus VI, fasc. 1 (Weimar, 1951), pp. 24–25. The problem of the dating is far from settled. Strecker placed it in Carolingian times, others in Ottonian. Cf. F. P. Magoun, Jr., and H. M. Smyser, *Walter of Aquitaine*, Connecticut College Monographs, IV (New London, Conn., 1950), p. 4.

[56] Otfried I.1, 87–93, in Oskar Erdmann, ed., *Otfrids Evangelienbuch*, 3rd ed. by Ludwig Wolff, Altdeutsche Textbibliothek, XLIX (Tübingen, 1957), p. 13. Cf. K. L. Roth, "Die Trojasage" p. 37 and Klippel, *Die Darstellung . . .*, p. 18.

diosity of his claims for Frankish distinction. Even in wording he approaches the nationalistic encomia of Conrad Celtis, who knew Otfried through Trithemius. Otfried may have been a source for Celtis, but closer studies than I have made would be necessary to prove the connection. The inchoate nationalism of the Carolingian Renaissance and the Renaissance proper, however, did have certain elective affinities which would explain the similarity of expression whether or not the connections were proved.

A similar nationalism moved Paul the Deacon to write his Lombard history, and with far greater effect in the politics of the future. Upon the retreat of Frankish power from Italy, the Lombards would remain for a thousand years one of the main contenders for control of the peninsula, and Paul's chronicle provided the necessary historical and mythical legitimation. That is only of peripheral interest here, since the myths of the Lombard past coincided only in part with the special interests of the myth-makers of the German past. The coincidence includes names and anecdotes which Renaissance men found useful for their patriotic ends.

He preserves for their use such names as the first King of the Lombards Agelmund, son of Aio, who chose for his successor Lamissio, a babe left to drown by his mother (Paul I.14ff., in Bethmann-Waitz, pp. 54ff.). Knowledge of Garibald of the Bavarians seems also to have been passed primarily by Paul (I.17 and III.10, in Bethmann-Waitz, pp. 56 and 97). The scant authentic details of Germanic worship available to the Middle Ages and Renaissance are directly traceable to Paul's recognition of "Godan" and "Frea" as divinities of the Lombards. He explains that Wotan or Godan was equivalent to Mercury and was thought to have lived in Greece ages before (I.9, in Bethmann-Waitz, p. 53). Paul took this, however, not from a popular source, but from a *Vita* of Saint Columban from about the year 664.[57] The Lombards as Christians venerated Saint Michael the Archangel (V.41, in Bethmann-Waitz, p. 161). At first glance this may not appear relevant. Saint Michael was, however, among the most popular objects of religious veneration among the Germanic peoples, even in the earliest years of their christianization, and his popularity continued throughout the Middle Ages. It has been suggested that the warrior divinities, Wotan and Tiu, found a safer identity in the valorous Michael.[58] The

---

[57] Cf. Foulke, *History of the Lombards*, p. 363, and Potthast, p. 1251; also, Jonas Bobiensis, *Vita S. Columbani Abbatis*, in Migne, *PL*, LXXXVII (Paris, 1863), 1041.

[58] Jacob Grimm, *Deutsche Mythologie*, 4th ed., 3 vols. (1875; reprinted Darmstadt, 1965), II, 698–99. Cf. Jakob Baechtold, *Die Stretlinger Chronik*, Bibliothek älterer Schiftwerke der Deutschen Schweiz, I (Frauenfeld, 1877), pp. li–lxii.

period in question here witnessed frequent reference to Michael, as for example, in the works of Gregory of Tours and Alcuin.[59] Although the Alsatian Anonymous of the time of Maximilian I probably did not know these works, his vision of Saint Michael at Belgrade seems clearly a continuation of the medieval Michael cult which they represent.

It is touching under the circumstances of the Frankish suppression of the Lombard Kingdom in Italy that Paul stresses among the virtues of the Lombards their love of freedom. The Lombards fought so fiercely not only for victory but also for the glory of freedom (Paul I. 10, in Bethmann-Waitz, p. 53). The Lombards had an easy solution for the problem of selecting men for single combat: a man of servile station would gladly volunteer to be the Lombards' man, because if he was victorious he and his progeny would be given their freedom (I.12, in Bethmann-Waitz, pp. 53–54). Paul extends the notion of warlike valor across other of the Germanic peoples. He describes the alliance of Saxons and Lombards for the march to Italy, and the later return of the Saxons to their homelands. These they found occupied by Swabians. When the Saxons were defeated in the attempt to retake the land, they vowed to cut neither beard nor hair until they avenged themselves on their Swabian enemies (II.6 and III.8, in Bethmann-Waitz, pp. 75–76 and 96–97). In his *Historia Romana*, a continuation of Eutropius's *Epitome*, Paul repeats Orosius on Alexander the Great's caution before the Goths.[60] Paul amplifies Europius's bare account of Marius's victory over the Germans with a description of the frenzied sense of honor among the defeated German women and the death of so many of them and their children (V.2, in Droysen, p. 85).

Paul the Deacon did not contribute anything noteworthy to the myth of the *Imperium*. A few years after his death, Rome witnessed on Christmas Day of the year 800 the fateful symbolic action that was to determine much of the subsequent history of Europe. With the coronation of Charlemagne, the Germanic assimilation of the Roman Empire signalled by Orosius and Cassiodorus was completed in a public, virtually sacramental gesture. The world of letters came to immediate support of the momentous action. In this triumph of prestige and myth, of the impractical and intangible in political science, the Troy legend of the Franks could find a useful place in the

---

[59] Gregory, VI.29: Buchner, II, 48–49; Alcuin in Dümmler, *Poetae Latini*, I.i, 348.

[60] Paul XI.15, in H. Droysen, ed. *Eutropi Breviarium ab urbe condita*, MGH auct. antiq., II (Berlin, 1879), p. 188.

service of the *Imperium*. Charlemagne's minister of education, so to speak, the Northumbrian ALCUIN (730–804) addresses Charles, a German Frank, with the title of Emperor Augustus, "pater patriae," calls him "decus ecclesiae," and places Charles over Rome, the "caput mundi."[61] Writing about 800, one of Alcuin's colleagues and successors, DUNGAL, also known as the Irish Exile (*Hibernicus Exul*), calls Charles Caesar and his just Frankish people the royal nation of Troy. As soon as Charles had been crowned, his ancient Trojan origin was summoned to affirm his worthiness for the new office. The *Romuleum Imperium*, Dungal continues, is ruled by the peaceful lord—Charles.[62] The Empire of Romulus, a descendent of Troy, is in the hands of Charles, a descendent of Troy.

Soon after Charlemagne's imperial coronation, a prayer for the Emperor and his Empire was inserted into the Canon of the Mass, the part that remains the same from day to day. Until recently—it was still optional in the nineteenth century—the Good Friday liturgy contained the prayer:[63]

Oremus et pro christianissimo imperatore nostro, ut deus omnipotens subditas illi faciat omnes barbaros nationes ad nostram perpetuam pacem.

[And let us pray for our most Christian emperor, that almighty God may make all barbarian nations subject to him toward our lasting peace.]

Charlemagne's counsellor and Alcuin's student EINHARD (770–840) composed what is considered the finest biography written in the Middle Ages.[64] Einhard's story of the life of Charlemagne adds relatively few details to the myth of the Empire. As soon as they are presented, it will be clear how influential they were. The Frankish King marched into Italy and defeated the Lombards. This march was in the service

---

[61] Dümmler, *Poetae Latini*, I.i.258. Poems of Alcuin were published in 1529; cf. Dümmler, p. 162. He was of course known to Trithemius (*Catalogus*, fol. LIIᵛf.). Cf. Manitius, I, 273ff.

[62] Dümmler, *Poetae Latini*, I.ii, 395, 398, 401. Cf. K. L. Roth, "Die Trojasage," p. 36, and Klippel, *Die Darstellung* p. 15; on Dungal, cf. Manitius, I, 370ff.

[63] Hans Hirsch, "Der mittelalterliche Kaisergedanke in den liturgischen Gebeten," in *Aufsätze zur mittelalterlichen Urkundenforschung*, ed. Theodor Meyer (Darmstadt, 1965), p. 3; Herbert Grundmann and Hermann Heimpel, eds., *Alexander von Roes: Schriften*, MGH Staatsschriften des späteren Mittelalters, I.1 (Stuttgart, 1958), p. 140 n. 1.

[64] Manitius, I, 642. Reinhold Rau, ed. and trans., *Einhard: Leben Karls des Grossen*, in *Quellen zur karolingischen Reichsgeschichte*, 3 vols. (Darmstadt, 1960–62), I, 157–211. It was first printed in Cologne in 1521 under the editorship of Hermann Count of Neuenar (Potthast, p. 395), one of the first scholars to explode the Hunibald of Trithemius (who also knew the *Vita* (*Catalogus*, fol. LIVᵛ). It is cited by Wimpheling and numerous other humanists.

of the Church, for it restored Italy to the popes (Einhard, ch. V, in Rau, pp. 172–73). His service to the Church is further illustrated by his construction of the basilica at Aachen, by his gifts of alms all over the world, and by his donations to the bishoprics (Einhard, ch. XXVIf., XXXIII, in Rau, pp. 196ff., 204ff.). Charlemagne took the town of Eresburg and baptized many of the pagan Northmen ("de Nordleudi"), according to the imperial annals sometimes ascribed to Einhard.[65] Einhard's biography tells the story of how Pope Leo, having lost his eyes and tongue to the fury of the Romans, turned to Charles for help, and of how Charles came to Rome, there receiving the titles of *Imperator* and *Augustus* (Ch. XXVII, in Rau, pp. 198–99). The imperial annals report as follows. Just as Charles was rising from prayer at the grave of Saint Peter, in order to hear the Christmas liturgy, Pope Leo placed the crown of the Empire on Charles's head, and the whole of the Roman people cried out (Rau, *Reichsannalen*, pp. 74–75):

> Carolo augusto a Deo coronato magno et pacifico imperatori Romanorum vita et victoria!

This acclamation was apparently the constitutive legal element in the creation of the Emperor.[66] The supremacy of the Empire was understood by Einhard and made by him to extend well beyond the actual borders of Charlemagne's formidable realm. The Spanish monarchs claimed the status of friends of the Empire. The Scots were pleased to consider themselves his subjects. Even Harun of the Persians granted Charles *potestas* over the holy places (Einhard ch. XVI, in Rau, pp. 184ff.).[67]

Up to this point, there has not been in the contemporary accounts any emphasis on Charles's being a Frank. Nor does Einhard stress it particularly. He mentions, however, that Charles named in his own language—"propriam linguam"—the twelve months and the twelve winds, e.g., "Ianuarium Wintarmanoth," "Februarium Hornung . . . subsolanum . . . ostroniwint," "eurum ostsudroni," etc. As soon as Charles had the imperial title, the new Emperor was concerned with

---

[65] Reinhold Rau, ed., *Reichsannalen in Quellen zur karolingischen Reichsgeschichte*, I, 1–155; see pp. 40–41. Potthast (p. 394) outlines the various attributions of authorship and mentions that the annals were printed in the same 1521 volume that contained the *Vita Karoli*. Manitius (I, 639) casts his vote on the authorship of the annals in favor of Einhard.

[66] Hans Hirsch, "Der mittelalterliche Kaisergedanke . . . ," pp. 8–9.

[67] Cf. Robert Holtzmann, *Der Weltherrschaftsgedanke des mittelalterlichen Kaisertums und die Souveränität der europäischen Staaten* (Darmstadt, 1953), p. 8.

establishing a uniform code of Frankish law and with collecting *barbara et antiquissima carmina*—by which Einhard must have meant Germanic poems of the type of the lone survivor, the *Hildebrandslied* (Einhard ch. XXIX, in Rau, pp. 200–201). Einhard was clearly aware that the Roman Emperor was German. Upon Charlemagne's death in 814, an anonymous poet launched into a lament. The Franks and Romans suffer at the death of Charles. Woe to Rome and the people of Rome. *Heu mihi misero!*[68] The identity of the Frankish-Germanic and the Roman in the new Emperor was obviously complete.

Implications of the supremacy of the Empire appeared in Alcuin with Charles's overlordship of Rome, the "caput mundi" and with Einhard's extension of his *potestas* over foreign lands. Standard terminology for the Emperor in the ninth century was "totius mundi dominus."[69] NOTKER I BALBULUS of St. Gall, the sainted writer of sequences, called Charles in his biography of the Emperor (ca. 884 A.D.), "caput orbis" and "episcopus episcoporum," underscoring both the supremacy and the sanctity of the Empire.[70]

By a gathering of some of Charlemagne's titles and a recollection of Einhard's description of Charles's interest in his German language, all the elements of the myth of the Empire fall into place: he who named the months and winds in German was *Caesar, Imperator, Augustus, pater patriae*, was *christianissimus, decus ecclesiae, episcopus episcoporum*, was *totius mundi dominus*, overlord of the *caput orbis*. In other words, almost as soon as Charlemagne was invested with the imperial distinction, the myth of the Empire as it would be passed on to the Renaissance and beyond sprang from the head of the medieval imagination, fully clad in its German, Roman, sacred, and supreme characteristics.

The remainder of the Carolingian period brings some added incidentals to various myths of the German past. HRABANUS MAURUS (784–865), a student of Alcuin, placed among those who speak a language derived from German ("theodisca") the Marcomanni whom he

---

68 Dümmler, *Poetae Latini*, I.ii, 407–8.

69 Pope John VIII summons Louis II, Charlemagne's great-grandson, to become Emperor and thus *totius mundi dominus*: Heinrich Finke, *Weltimperialismus und nationale Regungen im späteren Mittelalter*, Freiburger Wissenschaftliche Gesellschaft, IV (Freiburg/Br. and Leipzig, 1916), p. 16.

70 I.25–26, in Reinhold Rau, ed. and trans., *Notker: Taten Karls*, in *Quellen zur karolingischen Reichsgeschichte*, III, 359ff. On Notker, see Manitius (I, 354ff.) who is enthusiastic about Notker's stories of Charles, several of which anticipate important literary themes.

equated with the Nordmanni.[71] Although Hrabanus himself would hardly have thought in ethnic or nationalistic terms, his testimony may have provided grounds for the Renaissance to include the Normans among the Germans. In any case, he provides the important precedent of name transference. The Marcomanni were extinct as a separate entity by Hrabanus's time. Their name, however, survived in Latin historical writing. A newly important force on the continent, the Normans, who had no proper historical credentials, could be placed without difficulty into the known, learned tradition. They had to come from somewhere, and what was known about ethnology came from the classics—thus they had to appear somewhere in the classics. The medieval pattern had no more room for an ethnological nova than it did for an astronomical one.

Hrabanus is known as the first *Praeceptor Germaniae*, and with good reason, for most of the Germans of the Carolingian Renaissance were at one or other time under his tuition. His students also had the splendid habit of outshining their somewhat pedantic master. One of the brightest of these luminaries was WALAHFRID STRABO (ca. 808–49), whose early death was sorrowfully commemorated by Hrabanus. Walahfrid, like his master, made many greater contributions to medieval thought than these tenuous references to the myths of the German past may indicate. They, however, and not his great contributions are at issue here. Walahfrid perpetuated Gregory the Great's pejorative opinion of Theodoric the Goth. An equestrian statue presumed to represent Theodoric was brought from Ravenna to Aachen by Charlemagne back in 801. It was an event of some magnitude, and survived in living memory throughout the period. Theodoric was very much a popular hero. The transference of the statue and its presence in Aachen no doubt helped confirm this adulation. Walahfrid used a description of the occasion to denounce the Gothic king for his heresy and arrogance, contrasting him to the just and learned Emperor, Louis the Pious.[72] Theodoric's fame was preserved in the oral poetry of the vernacular, perhaps even in the *barbara et antiquissima carmina* which Charlemagne collected. This poetry was probably still in large part pagan, and as a consequence ordered destroyed by Louis. Walahfrid's

---

[71] Rabanus Maurus, *De Inventione linguarum* in J. P. Migne, *PL*, CXII (Paris, 1852), 518–19. Cf. Manitius, I, 288–89. Both Hrabanus and his student Walahfrid Strabo were known and admired in the Renaissance, e.g., Trithemius, *Catalogus*, fols. LVᵛ and LVIᵛ.

[72] *De imagine Tetrici* in Dümmler, *Poetae Latini*, II, 370ff. Cf. Manitius, I, 302ff. esp. pp. 310–11. On the symbolic significance of Theodoric's statue for Charlemagne's imperial policies, cf. Heinz Löwe, *Von Theoderich dem Grossen zu Karl dem Grossen* (Darmstadt, 1959), passim, esp. pp. 7–8 and 66–67.

poem is thus not only a eulogy of the new Emperor, but an act of Christian apologetics against a cherished secular tradition.

Yet another student of Hrabanus, RUDOLF OF FULDA (fl. 863) wrote an account of a more acceptable transference of monuments, the relics of Saint Alexander. His account described incidentally the origins of the Saxons, as we saw them mentioned by Meisterlin and rejected by Krantz: the Saxons stem from the Angles in Britain and were forced to leave their homeland because of famine. Upon their arrival in Germany, they battled against the Thuringians.[73]

Further anticipations of Renaissance conventions appear in a PSEUDO-ISIDORE of about 883, a list of the virtues and vices of nations. The Goths are known for their violence and sobriety; the Franks, for their ferocity, nobility, bravery, and seriousness; the Saxons, for their harshness and perseverance; and the Swabians, for their uncleanliness.[74] Such a list is a clear example of the Middle Ages' passion for organizing knowledge. A mutation of this or a similar catalogue erupts in the Renaissance judgement of peoples, as in various unkind remarks about the manners of the Saxons or the virtue of Swabian women. The convention of such catalogues was quite widespread in the Renaissance, and in fact, survives today on the lips of those willing to tell any listener the last word about the virtues and vices housed in neighboring cities, provinces, and countries. If Celtis's and Aventinus's extraordinary judgement on the teetotaling habits of the ancient Germans has any medieval source at all, it may lie in the equally extraordinary notion in Pseudo-Isidore that the Goths (or any Germanic nation) were renowned for their sobriety. From Tacitus on, the Germans are consistently criticized for their drunkenness.

The early Renaissance documents theorizing on the Empire were produced at a time of minimal imperial power. Aeneas Sylvius, Cusanus, and Hermann Peter aus Andlau wrote in the reign of Frederick III, whose power compared most unfavorably with that of his namesakes. Analogously, one of the earliest medieval documents theorizing solely on the newly revived Empire was written at low ebb, near the end of Carolingian authority. EUTROPIUS, a Lombard priest writing around 900, composed a brief tract similar in title to its Renaissance counterparts: *De Juribus ac Privilegiis Imperatorum in Imperio Ro-*

---

[73] Trans. by Paul Hirsch in *Widukind: Sächsische Geschichten*, 5th ed., Geschichtsschreiber der deutschen Vorzeit, XXXIII (Leipzig, 1931), p. 153. Cf. Manitius, I, 670–71 and Potthast, p. 1151.

[74] Mommsen, *Isidori ... Historia Gothorum*, p. 389–90.

mano.[75] The document itself does not seem very influential, discussing primarily the religious function of the Empire by the example of Charlemagne's defense of the Faith. I mention the work only because it prefigures the publicistic efforts not only of the Renaissance but also of the later Middle Ages. The next important propagandistic works on the Empire were written during or shortly after the Great Inter-regnum, when the political power of the Empire was at its absolute nadir. It may be unfair to generalize from this scanty evidence, but myths of political grandeur do seem to be of greatest interest to theo-reticians in periods of severest political impotence.

This impression I find confirmed in the world chronicle of a more renowned contemporary of Eutropius, REGINO OF PRÜM (fl. 906–908),[76] by contrast to the findings of an eminent historian—which findings I shall discuss in a moment. Regino's chronicle is reminiscent of the traditional forms of Orosius and Paul the Deacon. However, he lacks their relative originality in the presentation of older history, for which he depends upon them. In this way he anticipates the most conven-tional form of the medieval chronicle: straightforward imitation in the older epochs and some independence in the newer. His is one of the encyclopedic histories that saved the medieval man countless trips to the sources, and that, for our purposes, represents the status of the mythical past in the calm between Carolingian and Ottonian flowerings.

Regino repeats Paul the Deacon, and thus indirectly Isidore, on the etymology of the German name. Among the many peoples produced by the fecund land were the Scythians and Hungarians. The wives of these peoples founded the realm of the Amazons (Rau, pp. 282ff.). The moral lessons inherent in history find support in the damnable lives and deserved deaths of Theodoric, who persecuted Pope John and Boethius (not Symmachus—Migne, col. 26), and Brunihilde, who suffered just retribution for her many malefactions (col. 33).

Charlemagne is known to have entered Saxony and taken "Heres-burgh," where he baptized many of the Northmen—"de Nordliudis" —in the Elbe (Migne, col. 56). Regino extracts from Einhard also the

---

[75] J. P. Migne, *PL,* CXXIX (Paris, 1853), 961–68. Cf. Potthast, p. 437.

[76] I use the edition in J. P. Migne, *PL,* CXXXII (Paris, 1852), 9–172, and for the later parts, the edition and translation by Reinhold Rau, *Regino von Prüm: Chronik,* in *Quellen zur karolingischen Reichsgeschichte,* III, 179–319. Regino's chronicle was used by such historians as Hermann of Reichenau and Otto of Freis-ing. In the Renaissance it was published by Sebastian Rothenhan in Mainz (1521). Cf. Rau, *Quellen,* III, 10; Manitius, I, 695ff., Potthast, p. 956. Trithemius knew the work: *Catalogus,* fol. LX^r, and see Migne, *PL,* CXXXII, col. 178.

appeal of the mutilated pope Leo to Charles (col. 64). From the imperial annals he takes the acclaim of the Roman people, *Carolo Augusto a Deo coronato* . . . , including the detail that it was thrice repeated (col. 65). In the time of Charlemagne, Regino relates, all of "Brittania" was subject to the Franks (col. 64), forming this remark out of materials in the imperial annals (Rau, pp. 48ff.). He means, I assume, Britanny. This or a similar report led Bebel to declare that Britain was German.

In his description of the deeds of Charlemagne, Regino supports the myth of the Empire. Its Roman character is declared in the Roman coronation of Charles and his title "Augustus." Its sanctity is affirmed in Charlemagne's service to religion in general and the popes in particular. Its supremacy is exemplified in the extent of Charles's conquests, and its German character is bound up with this, when Regino makes "Brittania" subject specifically to the Franks rather than the Empire.

In connection with the Frankish suzerainty, Heinz Löwe has suggested that Regino did not identify the Carolingian realm with the *Imperium Romanum*, indeed, that he was able to tear himself entirely away from the traditional theological associations of worldly political power.[77] Löwe's arguments maintain that Regino saw the late Carolingians as Emperors in name only (Löwe, p. 118). In general reservation to this position, I suggest that names and titles in the Middle Ages were a very serious business. Modern distinctions between name and thing have an ancient history in philosophical discourse, but they can hardly be said to exist in the practical writing of the Middle Ages. The citations from Regino used by Löwe to prove his point (entries to the years 849 and 898: Rau, *Quellen*, III, 302–3 and 308–9) make it perfectly clear that Regino was no exception. Wido ruled Italy and bore the name of Emperor. Upon his death, Lambert went to Rome and had the Pope crown him with the diadem of the Empire. "Imperatoris . . . nomen" and "diadema imperii" are stylistic circumventions for *Imperator* and *Caesar*. When Ludwig defeated Berengar (entry to the year 898) he entered Rome where, crowned by the Pope, he was called Emperor. "Coronatus" and "appelatur" refer to the major symbolic actions of the creation of an emperor, the crowning and the acclamation, and do not imply "mere" naming. Löwe's remaining points seem to me to suffer from similar anachronisms. If title and

---

[77] Heinz Löwe, "Regino von Prüm und das historische Weltbild der Karolingerzeit," in *Geschichtsdenken und Geschichtsbild im Mittelalter*, ed. Walther Lammers, Wege der Forschung, XXI (Darmstadt, 1961), pp. 117–24.

office were indistinguishable to the Middle Ages, how much more so ancient and medieval Rome or secular and eschatological history.

Löwe's argumentation is based upon distinctions which, I believe, Regino could not have made. Of these, one between the Roman Empire and the German realm seems to me most anachronistic. To the best of my knowledge, only one German medieval historian after Charlemagne chose to separate the two concepts—and he did so under special circumstances. With the exception of Widukind of Corvey (to be considered below), the *Imperium* was regarded as wholly German and wholly Roman. Distinctions certainly existed between Roman and German, but the *Imperium* did not share them. A defense of Germans or an attack on Romans need not have implied either a denial of the Roman character of the Empire or the assertion of a separate German *Imperium*. To the mind of the Middle Ages a German Empire did not supersede the Roman Empire; the Empire of the Romans, in order to survive, came into the hands of the Germans. And that is an entirely different matter.

Without the category of the German-Roman *Imperium* it is impossible to understand such apparently inconsistent views as those held by Liutprand of Cremona. Liutprand, one of the most readable of medieval historians, relates that on his embassy to Constantinople for Otto the Great (A.D. 968) he told Emperor Nicephorus, who naturally considered himself Emperor of the Romans:[78]

> History tells us that Romulus, from whom the Romans get their name, was a fratricide born in adultery . . . we Lombards, Saxons, Franks, Lotharingians, Bavarians, Swabians and Burgundians . . . can find nothing more insulting to say than—"You Roman!"

These remarks were inspired by Liutprand's less than equivocal disaffection for the Greeks. He did not even shrink from using that old chestnut, "Learn the wiles of the Greeks and from one crime know them all" (*Aeneid* II.65; *Embassy*, ch. XXX, in Wright, p. 252). The anti-Greek feelings fashionable among some German Renaissance men had precedents. Modern Byzantinists have never quite forgiven "the ineptness of the hot-blooded diplomat," Liutprand.[79]

---

[78] *Embassy*, Ch. XII, in *The Works of Liudprand of Cremona*, F. A. Wright, trans. (London, 1930), pp. 242–43. Cf. Manitius, II, 166ff. Works of Liutprand were printed by Badius in 1512; see Potthast, p. 742 and Renouard, I, 79. Trithemius knew him under the name of "Eutrandus" (*Catalogus*, fol. LXIrf.).

[79] Karl Krumbacher, et al., *Geschichte der Byzantinischen Literatur*, 2nd ed., Handbuch der Altertumswissenschaft, IX.1 (Munich, 1897), p. 986.

Despite Liutprand's outburst against the Romans and his remarkable sense of Germanic identity, Otto remains for the West, as Liutprand reports, "august emperor of the Romans," and Nicephorus merely "emperor of the Greeks" (*Embassy*, ch. XLVII, in Wright, p. 263).[80] Among the titles preserved in Liutprand's account is "pale death of the Saracens," with which the Greeks acclaim Nicephorus (*Embassy*, Ch. X, in Wright, p. 241). I have found no earlier reference to this title in the main lines of western historical literature. Its application to the Ottos has later origins, which we shall consider in connection with Otto of Freising and Gotfried of Viterbo. I pass over the remainder of Liutprand's notions and prejudices, since they seem to have found little response in the Renaissance. He cannot be passed over altogether, however, because his history is incomprehensible outside the framework of the mythically charged *Imperium*. He represents the trend, and attention must be called to the trend before noting the exception.

Liutprand's equally readable, though less pungent contemporary, HROTSWITHA OF GANDERSHEIM (fl. 972), whom Conrad Celtis discovered and praised, also supported the imperial myth. In her metrical history of the deeds of Otto the Great, she addressed the Emperor straightaway as ruler of the Empire that stems from Julius Caesar, and that by divine ordination has passed from the Franks to the Saxons.[81] She clearly understood the harmony of the German possession of the Empire of Rome.

WIDUKIND, a third representative of the Ottonian learned flowering, does not permit such harmony. His view of the *Imperium francorum* is, as far as I can tell, a mythical hapaxlegomenon. Widukind in his Saxon history (ca. 958–73) passes over Otto the Great's Roman coronation altogether, and has the Saxon Emperor receive the Empire of the Franks at Aachen.[82] The other aspects of the imperial myth, the Em-

---

[80] Konrad Burdach, *Rienzo und die geistige Wandlung seiner Zeit* (Berlin, 1913–28), pp. 194–98 discusses Liutprand's sense of Germanic identity. Although a Lombard, Liutprand probably spoke Romance, since Lombardic was on the verge of dying out altogether. A family as high placed and politically active as Liutprand's would be likely to have accepted the language of international communication rather early. This makes his sense of Germanic identity in contrast to the "Romans" all the more remarkable.

[81] H. Homeyer, ed., *Hrotsvithae Opera* (Munich, 1970), p. 406.

[82] II.1, in Hirsch, *Widukind: Sächsische Geschichten*, pp. 64–66. Cf. Mario Krammer, ed., *Quellen zur Geschichte der deutschen Königswahl und des Kurfürstenkollegs*, 2 vols. (Berlin and Leipzig, 1911–12), I, 3. Cf. Manitius, I, 714ff. and Potthast, pp. 1113–14. The Saxon history was known to Gobelinus Persona and Albert Krantz; MSS were in the possession of Trithemius and Peutinger: Hirsch, *Widukind*, p. XXXVIf.; Manitius, II, 815; Trithemius, *Catalogus*, fol. LXIʳ. See also Oswald Holder-Egger, "Über eine zweite neue Widukind Handschrift (aus dem Besitze

pire's sanctity and supremacy, are maintained. Otto's duties include protection of the faith. His realm extends over most of Europe, specifically Germany, Italy, and Gaul. Distant nations send tribute (Widukind I.34, II.1, II.56, in Hirsch, pp. 49, 66, 134). For Widukind, however, the Empire was not that of the Romans but that of the Franks, by which he meant Germans.[83]

The importance of Widukind's Saxon history goes well beyond his extraordinary view of the Empire. As far as the Renaissance is concerned, Widukind is the remotest written source for one of the most popular myths of origin, the Macedonian ancestry of the Saxons. Certain Greeks in the army of Alexander the Great fled the conquered lands after the death of their king (*Widukind* I.2, in Hirsch, p. 7). Their course into Europe follows, where these Macedonians became known as Saxons. Their Greek origins seem supported by the fact that Apollo, Hercules, and Mars were worshipped among the Saxons. Widukind thought the Greek Mars to be Hermes, and hence called their famous sanctuary, the "Hirminsul," the columns of Mars (I.12, in Hirsch, pp. 23–24).

Widukind—rather original, indeed almost unique—was a most influential author. Trithemius may well have taken inspiration from him for the fiction of an independent Frankish Empire, and very probably used Widukind's reports of Frankish-Saxon alliances (I.14, in Hirsch, p. 26) as a basis for the mythical brotherhood of the two tribes. Widukind was a Saxon writing at a time of Saxon hegemony. As a self-conscious historian, he felt the need to justify the new authority, to make the Saxons as worthy as the Franks had been to bear world power. He minimized Charlemagne's bloody wars with the Saxons, certainly because the Saxons would appear in too unfavorable a light. They are made worthy successors to the Frankish *Imperium*. It is as though Widukind distrusted a double transference of the Roman *Imperium* from Romans or Greeks to Franks and then to Saxons. It seems that he somehow foresaw the catastrophic difficulties arising from the Roman pretensions of the German monarch. The Ottonians were among the most enthusiastic partisans of German-Roman assim-

---

Konrad Peutingers)," *Neues Archiv der Gesellschaft für ältere deutsche Geschichtskunde*, XXXVI (1911), 521–37. Cuspinianus and Irenicus were thought also to have used Widukind: Henricus Meibom, *Rerum Germanicarum Tomi III* (Helmstedt, 1688), I, 626. It was well enough known to enjoy a place on a sixteenth-century index of forbidden books: Fr. Heinrich Reusch, ed., *Die Indices Librorum Prohibitorum des sechzehnten Jahrhunderts*, BLVS, CLXXVI (Tübingen, 1886), p. 592.

[83] Fritz Vigener, *Bezeichnung für Volk und Land der Deutschen vom 10. bis zum 13. Jahrhundert* (Heidelberg, 1901), p. 13.

ilation,[84] so Widukind was writing for deaf ears. His opinions were so out of keeping with the accepted myth that he was violently attacked, even before his work was published in its final redaction.[85] As far as the creation of mythical origins is concerned, Widukind is fully in the tradition. His explanations are perfectly analogous to the Gothic, Lombard, and Frankish myths and to their rise at a time of political significance. They were a form of legitimation. Otherwise, he is a troublesome exception, not fully explained by the tradition. The precedents, such as do exist, regularly refer to an independent realm prior to Roman contact or, at worst, parallel to it. Widukind extends the principle in time and makes Otto's monarchy supersede the Roman power—an interpretation that would appear to be a mythical impossibility in the tenth century. Widukind describes an event that did not take place until Napoleon: the formal dissolution of the Roman Empire and the succession of an *Imperium Francorum*. This may have been mythically suitable for Napoleon's time and designs, but was premature for Ottonian Europe. I take comfort in the contemporary attacks on Widukind as an indication of his mythical aberrance.

A strongly independent spirit like Widukind does not appear again as an identifiable personality in medieval German historiography for many years. At the turn of the turn of the millennia, tradition has become the binding criterion. The texts preserve or recombine, but rarely produce something entirely new. Those rarities are, of course, of the greatest importance to our subject, but they do not make for a stable historical discipline. Without this stability, the tradition would have collapsed altogether. A characteristically unoriginal text from this period is the *Historia Miscella*, attributed to one LANDULFUS SAGAX. The work is in effect a third edition of Eutropius's *Breviarium* of Roman history, Paul the Deacon's *Historia Romana* being the second. The so-called Landulfus adds little of specific interest to our subject, although he seems to be the later historians' source for such information as the division of the Goths into four nations, the Gothi, Ypogothi, Gepides, and Wandali. His importance resides in his preservation of Germanic materials out of older texts. Authors relating the

---

[84] P. E. Schramm, *Kaiser, Rom-und Renovatio*, 2 vols., Studien der Bibliothek Warburg, XVII (Leipzig and Berlin, 1929), I, 109f.

[85] Cf. Helmut Beumann, "Widukind von Korvei als Geschichtsschreiber und seine politische Gedankenwelt," in Walther Lammers, *Geschichtsdenken und Geschichtsbild im Mittelalter*, Wege der Forschung, XXI (Darmstadt, 1961), pp. 160–61.

victory of Marius and the defeat of Varus, for example, cited him while seeming to quote the original sources, Eutropius, Orosius, and Paul.[86]

Within a few years (ca. 1004/8), a monk from the monastery at Fleury, AIMONIUS by name, composed a history of the Franks. He preserved Paul's tale of Lombard origins and combined the previous Troy myths of Frankish origins. Aimonius explained that the Lombards had been called Winili, came from an island called Scandinavia, were led out by Ibor and Aio, and were later ruled by Agelmund, son of Aio.[87] He explained the Frankish origins in the version with Priam and Anthenor leaving Troy, and then proceeded to identify Francio with Friga. These Franks then became the Macedonians (Phrygians?) and were ancestors of Philip and Alexander. Aimonius continued his history of the Franks through Marcomir, Sunno, Genebaud, Pharamundus, and Merovaeus (*Historia Francorum* II.13, in Migne, cols. 637–40).[88] Although the various elements are familiar, the combination of Frankish and Macedonian is rare. A German Alexander the Great appears in the Renaissance and in Otfried of Weissenburg. Renaissance authors were not likely to trouble themselves with Otfried's text, which was predominantly Old High German, but they knew and read Aimonius. Aimonius mentions also that these pagans worshipped the Sun, Vulcan, and the Moon (*Historia Francorum*, Preface, in Migne, col. 631).

Encyclopedic history is the common model for the chronicles of more limited political or geographic scope. Aimonius wrote in the service of young France. Far east of the Rhine, a contemporary bishop of Merseburg, THIETMAR (d. 1018), attempted the same service for his bishopric.[89] He explains that his city is supposed to have originated with Julius Caesar, who named it after Mars (*Thietmar* I.2, in Trillmich, pp. 360–61). Of other pagan antiquities, the Irminsul is still

---

[86] Complete text in J. P. Migne, *PL*, XCV (Paris, 1851), 734–1153. This immensely influential work was published in Paris in 1531 (Migne, col. 743–44) and in Basel in 1532 (Potthast, p. 612). For the extent of the distribution see Potthast, p. 612 and 902–3. I use the text by Droysen in MGH auct. antiq., II: Goths, p. 358; Marius, p. 266; Varus, pp. 296–97.

[87] Aimonius Monachus Floriacensis, *Historia Francorum libri quattuor*, in Migne, *PL*, CXXIX (Paris, 1853), 627–798; see col. 675. To Badius, who printed the work in 1514 (Renouard, I.81 and II.37; Potthast, p. 29), and Trithemius (*Catalogus*, fol. LXI^vf.), he was known as Ammonius. Cf. Manitius, II, 239ff.

[88] Cf. K. L. Roth, "Die Trojasage" p. 37, and Klippel, *Die Darstellung*, pp. 19–20.

[89] Werner Trillmich, ed. and trans., *Thietmar von Merseburg: Chronik* (Darmstadt, 1962), p. xxiii. Gobelinus Persona knew and cited the work (Trillmich, p. xxviii). On Thietmar, see Manitius II, 265ff., and Potthast, pp. 1061–62.

remembered: the church of St. Peter on the Eresburg stands on the spot where once stood the heathen sanctuary (II.2, in Trillmich, pp. 36–37). Among the most interesting items in Thietmar's chronicle is his description of Otto III's search, in 1000 A.D., for the grave of Charlemagne at Aachen. This he mentions shortly after reporting that Otto III was trying to reestablish the old customs of Rome (IV.47, in Trillmich, pp. 166ff.). Otto's attempt and tragic failure are well known.[90] Rome and Aachen, Otto III and Charlemagne are brought together in close quarters. The identity of the Roman Empire and the German monarchy is undamaged; Widukind's views on the subject had been forgotten or suppressed.

The Roman character of the imperial myth is repeatedly affirmed in Thietmar: *Inperator* and *Cesar* [in the spelling of the text] is the consistent terminology for the monarch. The sanctity and political might of the Empire work themselves out in the lengthy descriptions of the christianization and pacification of neighboring lands, particularly the Slavic (e.g., *Thietmar* VII.64ff., in Trillmich, pp. 424ff.). Emperor Henry II and his saintly Empress Kunigunde take a special oath to defend the Roman Church during their coronation in 1014 (VI, prologue, and ch. 1, in Trillmich, pp. 350ff.). While Thietmar was still working on his chronicle, an episcopal colleague in the missions, one Bruno, wrote to Henry II (winter, 1008) addressing him as "the pious," and "the strong custodian of the Church."[91] The myth of the Empire was intact at the turn of the millennia.

A further instance of the fundamental stature of the imperial myth in medieval writings comes in WIPO, the author of the famed sequence *Victimae paschalae laudes*. His history of the deeds of Conrad II (ca. 1049) praises the Emperor for his uninterrupted efforts in behalf of the faith.[92] Conrad, whose family stems from Troy, and whose excellence was surpassed only by Charlemagne, was elected Emperor by the people of Rome, hailed Caesar and Augustus in the presence of the Kings of Burgundy and England (*Wipo* Ch. 2, 6, 16, in *Quellen*, pp. 538–39, 556–57, 570–71). The Emperor is pious, and his Empire

---

[90] Schramm, *Kaiser, Rom und Renovatio*, I, 87–187.

[91] H. Ziessberg, "Die Kriege Kaiser Heinrichs II. mit Herzog Boleslaw I. von Polen," *SB der philosophisch-historischen Classe der kaiserlichen Akademie der Wissenschaften*, LVII (Vienna, 1868), 352–53.

[92] Werner Trillmich, ed. and trans., *Wipo: Gesta Chuonradi II Imperatoris* in *Quellen des 9. und 11. Jahrhunderts zur Geschichte der Hamburgischen Kirche und des Reichs* (Darmstadt, 1961), pp. 505–613—see pp. 550–51. The work was copied in MS about 1500 and used by Aventinus: Trillmich, pp. 516–17. Cf. Manitius, II, 318ff. and Potthast, pp. 1118–19.

is shown to be German with Charlemagne, Roman by the origin of the election, and supreme in the obeisance of great monarchs.[93]

Similarly, HERMANN OF REICHENAU (fl. 1050) simply accepts the imperial myth without propagandizing in its behalf. His chronicle proceeds through the alliance of Ostrogoths with Romans, the assumption of the Empire in the West by Odoacer, and the coronation of Charles and then Otto the Great, without any visible distinction between the old Emperors and the new.[94] By and large, Hermann's chronicle is too historical to be of much use to the discovery of myths of the German past. It clearly reflects the view of history of a sober scholar of the eleventh century, including the unquestioning acceptance of the mythically charged *Imperium*.

Hermann's history has a less reserved counterpart in a brief anonymous text, the *Excerpta ex Gallica Historica*, with a manuscript tradition reaching back into the eleventh century.[95] The Anonymous tells us of a defeat handed to the Roman people in the time of the praetor Titus Annius. The *legio Martia* attacked the upper German town called Zizaris (Cizaris) in honor of the local goddes Ciza. In aid of the Romans came the royal son Avar with his Macedonian force. The princes of the defending city, Habino and Caccus, were killed by the Romans, but the attacking forces were eventually defeated and Prince Avar was captured and slaughtered like a head of cattle (Grimm, I, 242–43). The historiography of Augsburg in the fifteenth century is clearly indebted to this text and its elaboration in later histories (see Grimm, I, 244–46).

In the final quarter of the eleventh century, in what might seem the darkest corner of the dark ages, in a location apparently remote from the main sources of enlightenment, a German monk informs us, virtually in one breath, of the roundness of the earth and the recent discovery of America.[96] I must admit that the first is surprising only to

---

[93] Cf. Holtzmann, *Der Weltherrschaftsgedanke des mittelalterlichen Kaisertums* . . . , p. 20.

[94] Georg Waitz, ed., *Hermanni Augiensis Chronicon*, MGH SS, V. 67–133 (Hannover, 1844), pp. 68, 81, 84, 101, 115. Cf. Manitius, II, 756ff. and Potthast, pp. 587–88. Hermann was published by Sichard, *En damus Chronicon* (1529) and was known to Trithemius (*Catalogus*, fol. LXIIIᵛf.).

[95] Grimm, *Deutsche Mythologie*, I, 242.

[96] IV.38–39, Werner Trillmich, ed. and trans., *Adam von Bremen: Bischofsgeschichte der Hamburger Kirche* in *Quellen des 9. und 11. Jahrhunderts* . . . , pp. 488–89. Cf. Manitius, II, 398ff. and Potthast, pp. 10ff. Adam's history was often transcribed in the fifteenth and sixteenth centuries, but was not printed until 1579.

those who underestimate the Middle Ages, and that the second is still dubious. ADAM VON BREMEN is nonetheless a fascinating writer and happens to contribute some important notions to the Renaissance myths of the German past. The original neighbors of the Saxons, Adam tells us, were the Druids, Bards, and Sicambri, among others. The Saxons later conquered Britain, where they were called Angles. There are also reports that the Saxons originally came from Britain and upon their arrival on the continent did battle with the Thuringians, whose lands in part they settled (*Adam von Bremen* I.3–4, in *Quellen*, pp. 166ff.). Adam took the latter version from Rudolf of Fulda's *Translatio Sancti Alexandri* (*Quellen*, p. 147), and seems markedly undisturbed by the inconsistency of his authorities.

The Saxons, Adam continues, worshipped Mercury, who accepted human sacrifice. They did not require great temples, but chose to worship in groves. Their abilities in augury were renowned (*Adam* I.7, in *Quellen*, p. 170–71). Tacitus is the ultimate source for these observations, but they seem to come more proximately from a lost redaction of the above mentioned *Translatio*.[97] Adam interprets the name of the famous Irmensul to mean "universal column," for it bore everything (I.7, in *Quellen*, pp. 172–73). Wodan was equivalent to Mars, Thor to Jupiter, and Fricco was the divinity of love (IV.26–27, in *Quellen*, pp. 470–71). Adam realized that Fricco was the male divinity of fertility (Freyr), but this was not clear to Krantz, who is at least indirectly indebted to Adam for his description of Scandinavian worship. We shall touch below on the possible intermediary, Saxo Grammaticus. Adam describes a grave sacred to the pagans, the trees of which were especially venerated and decorated with the heads of cows, horses, and men. Simon Grunau's sources may of course have been popular and authentic, or they may have been mutations of a written source such as Adam.

Adam von Bremen states in the clearest terms the German character of the Empire: the grandeur of the Roman Empire now flourishes among the Germans who once were pagans (*Adam* I.10, in *Quellen*, pp. 174–75). The services of the Emperors to the Scandinavian and Slavic missions were of extreme importance to Adam. He gives Charlemagne due credit for the privileges to Hamburg, and Otto for those to Magdeburg (I.14, II.15, in *Quellen*, pp. 184–85, 244–45). Thus the sanctity of the Empire is affirmed as well.

---

[97] Cf. Trillmich, *Quellen*, pp. 147 and 170–71, notes 40 and 42, and p. 205, note 159; and Manitius, II, 407 and 411, who argues convincingly that Adam had an actual Tacitus MS before him.

That the myth of the Empire was firmly established in the medieval mind does not mean that, individually, Emperors could not be attacked. Quite the contrary. It is conceivable that the very prestige of the imperial title invited attacks. This was surely in part the case with Henry IV and his grave difficulties with the papacy. One of Henry's many articulate enemies was LAMPERT VON HERSFELD (ob. before 1085), himself like Henry a victim of the political and ecclesiastical upheavals of the age. Lampert wrote among other works a book of annals which state concisely several incidents in Germany's mythological history. They include the familiar capture of the Eresburg by Charlemagne and the destruction of the idol there called Irminsul; the event was dated by Lampert to the year 772.[98] In the year 800, Charles was hailed Augustus (Schmidt/Fritz, pp. 20–21). This report is echoed almost identically by the chronicle of Lampert's contemporary Marianus Scotus (fl. 1082).[99] This kind of wording underlies Cusanus's opinion that Charles was not actually made Emperor, although Lampert also calls Charlemagne *Imperator*. In the year 1000, Otto found in Aachen the bones of Charlemagne, the location of which had been known to few before that (Schmidt/Fritz, pp. 38–39).

Lampert has in common with most of the chronicles and annals of the next several centuries the six traditional ages which bring the most general order to the first parts of his work. After the fifth age and the decline of the Empire of the Greeks (Macedonians), the Empire of the Romans rises. From that point on, the chronicle is organized by the reign of Roman Emperors, from Julius Caesar through Constantine to Charlemagne and Otto. Lambert varies this pattern slightly when he moves into the history of the Frankish majordomos (Schmidt/Fritz, pp. 14ff.). The medieval universal chronicle was commonly ordered under the six ages, then perhaps by the reign of a local prince or national monarch, by the tenure of a bishop or abbot, or simply by year. The pontificate of the Roman Pope and the reign of the Roman Emperor were, however, the generally acceptable temporal milestones. The continuity of the papacy from the time of the apostles had, by the late eleventh century, become a fixed point in Christian faith. The

---

[98] Adolf Schmidt and Wolfgang Dietrich Fritz, eds. and trans., *Lampert von Hersfeld: Annalen* (Darmstadt, 1962), pp. 18–19. Lampert's work passed through the hands of Schedel, Trithemius, and Naucler before being printed under Melanchthon's patronage (Tübingen, 1525): Schmidt/Fritz, p. XVIf. Cf. Manitius, III, 322ff. and Potthast, pp. 705ff.

[99] Georg Waitz, ed., *Mariani Scotti Chronicon*, MGH SS, V.481–568 (Hannover, 1844), p. 549. Cf. Manitius, II, 388ff. and Potthast, pp. 766–67. Marianus was exploited by Werner Rolevinck for his *Fasciculus Temporum* (1474), and was known to Trithemius (*Catalogus*, fol. LXVIv).

continuity of the Empire from the time of the first Caesars was, as many chronicles attest, no less a fixed notion.[100]

The Roman coronation of the Emperors ceremonially represented the continuity, indeed all the constituents of the imperial myth. According to the description of BENZO OF ALBA, an Italian and fanatic partisan of Henry IV, the sceptre held in the right hand demonstrated the succession of the Empire from Julius, Octavian, and Tiberius. The golden apple held in the left signified the rule over a multiplicity of kingdoms. The procession introducing the coronation was led by a crucifix laden with the wood of the true cross. At the conclusion of the procession the clergy sang a hymn and the Germans cried out, "Kyrie eleyson, helfo. . . ."[101] In all ways the Empire was Roman, German, sacred, and supreme.

The twelfth century produced historical works pertinent to our subject in a concentration surpassing even the richest of previous periods. The author who will serve as an introduction to the century is SIGEBERT OF GEMBLOUX (d. 1112). Like Benzo of Alba, Sigebert was no German, but nonetheless chose to side with the Emperors against the papacy. Both he and Benzo make curious counterparts to the German but anti-imperial Lampert. Many of the myths of the German past thus far evolved in the Middle Ages came together in Sigebert's chronicle. It is little wonder considering his sources. A partial list includes Jerome, Augustine, Orosius, Cassiodorus, Jordanes, Gregory the Great, Gregory of Tours, Fredegarius, Bede, Paul the Deacon, Einhard, Regino, Liutprand, Widukind, and Aimonius.[102]

Sigebert repeats the Troy myth of the Franks in two of its versions, obviously preferring the first. After the destruction of the city of Troy

---

[100] Georg Waitz, ed., *Chronica minora saeculi XII et XIII*, MGH SS, XXIV.81–288 (Hannover, 1879), passim. This prevails not only of imperial lands but of France as well, e.g., Georg Waitz, ed., *Hugo Floriacensis: Opera Historica*, MGH SS, IX. 337–406 (Hannover, 1851), pp. 355ff. [A.D. 1109]; cf. Manitius, III, 518ff.

[101] Karl Pertz, ed., *Benzonis Episcopi Albensis ad Henricum IV Imperatorem Libri VII*, MGH SS, XI.591–681 (Hannover, 1854), pp. 602–3. Cf. Manitius, III, 454ff. and Potthast, pp. 147–48. Trithemius owned and used Benzo's autograph MS.

[102] L. C. Bethmann, ed., *Sigeberti Gemblacensis Chronographia* MGH SS, VI.268–474 (Hannover, 1844), p. 275. Cf. Trithemius, *Catalogus*, sig. B 3ᵛ and fol. LXIXᵛf., where Sigebert is made a conscious object of imitation by the learned biographer. The *Chronographia* was printed in Paris in 1513 (Potthast, pp. 1016–17), and was used by Cuspinianus; Cf. Hans von Ankwicz-Kleehoven, *Der Wiener Humanist Johannes Cuspinianus* (Graz and Cologne, 1959), p. 312. On Sigebert in general, see Manitius, III, 332ff.

—an event known by all ages and all peoples—a part of the Trojans conceding the victory of the Greeks set out with Aeneas to found the Roman Empire. Another part, 12,000 Trojans, set out with Duke Anthenor and arrived at the Maeotian swamps on the borders of Pannonia. There they built a city which they called Sicambria. They dwelt there for many years, growing into a great people. With increasingly frequent incursions onto Roman soil, they made their ferocity felt as far away as Gaul. After some time, the Emperor Valentinian called on anyone to free the Romans of the barbarous Alani. The formerly Trojan people of Sicambria crossed the impenetrable Maeotian swamps and annihilated the Alani. Valentinian was pleased and called these people—once Trojans, then Antenoridae, then Sicambri—Franks, an Attic word which means "fierce." Others say that the nation was named after its king "Frantio," who later rebelled against the Romans (Bethmann, p. 300).

Abbreviated versions of several other myths of origin appear in Sigebert, such as that of the Lombards after Paul the Deacon and that of the Goths after Jordanes. The Langobards come from the island of Scandinavia in Scythia, and the Goths from the island of "Scancia," also in Scythia. The Huns are derived from the Goths over a tribe of witches called Alirunae in Gothic (Bethmann, p. 301). From Fredegarius and related texts Sigebert took not only the Troy myth, but also the early history of the Franks including Sunno and Marcomir, the latter's son Pharamund, the law makers Bosogast, Widegast, Salagast (p. 307), the execution of Brunihilde (p. 322), and more.

Certain traits of Sigebert's chronicle, particularly his principles of selection from the sources, reveal a strongly pro-imperial, perhaps even pro-German attitude. He tells us that Emperor Zeno made Theodoric, King of the Ostrogoths, into *consul ordinarius*, the highest rank in the Empire, save for the imperial dignity itself. After this, Theodoric had himself immortalized in an equestrian statue (Bethmann, p. 311). When Sigebert reaches the time of Charlemagne, he chooses to perpetuate Einhard's information on Charles's naming the months and winds in the language of his fatherland, that is, Teutonic (p. 335). Charles converted the Saxons to the true faith and built the great basilica at Aachen. The Romans acclaimed Charles; he was crowned by the Pope and named Caesar and Augustus. Henceforth the realm of Constantinople is to be distinguished from that of Rome. Henceforth the Kingdom of the Franks and the Kingdom of the Romans are identical. Charles is called *Karolus Imperator* (pp. 335–36). And as in our other authors, the myth of the Empire pervades Sigebert's work.

Yet another encyclopedic history of the period represents the status of historical knowledge for several generations. It is a work attributed until recently solely to Ekkehard of Aura (d. 1125) and now generally known as EKKEHARD AND FRUTOLF, under the names both of the original compiler and the later reviser. The sources of their chronicle are almost identical to those of Sigebert, and hence there is considerable duplication.[103] While Sigebert was not without influence, he pales beside this work which was to remain normative for the "scissors and paste" school of historical writing until the end of the thirteenth century, when a new encyclopedia took its place. By their important place in medieval historiography, Ekkehard and Frutolf participated extensively in the reconstruction of the mythical German past. They wrote without overt propagandistic or homiletic intention, and their work became a convenient reference tool.

Ekkehard and Frutolf repeat two tales of the Trojan origins of the Franks. According to some sources, Aeneas and Frigas were blood brothers, the one reigning in Latium, the other in Frigia. When the descendents of Frigas reached the territories between the Rhine and the Danube, they elected Francio their King, and from him they took their name (Waitz, *Ekkehardi*, p. 44). Elsewhere the report is as follows: When Aeneas went to Italy after the fall of Troy, some other Trojans in like fashion fled, but to the Maeotian swamps. There they settled, spreading their borders even to Pannonia. They built a city called Sicambria where they dwelt for many years, growing into a great nation. These Sicambri expelled the Alani from the Maeotian swamps, and for this victory Valentinian called them Franks and remitted their tribute for ten years. Two princes reigned over them at this time, bearing the distinguished ancient names Priam and Antenor. When the ten years had passed, Valentinian sent an embassy to exact tribute. The ferocious Sicambri were indignant at being subject to another tribute and promptly killed the ambassadors. Valentinian in his turn was furious and gathered a great host to defeat them. Many died on both sides, but the Franks were not up to the greater number of the enemy

---

[103] Georg Waitz, ed., *Ekkehardi Uraugiensis Chronica*, MGH SS, IV.1–267 (Hannover, 1844), pp. 4–5. Cf. Manitius III, 350ff. Potthast (pp. 400–401) still used the old nomenclature. The chronicle was one of the great best-sellers of the Middle Ages and was not without influence in the Renaissance, when it was variously ascribed to Saint Jerome, an uncertain Abbas Urspergensis, and the later continuators. It was known to Trithemius (Waitz, *Ekkehardi*, p. 1), Cuspinianus (Ankwicz-Kleehoven, p. 312), and Peutinger (Potthast, p. 400) whose MS was the model for the 1515 Augsburg edition. The humanist and later Protestant interest in the work caused it to be proscribed by Catholic authorities later in the sixteenth century: Reusch, *Indices*, p. 219.

and fled. Their King Priam fell in the battle. They left Sicambria and came to the land of Germany, to the people most hostile to the Romans. For a while they dwelt in Thuringia under Marcomed, son of Priam, and Sunno, son of Antenor. All the people living in that section of the Rhineland are called Germans because they have great bodies and are always brave and indomitable. In the meantime Sunno died, and the Franks took counsel among themselves in order to have one king like other nations. They took the advice of Marcomed and made his son, Faramundus, their king. The Franks began at that time to have laws. Wisogastaldus and Salegast are two of their ancient law makers; the latter gave his name to Salic law. After the conquest of the surrounding areas, the Franks began to mix with the local populations. Those who joined the Teutonici were properly called Franci; those who joined the Gauls were properly called Francigenae (Waitz, *Ekkehardi*, pp. 115–16).

This is a seminal form of the application of the Frankish Troy myth to the Germans at large. Later in the twelfth century the application comes to full bloom. Ekkehard and Frutolf apply the myth directly to Charlemagne by identifying his ancestor Ansgisus as a namesake of the family's Trojan ancestor Anchises (Waitz, *Ekkehardi*, p. 118). The Chroniclers had similarly drawn the only somewhat less apocryphal Roman Troy legend to Caesar Augustus by making him a direct descendent of Aeneas on his mother's side (p. 91). The name of Salic law and the distinction between Frankish and French had not appeared too frequently in the chronicles before Ekkehard and Frutolf. A sign of their effect is the frequency with which these explanations appear in the subsequent historiography. Their versions of the names of the Salic law makers, with "-ald" added to Wisogast, gave Trithemius a model for the names of his no less mythical jurists, scholars, and warriors.

The Chroniclers preserved and adapted Orosius and Jordanes on the subject of Scanzia, also called Scandinavia. This "womb of nations" gave birth to the Goths, as well as the Huns, Gepidi, and Amazons—all of whom stem from the Goths—the Dani, Wandali, and Winili who became the Lombards (Waitz, *Ekkehardi*, pp. 119–20). The tale of the origin of the Amazons is told at some length, with the adventures of Marpesia and Lampedo, but Orosius's Scythian princes, Plinus and Scolopetius, are made unequivocally Gothic (p. 121). The origins of the Saxons are also chronicled in the two contradictory versions: the first out of Widukind's Saxon history with the Macedonians dispersing after the death of Alexander the Great, the second out of Rudolf of Fulda's *Translatio*, with the Saxons breaking away from the Angles in Britain and settling in Thuringia (p. 176). In the way of heroic figures, Brunihilde and Theodoric appear as negative examples, the first in her hideous execution, an event greeted with universal acclaim (p. 118), the second in his violent and unchristian death (p. 129).

Theodoric appears in another context, however, and Ekkehard and Frutolf demonstrate their membership in the tradition of Orosius, Cassiodorus, and Jordanes. On the one hand, they preserve the conflicts of German and Roman, including Augustus's cry, *Quintili Vare, redde legiones* (Waitz, *Ekkehardi*, p. 93) and they remark, after describing the fall of Rome to Odoacer, that the Empire founded by Augustus perished with Augustulus. On the other hand, the situation seems reversed within a few years, for the Chroniclers have Theodoric with his Goths presiding over the *Imperium Romanum* (p. 138). Later, in the time of Charlemagne, the Roman Empire (in the possession of the Greeks since Constantine, son of Helena) is clearly in the hands of the Germans, that is, of the Emperors of the Franks and of the Saxons later on (pp. 169, 175). Ekkehard and Frutolf carefully describe the Roman coronation and acclamation of Charlemagne with the familiar cry, *Karolo augusto a Deo coronato, magno et pacifico imperatori imperatori Romanorum, vita et victoria* (p. 169). The removal of the *Imperium* from the Greeks and the distinction between the Frankish and the Saxon tenure had serious political implications, some of which we have observed in the Renaissance, others of which will be discussed as we proceed through the Middle Ages.

The first half of the twelfth century in historical writing in Germany is, as I have suggested, characterized by encyclopedic zeal and a minimum of originality. That minimum, however, reveals a strong undercurrent of imaginative history. Historical frauds and fictions seem regularly to be a sign of intense political activity. In the earlier Middle Ages and in the Renaissance, fictitious history indicates burgeoning ethnic, dynastic, or provincial loyalties, as with Jordanes, Fredegarius, and Paul the Deacon or Celtis, Trithemius, and Aventinus. In the early twelfth century, new fictions appeared alongside the tradition- and authority-minded works of Sigebert of Gembloux and Ekkehard of Aura. The world-chronicles suggest a continuation of the universal view of history; the novelties suggest a local patriotism opposing the universal view and anticipating both the local patriotism of the Renaissance and the Renaissance dichotomy of universal and provincial history.

In the myths of origin common among the Germanic invaders, several motifs stand out by their relative frequency. The basic configuration of the Langobardic myth contains most of these motifs. A nation in Scandinavia suffers from a great famine. A certain portion of the nation is obliged to leave that the rest may survive. The portion is selected and leaves under distinguished leadership. When it reaches the continent, it confronts a nation with which it makes war and which it defeats.

The same basic configuration gives form to an ANONYMOUS DESCRIPTION OF THE ORIGINS OF THE SWABIANS, produced by a contemporary of Ekkehard.[104] On the northern shore, there is a province called Swevia (here, Sweden). Its idolatrous populace was in the habit of sacrificing Christians in its rituals. God eventually sent a punishment in the form of famine (Müllenhoff, p. 57). The nation decided to sacrifice its youngest sons in order to avoid starvation. The monarch, Rodulf, could not conceal his sorrow from his own youngest son, Ditwin. Ditwin took the opportunity to leave the province with the other youngest sons. They departed by ship (p. 58), landed in Schleswig, and migrated to the Elbe, where they joined Theodoric of the Franks in his battle against Irminfrid of the Thuringians. Together they defeated the Thuringians, and Irminfrid fled to the court of Attila (pp. 59–60).

The last details of this early twelfth-century fiction are not important here, although they are revealing for other subjects. The defeat of the Thuringians by an alliance with the Franks seems to be lifted directly from Rudolf of Fulda, who, however, credits the Saxons with the victory. The oral literature of the time seems to be the direct source for the flight of Irminfrid to Attila. Irnfrid, Landgrave of Thuringia, appeared at Etzel's court in the XXXVth adventure of the *Nibelungenlied*, which was not given its known written form until the end of the twelfth century. For our purposes, the significance of this little text resides in the supposed Swedish origins of a German tribe or nation. The text clearly reflects living oral tradition (see Potthast, p. 108), however corrupted and mediate. The simple form—the configuration of the Lombard tale of origins—seems to have been common upper German property. If this is so, then the fifteenth-century fable of Swiss origins from Sweden has an identifiable provenance. Written antecedents for the Swiss myth have not survived and may conceivably never have existed. Gothic, Lombard, and now Swabian origins had been sought in Scandinavia. All three tribes spent some time in Swit-

---

[104] K[arl] M[üllenhoff], ed., "Von der Herkunft der Schwaben," *Zeitschrift für deutsches Altertum*, N.F. V [XVII] (1897), 57–71. Comp. Paul Hirsch, *Widukind*, pp. 160–67. Cf. Potthast, p. 108.

zerland; indeed, the Swabians never left. It is more than possible that popular memory preserved these fables, particularly their common motifs. When the Swiss emerged as an entity apart from their neighbors, the skeleton of a myth of origins was available and needed only the flesh of new patriotic names and nationally significant details. To imply a direct connection between Swabian and Swiss myths of origin would go beyond the evidence. Both can, however, be said to represent the same popular tradition in distinct, patriotically determined manifestations.

The mythical pre-history of the Germanic peoples is too eclectic to permit rigid categorizations. Nevertheless, whether Scandinavian, British, biblical, Vergilian, Alexandrian, or any combination of these, all origins came from only two directions, North and East. The South and West were ruled out because the ancient and medieval worlds considered them uninhabitable. The North and East still suggest somewhat meaningful categories. In the first case, the issue is Scandinavia for the Goths, Lombards, Swabians, and later the Swiss, and Britain for the Saxons. In the second case, this issue is Noah for all peoples, Troy for the Franks, and Macedonia for the Saxons. The tales of the North leave the impression of being somewhat closer to popular tradition, if only because the tales of the East all have some non-Germanic precedent, Greco-Roman or ancient Judeo-Christian. To be sure, the Swabian origins tale is replete with oppression of the chosen people and pharaonic plagues, biblical motifs which demonstrate medieval syncretism, and the splendid dearth of inhibitions among medieval myth-makers. Until the twelfth century, German myths of origins were compiled primarily for the tribes or nations, and then applied to dynasties. In the twelfth century itself, the cities began to demand similar glories. Curiously, they all chose Eastern origins, perhaps because the very concept of the city was attached to Babylon. The first major fiction for a city is GESTA TREVERORUM by an anonymous (ca. 1132), which tells of the fabulous beginnings of Trier (Trèves). The Anonymous taps classical sources through their Christian intermediaries for the raw materials of his fabrication. His direct model is Orosius through whom he cites Justin's *Epitome* of the universal history of Pompeius Trogus.[105] About 1300 years before the founding of Rome, Ninus was King of the Assyrians. He was survived upon his death by Semiramis, his Queen, and two sons, Ninas and Trebetas, the latter being a son by a previous marriage to a Queen of the Chal-

---

[105] Orosius, I.4.1–8, in Zangemeister, pp. 42–44 and notes there. On Justin's *Epitome* cf. Schanz-Hosius, II, 320–25.

deans. Semiramis lusted after her stepson. He was quite disgusted at this, and was therefore driven from his country and kingdom. Trebetas wandered abroad, seeking a place to settle. Eventually he put the matter in the hands of fate, which directed him to find Europe, the third part of the earth. He came to the river Mosel on whose shores he found a pleasant landscape, and there he founded a city called Treberis after himself. The city is hence some 1250 years older than Rome. It was founded in the seventh year of the era of Abraham the patriarch. The people who lived about Treberis traced their origins from Gomer, son of Japhet son of Noah, and they were called Gauls on account of the whiteness of their bodies.[106]

Whatever the linguistic frontier may have been when the Anonymous was writing, Trier was consistently known as a city of Gaul. The ideal of universality for the Holy Roman Empire was in part supported by the denomination "Gaul" for the Trier district. Three "nations" had the Emperor as overlord: Germany, Italy, and Gaul. This concept was legalized in the titles of the three ecclesiastical Prince-Electors; the Archbishops of Mainz, Cologne, and Trier were, familiarly, imperial chancellors for Germany, Italy, and Gaul respectively. The "Gaul" over which the Archbishop of Trier had real or nominal authority was the German area west of the Rhine. Trier's presumably Gallic character does not remove it from Germany's mythical past.

When Trebetas died, the Anonymous continues, his son Hero succeeded to the office of Prince. Hero buried his father on the summit of Mount Jura, having cremated him according to the ceremonies of the gentiles. Hero had his father worshipped as a god, and thereby repeated the error of Ninus who had done the same for his own father. The story of the founding of Trier was, on Hero's order, inscribed in marble to honor the memory of Trebetas. In the course of time, the city was fortified with walls and towers. Among the various gates was the *Porta Nigra*, called the "Gate of Mars." The field before the gate was known as the *Campus Martis* (Waitz, *Gesta*, p. 131). The inhabitants worshipped many gods, foremost among them, Mercury. A temple

---

[106] Georg Waitz, ed., *Gesta Treverorum*, MGH SS, VIII.111–260 (Hannover, 1848), p. 130. Cf. Potthast, pp. 522–23. Familarity with this myth in the Renaissance hardly needs verification, but see Manitius, III, 518, on Trithemius. The motif of the chaste youth and the lustful stepmother was given a splendid comparative-literature evaluation with commentary and texts by John D. Yohannan, ed., *Joseph and Potiphar's Wife* (New York, 1968). However, Yohannan seems to have missed Semiramis, even though her lechery won her a place in Dante's Hell (Canto V) and on every important operatic stage of the eighteenth and nineteenth centuries in no less than forty operas, several based on a play by Voltaire.

they constructed contained no less than a hundred idols (p. 132). The Trebiri were a brave people and expanded into the nearby territories conquering five cities: Basel, Strassburg, Worms, Mainz, and Cologne. These cities henceforth paid tribute to Treberis. Belgus, a leader of the Trebiri, gave his name to Belgium (p. 133).

The Christian era begins most auspiciously among the Trebiri. Saint Peter himself sent the third member of the order of the seventy-two disciples to preach in the North. His name was Eucharius, and sent to preach with him were Valerius and Maternus. Peter ordained Eucharius bishop, Valerius deacon, and Maternus subdeacon. The missionaries went to "Elegia" in Alsatia to preach the word of truth (Waitz, *Gesta*, pp. 145–46). There Maternus grew sick and after a few days died. The holy Eucharius commended him to the earth with much weeping and lamentation. Valerius sped to Rome to bring Peter the sad news. Peter gave Valerius his staff to bring back to the North. Upon his return, the staff was placed over the corpse of Maternus, and he was revived in the name of the Lord. In 54 A.D., the three holy men went to preach in Trier (pp. 146–47) and convert the city where Saint Helena, mother of Emperor Constantine, first saw life (pp. 151–52).

The Anonymous of the *Gesta Treverorum* was, all appearances to the contrary, no lunatic. His forgery was not a game played for its own sake; it was played for high stakes—the primacy of the Trier episcopate north of the Alps. The years 1130 to 1140 were filled with intrigue among the Rhenish bishops as the Investiture Controversy dissipated and the papacy suffered under one of its periodic schisms. Power passed quickly between Mainz, Cologne, and Trier.[107] The instruments of policy were employed, and propaganda was one of them, then as now. The *Gesta* are hardly the first forgery to serve political interests. The Anonymous had every reason to trace the origin of Trier to pre-Roman times, in case it was necessary to declare relative independence of the Roman Empire. Similarly, the christianization of Trier under Eucharius was to give a direct link to Saint Peter's Rome, and thus guarantee a primacy of chronology and prestige over other northern bishoprics. The cities supposedly paying tribute to the Trebiri were important sees, Mainz and Cologne, Trier's main contenders for power, not least among them. As it happened, the gamble of the Anonymous and his party was lost, and Trier continued to enjoy an existence of genteel mediocrity. The *Gesta* have therefore become a historiographic

---

[107] Charles C. Bayley, *The Formation of the German College of Electors in the Mid-Thirteenth Century* (Toronto, 1949), pp. 98–99.

curiosity, although yielding some influence in the later construction of Germany's mythical past. Their character as a propagandistic work has been recognized and fairly evaluated.[108] Why the corresponding Renaissance phenomena—Annius of Viterbo's Berosus and Trithemius's Hunibald, for example—elicit annoyance rather than a similar evaluation is difficult to understand.

The Anonymous of the *Gesta*, as well as the Anonymous of the origin of the Swabians, cannot be considered typical of the period. Partisan interests were likely to invade any historical work, but few engaged in such wholesale invention. Modern scholarship congratulates the work of the ANNALISTA SAXO (fl. 1139) for its objectivity, discriminate derivativeness, and absence of fable.[109] The Annalista Saxo does, however, tell us that Saint Peter himself founded the Trier archbishopric, and that it hence had primacy over Cologne and Mainz.[110] Although this seems somewhat neologistic, the larger part of his chronicle does incline simply to preserve traditional notions. He tells us, for example, of Charlemagne's service to religion in the destruction of the Irmenseul in the year 772 and then of the thrice acclaimed coronation by God of the great and peaceful Emperor of the Romans, the august Charles (Waitz, *Annalisto Saxo*, pp. 563–64).

As traditional and even more encyclopedic is the work of the Bavarian polyhistor, HONORIUS AUGUSTODUNENSIS (fl. 1130–50), who also tells of Charlemagne's elevation to the title of Augustus.[111] Adapting Isidore, Honorius derives the name of the Germans from "a germinando" (Migne, col. 128). The Troy myth of the Franks also received learned support from Honorius, when he chose the version of Aethicus Cosmographicus, with Francus leaving Troy in the company of Aeneas, coming to the Rhine, and there founding New Troy (Migne, col. 130). Another close contemporary, an Anonymous of Paris (fl. 1108–37) preserves the Troy myth more or less in the version of the *Liber historiae Francorum*, with Anthenor leading the Franks and continuing through the leadership of Francio, "Sumno," Genebald, Marcomir, Phara-

---

108 [Wilhelm] Wattenbach and Robert Holtzmann, *Deutschlands Geschichtsquellen im Mittelalter: Die Zeit der Sachsen und Salier*, 4 pts. in 2 vols. (Darmstadt, 1967), II [pt. 4], 621–22.

109 Manitius, III, 486.

110 Georg Waitz, ed., *Annalisto Saxo*, MGH SS, VI.542–777 (Hannover, 1844), p. 599. Cf. Potthast, p. 99.

111 Honorius, *Didascalia et Historica*, in J. P. Migne, *PL*, CLXXII (Paris, 1848), 190. Cf. Potthast, p. 620 and Manitius, III, 364ff. Honorius was well known to Trithemius (*Catalogus*, sig. B 3ᵛ and fol. LXIXᵛ) and was often printed in the Renaissance (e.g., 1470, 1491, 1497).

mundus, and Merovaus.[112] Despite the originality of several early twelfth-century texts—usually anonymous ones—the great majority of historians and chroniclers chose to walk the path of tradition.

This tradition reaches an apex in the middle of the twelfth century in perhaps the greatest synthesis of medieval historical writing, OTTO VON FREISING's *Chronica sive Historia de duabus Civitatibus.* Otto (d. 1158), uncle of Emperor Frederick I Barbarossa, brings together in his chronicle the vast majority of the earlier myths of the German past, and adds some of his own. Otto informs us of the origins of the Galatha and Scythians from Gomer and Magog.[113] He tells us of the origins of Trier from Trebeta, stepson of Semiramis (*Chron.* I.8, in Schmidt and Lammers, pp. 74–75), and of Saint Helena's birth in that city (II.43, pp. 282–83). The Franks of course stem from Troy, and their name means "fierce" in Attic or "noble" in their own language (I.25, pp. 90–91). The Lombards and Goths are known to stem from the isle of Scanzia (V.4, pp. 384–85). Otto also knows the Lombards to have received their name from the occasion at which their women tied their hair about their chins.[114] The cities of Augsburg and Mainz are said to have been founded by Drusus (*Chron.* III.3, pp. 220–21). Frankfurt was so named when Charlemagne forded the river Main in battle once with the Saxons (*Gesta* I.46, in Schmidt and Schmale, pp. 216–17).

Among Otto's figures of more than ordinary historical importance, men of learning and law appear alongside political and military heroes. Gulfilas, Bishop of the Goths, invented letters for his people (*Chron.* IV. 16, in Schmidt and Lammers, pp. 332–33). Wisogastaldus and Salagastus composed the law for the Franks, and the latter gave his name to Salic law (IV.32, pp. 366ff.). Alexander the Great, we are told, received emissaries from Germany (II.25, pp. 152–53). Otto finds room for the story of the death and burial of Alaric in the diverted

---

112 Georg Waitz, ed., *Historia regum Francorum Monasterii Sancti Dionysii,* MGH SS, IX.395–406 (Hannover, 1851), p. 395. See Potthast, pp. 615 and 626 s.v. "Hugo Floriacensis."

113 Otto von Freising, *Chronica* . . . I.4, in Adolf Schmidt and Walther Lammers, eds. and trans., *Chronik oder die Geschichte der zwei Staaten* (Darmstadt, 1961), pp. 66–67. Cf. Manitius, III, 376ff. and Potthast, pp. 885ff. Otto's works were first published in 1515 in Strassburg under the editorship of Cuspinianus. Trithemius knew Otto at least by reputation, but dates him incorrectly (*Catalogus,* fol. XCIᵛ).

114 This appears in the *Gesta Frederici,* the history of Frederick I's deeds by Otto and his student Rahewin, Bk. II, ch. 14, in Adolf Schmidt and Franz-Josef Schmale, eds. and trans., *Die Taten Friedrichs oder richtiger Cronica* (Darmstadt, 1965), pp. 308–9 [henceforth "*Gesta*"].

river Busentus (IV.21, pp. 348–49). Although in no way associated with Germany, Prester John is mentioned at some length in Otto's chronicle, apparently for the first time in western written literature (VIII. 33, pp. 556–57). Otto preserves Gregory the Great's story of Theodoric's end, how he was hurled into Mount Etna by John and Symmachus, and adds that this is probably the source of the fable of Theodoric riding alive into the mouth of Hell (V.3, pp. 381–82). The Bishop of Freising moralizes on the miserable death of Brunihilde, an admonition to refrain from atrocity (V.7, pp. 392–93). Emperor Otto II had grave problems with the Saracens, but tradition quite contrary to fact made him *pallida mors Sarracenorum*. Otto von Freising is among the first to apply this title to a western Emperor (VI.26, pp. 470–71).

Curiously, Otto's chronicle tells us nothing of the ancient religion of the Germans, but it does repeat the traditional tales of Germanic valor. Marius's victory over the Cimbri and Teutoni was effected only after disastrous Roman defeats (*Chron.* II.44, in Schmidt and Lammers, pp. 186–87). The Germans later aided Caesar when he attacked Pompey (II.49, pp. 198–99). Out of Orosius, Otto tells of the Germanic victory which led Augustus to cry out, *Quintili Vare, redde legiones!* Local tradition places the event near Augsburg (III.3, pp. 220–21). Otto chooses also to mention the detail that the Germans in their attacks on Italy reached as far as Ravenna (III.37, pp. 278–79).

As befits his place in the imperial family, Otto fully elaborates the myth of the Empire. Empire as such moved westward from the Babylonians to the Romans (*Chron.* I, Prologus, in Schmidt and Lammers, pp. 16–17). The fall of the realm in the East was accompanied by the rise of the realm in the West (II.13, pp. 128–29). Whereas nations had once gone to Babylon in the farthest east to seek peace, they came in the time of Augustus from the farthest east to western Rome to give tribute (III.4, pp. 222–23). Otto applies this doctrine of direction also to the later possession of the Empire by the Germans. While Rome fell under Augustulus, the Kingdom of the Franks rose (IV.31, pp. 366–67). As Rome declined, Francia arose to take its crown (IV.33, pp. 370–71). A Frankish crown does not supplant Rome's; rather, Rome's crown comes to the Franks. The catalogue of Emperors appended to Book VII of the *Chronica* moves without hesitation from Augustus to Frederick I (pp. 568ff.). Otto clearly sees his German nephew as legitimate and linear descendent of Augustus.

There is one curiosity in Otto's description of the *translationes* of the Roman Empire. He has it transferred from the Romans to the Greeks, then to the Franks, then to the Lombards, and then to the German Franks (*Chron.* I, Prologus, in Schmidt and Lammers, pp. 12–

13). This is the very view held by Andreas of Regensburg in the fifteenth century. As with Andreas, Otto's view does not imply a radical distinction between Franks and German Franks. The Ottonians are merely the successors to the Carolingians (VI.17, pp. 456–57).

The legend of Saints Valerius, Maternus, and Eucharius and the staff of Saint Peter reappears in Otto's chronicle (*Chron.* III.14, in Schmidt and Lammers, p. 240–41). Otto does not, however, analyze the legend for its implications of the German possession of the Empire, as we have seen Renaissance authors do. Otto supplied the source for them, including the detail that the staff was left in Germany, the upper half in Trier and the lower half in Cologne. The implications for imperial policy were drawn out later in the Middle Ages, and we shall consider them in the next chapter.

Otto supports the sanctity of the Empire in Charlemagne's aid to Pope Leo and his subsequent coronation by God (*Chron.* V. 30–31, in Schmidt and Lammers, pp. 418ff.). The entire eschatological theology of Otto's chronicle is directed away from the Empire, the earthly city, so that he does not unreservedly accept the special function of the Empire as the one who holds off Antichrist, the false prophet of *pax et securitas* (VIII.2, 8, pp. 588ff., 598–99). Indeed, Otto refuses to reject the theory that the Roman Emperor himself will be the apocalyptic beast, the servant of Antichrist (VIII.3, pp. 592–93). He goes so far as to relate Saint Augustine's story (without Augustine's rejection of it) that Nero never died and awaits the last days to be Antichrist himself (III.16, pp. 246–47). Little did Otto realize that one day the story would be applied to his imperial nephew.

The supremacy of the Empire is affirmed by Otto on various occasions, despite his other-worldly view of history. Conrad II, for example, was crowned in Rome, receiving the obeisance of kings Knut of England and Rudolf of Burgundy (*Chron.* VI.29, in Schmidt and Lammers, pp. 474–75). France, Spain, England, Denmark submit to the authority of Frederick (*Gesta* I.26, in Schmidt and Schmale, pp. 172–73). Frederick is prince of the earth (*Gesta* II.26, pp. 332–33), Emperor, prince of the whole world (III.23, pp. 446–47), holding the government of the city and the globe (II.52, pp. 348–49). The *Gesta* also preserve a letter from Henry II of England to Frederick (III.8, pp. 406ff.), declaring Frederick's greater excellence, specifically his *auctoritas imperandi*, and Henry's willingness to serve the Emperor.[115] This letter is, by the way, witnessed by the English Chancellor, Thomas à Becket.

Much remains to be said about Otto von Freising, his histories, and

---

[115] Cf. Holtzmann, *Der Weltherrschaftsgedanke* ..., p. 14.

their influence in the Renaissance. This sketch purports only to capture several highlights which visibly shone on into the fifteenth and sixteenth centuries. To the best of my knowledge, no exhaustive study has evaluated Otto's impact on Renaissance historiography as it has been limited here. His work is many-faceted and may have been greeted with mixed feelings among secular-minded historians in Germany, who were, on the other hand, proud indeed of so distinguished a scholarly ancestor. The extent of their debt to Otto should be established, if only to see if pre-Reformation historians could understand Otto's ambivalent philosophy of history that touched closely on their patriotic optimism and their eschatological pessimism. The Empire was a point of focus for both these moods among Germans of the Renaissance, and Otto was a monumental authority on the subject.

The mid-twelfth century produced a multiplicity of texts which demonstrate the extent to which the myth of the *Imperium* was taken for granted. HILDEGARD OF BINGEN (1098/9–1179), a major mystic and scientist of the Middle Ages, predicted the decline of the Empire, its division and impotence, and the subsequent arrival of Antichrist.[116] For her, the fate of the Empire was intrinsically wound up with the history of salvation. The less pious ARCHPOET, who proposed to die in a tavern (fl. 1160), addressed Emperor Barbarossa as follows:

Salve mundi domine, Cesar noster ave . . .

[Hail Lord of the world, Hail to thee our Caesar . . .]

and called him another Augustus.[117] It is the Archpoet's immediate patron, Rainald, Archbishop of Cologne and Frederick's chancellor, who used his authority in Italy to take the relics of the Three Magi from Milan to Cologne.[118]

---

116 *Visio* X.25, in *Liber Divinorum Operum* in J. P. Migne, *PL*, CXCVII (Paris, 1882), 1026f. Cf. Potthast, p. 598 and Manitius, III, 228ff. Hildegard was quite well known in the Renaissance—various of her works were published by Lefevre d'Étaples and Hieronymus Gebwiler, among others: Ernst P. Goldschmidt, *Medieval Texts and Their First Appearance in Print*, Bibliographical Society Transactions, Supplement, XVI (London, 1943), pp. 57, 123.

117 Karl Langosch, ed. and trans., *Hymnen und Vagantenlieder*, 3rd ed. (Darmstadt, 1961), pp. 248–49 and 254–55. Cf. Manitius, III, 978ff. We have no reason to believe that the Archpoet was known in the Renaissance, but cf. Goldschmidt, *Medieval Texts*, p. 85.

118 L. C. Bethmann, ed., *Roberti de Monte Cronica*, MGH SS, VI.475–535 (Hannover, 1844), p. 513. Cf. Potthast, pp. 976–77 and Manitius, III, 442ff. The pertinent section of the chronicle of Robert [ob. 1186] was printed in 1513.

The myth of the Empire extended well beyond the court and family of the Emperor. Charlemagne remains in this period a symbol of the Empire and continues to have sacred attributes applied to him. It is Charlemagne who is called the Liberator of Christianity and who receives a vision of Saint James in the history of Charlemagne's deeds by Pseudo-Turpin.[119] Extant from the mid-twelfth century are Ordines, formal liturgical texts, for the consecration and coronation of emperors. The rubrics to one such *Ordo* read: [120]

> Incipit ordo qualiter rex teutonicus Roman ad suscipiendam Coronam imperii venire debeat . . .
>
> [Here begins the rite (or protocol) describing the manner in which the German king is supposed to come to Rome for the purpose of receiving the Crown of the empire . . .]

The rubrics specify that the monarch is German, that the imperial crown is given, and that Rome is the seat of the Empire. The sacred stamp of the Empire clearly reveals itself in the very fact that the coronation was a liturgical act. As for the supremacy of the Empire, it is more or less in these years that Eloise is presumed to have written Abelard (d. 1142): [121]

> Deum testem invoco, si me Augustus universo praesidens mundo matrimoni honore dignaretur, totumque mihi orbem confirmaret in perpetuo praesidendum, charius mihi et dignius videretur tua dici meretrix quam illius imperatrix.
>
> [I call upon God as my witness, if Caesar, ruling over the entire world, were to award me the honor of marriage and promise me forever the government of the whole globe, it would nonetheless seem more pleasing to me and more honorable to be called your whore than his empress.]

Eloise may merely be using a literary figure, but that alone confirms the currency of the idea.

The continuity of the *Imperium* from Julius Caesar to the emperors of the twelfth century is confirmed once again in the Middle High

---

[119] H. M. Smyser, ed., *Pseudo-Turpin*, Medieval Academy of America, Publications, XXX (Cambridge, Mass., 1937), p. 57, cf. p. 18. Cf. Potthast, pp. 1075–76 and Manitius, III, 487ff.

[120] Reinhard Elze, ed., *Die Ordines für die Weihe und Krönung des Kaisers und der Kaiserin*, MGH Fontes iuris Germanici antiqui, IX (Hannover, 1960), p. 48.

[121] Epistola II: Petrus Abaelardus, *Epistolae*, in J. P. Migne, *PL*, CLXXVIII (Paris, 1855), 185. Comp. Finke, *Weltimperialismus . . .*, p. 13. Cf. Trithemius, *Catalogus*, fol. LXXIV^v, and Manitius, III, 105ff.

German KAISERCHRONIK. Vernacular verse chronicles did not generally play a large part in the Renaissance revival of the German past, although there are important exceptions. But it would be difficult to prove that the *Kaiserchronik* was the immediate source for any Renaissance speculation about German antiquity. It does deserve some mention, however, for it provides the earliest record of several fictions which made their way into the Renaissance. The Bavarians, it tells us, stem from Armenia, where Noah landed with the Arc. The heroes of this people include the war-lords, Boimunt and Ingram, who did battle with Julius Caesar.[122] Adelger, another Bavarian duke, made war with Emperor Severus (*Kaiserchronik*, ll. 6622–29, in Schröder, pp. 202–3). Prenne (Brennus), who attacked the Romans, was not quite a Bavarian, but a Swabian, presumably the next best thing (ll. 267–76, p. 84). Such stories appeared with great frequency in the Renaissance, as in the works of Andreas of Regensburg, Veit Arnpeck, and Aventinus.

The *Kaiserchronik* preserves also the myths of Saxon origins from Alexander (ll. 325–31, in Schröder, p. 86), of Frankish origins from Troy (ll. 343–48, p. 86), of King Franko on the Rhine (ll. 373–78, p. 87), of Caesar's founding countless Rhenish cities (ll. 379–94, p. 87), of German aid in Caesar's victory over Pompey (ll. 469–514, pp. 89–90), of Theodoric's fiery vigil in a volcano awaiting the end of the world (ll. 14,164–75, p. 337), and of Charlemagne's glorious career (ll. 14,278–15,087, pp. 340–54). The chronicle is one of the major monuments of imaginative history. To judge from the number of surviving manuscripts (Potthast, p. 694), it must have been extremely popular and hence must have satisfied a certain segment of vernacular historical demand. Latin historical writing in the period—while hardly a model of critical method—rarely immersed itself so completely in legend. There are, as usual, exceptions, and the *Gesta Romanorum* or Pseudo-Turpin could be summoned as examples. They both carried authority as histories and are even more fabulous than the vernacular *Kaiserchronik*. But they are explainable exceptions to the Latin historiography: neither is of learned Latin provenance.

This is not to imply that learned historical writing was without imaginative and legendary qualities. Extremely erudite historians made more than few leaps into fancy in their attempts at serious history. Such a one is GOTFRIED OF VITERBO, a rather pro-German, pro-Imperial

---

[122] *Kaiserchronik*, ll. 297–322, in Edward Schröder, ed., *Die Kaiserchronik eines Regensburger Geistlichen*, MGH Deutsche Chroniken, I.i (Hannover, 1892), p. 85. The classic discussion is Ernst Friedrich Ohly, *Sage und Legende in der Kaiserchronik* (1940; reprinted Darmstadt, 1968).

Italian resident. He had been in the service of Frederick Barbarossa as chaplain and notary, and survived the Emperor by a few years, dying in the last decade of the twelfth century.[123] Gotfried begins his *Speculum Regum*, dedicated to Emperor Henry VI (1190–97), with a promise to trace the genealogy of his patron from the time of the flood to the flourishing of Troy and Athens, and finally to the present (Waitz, *Gotifredi . . . Opera*, p. 21). In his *Pantheon*, he more than keeps the promise, beginning with Adam and proceeding to the present over Noah, Sem, Nimrod, Saturn, Jupiter, Troius, Priam, Salgast, and Charlemagne (pp. 300ff.).

Gotfried preserves the myths of origin associated with Trier and adds an important item. "Troletus," that is, Trebeta, son of Ninus, fled Semiramis and founded Trier some two thousand years before Christ. During his exile, he also founded Troy, which took its name from him (Waitz, *Gotifredi . . . Opera* pp. 34, 138). Troletus-Trebeta founded Troy first; so Trier is younger—an extraordinary admission for a myth-maker. The connection between Troy and Trier is significant in Gotfried, for he is the first to suggest that the very founding of Troy is historically tangent to a moment in "German" history. He could thus be a support for the pan-German antiquity of certain Renaissance thinkers. Other familiar myths of origin appear dispersed in Gotfried's work. The Saxons stem from the army of Alexander the Great (pp. 106, 119, 147–48). The origins of the Swabians are also connected with Macedon (p. 141). The Lombards originate in Scandinavia and received their name because of their long beards, some say, from their divinity Godan, who was equivalent to Mercury (pp. 212ff.). The Goths stem from "Got," who is equivalent to Magog, son of Japhet (p. 276). Aachen, Aquis Grani, received its name from the Roman prince Granus, who ruled among the Franks in the time of "Cletus," the first pope after Saint Peter (p. 158). The Alemanni are an ancient people, and their name means "all man" (p. 142).

The most important myth of origins for Gotfried is the Troy myth of the Franks. The Trojan Empire is the antecedent of Henry VI's realm (Waitz, *Gotifredi . . . Opera*, p. 31). This is so because the Teutonici and Franci are one and the same thing (p. 61). Germani

---

[123] Georg Waitz, ed., *Gotifredi Viterbensis Opera*, MGH SS, XXII.1–376 (Hannover, 1877), p. 1f. Cf. Potthast, pp. 533–34 and Manitius, III, 392ff. Although Gotfried was not printed in the Renaissance, at least not in the years at issue here, he was very well known indeed, better than these few indications might imply: Waitz (p. 3) lists Trithemius and Gobelinus Persona among those who used him; cf. Trithemius, *Catalogus*, fol. LXXVIII^r. Naucler, too, knew and used Gotfried: cf. Naucler's *Chronicon*, 2 vols. (Cologne, 1584), II, sig. XXX^vf. [following the numbered pages].

and Franci are interchangeable words (p. 66), and Sicambri was a term which covered both (p. 105). The younger Priam and Anthenor fled Troy together (p. 61). Priam, who was a son of Anchises (and hence a brother of Aeneas), became *Rex Alamannorum* (p. 44). Priam founded Sicambria, where the common good flourished. These Sicambri mingled with the Germani, also called Theutonici (p. 63), and assumed the manners and the language of the Germans (p. 64). When the Roman Empire was once threatened by the Alani, the "Ierman" came to the aid of Emperor Valentinian. For this aid they were called "Francus," that is, "audax" (p. 65). Such aid was only meet, since the "Iermani" and the Romans were brothers from Troy (p. 119). Aeneas and Priam the Teuton personified this brotherhood (pp. 61–62). Romans and Germans rejoice when they discover one another (p. 64). Gotfried's extensive and somewhat confusing Troy myth seems to be the first to identify the Franks of antiquity wholly with the Germans.

Gotfried counts among his heroic figures not only the many Frankish kings of antiquity, but also the traditional non-Romans who could in any way be made into Germans. Brennius of the Svevi threatened Rome, but was also known for the founding or fortification of Milan, Verona, Pavia, Brixen, and other cities (Waitz, *Gotifredi . . . Opera*, p. 118). Alaric and Theodoric were leaders of great virtue (p. 102), and of the latter king of the Goths many wondrous tales are told by the Germans (p. 188). Merlin is definitely identified as Anglo-Saxon (p. 127). Salegast and other law-makers appear (p. 201). Otto II is called, after Otto von Freising, *pallida mors Sarracenorum* (p. 238).

Not included among the Germans but among the pagan chroniclers is Berosus (Waitz, *Gotifredi . . . Opera*, p. 133). Annius of Viterbo lived three hundred years after Gotfried of Viterbo. The Berosus of Annius is hardly less imaginative than Gotfried; it is only less traditional. Perhaps the Renaissance inclined toward forgery, where in the Middle Ages tradition could fill the same needs. This is, incidentally, not a suggestion of any direct relationship between Gotfried and Annius: imaginative history may merely have been in the air of Viterbo.

The Troy myth reappears in Gotfried's enthusiastic affirmation of the imperial myth, in a fashion which links him closely to his Renaissance successors. The seed of Troy gave off two sprouts. The one grew into the diadem of Rome, the other into the Teutonic kingdom. In ancient times, the Germans and the Romans held power communally. The two powers were united in Charlemagne, who was *Romuleus matre, Teutonicus patre* (Waitz, *Gotifredi . . . Opera*, pp. 61–62, 65). In the fifteenth century, Hermann Peter of Andlau chose the same words to express a similar idea. Charles's German nationality is stressed above his Roman ancestry, however, for Gotfried reports—and is apparently the first to do so—that Charles was born at Ingelheim (p. 209). Charles sums up in himself the fully Roman and fully German aspects of the *Imperium*. He was also liberator of Rome and its Church, and so personifies the sacred duty of the Empire as well.

The Sibylline prophecy that the last Emperor will subdue the pagans and convert the Jews is substantially older than Gotfried.[124] He is, however, largely responsible for introducing, or reintroducing, this concept into western historiography. His Sibylline prohecy is a pointed counterpart of Otto von Freising's less happy view of the fate of the Emperors. The last Emperor, according to Gotfried, will struggle with Antichrist, but only Michael the Archangel will conquer the fiend (Waitz, *Gotifredi . . . Opera*, pp. 146f.). There can be no doubt about the sanctity of the Empire. As for the supremacy, four cities are the capitals of the Empire: Aachen, Arles, Milan, and Rome (p. 221), which shows that the Empire was above at least certain kingdoms. The symbolic if not the practical political gestures of history in Gotfried's time tended to support the supremacy: Henry VI, Gotfried's last sponsor, accepted the obeisance of Richard Lionheart, and the contemporary Leo of Armenia called himself King *per Romani imperii gratiam*.[125]

As was the case with Otto of Freising, this discussion of Gotfried of Viterbo has been painfully superficial. Even more than Otto, Gotfried deserves a closer investigation, particularly for his influence on the Remaissance. Otto's work is recognized for its importance at least in the Middle Ages, and Gotfried has been largely ignored, and this even though he left a notable impression on subsequent historiography. Such elements as Charlemagne's birth at Ingelheim and the formal component of Sibylline prophecy point out the extent of Gotfried's influence on later texts.

One of the few imaginative historians of the Middle Ages to enjoy abiding esteem is SAXO GRAMMATICUS (fl. 1200). Saxo is the main continental source for the deeds of the Germanic gods and has the distinction of preserving the Hamlet saga in its earliest form. He has been taken largely on his own terms and is considered a serious source

---

[124] Ernst Sackur, *Sibyllinische Texte und Forschungen* (1898; reprinted Turin, 1963), pp. 126–27.

[125] Finke, *Weltimperialismus . . .*, p. 12.

for folk tradition.[126] His colleagues to the south are rarely accorded such unprejudiced treatment.

Saxo does his best to satisfy the abiding curiosity about national or ethnic origins. Dan and Angul, sons of Humblus, are fathers of the Danes. Some say that they are named after the Danai of ancient Greece. The Angles stem from Angul.[127] The origin of the Lombards is also known to Saxo, but in an imperfect form. Aggo and Ebbo were of noble family in the North, and, in the course of a famine, they suggested to the assembly that the young and old be killed in order to allow the rest to survive. Their mother, Gamburuc, condemned the plan. It was decided that lots should be drawn, and that those selected should leave the land under Aggo and Ebbo. The goddess Frig later gave them their name, Langobards (*Saxonis Gesta* VIII.xiii. 1–2, in Olrik, I, 237–38). Saxo has confused Paul—whom he gives credit—and a story similar to that of the early twelfth-century origin of the Swabians, preserving the elements of the famine, the elimination of a part of the nation, the drawing of lots, the exodus under known leaders, and the arrival on the continent.

Among Saxo's heroic figures are King Wermund and his strong but stupid son Uffo. The Saxons, hereditary enemies of the Danes, challenged Wermund when he was old and blind. Uffo defended his father eloquently in council and bravely on the field, although he had been thought to be an idiot. He explained that when his father was strong he had no need for a strong son, but now in his dotage, the father required and had an eloquent and brave son (*Saxonis Gesta* IV.iii.i, and IV.iv–v, in Olrik, I, 92, 97–100). Albertus Krantz told the same story some three hundred years later.

Saxo's many tales of the gods seem to have confused the Renaissance. It remembers little of them, and we need only mention several curiosities. Othin and his wife Frigga were ordinary people who falsely took the dignity of godheads. They spent most of their time in Upsala (*Saxonis Gesta* I.vii.1, in Olrik, I, 25), although the seat of the gods

---

[126] Cf. the German translation by Hermann Jantzen, *Saxo Grammaticus* (Berlin, 1900) and the English translation by Oliver Elton, *The First Nine Books of the Danish History of Saxo Grammaticus* Publications of the Folk-Lore Society, XXXIII (1893; reprinted Nendeln/Liechtenstein, 1964) with introductory remarks by F. Y. Powell.

[127] *Saxonis Gesta Danorum* I.i.1–2, J. Olrik, et al., eds., 2 vols. (Copenhagen, 1931–57), I, 10. That we have a complete Latin text at all is due to its preservation in Badius's 1514 Paris printing (Renouard, I, 79 and III, 249). Cf. Manitius, III, 502ff. and Potthast, pp. 999ff. Substantially the same story of Danish origins appears in a later thirteenth-century text: Stephanus I. Stephanius, ed., *De Regno Daniae et Norwegiae* ... (Leyden, 1629), pp. 119–20.

was properly Byzantium (III.iv.9, in Olrik, I, 72). Thor was supposed to be equivalent to Jupiter and Othin to Mercury; but this is patent nonsense since Thor was Othin's son and Mercury was Jupiter's (IV.v.3–5, in Olrik, I, 152).

The myth of the *Imperium* was as alive in Denmark around 1200 as anywhere else in Europe, despite Denmark's relative distance from the main cultural highways and despite its extreme hostility to Germany. Charlemagne was known as Caesar (*Saxonis Gesta* XIV.xxxix.13, in Olrik, I, 467). He christianized Germany and protected the Rome of Pope Leo (VIII.xvi.5, in Olrik, I, 248). The prestige of the Empire was such that a marriage into the imperial house was a matter of great importance to neighboring monarchs. Canute's daughter, Gunnihild, was married to Henry, Prince of the Romans, who was to become Emperor Henry III (X.xvii.1, in Olrik, I, 291). Saxo was writing specifically for Denmark, and few of his many legends touch Germany directly. When they do, they are rarely flattering enough to the Renaissance sense of antiquity for the Germans to have accepted them wholeheartedly. Albertus Krantz was, however, in considerable debt to Saxo.[128]

In the course of the thirteenth century, the myth of the *Imperium* became quite literally canonized. That is to say, policy statements of Pope Innocent III were promulgated not long after his death as part and parcel of Canon Law. Such curiosities as the legend of Saints Eucharius, Valerius, and Maternus appear as legal explanations for the pope's never carrying a staff.[129] The myth of the *Imperium*, particularly the aspect of its supremacy, had become such a serious political issue that Innocent found it necessary to make some kind of clarification, one that would speak to the independence and rising power of other European crowns, while preserving appearances for imperial supremacy. This resulted in documents (1202/4) which came to mean that every king was emperor in his own realm.[130] Herewith Innocent eliminated the basis for imperial intervention in the affairs of monarchs not immediately subject to the emperor without denying, indeed while affirming the emperor's supremacy—an example of the Pope's renowned political acumen. The authority of the emperor, such as it was

---

[128] Paul Schaerffenberg, *Die Saxonia des Albert Krantz* (Meiningen, 1893), p. 12.
[129] Cf. Grundmann and Heimpel, *Alexander von Roes*, pp. 6 and 14 with notes.
[130] Richard Scholz, *Die Publizistik zur Zeit Philipps des Schönen und Bonifaz' VIII* (1903; reprinted Amsterdam, 1962), p. 232. cf. also Percy Ernst Schramm, *Der König von Frankreich*, 2nd ed., 2 vols. (Darmstadt, 1960), I, 181.

even in his own realm, remained untouched, as did the theoretical jurisdiction of the imperial chancellors over territories rarely under firm imperial control. The archbishops of Cologne, for example, continue to wear their title as imperial archchancellor for Italy.[131]

Perhaps the single most important document for the myth of the Empire is Innocent III's letter of 1202 which entered Canon Law as the decretal "Venerabilem."[132] It states that the Apostolic See:

> Romanum imperium in persona magnifici Karoli a Grecis transtulit in Germanos . . .

> [transferred the Roman Empire from the Greeks to the Germans in the person of the magnificent Charles . . .]

Henceforth, anyone who wished to argue the point had papal and later canonical support for at least two aspects of the imperial myth: that the Roman *Imperium* was transferred, and that the Germans received it. That Charles was German was obviously taken for granted.

The myth of the *Imperium*—and many others we have seen—rested on a broad base in the thirteenth century. Neither geography nor language restricted acceptance of the myths or their subjection to political designs. In Lombardy, which had long since been romanized, the myth of the Scandinavian origins of the Goths and Lombards remained very much alive. SICARDUS, Bishop of Cremona (d. 1215) preserves the story and points with pride to Aio and Agelmund as founders of the royal nation of the Lombards.[133] He has no objection to the grandeur of Charlemagne and to the importance of his imperial coronation (col. 493). The subjugation of the Lombard Kingdom under Charles perpetuated the unhappy interference in Italian affairs that was to cost both Germany and Italy genuine political independence for a thousand years. As Roman Emperors, the Germans had little choice but to establish their authority in Italy, or rather, to attempt to. The Italian policy of the Emperors represents one of those cases where myth overwhelms practical advantage. Emperor Frederick II, hardly an impractical dreamer, used every imaginable device to subjugate his Italian territories, and did not fail to remind the Romans of their Trojan

---

[131] Eduard Winkelmann, ed., *Acta imperii inedita*, 2 vols. (Innsbruck, 1880–85), I, 526 and II, 888, documents from the years 1220 and 1238.

[132] Krammer, *Quellen*, I, 53ff. and cf. Georgine Tangl, *Das Register Innocenz' III. über die Reichsfrage, 1198–1209*, Geschichtschreiber der deutschen Vorzeit, 2. Gesamtausgabe, XCV (Leipzig, 1923), pp. 117ff.

[133] *Chronicon*, in J. P. Migne, *PL*, CCXIII (Paris, 1855), 484. Sicardus was known and used by Cuspinianus, see Ankwicz-Kleehoven, *Cuspinianus*, p. 317.

origins over against the inferior Scandinavian origins of the Lombards, in order to win Roman support for his war against Lombard Milan (1234 A.D.).[134]

Still in the reign of Frederick II, there appeared a pair of texts in Saxon, "the Greek of German languages," that illustrate, first, the abiding popularity of a mythical view of history, and second, the increasing sophistication of vernacular technical literature. The creation and transmission of fictitious history in the Middle Ages was largely the doing of the learned tradition. A vernacular monument like the *Kaiserchronik* of the twelfth century is without serious competition until the *Sachsenspiegel* and *Sächsische Weltchronik* of the thirteenth (ca. 1220–48). The latter works are generally attributed to EIKE VON REPGOW (Potthast, pp. 992, 1109). The ancestors of the Saxons, Eike tells us, came from Alexander the Great's army.[135] Of the three hundred ships that left the conquered lands after Alexander's death, few survived; eighteen of the ships came to Prussia, and twenty-four eventually arrived in Saxony. Not only the Saxons, but also the Swabians stem from Alexander's army, according to Eike elsewhere.[136] Some say, however, that the Saxons originated among the Danes and Northmen, and others, that they came from Britain (Weiland, p. 85).

The major personages of Eike's history include Julius Caesar, who built many cities on the Rhine (Weiland, p. 85). Saints Eucharius, Maternus, and Valerius were sent by Saint Peter himself "to duischeme land" to convert the people (p. 95). After Augustulus ended in the year 476 what Augustus had begun, Theodoric held the "Rike" for thirty-one years "mit der dudischen helpe." Some say that Theodoric still lives in Hell, having fallen into a volcano (pp. 133–34). Eike mentions in passing Adelger of the Bavarians, who did battle against Emperor Severus (pp. 107–8). A close contemporary of Eike provides another authority for the list of Bavarian heroes: Udo, Geriwald (Garibald), Tassilo, and most importantly, Theodo—all princes of the Warwari or Bawari.[137]

---

[134] Burdach, *Rienzo*, p. 322.

[135] See Ch. XLIV, in C. von Schwerin, ed., *Sachsenspiegel* (Stuttgart, 1962), pp. 117–18. As a major document of common law, Eike's work was printed many times in the Renaissance. No fewer than 41 editions and translations appeared before 1600, some in Dutch, Latin, even Polish (Potthast, p. 992). Albert Krantz was proud of the Saxon accomplishment but felt he had to reject the myths of origin found there; see *Saxonia*, Basilius Faber, trans. (Leipzig, 1563), fol. XIXᵛ.

[136] L. Weiland, ed., *Sächsische Weltchronik*, MGH Deutsche Chroniken, II.1–384 (Hannover, 1877), p. 83.

[137] Wilhelm Wattenbach, ed., *Annales Austriae*, MGH SS, IX.479–843 (Hannover, 1851), p. 550, and cf. Potthast, p. 53.

The Empire is likely to play some part in any work as legally oriented as Eike von Repgow's. He preserves the westward move of the Empire from Babylon to Rome (Schwerin, p. 117). His catalogue of Roman rulers begins with Romulus and continues over Julius Caesar, Charlemagne, and Otto to Frederick II (Weiland, pp. 273–74). For Eike then the *Imperium* of the Romans is the Roman state and not simply the Empire. This political entity passed to the Franks and later to the Germans. One wonders whether Eike had any idea of the problems such phrasing would create in later times. Since his chronicle does not yet reflect the propagandistic historiography of the next generations, Eike's thought about German aid to Caesar and Theodoric's rule of the "Rike" probably cannot be called an intentional prototype of German possession of the Empire. On the other hand, the defensiveness characteristic of propagandistic writers enters Eike's description of the transference of the Empire. As soon as he states that the Germans have the Empire, he informs us of the covetousness with which France and others regard the imperial crown (Weiland, p. 150). Although this was true and was to become progressively more serious an issue, such a written statement is exceptional for the historical writing of Germany in the days before the *Interregnum*.

The encyclopedic trends of the Middle Ages reach a kind of peak in the thirteenth century. Eike's *Sachsenspiegel* is one of several attempts to codify common law in the vernacular. In the course of the century, the Corpus of Canon Law begins to receive the form it will keep until the Council of Trent. It is the century of Thomas Aquinas, indeed, a century of *summas*. VINCENT OF BEAUVAIS produced such a *summa* in his *Speculum Historialium* (1244). It preserves the story of the translation of the relics of the Three Magi from Milan to Cologne under Frederick I and his Chancellor Rainald, as well as the Troy myth of the Franks in the version with the younger Priam, son of Hector, leaving the fallen city.[138] A similar encyclopedia is BARTHOLOMEUS ANGLICUS's *De Proprietatibus Rerum* (ca. 1250). It preserves the tales of the Gothic women, the Amazons, and their leaders, Marpesia and Lampeto.[139] France, which used to be called Gaul, is named after

---

[138] O. Holder-Egger, ed., *Vincenti Bellovacensis Memoriale Omnium Temporum*, MGH SS, XXIV.154–67 (Hannover, 1879), p. 164, comp. Klippel, p. 32. The *Speculum Historialium*, of which the *Memoriale* is an excerpt, was published eight times by 1496 (Potthast, p. 1095). Vincent was known to Trithemius (*Catalogus*, fol. LXXXVI r f.).

[139] Robert Steele, *Medieval Lore from Bartholemew Anglicus* (London, 1924), pp. 82–83. Steele (p. 181) lists sixteen Latin editions before 1519, all but three of which appeared in Germany. Bartholomeus appears in Trithemius's *Catalogus* (fol. CXVI r).

a nation of Germany (Steele, p. 91). The origin of the name of England as it appeared in Werner Rolevinck, for example, shows a precedent in Bartholomeus: Engelia, daughter of the Duke of Saxony, gave her name to the island which Brute of Troy had originally named (Steele, p. 85).

Within the encyclopedic tradition, but more specifically in the lineage of the *Kaiserchronik* and its continuators, is RUDOLF OF EMS (fl. 1250–54) and his universal chronicle. He passes on the Troy myth, with Aeneas's brother Frigias of Phrygia as ancestor of "Franze," who named France.[140] Rudolf touches on the myth of the Empire in Conrad of Hohenstaufen, son of Frederick II, chosen by God to rule Jerusalem, Sicily, Arles, Rome, and Milan (Ehrismann, pp. 301–2). The first to rule over Greece, Rudolf tells us, was "Demorgon" (p. 45), not quite Boccaccio's and Celtis's Demogorgon, but surely the same "grammatical error become god."[141]

In 1245, Pope Innocent IV declared FREDERICK II deposed from the imperial throne. Within the very documents warning against obedience to the deposed Emperor, Innocent IV affirms the sacred ideals of the Empire, needless to say denying Frederick's adherence to them.[142] From Frederick's death in 1250 until the accession of Rudolf of Hapsburg in 1273, the Empire was without a head. In the absence of even a semblance of unity, imperial Europe fell on bad days indeed. The *Interregnum* marked the end of any lasting consequences of imperial political ambitions. Roman coronations continued to drain the coffers of the Emperors, and Italian interests continued to plague them, but a new Barbarossa or Frederick II was unthinkable. The beginnings of a major social change accompanied the political chaos of the *Interregnum* in imperial lands. In all of Europe, the knightly classes were giving way to the rising burghers. Thirteenth-century German letters widely reflect this change, and of our authors here Rudolf of Ems provides a clear example with his *Der gute Gerhard*. An age was ending, and a new one was beginning. Like the German authors of the *fin de siècle* with their Cassandra-cries at the end of the old order, the historians of the mid-thirteenth century in German lands detected the cataclysm and chronicled the demise of the traditional political and social universe. Another CONTINUATOR OF GOTFRIED OF VITERBO, writ-

---

[140] Gustav Ehrismann, ed., *Rudolf von Ems Weltchronik*, Deutsche Texte des Mittelalters, XX (Berlin, 1915), p. 370.

[141] Cf. Ch. III supra, notes 16–17.

[142] Winkelmann, *Acta imperii inedita*, I, 576.

ing in the midst of the *Interregnum* (ca. 1261), states that Frederick II was the final "ultimus" Emperor, having reigned for thirty-three years.[143] This continuator certainly meant "final" and not "most recent" when he wrote "ultimus." He knew Gotfried's Sibylline oracle and sensed that Frederick was the object of the prophecy. As the continuator was writing, the first false Emperor Frederick appeared in southern Italy with a considerable army.[144] It is little wonder that a Frederick myth grew up. An anonymous Franciscan chronicler of Erfurt tells us, also in 1261, that Henry Raspe, Landgrave of Thuringia (son of the Wagnerian Hermann I, Landgrave of Thuringia) had visited Frederick II and been told by him:[145]

> . . . tres . . . seduxerunt totum mundum, videlicet Moyses Hebreos, Christus Christianos et Machometus Barbaros.

> [. . . three have "seduced" the whole world, that is, Moses the Hebrews, Christ the Christians, and Mohammed the heathens.]

The ERFURT ANONYMOUS touches on other aspects of the imperial myth when he explains that Octavian took the title Augustus and thus gave it to all subsequent emperors, just as they are called Caesar in honor of Julius (Pistorius, pp. 706–7). The catalogue of Emperors naturally passes uninterruptedly from Caesar and Octavian through Charlemagne. The Roman Empire, which had since the time of Constantine, son of Helen, been in Constantinople, was transferred to the Germans in the person of Charles. To underscore the importance of the event, the Anonymous follows his citation of the "Venerabilem" with the usual description of the Roman acclamation and coronation of Charles by God (p. 728). Charlemagne remained the perfect symbol of the Roman and German in the Empire, and precisely these traits seem to have moved Otto III to search for Charles's bones in Aachen (p. 733). The sanctity of the Empire is shown to some extent by Frederick I's attributive, *vir catholicus*, by which the Anonymous surely

---

[143] Waitz, *Gotifredi Viterbensis Opera*, p. 24.

[144] This is reported in a Thuringian continuation of Eike von Repgow's *Sächsische Weltchronik* (Weiland, p. 296). Cf. Hermann Grauert, "Zur deutschen Kaisersage," *Historisches Jahrbuch*, XIII (1892), 108.

[145] Ed. by Johannes Pistorius in his *Illustrium veterum scriptorum ... tomus unus* (Frankfurt, 1583), p. 743. Cf. Potthast, pp. 235–36. The story seems to go back to a tenth-century Arabic text and was first applied to Frederick by Pope Gregory IX; see D. C. Allen, *Doubt's Boundless Sea* (Baltimore, 1964), pp. 224–25. Its regular appearance in German historiography is traceable to the Erfurt Anonymous. The elusive book inspired by the story has recently been edited and translated by Gerhard Bartsch and Rolf Walter, *De Tribus Impostoribus Anno MDIIC—Von den drei Betrügern 1598*, Quellen und Texte zur Geschichte der Philosophie (Berlin, 1960).

meant a religious and not a humanistic character. Frederick's chancellor Rainald brought the relics of the Three Magi from Milan (p. 737). Certainly among the best examples of piety in the Empire was the canonization of Saint Kunigunde, Empress of Henry, eighty-eighth Emperor since Caesar Augustus (p. 733).

A vague feeling of the troubles of the time imbues the work of the Anonymous of Erfurt, if only in the disparity between the reality of the headless Empire and the theoretical grandeur remembered by the learned tradition. The sudden appearance of a body of legend surrounding Frederick II also indicates a growing concern over the confused political conditions of the time. These worries developed into a sophisticated publicistic and theoretical literature which, however, points forward in time and which we shall consider shortly. As the *Interregnum* was drawing to a close, traditional historical learning was not quite ready to leave the stage. It produced, in the work of the Dominican monk, MARTINUS POLONUS, the last Latin universal chronicle written in German lands before the arrival of humanism. Martinus compiled much and added little. His chronicle was so extensive a summary that it replaced many of its sources and became nothing less than a medieval best-seller.

Martinus preserves Orosius's division of the four realms, Babylon in the east, Carthage in the south, Macedon in the north, and Rome in the west, with Orosius's westward move of Empire.[146] Within this temporal framework, Martinus proceeds through the history of Rome from Romulus. This includes the immolation of the Cimbrian and Teutonic women after the battle with Marius. The Germanic defeat seems almost to be presented in balance to Octavian's loss of three legions in Germany, Rome's worst defeat since the Punic wars. In the reign of Augustus, at a time when peace prevailed over the whole world, Christ chose to be born among men. Martinus is aware of the divine plan manifest in this coincidence, for he proceeds immediately to explain the "two swords" as the two powers in the world, Christ and Octavian—and their successors, the popes and the emperors (Weiland, p. 405).

The continuity of the Empire is a problem in Martinus. On the one hand he moves his catalogue of *Imperatores* from the beginnings over Augustulus, Odoacer, and Theodoric, as though the Germanic

---

146 L. Weiland, ed., *Martini Oppaviensis Chronicon*, MGH SS, XXII.377–475 (Hannover, 1872), p. 398. On knowledge of Martinus in the Renaissance, cf. Weiland, pp. 378, 380; Potthast, p. 772; and Trithemius, *Catalogus*, fol. CIIᵛ.

invaders wore the imperial crown of Rome (Weiland, pp. 443–51). On the other hand, Martinus explains that Otto I was the first Emperor of the Germans—"Theotonicorum" (p. 465). This represents a political development of the *Interregnum*, when the non-German peoples of the Empire used the chaos to extricate themselves from German control. They remained subjects of the Roman Empire but denied allegiance to the German King. The distinction could not exist in Germany since there was no separate German crown. Martinus shows elsewhere that he implies no such distinction, but his wording reflects the developments abroad and becomes a major historiographic source for the later confusion and debate about the starting point of German possession of the Empire.

The identity of ancient Roman and medieval German Empires may not be involved in Martinus's placing of Odoacer and Theodoric in the Roman lineage, particularly since he does not idealize Theodoric and preserves the story of his unholy demise (Weiland, p. 420). Nor does he necessarily imply the same identity when he reports Emperor Henry's discovery of the body of Pallas (pp. 399, 467). This report, however, contains an intrinsic implication of the special relationship between the German Emperors and the origins of Roman power. Whatever the trends of contemporary politics may have been, and however they may have induced Martinus to subdue this or that part of the imperial myth, its basic thrust was too strong to be suppressed altogether.

It is more than a manner of speaking to suggest that Martinus's world chronicle spells the end of medieval historiography in German lands—which is not to say that all subsequent historians were Leonardo Brunis. Many, perhaps most medieval preconceptions survived well into the Renaissance, particularly in vernacular historiography, which lacked even the semblance of a critical tradition. For Latin historiography in Germany, Martinus had accomplished his task so well that it did not need to be repeated until Gobelinus Persona, more than a century later—and Gobelinus wrote in a new spirit. The intervening years mark a series of important changes. The vernacular, however old-fashioned its viewpoint, begins to appear experimentally in a growing variety of technical jobs, including history and propaganda. Local history in the vernacular and in Latin rises, while universal history goes into temporary decline. Propaganda wars consume the energies of historians who simultaneously plunder and enrich the mythical past for their own purposes. Nevertheless, Martinus's work—a summary of medieval historical knowledge—keeps its authority over a long period of time, while a new world-view is evolving.

V

The renaissance myths of the german past from the interregnum to the council of constance

Most divisions into periods seem arbitrary. Some, however, are less arbitrary than others. The span of time from the Interregnum (1254-73) to the Council of Constance (1414–17), anchored partly in the northern Middle Ages and partly in the southern Renaissance, deserves special scrutiny. It is a period of extraordinary transitions, set between the specifically literary flowering of medieval Germany in the decades surrounding the year 1200 and the broader cultural flowering in art, music, scholarship, and religion in the fifteenth and sixteenth centuries.

In German literature, there is a clear continuity of undisturbed courtly tradition in the romance and lyric, from the time of Konrad von Würzburg (d. 1287) to Oswald von Wolkenstein (d. 1445), binding this period to the past. But there are also innovations pointing forward. In 1310, Frauenlob is reported by legend to have founded a school for "Meistersang" in Mainz. The event heralds symbolically the burghers' claim to the right of literary expression. As the century proceeds, the vernacular rises dramatically in importance, palpably in the service of the cities and their citizens. Early New High German comes into being out of and alongside late Middle High German. Historiography turns with greater frequency to the vernacular and is increasingly under the patronage of the burghers rather than of the feudal courts. It records historical moments in vernacular literature (e.g., the *Limburger Chronik*, ca. 1398, and Jacob Twinger)—rarely, to be sure; nevertheless, for the first time in Germany, literary history becomes a part of history proper.

Latin historiography in the North undergoes a real change during and after the Interregnum. The encyclopedic tradition falls victim to its periodic hypertrophy in the thirteenth century—witness the completely unmanageable *Speculum Universale* of Vincent of Beauvais. Universal history, as a subspecies of the encyclopedia, temporarily exhausts itself in the comprehensive and wholly derivative chronicle of Martinus Polonus, and seems to disperse its energies in florilegia, continuations of Martinus and his peers, and attention to local or contemporary history.

Thus the Interregnum provides one terminus for periodization. Contemporary Germans blamed much of their grief on the vacancy of the imperial throne. The confusions certainly abetted the fragmentation of imperial lands within and without Germany, and more than any other event encouraged the ideal of a unified Empire, free of internal strife. In direct proportion to the rise of the competing cities and new dynasties, certain intellectual forces fostered the myth of the Empire. It was perhaps a reaction against the political, social, and economic changes that were everywhere evident but not necessarily comprehensible to the observers at the time. For the myths of the German past, this one preoccupation overshadows the Latin historiography and, for most of the fourteenth century, the vernacular historiography as well. Polemicists take a most important place beside other sources of speculation about the German past. The relative stability of history as a discipline in the Middle Ages, a result perhaps of its patronage by theology, begins to be shaken by a panoply of partisan interests which force historical argument to serve their own ends: curial, imperial, dynastic, national, provincial, and civic. In Germany, the partisan interests are inevitably and inextricably bound up with the *Imperium* and its politics. Thus, with a few important exceptions, the myths of origins, heroes, religion, and virtue and vice are subordinated to the myth of the *Imperium*.

The other terminus, the Council of Constance, with its importation of learned men from all over the world, especially the south, into German lands, is conventionally regarded as the first large-scale entry of the new learning into Germany.[1] That this conventional view leaves something to be desired has been proven by Konrad Burdach and his

---

[1] As examples of this view Johannes Maasen, *Drama und Theater der Humanisten-Schulen in Deutschland* (Augsburg, 1929), p. 9, and R. F. Arnold, ed., *Das deutsche Drama* (Munich, 1925), p. 122, can be cited.

colleague Paul Piur.[2] Despite numerous assaults on their work, no question remains but that early figures of the Italian Renaissance— Petrarch in literature and Rienzo in visionary politics—left in their own lifetimes an indelible impression on German lands. The time of the Council of Constance may, however, be considered if not the first then the second dawn of the Renaissance in Germany. It certainly marked the end of a greater period of transition, when the medieval still controlled the minds of men; and just as certainly, it marked the beginning of an age, when the new could survive side by side with the old and, in some cases, prevail.

Between these two *termini*, the elements of the imperial myth created by the tradition were gathered together and forged into the structures they would carry into the Renaissance. Since the codification of this myth's symbolic content seems to be the largest contribution to the myths of the German past made by the fourteenth century, the *Imperium* will be our main concern. The myth in its overall framework supports, as we have seen, the belief that the Empire is Roman, German, sacred, and supreme. The Emperor stands in uninterrupted succession with Caesar, Augustus, Constantine, and Justinian. Since the time of Charlemagne or Otto, the Emperor and his electors have been German. The Emperor's office is virtually sacramental, charged with ecclesiastical responsibilities and religious connections of a high order. The Emperor's crown is the most prestigious in Christendom, of higher dignity than any other—a concept best articulated in this period. The quixotic defenders of an impotent Empire never made more extravagant claims in its behalf. These were angrily reacted against by the defenders of national sovereignty. It is only after the Interregnum that the supremacy of the imperial *auctoritas* genuinely troubled other states.[3]

The continuity of the Empire from Roman times was axiomatic in the Middle Ages, so much so that, as we have seen, it eventually be-

---

[2] For their work in substantiating the new view, see Konrad Burdach, *Vom Mittelalter zur Reformation*, 11 vols. (Berlin, 1893–1935), e.g., II.i, 16–17; IV, 35ff., 59–60, 65–66; V, intro., pp. xxixff. Burdach has been widely attacked: e.g. Paul Joachimsen, *Vom Mittelalter zur Reformation* (Darmstadt, 1959), pp. 31, 41, 45, and passim (reprint of article in *Historische Zeitschrift*, XX [1920/21], 420–70).

[3] Robert Holtzmann, *Der Weltherrschaftsgedanke des mittelalterlichen Kaisertums und die Souveränität der europäischen Staaten* (Darmstadt, 1953), p. 29.

came canonical. Innocent III's Decretum *Venerabilem* was taken into the corpus of canon law by the middle of the thirteenth century and remained there until the canonical reforms of the late nineteenth and early twentieth centuries.[4] The Empire that was transferred from the Greeks to the Germans was clearly the Roman Empire and none other. In Jansen Enikel's Middle High German chronicle (last quarter of the thirteenth century), the presentation of the history of the Emperors proceeds traditionally over Constantine the Great to Charles the Great.[5] Although the medieval Emperors were, by and large, ostentatiously German, and although the Germans were roundly condemned for their ignorance of Roman law, the German Emperor, like Justinian before him, was universally considered the protector of the Roman law.[6] The Emperor swore an oath to preserve the Justinian code. When a non-Roman wished to be judged under Roman law, he required the German Emperor's consent.[7] John of Paris (fl. 1303) in asserting French independence of the Empire, explained that the French crown had the right to do away with imperial, that is, Roman law, and to establish a national law of its own.[8] The notion that the Emperor, himself a German functioning with Germanic law, might not be the embodiment of the Justinian code never occurred to John of Paris. The mystical connection between the medieval Emperor and ancient Rome finds further expression in these years (ca. 1300) in a retelling of the incident where Emperor Henry finds the remains of Pallas.[9]

The *Venerabilem* makes it unequivocally clear that the Empire had been transferred into German hands. The transference was not always readily acknowledged, but ultimately the papal utterance left no alter-

---

[4] Mario Krammer, ed., *Quellen zur Geschichte der deutschen Königswahl und des Kurfürstenkollegs*, 2 vols. (Berlin and Leipzig, 1911–12), I, 53ff. [henceforth "Krammer, *Quellen*," with appropriate vol. number].

[5] Philipp Strauch, ed., *Jansen Enikels Werke*, MGH Deutsche Chroniken, III (Hannover and Leipzig, 1900), foreword and pp. 498ff. (ll. 25, 539ff.).

[6] Konrad Burdach, *Rienzo und die geistige Wandlung seiner Zeit* (Berlin, 1913–28), pp. 184 and 189.

[7] *Ibid.*, pp. 185–86.

[8] Richard Scholz, *Die Publizistik zur Zeit Philipps des Schönen und Bonifaz' VIII* (Stuttgart, 1903), pp. 384–85 [henceforth "Scholz, *Publizistik*"]. Cf. Fritz Bleienstein, ed. and trans., *Johannes Quidort von Paris: Über königliche und päpstliche Gewalt (De regia potestate et papali)*, Frankfurter Studien zur Wissenschaft der Politik, IV (Stuttgart, 1969), pp. 190–91.

[9] Oswald Holder-Egger, ed., *Flores Temporum*, MGH SS, XXIV.225–50 (Hannover, 1879), p. 237.

native. Various curiosities show the reluctance of some to accept the German possession of the Empire. A protocol from Siena on the reception of Rudolf of Hapsburg's daughter in 1281 alters *imperatoris* to *regis Alamaniae electi*.[10] It was an obvious avoidance of diplomatic recognition, an attempt to deny Rudolf authority in Siena. Philipp IV of France uses in a treaty of 1305 *rex alemannus* as the consistent nomenclature for Albert of Hapsburg.[11] Albert at the same time naturally refers to himself as *Romanorum rex*.[12] After his Roman coronation (29 June 1312), Henry VII calls himself *Henricus Dei gratia Romanorum imperator semper augustus* in a complaint to Philipp IV. Philipp in his reply addresses Henry *Victorissimo principi regi Alemanie et Romanorum imperatori semper augusto. . . .*[13]

Philipp was dividing the functions of German King and Roman Emperor. This division was a necessity for a French King with ambitious designs on the imperial crown, and a great convenience for those princes and cities long unaccustomed to imperial interference. Such arguments enjoyed the widest circulation in these years, particularly in the non-German territories of the Empire. The underlying intent was to preserve the independence acquired by default in the Interregnum even now, in the presence of a legitimate ruler. The legal neologism maintained that the head of the Empire possessed rightful authority only over those who elected him and participated in his coronation at Aachen, in other words, only the Germans, until such time as he had undertaken the costly business of a Roman coronation.[14] This made him Emperor with titular authority over the whole Empire, which authority was, however, remote and general, distinct from his proximate and specific authority in Germany.

The very attempt to separate the titles betrays a sharp if reluctant awareness of the German character of the Empire. The Emperor, while in fact some sort of King of the Germans, nowhere received such a title. His election and coronation at Aachen made him King of the Romans, his coronation in Rome made him their Emperor. By pretending to recognize a non-existent German crown distinct from the Roman crown, this policy succeeds only in identifying the Roman crown as German.

---

[10] Fritz Kern, ed., *Acta Imperii, Angliae et Franciae ab a. 1267 ad a. 1313* (Tübingen, 1911), p. 168, item 248.

[11] *Ibid.*, pp. 102–3, item 155.

[12] *Ibid.*, p. 107, item 161.

[13] *Ibid.*, pp. 151–52, items 228, 229.

[14] Fritz Kern, *Die Reichsgewalt des deutschen Königs nach dem Interregnum* (Darmstadt, 1959), p. 30 and passim.

The sanctity of the Empire takes on new dimensions in this period as old and new arguments are brought together to guarantee it a divinely ordained place in a divinely ordered universe. The attraction of the name "Roman Emperor" was no doubt explained at least in part by the sacramental character it bore. All through the first third of the fourteenth century, while the French crown was consolidating its power at home, it kept one eye on possible seizure of the imperial crown.[15] This attraction was not a new one, generated only by the political, social, and economic chaos of the Empire that attracted contestants for the imperial title from all over Europe during the Interregnum. The mystical associations quite transcended practical material realities. Richard of Cornwall, for example, proudly saw himself as King of the Romans, however useless, in fact burdensome the honor was to him.[16]

The primacy of the imperial crown was repeatedly at issue in these years, symbolically affirmed in inverse proportion to its political might. The French found it necessary to make assertions of independence from the Emperor, despite the fact that the Emperor was far too weak to threaten the power of any monarch. John of Paris cited canon law to support his sovereign.[17] It seems to have made no difference that the canonical bases of national monarchial independence were at least a century old, or that the Empire had not yet recovered from the political debacle of the Interregnum.

A few years before John of Paris, another French publicist produced a document supporting France's claims on Lyons (ca. 1296/7). The document explained that civil law guaranteed the King of France all the *imperium* (power) in his kingdom, just as the Emperor was in possession of the same in the *imperium* (Empire):[18]

Rex Francie est in loco imperatoris in regno suo et sicut imperator est dominus mundi quatenus extenditur imperium suum. . . .

[The King of France is in his own kingdom in the place (position) of the Emperor, and like the Emperor he is lord of the world insofar as his realm extends. . . .]

---

15 Hermann Grauert, "Dubois (p.) de recuperatione terre sancte," *Historisches Jahrbuch*, XII (1891), 809 and 812; cf. Attilio Hortis, ed., *Scritti inediti di Francesco Petrarca* (Trieste, 1874), p. 190.

16 In 1272: see Hermann Grauert, "Zur deutschen Kaisersage," *Historisches Jahrbuch*, XIII (1892), 118–19.

17 Scholz, *Publizistik*, p. 328.

18 Fritz Kern, ed., *Acta Imperii*, pp. 199–200, item 271.

The entire argument purposes a removal of incursions on royal authority, with an assertion of independence and equal dignity. The chosen vocabulary, however, goes farther toward affirmation of the imperial myth than toward political reality. The French King was, after all, independent of the Emperor and more than his political equal. The argument's antistasis of *imperium* (power) and *imperium* (empire) indicates that the power of the monarch is imperial. The back-handed admission that the emperor is lord of the world is almost startling from the pen of an anti-imperial polemicist. The difficulties of the phrase *in loco* may be circumvented by saying that the king "represents" the emperor. This may mean that the king reigns in his own kingdom as the emperor does in the empire, the connection between the two being only simile. On the other hand, it may mean quite literally that the king reigns in the emperor's stead. Both interpretations reside in the wording and seem to be implied by it, however different the ramifications. At the roots of the whole argument is the unavoidable supremacy of the imperial office. This cannot be disputed; only what the supremacy may imply is the subject of dispute.

Aegidius Romanus, a curialist of French sympathies, hence doubly anti-imperial, writes (ca. 1300) that the *imperium* enjoys a place above all *regna*, this despite the fact that the document was intended for French eyes.[19] John of Paris momentarily forgets his doctrine of French sovereignty by admitting that the emperor, like Caesar Augustus, had the right to tax the whole world, if he saw fit.[20] Hardly a friend of the Empire, John had to admit, if indeed one lord ruled the world, he could be none other than the emperor.[21] Edward II (1307–27) formally submitted to Emperors Henry VII and Ludwig the Bavarian in the first decades of the fourteenth century, as his predecessor Henry II had to Barbarossa in the twelfth.[22] Boniface VIII (1249–1303) was hostile to all secular monarchy, but made it clear that the emperor was ruler over kings and princes and that all Christians were subject to him.[23] The King of Naples is supposed to have written at this time:[24]

---

[19] Scholz, *Publizistik*, p. 106.
[20] *Ibid.*, p. 351.
[21] *Ibid.*, p. 326.
[22] H. Finke, *Weltimperialismus und nationale Regungen im späteren Mittelalter*, Freiburger Wissenschaftliche Gesellschaft, IV (Freiburg/Br. and Leipzig, 1916), p. 45.
[23] *Ibid.*, p. 16.
[24] Edwin H. Zeydel, *The Holy Roman Empire in German Literature* (New York, 1918), p. 13.

Nos reges omnes debemus reverentiam Imperatori, tamquam summo regi, qui est Caput et Dux regum. . . .

[We kings all owe reverence to the emperor, as to the highest king, who is the head and leader of kings. . . .]

The Empire was a direct descendent of its Roman ancestor; it was in the hands of the Germans; its specially religious character made it the foremost crown in Christendom; and all lands were somehow subservient to it. The myth of the *imperium* had a hard political reality in the generations after the Interregnum just as it had in those before. Each element was a matter of absolute conviction among the Germans and among many others in the fourteenth century and onwards. The others did not always profess this conviction, but had often to confront it, as though it were practical reality.

The general theory of the Empire as expressed in the political thought and practice of the day was a setting for activities other than political wrangling. As an inescapable part of the medieval universe, it penetrated the work of countless authors of varying interests and pretensions. From the general framework of the Empire, I move now to consider some authors who touch upon things German and who wrote within that overall framework.

JANSEN ENIKEL's Middle High-German chronicle is solidly rooted in the older period, but adds something of the new. Most of what was said about the *Kaiserchronik* in the previous chapter prevails for Jansen's work, since he was heavily indebted to it.[25] For example, he repeats the tale of the Trojan origin of the Franks much as he found it in the *Kaiserchronik*: after the fall of Troy, Aeneas and Franco flee westward, the latter to the Rhine (Strauch, pp. 320–21). He similarly preserves the high respect for Julius Caesar and his founding of Rhenish cities. From another source, the popular epic *Herzog Ernst*, Jansen takes some mythological monsters, the dreadful "Plattfüsse," and attributes their expulsion from Germany to Caesar, for which service future generations were no doubt profoundly grateful. Caesar

---

25 Philipp Strauch, ed., *Jansen Enikel*, p. lxiii. Enikel's work continued to be read in the Renaissance, e.g., by Cuspinianus (Strauch, pp. iv, xvii, c). A copy of the chronicle was in the possession of Maximilian I: see Theodor Gottlieb, *Büchersammlung Kaiser Maximilians*, Die Ambraser Handschriften—Beitrag zur Geschichte der Wiener Hofbibliothek, I, (1900; reprinted Amsterdam, 1968) p. 101, item 212; cf. p. 162, s.v. "Jansen der Enenkel."

was also known to have battled with the Bavarian heroes Ingram and Boimunt (Strauch, pp. 402ff.).

The deeds of the Bavarians are treated with some elaboration not long after Enikel's work. In the first years of the fourteenth century, a chronicle appears which traces Bavarian origins back to Armenia, as had been done in the *Kaiserchronik*, and names the heroes connected with the origins: Warwarus led his people out of Armenia to Noricum, which takes its name from Norix, son of Hercules.[26]

Jansen Enikel does not dwell on the history of any one German people. His chronicle is more generally directed to the history of the Empire at large. I mentioned above Jansen's sense of imperial continuity between Constantine and Charlemagne. While this is most traditional, Jansen takes some liberty with the tradition and his model in the *Kaiserchronik* by making the continuity immediate. No apparent publicistic reason exists for this extraordinary anachronism in a purportedly historical work like Jansen's. Of course, he may have leafed through his sources carelessly and picked up after Constantine VI when he meant to begin again after Constantine I. The difficulty with such an explanation is that it implies a most faulty sense of history in Jansen without revealing the principle upon which such an error could be made. The loss of 500 years of imperial history is perfectly understandable and not really unhistoric within the framework of the myth of the Empire: the myth maintains an uninterrupted succession between Byzantium and Aachen. Jansen merely extends the principle of immediate succession from the possessors of the Empire (Greeks and then Germans) to the notable individuals who marked the change of possession (Constantine, who brought the Empire to the Greeks, and Charlemagne, who brought it to the Germans).

The place of Charlemagne is customarily large in Jansen's chronicle and ties it to the tradition. He remembers, for example, how the Frankish King acquired the Empire by the defeat of the Lombards in aid of the mutilated pope (Strauch, pp. 498ff.). Jansen goes beyond the tradition, however, by introducing material alien to the historical conventions, such as the popular tale of the "Liebeszauber."[27] Charlemagne's beloved has died. The great King continues to dote over the dead woman, until a pious cleric discovers a magic charm under her

---

[26] Georg Waitz, ed., *Historiae Patavienses et Cremifanenses*, MGH SS, XXV.610–78 (Hannover, 1880), p. 639. This and not the *Kaiserchronik* seems to be the immediate source for these stories in the Renaissance, as in the *Mühldorfer Annalen* (1428), the Schedel chronicle, Aventinus, and others.

[27] Cf. F. H. von der Hagen, ed., *Gesamtabenteuer*, 3 vols. (1850; reprinted Darmstadt, 1961), I, intro., p. li; II, 614–34; III, intro., p. clxiif.; also Gaston Paris, *Histoire poétique de Charlemagne*, 2nd ed. (Paris, 1905), pp. 383ff.

tongue. When the charm is removed, Charles comes to his senses, the body decays, and the monarch submits to humble penance. Jansen's modification of history in favor of fable is not necessarily as retrogressive as it may first appear. This very tale caught the ear of Petrarch and thus entered German Renaissance historiography. Further, relative originality and the exploitation of new sources for historical writing are much more characteristic of the practice of history after the Council of Constance than before the Interregnum.

Jansen Enikel concludes his chronicle with another extraordinary tale, but one we have often seen. FREDERICK II, it seems, never died but is wandering about the Empire (Strauch, p. 574). A continuator of the anonymous Franciscan chronicler of Erfurt (the one who introduced the "three seducers" story) relates a prophecy that a branch would grow from the tree of Frederick, a branch that would prevail over the whole world and humble even the pope.[28] This was written about 1272. The anonymous author of the epic *Reinfrid von Braunschweig* (ca. 1300) reports similarly that Frederick would return to plague Christianity.[29] A north German chronicle (from Lübeck), composed about 1276, relates (as Enikel does) that long after Frederick II's death people said he lived on.[30]

A continuator of Eike von Repgow reports (to the year 1275) that Frederick's death was not universally accepted.[31] The second redaction of the above-mentioned north German chronicle (from Lübeck) tells the story that a man came to Lübeck claiming to be Frederick the Emperor and that the people did him great honor. Later, the word came that he had been burned somewhere along the Rhine.[32] The Austrian chronicler Ottokar (fl. 1309) reports a fine reception of the false Frederick among the nobles.[33] A continuator of Martinus Polonus writes (ca. 1308–23) that the man claiming to be Frederick said that he would

---

28 Oswald Holder-Egger, ed., *Chronica minor auctore Minorita Erphordiense*, MGH SS, XXIV.172–213 (Hannover, 1879), p. 207.

29 Karl Bartsch, ed., *Reinfrid von Braunschweig*, BLVS, CIX (Tübingen, 1871), p. 524; cf. Franz Guntram Schultheiss, *Die deutsche Volkssage vom Fortleben und der Wiederkehr Kaiser Friedrichs II.*, Historische Studien, XCIV (Berlin, 1911), pp. 49–50 [henceforth "Schultheiss, *Die deutsche Volkssage*"].

30 K. Koppmann, ed., *Detmar-Chronik*, Chroniken der deutschen Städte, XIX (Leipzig, 1884), p. 95.

31 L. Weiland, ed., *Sächsische Weltchronik*, MGH Deutsche Chroniken, II.1–384 (Hannover, 1877), p. 285.

32 Koppmann, *Detmar-Chronik*, pp. 151 and 367.

33 Joseph Seemüller, ed., *Ottokars österreichische Reimchronik*, MGH Deutsche Chroniken, V. i (Hannover, 1890), pp. 421ff.

stay a little while and return in the future.[34] The earliest report of this false Frederick seems to be in the anonymous continuation of the chronicle of Girardus of Arvenia. Written in 1287, it announces the appearance in 1284 of the false Frederick at Cologne and Neuss. The report is repeated by Sigfrid von Balnhusen in 1307.[35] The older "three seducers" story appears again in these years in a ca. 1300 redaction of a popular historical anthology.[36]

These are the more or less historical reports concerning Frederick from a time when many people were still alive who could have been late contemporaries of the dead Emperor. The extensive distribution of the Frederick myth such a short time after his death points toward a need in the popular mind for a salvation-bringing hero. The breadth and depth of this myth clearly reflect the sense of political disorder felt throughout German lands in and after the Interregnum. The threat of the mythical Frederick to the pope is one of the early signs of popular disenchantment with prevailing religious custom, a sign of popular demand for renewal. The myth did not remain in the province of folklore but spread to the hands of the most sophisticated propagandists, who expressed these demands for the formal literary tradition.

Of these propagandists, one of the earliest and most important is ALEXANDER VON ROES (fl. 1281).[37] Alexander's *Memoriale de prerogativa Imperii Romani* articulated the eschatological characteristics of the legend surrounding Frederick II: an "old" German prophecy claimed that out of Frederick II's seed another Frederick would come to humiliate the clergy in Germany, cause great trouble for the Roman Church, and signal the end of the Empire.[38]

---

[34] L. Weiland, ed., *Continuationes Chronici Martini Oppaviensis* MGH SS, XXIV. 251–65 (Hannover, 1879), p. 263.

[35] Oswald Holder-Egger, ed., *Sigfridus de Balnhusin: Historia Universalis*, MGH SS, XXV.679–718 (Hannover, 1880), p. 710; see n. 4 there for the report of the continuator of Girardus.

[36] Holder-Egger, *Flores Temporum*, p. 241.

[37] Alexander's identity was submerged under that of Jordanus of Osnabrück until the studies of Wilhelm Schraub, *Jordan von Osnabrück und Alexander von Roes: Ein Beitrag zur Geschichte der Publizistik im 13. Jahrhundert*, Heidelberger Abhandlungen zur mittleren und neueren Geschichte, XXVI (Heidelberg, 1910), pp. 26, 36, and passim. On Trithemius's and Hermann Peter aus Andlau's relations to these texts, cf. Georg Waitz, "Des Jordanus von Osnabrück Buch über das Römische Reich," *Abhandlungen der historisch-philologischen Classe der königlichen Gesellschaft der Wissenschaften zu Göttingen*, XIV (1868/9), 3–4, 17.

[38] I cite regularly the earlier ed. and trans. by Herbert Grundmann and Hermann Heimpel, *Die Schriften des Alexander von Roes*, MGH Deutsches Mittelalter, IV (Weimar, 1949), here pp. 56–57 [henceforth "Grundmann/Heimpel"].

The last Emperor marks a special event, the coming of Antichrist. The sacramental dignity of the Roman Empire is such that God gave it the following privilege: not until the Empire is completely ended can the Adversary come (Grundmann/Heimpel, pp. 30–31). Leaning on II Thess. ii.7–8 and the traditional exegesis, Alexander explains that the one who is now holding off the Adversary is the Empire. When it has ceased to be, the Antichrist comes (pp. 26–27, 96–97).

Alexander took up his pen in defense of the Empire when he felt its sacramental character slighted. While celebrating the liturgy in Viterbo in 1280, he found that the prayer for the Emperor had been struck from the missal he was using (Grundmann/Heimpel, p. 20 and n.3). In distress over the omission, he composed his *Memoriale* and included in it a brief polemic by Jordanus von Osnabrück. The sanctity of the Empire was of prime importance to both polemicists. Christ Himself placed His approval on the Roman Empire in at least two ways: by choosing to come to earth in the period of the Roman peace, and then by choosing within that period the very time of an imperial census (Grundmann/Heimpel, pp. 22ff.). Not only the sanctity of the Empire, but its continuity from antiquity find emphatic support in these views. Alexander and Jordanus saw no basic difference between Augustus's Empire and that of Frederick II.

The sanctity and the German character of the Empire become one in Alexander's explanation of the transference of the Empire. It has been given over into German hands until the second coming of Christ:

> Sic manifestum est . . . quod Romanum imperium in fine seculorum transferri oportuit in Germanos (Grundmann/Heimpel, pp. 66–67).

To support the transference of the Empire to the Germans, Alexander relates the legend of Saint Maternus (pp. 60ff.). Saint Peter sent Eucharius, Valerius, and Maternus to Alsatia to preach the Holy Trinity. Maternus sickened and died in the town of Legia (Ehl). The two survivors returned to Rome, where Saint Peter gave them his staff to revive Maternus. They returned and raised him from the dead. When Maternus had finished his work, he died in Cologne. According to the instructions of an Angel, his body was brought to Trier for final burial. Saint Peter's staff, however, was divided. The lower half was sent to Trier with Maternus, and the upper half remained in Cologne.[39] The legend is raised in importance somewhat over the

---

[39] Grundmann/Heimpel, pp. 64–65 and notes 1 and 2 there. We may note in passing that Alexander preserves the tale of the founding of Trier by Trebeta (pp. 36–37), and names the Palatinate after the palace in Trier (pp. 30ff. and 40ff.). Aventinus took this notion directly from Alexander (*Werke*, VI.i [Munich, 1882], 96), crediting "Jordan von Osnaburg." Otto of Freising reports (above, p. 232) the reverse fate for the two halves of the staff, but he seems to be in error.

norm of medieval legend by the convention that the pope (despite Wagner's *Tannhäuser*) not carry a staff. This convention with the explanation provided by the Maternus legend was incorporated into canon law.[40] Alexander explained that, long before the fact, the Empire had been transferred to Germany by the sending of Saint Peter's staff to northern lands:

> Et hec est causa, quare Romanus episcopus baculum non habet pontificalem, quem utique beatus Petrus spiritu prophetico transmisit ad Germanos. . . .
>
> Hunc itaque baculum beatus Petrus Romanus et Antiochenus episcopus per Eucharium et Valerium transmisit ad Galliam Belgicam, dum Romanus pontifex per manus magnifici Karoli Romanum imperium de Grecis transtulit in Germanos . . . (Grundmann/Heimpel, pp. 64ff.).
>
> [And this is the reason why the Bishop of Rome does not have an episcopal staff, for Saint Peter, truly, sent it in the spirit of prophecy to the Germans. . . .]
>
> [And just as the blessed Peter, Bishop of Rome and Antioch, sent his staff to Belgian Gaul through Eucharius and Valerius, just so did the Roman Pontiff transfer the Roman Empire from the Greeks to the Germans through the hands of the magnificent Charles. . . .]

Alexander interprets the legend himself with this reference to the *Venerabilem*. He makes it unequivocally clear that the Empire was a sacred institution (*sacerdotale regnum*) and German. The raw materials of the Maternus legend remained in widespread circulation. A contemporary of Alexander, Gotfrid Hagen (fl. 1277–87), incorporated them into his much read German verse chronicle, assuring the survival of the legend in vernacular historiography, particularly in Cologne where it would be treasured.[41]

The course of Alexander's polemics reveals his angry insistence that the transference of the Empire was to the Germans and not to the French, despite their preemption—as Alexander saw it—of Charles in whom the transfer was effected (Grundmann/Heimpel, pp. 32–33). In discussing this problem I make use of Alexander's second known work, the *Notitia Seculi* of 1288. In both this and the *Memoriale* Alexander uses a combination of Troy myths to distinguish between Franks and

---

[40] Grundmann/Heimpel, p. 65.

[41] H. Cardauns and K. Schröder, eds., "Gotfrid Hagen: Dit is dat boich van der Stede Colne," *Chroniken der deutschen Städte*, XII (Leipzig, 1875), 24–26. Cf. pp. 6 and 14 there on the dating and the survival of Hagen's chronicle into the *Koelhoffische Chronik* of 1499.

French.[42] Aeneas and Priam (no mention of Francio), grandson of Priam the Great, flee Troy after its fall, migrate through Africa, and then Italy where Aeneas remains. Priam moves on to the Rhine where he forces the Gauls westward. Here he founds two cities; one is called the other Troy (Xanthen) and the second, Verona (Bonn). These Trojans take wives from among the Teutons, who are descendents of giants. Alexander explains elsewhere that Teutonic and German are the same thing (Grundmann/Heimpel, pp. 90–91). These Trojans assume the language of their wives. They are called German because they spring from the same seed, "germen," as the Romans. Alexander rejects Isidore of Seville and Honorius of Autun on this etymology, calling their version contradictory to the truth of the matter. He thus provides one of the rare medieval instances of *anasceua*.

The Germans, Alexander continues, then become known as Franks when, having aided their brother Romans against the Alani, they are freed of tribute. Those who moved on to the lands between Seine and Loire and who married Gallic women are called French—"Francigenae." They are French and not Franks because they only stem from the Franks.

Alexander then proceeds through the traditional and vaguely accurate history of the Franks through Hildricus (Chilperich) and Pippin to the time of Charlemagne (Grundmann/Heimpel, pp. 40–45). In making one of his main points, that Charlemagne was of the German nation, the publicist tells a pleasant story of Charles's forefathers. The messenger announcing to Pippin II the birth of his son calls out *Vivat rex quia karl est!* (pp. 42–43). Alexander explains that "karl" in German is a compliment to a robust man (modern German "Kerl"?), and thus in disguised fashion informed Pippin of his paternity. *Bonum nomen est Karl!* exclaims Pippin. The child was Charles Martel. Thus also Andreas of Regensburg, a century and a half later.

Charles Martel's son Pippin freed the Roman Church from the Lombards. His son Charlemagne, in turn, did the same when the Greeks steadfastly refused their aid to the pope. For his services, Charles was first named Patrician of the Romans. Later, the Pope withdrew the Empire from the Greeks and crowned Charles Emperor of the Romans (Grundmann/Heimpel, pp. 44–45). The Emperors seem constantly to be freeing Rome of the Lombards. This activity is in any case one of the constant accoutrements of the imperial myth, at least in the presence of Charlemagne or Otto the Great. It is sometimes

---

[42] Grundmann/Heimpel, pp. 34ff. and 80ff. Alexander's version is the immediate source for Rothe's version of the Troy myth in the *Düringische Chronik*.

employed to prove that Lombardy is papal,[43] sometimes to prove that it is imperial,[44] always implying the pious mission of the Emperor. In connection with Charlemagne's work in Italy, a markedly anti-Greek feeling becomes apparent in Alexander. Greece's failure to aid the pope and the Byzantine schism with the West left considerable ill feeling which prevailed throughout the period under discussion here and to some extent on into the Renaissance. Alexander concludes his discussion of Charlemagne in the *Memoriale* with a suggestion that one go to Aachen to hear all the wonderful stories about Charles (pp. 44ff.). This is just what Petrarch did a half century later.[45]

In the *Notitia Seculi* Alexander makes the plain statement on which his history of the Frankish realm rests:

> Nec est dubium, quin Karolus fuisset Theutonicus, licet ipse super Gallicos regnaverit (Grundmann/Heimpel, pp. 94–95).

> [There is no doubt but that Charles was German, even though he reigned over Gauls (the French).]

For Charles named in his mother tongue, that is, German, the months and the days of the week [sic]. Alexander was compelled to make Charles's German nationality transparently clear, since Charlemagne was, in living tradition, ancestor of the French kings. A document of 1267 addresses to Philipp of France mentions *attavus regis Francie Karolus Magnus*.[46] A somewhat later document (1328) announces:[47]

> O Francorum rex excellentissime . . . Te enim pre ceteris mundi regibus timent et omnes alii credentes semper videre in te Karolum et Pippinum et in tuis militibus Oliverum et Rolandum.

> [O most excellent King of the French . . . All others do fear you before the remaining kings of the earth, believing always to see in you Charles and Pippin and in your knights Oliver and Roland.]

---

[43] One papal publicist denied all imperial claims to Lombardy, declaring that Charlemagne conquered it for the Church: Richard Scholz, ed., *Unbekannte kirchenpolitische Streitschriften aus der Zeit Ludwigs des Bayern 1327–1354*, 2 vols., Bibliothek des königlichen preussischen historischen Instituts in Rom, X–XI (Rome, 1911–14), I, 46; II, 106 and 109 [henceforth "Scholz, *Unbekannte . . . Streitschriften*"].

[44] For Alexander of Roes, Milan is one of the four capitals of the Empire, along with Aachen, Arles, and Rome: Grundmann/Heimpel, pp. 48–49.

[45] Paul Piur and Konrad Burdach, eds., *Petrarcas Briefwechsel mit deutschen Zeitgenossen*, Vom Mittelalter zur Reformation, V (Berlin, 1933) pp. 162ff. [henceforth *PBW*].

[46] Fritz Kern, *Acta Imperii*, p. 1, item 1.

[47] Scholz, *Unbekannte . . . Streitschriften*, II, 177; cf. I, 62.

Both documents were petitions. The requisite flattery of such productions aside, the whole Carolingian mythical complex clearly enjoyed great vitality in the French monarchy. This tradition continued to be attacked by most pro-German authors, regardless of party, papal or imperial, throughout the next centuries.

French authors used the traditions of both the French Charlemagne and the Frankish Troy myth to prove their independence of the Empire. The French, that is, the "Franci" have an antiquity coeval to the Romans. Moreover, the Roman Empire never ruled over the Frankish realm of antiquity. Why then should the Roman Empire of the fourteenth century have any authority over France?[48] Such ratiocination took it entirely for granted that the medieval Empire was unconditionally equivalent to the Roman Empire of antiquity. The separation of the French realm from the Roman Empire was, however, not consistently maintained, since certain publicists supported French designs on the imperial crown. There are calls in the early fourteenth century for the Germans to abandon the Empire to the French.[49] They appeal to the interpretation of the transference of the Empire at the time of Otto the Great *de Gallicis in Germanos,* making Charlemagne and the Carolingians something other than German.[50]

Such publicistic writings surely moved Alexander of Roes to emphasize the German character of the Empire, to the extent of claiming German possession of the Empire until the end of time. French hostility caused him great distress. The sorry state of the Empire, he maintains, is partially their fault, and its threatened collapse a grave responsibility. Only when sin has triumphed altogether will the Roman Church complete its already begun destruction of the Empire—and the French will lend their arms (Grundmann/Heimpel, pp. 96–97). The gravity of this charge is evident only when the end of the Empire is seen in the perspective of the last days, as it was by Alexander. The Empire alone is holding off Antichrist. Alexander says outright that those who combat the Empire are his forerunners (pp. 30–31).

The remedy Alexander proposes to avert this catastrophe is an extraordinary tripartite division of the world's faculties. The *Sacerdo-*

---

48 Scholz, *Publizistik*, p. 239.

49 Walther I. Brandt, trans., *Pierre Dubois: The Recovery of the Holy Land,* Columbia University Records of Civilization, Sources and Studies, LI (New York, 1956), pp. 80 and 215.

50 Mario Krammer, ed., *Determinatio Compendiosa de Iurisdictione Imperii auctore anonymo ut videtur Tholomeo Lucensi O.P.; Tractatus Anonymus de origine et translatione et statu Romani Imperii,* MGH Fontes iuris germanici antiqui, I (Hannover and Leipzig, 1909), p. 72 [henceforth "Krammer, *Determinatio*"]. The document in question here is the *Tractatus Anonymus* (ca. 1308).

tium is the office of Italy; the *Studium* belongs to France, since Charlemagne transferred it thither; and the *Imperium* belongs to Germany:

> . . . quia nullatenus veniet Antichristus quamdiu ecclesia Romanum imperium habet defensorem in temporalibus et studium Gallicorum in spiritualibus adiutorem (Grundmann/Heimpel, pp. 98–99).

> [. . . for Antichrist would never come as long as the Church had the Roman Empire as its defender in temporal matters and the learning of the French as its helper in spiritual matters.]

In some ways, this notion sums up Alexander's view of the Empire, excepting its presupposed continuity from Roman times. The Germans hold the Empire; its mission is sacred; in temporal affairs it is, or should be, superior to other powers.

I now abandon Alexander and Jordanus with my, alas, formulaic apology for the brevity and superficiality of the consideration. The influence of these writings is out of all proportion to their length and renown. German Renaissance historians embraced Alexander as one of their own, and in truth, he is more at home in their company than in the more irenic tradition of medieval historiography. I consider his work a turning point, indeed a normative model for polemical historiography in Germany until the Reformation.

Alexander of Roes had an anonymous contemporary (thought to be Ptolemy of Lucca), who wrote a DETERMINATIO COMPENDIOSA DE IURISDICTIONIS IMPERII. It is as strong a defense of the papacy as Alexander's was of the Empire. Yet the Anonymous (or Ptolemy) avoids being overly anti-imperial or anti-German.[51] For him, the intervention of the Papal See understandably plays a central and indispensable part in the transference of the Empire. The Germans are considered worthy of the Empire, however, having earned it by their pious aid to the pontiff. Princes from Germany have always liberated the Church from its servitude to others, Lombards and impious Romans, as witness Pippin, Charlemagne, and Otto. The author of the *Determinatio*, like Alexander of Roes, found it necessary to exclude all doubt about Charlemagne's German nationality. He first quotes the *Venerabilem*, which assumes that Charles was German; he then mentions Charles's birth, death, and burial in German lands to confirm the certainty (Krammer, pp. 30 and 60–61). The basically cordial disposition to-

---

[51] Krammer, *Determinatio*, p. V. The document was published in 1281.

ward the Empire, despite the curial bias, expresses itself most specifically when the author states that no right to Empire exists at all, if it is not in the royal power of Germany (p. 23).

No confusion prevails in the *Determinatio* on the issue of distinction between the Roman Empire and the German royal power. Empire *simpliciter* was first held by the Assyrians, then by the Medes; later it was transferred to the Greeks, then the Egyptians, and is now, finally, in the hands of the Romans (Krammer, pp. 48–49). In other words, Empire *simpliciter* was last transferred to the Romans, and what the Germans now have is the Romans' Empire. By choosing Pippin, Charlemagne, and Otto as examples of German and imperial piety, the author of the *Determinatio* also demonstrates his belief in the religious duties of the Empire, whose myth thereby remains intact.

A major repercussion of the myth, one to which the author of the *Determinatio* contributes, is anti-Greek sentiment. Our author, like Liutprand before him, and Occam, Konrad of Megenberg, and Petrarch after him, charges the Greeks with impiety. Byzantium, not Rome produced the Arian Emperors and Julian the Apostate (Krammer, p. 25). For this period, heresy was, of course, among the most heinous crimes, condemning the heretic's soul to eternal flames and his body, as often as not, to their earthly counterpart. In the previous chapter, we saw that Liutprand had little affection for the Greeks. Alexander of Roes implied a certain anti-Greek opinion in his expression of the imperial myth. Such feelings are generally contained in the *Venerabilem*, since the Empire was wrenched from the Greeks when the Germans received it. A few publicists contest this, such as John of Paris, who maintains in his anti-imperial program that there were still Emperors in Greece after the *translatio*.[52] John's view, however, is rare among pro- and anti-imperialists alike. Alexander of Roes, for example, utterly rejected the Greeks' right to the imperial title. The ANTHOLOGIST OF THE FLORES TEMPORUM states simply that a Nicephorus or a Michael could not be called Emperor because the title had devolved on Charles.[53] According to the Anthologist, the author of the *Determinatio*, and Alexander of Roes, the refusal to aid the Roman Church cost the Greeks the Empire.

Unfortunately, wherever larger identities are sought—be they local, national, or international—the formation of the identity springs largely from the assertion of the inferiority of others. The growing awareness of a cultural identity in the West seems to underlie much

---

52 Scholz, *Publizistik*, p. 327.
53 Holder-Egger, *Flores Temporum*, p. 234.

of the hostility of Westerners toward the culturally superior Byzantine. Similarly, the reciprocal hostility between the Empire, the Papacy, and France resides perhaps in the gradual growth of modern political identities.

Such seems to be the case with an ANONYMOUS FRENCH PUBLICIST of ca. 1308, who went about raising the French royal dignity by lowering the dignity of the Germans and by assuming the aura of the imperial myth for France. He borrows from the canonists to prove that the Empire had been transferred to the French before it came to the Germans. The text he cites speaks of a transference of the Empire *de Grecis in Francos*.[54] In connection with the *Venerabilem* and its transference of the Empire *de Grecis in Germanos*, the phrase *de Grecis in Francos* presents no difficulties: "Germani" and "Franci" were not mutually exclusive terms. The French Anonymous, however, evades the *Venerabilem* and declares a transference of the Empire *de Grecis in Gallicos*, preceding the transference *de Gallicis in Germanos*. "Gallici" and "Germani" were mutually exclusive, and the Anonymous so uses them. His analogy of "Franci" and "Gallici" is a transparent attempt to make "Franci" and "Germani" just as mutually exclusive. His analogy represents no neologism. The King of France was, after all, *Rex Francorum* and not properly *Rex Gallicorum*. Out of these interpretations, the Anonymous can prove that the Empire was once in French hands and could be there again.

The chronicle of Martinus Polonus had listed Charlemagne as *Rex Francorum* before his imperial coronation, and then said that Otto was the first Emperor *Theotonicorum*. Martinus wrote during the *Interregnum*. Toward the end of this period, Dietrich von Nieheim wrote a distinctly pro-imperial tract, mentioning *imperii mutatio* (but not *translatio*) . . . *de Francis seu Gallicis in Germanos* at the time of Otto the Great.[55] The shift from Frankish to Gallic or French is logical and defensible in the tradition for French publicists. Its appearance among those writing in behalf of the Empire shows the strength of this view. Occasionally it is an embarrassment, as in Dietrich, and occasionally a weapon, as in Cusanus. In any case, the imperial publicists leave the Empire in the hands of the Germans, even if through Otto and not Charles the Great, and thus do not disturb the German aspect of the imperial myth.

---

[54] Krammer, *Determinatio*, pp. 68 and 72. The text in question is again the *Tractatus Anonymus*.

[55] Alphons Lhotsky and Karl Pivec, eds., *Viridarium Imperatorum et Regum Romanorum*, MGH Staatsschriften des späteren Mittelalters, V.i (Stuttgart, 1956), p. 24 [henceforth "Lhotsky/Pivec"].

The French Anonymous strays into one thorny patch through his insistence on the equivalence of *Franci* and *Gallici*. By mentioning the office of the electors he implies, surely unintentionally, imperial authority over France.[56] He is faced on the one hand with his unequivocal understanding of "Gaul" and on the other with the unquestionable validity of the archbishop of Trier's title. The traditional titles of the ecclesiastical electors were present to the Anonymous in his source, Martinus Polonus.[57] The clerics in question used their titles in a treaty of 1273.[58] Alexander of Roes employed them in the *Memoriale* (Grundmann/Heimpel, pp. 46–47). They appear in the *Determinatio* just discussed.[59] In a letter of about 1306 from the Archbishop of Cologne to Edward I of England the title appears *sacri imperii per Italiam archcancellarius*.[60] Emperor Henry VII confirmed the titles in 1310, and they were used throughout 1314 in the dispute between Ludwig the Bavarian and Frederick of Austria for the imperial crown.[61] The French Anonymous lived in a time when the theoretical power of the Empire extended over Italy and Gaul, as well as Germany. His interpretation of Gaul only underscores the validity of the myth.

In the preceding pages I have surveyed a series of documents extending from the Interregnum approximately to the death of Henry VII, with a few excursions beyond those times. The different character of the myths of the German past in this period, distinguishing it from the surrounding epochs, is, I think, already clear. The tales of the Scandinavian origins of Germanic peoples seem to have given way altogether to the pseudo-classical myths—although this is only partly true. Even some of those seem temporarily to have passed from attention, such as Saxon origins from Alexander the Great. The Goths seem to be remembered at best as Spanish national heroes,[62] at worst as enemies of ancient Rome,[63] and apparently not at all as mythical cousins of those who now hold the Empire. Remaining as important

---

[56] Krammer, *Determinatio*, p. 72.

[57] L. Weiland, *Martini Oppaviensis Chronicon*, MGH SS, XXII. 377–475 (Hannover, 1872), p. 466.

[58] Krammer, *Quellen*, II, 2.

[59] Krammer, *Determinatio*, p. 29; cf. Krammer, *Quellen*, I, 96.

[60] Fritz Kern, *Acta Imperii*, p. 109, item 156.

[61] Krammer, *Quellen*, II, 54ff. and 57–58.

[62] Scholz, *Unbekannte . . . Streitschriften*, II, 514–15.

[63] Horst Kusch, ed. and trans., *Marsilius von Padua: Der Verteidiger des Friedens*, 2 vols. (Darmstadt, 1958), I, 338–39, 424–25; II, 854–55, 992–93. The *Flores Temporum* (Holder-Egger, p. 250) remember Theodoric as a heretic, a persecutor of John, Symmachus, and Boethius, popularly sung *a ioculatoribus*.

from the previous age is what had been one of many myths, that of the Empire.

The situation does not continue to be quite so simple in the remainder of the fourteenth century. The abiding conflicts between Pope and Emperor, the unhappy condition of Rome, and the papal exile at Avignon led to the writing of many documents in defense of various programs. When they referred to the Empire, they called attention to Germany, one way or the other. This attention brought with it the mythical complex that appears in the documents to be examined now.

The disparity between political fact and imperial theory could conceivably lead one to believe that the documents discussed above are not truly representative of the feelings of the time. From our point of view in the twentieth century, the medieval German monarchy was most obviously not Roman, and just barely an empire. The people who called themselves emperors were, by and large, patently German, and must have been viewed as unwanted foreigners by the other peoples of the realm, particularly the proud Italians. The imperial crown could hardly have been considered the first in Europe when it controlled no armies of its own and was constantly being bickered over by petty German princes. Let anyone who thinks that practical politics wholly determined the fourteenth century's picture of itself read DANTE. The singer of Beatrice, in his important seventh epistle, addresses the Luxemburger Henry: [64]

> Gloriosissimo atque felicissimo triumphatori et Domino singulari, Domino Henrico, divina providentia Romanorum Regi et semper Augusto . . . tu, Caesaris et Augusti successor. . . .

> [To the most glorious and happy victor and distinguished lord, Lord Henry, by divine providence, King of the Romans and ever august . . . You, successor of Caesar and Augustus. . . .]

In these few words, Dante reveals his unconditional acceptance of the imperial myth: the divine ordination of the monarch, his succession

---

[64] *Epistolae*, VII, salutation and sect. 1, in E. Moore, ed., *Tutte le Opere di Dante*, 4th ed. (Oxford, 1963), p. 409 [henceforth "Oxford Dante"]. Morimichi Watanabe's suggestion in *The Political Ideas of Nicholas of Cusa with Special Reference to his "De Concordantia Catholica,"* Travaux d'Humanisme et Renaissance, LVIII (Geneva, 1963), p. 124, that Dante could distinguish between the Roman Empire and the German Emperor is, I believe, anachronistic. Contrast Nancy Lenkeith, *Dante and the Legend of Rome*, The Warburg Institute: Medieval and Renaissance Studies, Supplement II (London, 1952), p. 85.

in the line of Julius and Augustus Caesar, and thus the identity of the medieval empire with its eminent forebear.

Like most authors who touch on the Empire, Dante makes reference to Charlemagne and his liberation of the Roman Church from Lombard oppression.[65] Two motives, at least, induced Dante to mention imperial domination of the Lombards. The first reflects his program for cooperation between Church and Empire. The second reflects Italy's internecine strife and his own partisanship. In the fifth epistle addressed to all the people of Italy, Dante, having designated Henry *Divus et Augustus et Caesar*, cried out against the barbarity of the Lombards: when will they, insubordinate, remember their Trojan and Latin blood? Dante in the same breath reminds them of their Scandinavian origins (Oxford Dante, pp. 405–6).

The reminder may well be associated with Lombard ambitions toward a separate Italian kingdom under their own crown. The Lombards claimed origin from Anglus, a grandson of Aeneas and ancestor as well, in myth, of the Angles and Saxons.[66] They had every reason to assume parity with any other royal nation. Memories of the Germanic Lombard kingdom in old Italy played an active part in the politics of the time. They were made an alternative to imperial suzerainty in Italy. Occasionally the alternatives combined, when for example the Lombard Visconti disguised their ambitions for an independent and unified Italian crown behind the facade of imperial loyalty: their name, so they claimed, meant "vice-counts," vicars of the Emperor in Milan.[67] Dante's intention may have been to remind the Lombards simultaneously of their past glories and of their present duties to the Empire.

Dante showed himself to exist totally within the framework of the myth of the Empire. Repeatedly he confuses the Rome of antiquity with the Roman Empire of his own day. Within this confusion he seeks to prove divine approbation of the Empire, using such familiar arguments as the divine choice for the moment of Christ's birth and the submission of Christ to Roman law.[68] Ideally, the monarch of the world should be the Roman Emperor. And there we have the myth: the continuity from ancient Rome; the residence of that Empire

---

[65] *De Monarchia*, III.xi, in Oxford Dante, p. 372. The work was largely suppressed in Catholic Europe and did not see print until 1559, when Oporinus printed it and a German translation in Basel: cf. Johannes Oeschger, "Nachwort," in *Von der Monarchey—deutsch durch Basilius Johann Heroldt, Basel, 1559* (Basel and Stuttgart, 1965), p. 251.

[66] Cf. Konrad Burdach, et al., eds., *Aus Petrarcas ältestem deutschen Schülerkreis, Vom Mittelalter zur Reformation*, IV (Berlin, 1929), p. 102.

[67] *Ibid.*, pp. 229 and 233.

[68] *De Monarchia*, II.xiif., in Oxford Dante, pp. 362–63.

among the Germans, where it was in the poet's time; the divine stamp on the Empire; the primacy of its crown above all others.

A close Italian contemporary of Dante, LANDULPHUS of the pro-imperial COLONNA family produced, about 1320, a document theorizing about the translation of the Empire.[69] Landulphus presents various traditional thoughts on the founding of the Empire—that it was established by Aeneas according to some, and according to others by Julius or Octavian (Schard, p. 285). This very Empire was transferred from the Greeks to the Franks in the person of the magnificent Charles, the great king of France and Germany, and this was the transference of the Empire *de Grecis in Francos.* Later the transference took place *de Gallicis in Germanos* or *de Francis in Germanos* (pp. 296, 289).

The sanctity of the Empire is preserved by Landulphus in the history of the transference of the Empire from the Greeks: they lost the Empire by the iconoclast heresy (Schard, p. 289). Conversely, Charles who won the Empire was *ecclesiae defensor* (p. 293). At Charles's coronation *a Deo,* the life and victory wished him were accompanied by the wish that heaven itself minister to him (p. 294).

Landulphus leaves no doubt about his views on the supremacy of the Empire. The ecclesiastical electors hold sway over Gaul, Germany, and Italy (Schard, p. 296). The *regnum mundi* was transferred *ad Germanos vel Theutonicos* at the time of the Ottos. The Roman Emperor is over all kings, and all nations are subject to him (p. 297). It might be added that almost identical views on the above subjects were expressed by Marsilius of Padua in his own essay *De translatione imperii* (1325/6).[70]

As in Dante, Landulphus, and Marsilius, Charlemagne's service to the Church was a critical element in the publicistic work of KONRAD OF MEGENBERG who, unlike these Italians, was pro-papal. In his *De translatione Romani Imperii* (1354), Konrad had implications in mind other than the glorious victories of a secular monarch or the simple interdependence of Pope and Emperor. For him, the Emperors were totally inferior to the Pope.[71] Konrad was, however, a pro-German curialist

---

[69] In Simon Schard, *De iurisdictione, autoritate, et praeeminentia imperiali* (Basel, 1566), pp. 284–97; cf. August Potthast, *Bibliotheca Historica Medii Aevi*, 2nd ed. (Berlin, 1896), pp. 709–10 [henceforth "Schard, *De iurisdictione*," and simply "Potthast"].

[70] Schard, *De iurisdictione*, pp. 224–37.

[71] Scholz, *Unbekannte . . . Streitschriften*, II, 249ff., 288, and 585.

like the Anonymous of the *Determinatio*, not nearly so hostile to the Empire as most of his curialist colleagues. His belief that the Empire should be subordinate to the Church in no way interferes with his supporting the imperial myth at every turn.

For Konrad, the Empire belongs to God and is in some fashion coordinate to the Universal Church (Scholz, *Unbekannte . . . Streitschriften*, II, 251). He goes so far as to maintain that all nations must somehow signify their submission to the Emperor, for he is the *princeps mundi* (Scholz, I, 99; II, 253). Konrad proceeds to show that the Empire has always been in German hands since the time of Charlemagne Scholz, I, 100–101; II, 260ff.). He explains, loosely quoting the *Venerabilem*, the German character of the transference. Central to this argument is the proof of Charlemagne's German nationality: Charles named the months and winds in his own language, German, and was born in German lands. The French—who claim Charles—must be distinguished from the Franks. They are properly called "Francigenae," that is, Trojan Franks who married Gallic women and who are thus not strictly Franks, but rather a people who stem from the Franks. The true Franks are the "Franci Germani" (Scholz, II, 262–63, 267–68). Konrad explains that those Germans who helped Rome against the Alani were granted freedom of tribute and hence were called "Franci." If all of this looks exceptionally familiar, let us look farther.

The Empire came to Charlemagne after the Greeks lost it because of their heresy (Scholz, *Unbekannte . . . Streitschriften*, II, 275). Konrad proceeds through an approximately accurate history of the predecessors and successors of Charlemagne to illustrate exactly how the Empire is German and cannot be Gallic (Scholz, II, 267ff.). There is no need to review Alexander of Roes. The main lines of argumentation were repeated by Konrad with a few large omissions and a few (by that time) traditional additions. I have no doubt that Konrad had some knowledge of Alexander's works. Even though Konrad wrote from a pro-papal point of view and Alexander from a pro-imperial one, he discovered in his source sufficient pro-German material to satisfy at least that part of his bias. It is not at all unlikely that one of the dozens of manuscripts that have survived from the fourteenth century fell into Konrad's hands.[72] Even if this is not necessarily the case, German authors of the fourteenth century converge on Alexander's formulation of the problems of the Empire. They may not have known his name or read his work, but may well have read and imitated

---

[72] Grundmann/Heimpel, p. 9, and Schraub, *Jordan von Osnabrück und Alexander von Roes*, p. 5.

those who had. The chief arguments were, of course, available in the historiography, but Alexander's organization of them seems to supply the model for later publicists. The rarity of his tripartite attribution of the world's faculties in later historiography proves not that he was unknown but only that his suggestion was too neologistic and repercussive to find a comfortable place in the propaganda.

Whether or not Konrad is in immediate debt to Alexander, he is certainly in his lineage as an emotional publicist. An earlier work of Konrad's, a *Planctus Ecclesie in Germaniam* (1337/8), was written in the form of a dramatic disputation between Lady Ecclesia, the Pope, and Germany.[73] To my mind, it is no mean artistic achievement. Had it been written in German, like his scientific works, rather than in difficult and affected Latin, it would have been a highlight of German letters in the fourteenth century. I give examples of Lady Ecclesia's condemnation of Lady Avarice-and-Vainglory, her main rival for the affection of the clergy. The English translation is inspired by the spirited German of Horst Kusch (pp. 26–29):

Alleph, sed meretrix viciorum pessima nutrix . . .

[Ach! that whore, that wretched nurse of vice . . .]

O nimis immunda mulier, tibi nulla iocunda . . .

[O you filthy female, you should never know any joy . . .]

Phach, mala rach, misera tu pessima tu pharisea!

[You miserable wretch, ach, you superlative evil, you hypocrite!]

Lady Church has little but unladylike words for the clergy as well. Instead, she praises the simplicity and loyalty of the Germans and their eagerness for battle, for which others call them crude. On the contrary, they ought to be called noble, since they are sprung from the very seed of knighthood, Lady Church's etymology of German: *"Germen milicie" Germanus dicitur unde*. Another *Planctus* by Alvarus Pelagius (fl. 1332–40) explained *a nobili germine Germani dicti sunt*, which was the opinion of the scholiasts of canon law (Kusch, pp. 40–41, 60–61, and intro., p. xxix). Elsewhere Konrad assures us that, without the Germans, the Church is quite betrayed to thieves, dogs, and pigs (Scholz, I, 86). In the *Planctus* of Konrad, matters are so serious that Germany threatens—even though Greece lost the *Imperium* to Charlemagne through heresy—to join the Greeks in schism, and only the

---

[73] Horst Kusch, ed. and trans., *Konrad von Megenberg: Klagelied der der Kirche über Deutschland* (Darmstadt, 1956), pp. VII, 11, 151.

blood of many martyrs will ever bring her back (Kusch, pp. 66–67 and 92–93). Tradition makes the Empire the defender of the Church with the German princes as the first of those defenders. Konrad presents the obverse of that tradition and therein resembles the Christian humanists and Catholic propagandists of the Reformation more, perhaps, than the typical fourteenth-century curial publicist.

The work of the German princes for the Church is the main issue in a work by a friend and disputant of Konrad, LUPOLD OF BEBENBURG. His *Libellus de Zelo Catholicae Fidei veterum Principum Germanorum* (1340) is the fullest elaboration of this tradition and found considerable response in the Renaissance proper.[74] Lupold, who was to become Archbishop of Bamberg under Charles IV, shows himself to be a faithful son of both Church and Empire.[75] In his preface, Lupold explains what he understands by "German" princes (de la Bigne, p. 88). Charlemagne was a German Frank. Insofar as the French kings are descended from him, they too are German. The kings of England as well are Germans, insofar as they are of German Saxon origin. His essay might thus include the deeds of French and English princes, but he chooses to limit his discussion to a stricter sense of "German," coinciding in part with the Renaissance sense of the term, in part with the modern.

Lupold begins his first chapter with the patriotic remark that the German princes do indeed stand above others in the zeal for defense of the faith (de la Bigne, p. 89). Before the transference of the Empire, Lupold explains quoting the *Venerabilem*, the Emperors were forever falling into heresy. Those in Constantinople were the worst of the lot, virtually all Arian and some, like Julian, worse. Citing Martinus among others, Lupold proceeds through a catalogue of heretical Emperors. Valens sent heretical missionaries to the Goths. Even Justinian was in doctrinal error until corrected by the pope. The tribal cousins of the Germans all suffer Lupold's condemnation as enemies of the Church, with the sole exception of the Franks whom he is about to make the equivalent of the Germans (de la Bigne, p. 90). Ostrogoths, Visigoths, Vandals, and Lombards were all heretics and persecutors

---

[74] I use the edition in Margarinus de la Bigne's *Maxima Bibliotheca Veterum Patrum*, XXVI (Lyons, 1677), 88–108. Wimpheling and Brant published major works of Lupold in 1497 and 1508; see Potthast, p. 752. See also Hermann Meyer, *Textkritische Studien zu den Schriften von Lupold von Bebenburg* (Freiburg/Br., 1908), pp. 2–3. The hot-headed Reformer Mathias Illyricus Flacius edited Lupold, and this edition enjoyed a German translation (1566 and 1567 resp.).

[75] Scholz, *Unbekannte ... Streitschriften*, I, 97.

of the Roman Church. Theodoric was a wretched man, inflamed with iniquity. Leonigildus of the Spanish Visigoths, Hunerich of the African Vandals, and Ruther of the Italian Lombards are singled out for reproach.

When Lupold turns to the Franks in his second chapter, he calls them not "Franks" but "Germans." In distinction to the Renaissance sense of "German," he does not associate the West Germanic peoples with their East or, as we shall see, their North Germanic cousins. Clovis, the first Christian king of all the Germans, begins the pious tradition that extends through Pippin and Charlemagne on to Lupold's time. Despite Clovis's great efforts, idolatry prevails until the time of Pippin and Saint Boniface. With Charlemagne, the great triumphs begin. He subdues the Frisians and Saxons for the faith. The Spaniards and the Arian Huns (pagan Avars?), and later the Danes are all conquered by Charlemagne for Christianity (de la Bigne, p. 91).

Charles's sons and grandsons did the same for the Bohemians, Bulgars, and Normans. The Danes and the Normans are clearly not regarded as the Germanic cousins of their supposed conquerors, but as equivalent to Huns and Slavs. When it pleased God to let the Empire pass from the German Franks to the Saxons, the latter continued the work on the Normans and Danes, who were constantly relapsing into superstition. Otto the Great won the Slavs for Church and Empire in his pious zeal. Henry II did the same for Prussia and Livonia (de la Bigne, p. 92). Ignoring popular, curial, and literary tradition, Lupold praises Frederick II as a good law-giver and an enemy of heresy. Dante, it will be remembered, numbers Frederick among the heretics in Hell (*Inf.* X.119, in Oxford Dante, p. 15).

Continuing resolutely to ignore unfavorable tales and the unpleasant realities of political history, Lupold reviews in his third chapter the contemplative piety of the German princes, just as he had reviewed their activist piety. Contenders for Merovingian and Carolingian power were continually withdrawing to the monastic life—for none but the most religious motives (de la Bigne, pp. 92–93). Lupold tells of the pious practices of the Emperors in their private lives, their keeping of monastic hours, their celebration of all elements of the liturgy, matins, vespers, mass. In these chapters he underscores from without and within the religious characteristics, not merely of the German princes as local rulers, but as holders of the imperial reins.

Lupold returns to the activist role in his fourth chapter, surveying the Germans' more direct services in the protection of the Church (de la Bigne, pp. 83–84). The Germans won distant nations for Christianity and defended nearby Rome and its Church once against the Goths with the arm of Charles Martel, twice against the Lombards with Pippin and Charlemagne. Louis the Pious performed similar services against the Saracens, the first and third Ottos the same in their turn against the Lombards. The German princes exhibited their Christian zeal in their habit of bestowing great gifts on the Church. Pippin, Charlemagne, Henry II, Otto IV, Frederick II, and Rudolf all made famous donations. They followed a good example: Constantine, certainly the most famous donor of all time, was on his mother's side a German, since Saint Helena was born in Trier (p. 95).

For the remainder of the essay, Lupold intertwines politics and commendations for piety. The chronicles and canon law show that only Germans have been anointed to the imperial honor since the transference of the Empire. In that transference, the pope gave up the right to name the emperor in favor of the German electors, just as Louis the Pious and Otto the Great's descendents relinquished their privileges in papal elections.[76] Lupold concludes with an exhortation that his contemporaries among German princes follow the glorious example of their predecessors (de la Bigne, pp. 107–8).

In another essay, *De iure regni et imperii Romani*, Lupold stresses the German character of the Empire, while attempting to maintain a friendly aspect toward France.[77] Lupold recounts the Trojan origin of the Franks as he found it in "Eusebius" (Ekkehard and Frutolf): the flight from Troy, the building of Sicambria, the freedom from tribute, the flight to Germany, the reigns of Priam and Anthenor, Marcomed and Sunno (Schard, p. 333). He tells also of Aeneas's brother, Phryges, who named the Franks, and Salagast, who named Salic law (pp. 333–34). It is made clear in Lupold's essay that he considered the Trojans who married Gallic women to be French and those who married German women to be Franks, properly so-called (p. 334). Lupold cites Gotfried of Viterbo on Charlemagne's birth in Ingelheim, his German parentage, and the naming of the months and winds in his own language (pp. 340–41). Thus the transference of the Empire to the Franks is equivalent to the transference of the Empire to the Germans (p. 329). Lupold is, however, conciliatory, and chooses to praise the common origins of the German Franks and the Gallic French from the glorious Trojans (p. 342). Why the Trojans who, after all, lost the war were glorious to the warlike Middle Ages is unexplained by Lupold.

Of the other aspects of the imperial myth Lupold stresses in this

---

[76] De la Bigne, pp. 96–97. Cf. also p. 100, where Charlemagne calls an ecclesiastical council in Gaul. He has the authority to do so, but it is considered an act of piety. Marsilius of Padua (Kusch, II, 743ff.) lays great weight on the ruler's right to call a synod.

[77] Schard, *De iurisdictione*, pp. 328–409.

work only the religious attributes of the Emperors. Charlemagne and his divine coronation appear (Schard, p. 335), as do the battles of the Ottos against heretics and other enemies of the Church (p. 339). The very basis of the German possession of the Empire was the heterodoxy of the Greeks and the aggression of the Lombards (pp. 346ff.).

Lupold seems to have intended these works to heal some of the wounds suffered in Ludwig the Bavarian's controversial bid for the imperial crown. Neither these documents nor any like them could resolve such a major dispute, but his works remain a vivid example of the political theorizing of the day. Lupold's factual foundations and his interpretation of them would certainly be unsatisfactory for a modern historian. His sources, Martinus Polonus and Gotfried of Viterbo, are today considered most unreliable. Unadorned political power, which must have been a conceptual reality to Lupold—piety and merit alone rarely led to the prestigious archbishopric of Bamberg —plays no role in his writing. The one and only reality was myth, the myth of the Roman State and Church. Lupold, like the rest of his contemporaries, assumed the fundamentally uninterrupted continuity of the Empire from Roman times. Like his friend Konrad of Megenberg, Lupold glorifies the German character of the Empire—the one aspect of the imperial myth least contradicted by pragmatic history. Lupold's major message seems to be the pious mission of the Empire. The mission is so important, so well documented by history, as Lupold thinks, that it becomes the primary function of the Empire. Frankish and Saxon imperialism, colonialization, and wars of aggrandizement, are all given a charismatic stamp. The almost sacramental Empire has the duty of winning souls for the Church, of keeping the peace in such a way that Rome and her Church may flourish.

Establishing and maintaining order remained a duty of German princes on through the fourteenth and fifteenth centuries. Such at least was the mind of Petrarch and his friend Cola di Rienzo. The Italians, in contrast to their German contemporaries Konrad and Lupold, inclined to disregard the identity of the Emperor with his German tradition. Insofar as Charles IV was Emperor, he was Roman; insofar as he was Bohemian king or the like, he was barbarian. Charles may indeed have agreed with them in part. What he probably believed to be his true pedigree was far from purely German. The Emperor commissioned genealogical investigations and had the findings painted in fresco in one of his castles. His ancestors included Noah, which is not surprising, and the Trojan refugees of the Frankish origins myth.

He was thus Maximilian's immediate model for the outrageous genealogical speculations of the Hapsburgs.[78]

PETRARCH was surely too critical to accept such fantasies, but he was not nearly critical enough to reject the little less fantastic notion that Charles was Caesar. In a letter to Charles (dated in Venice, 1363) the poet cries out to the sovereign:

> Tua te, inquam, Italia, Cesar, vocat—
> Cesar, Cesar, Cesar meus, ubi es? cur me deseris? . . .[79]

[I tell you, your Italy calls you, O Caesar—/Caesar, Caesar my Caesar, where are you? Why have you forsaken me? . . .]

On one occasion Petrarch gave to Charles, whom he called "truly a valid successor of the Caesars," ancient Roman coins with the portrait of Augustus, urging Charles to follow his predecessor's distinguished example (*PBW*, p. 185). But not all is praise. Petrarch condemns Charles for his hasty return to Germany after his first Italian coronation (1355)—there goes Charles, back to his barbaric realm (p. 52). If, content with his Germany and the mere limbs of the Empire, Charles should abandon Italy, the head, then he might be German King but never Roman Emperor (p. 175):

> Certe si Germania sua et membris Imperii contentus rerum caput linquit Italiam, rex teutonicus poterit esse, Romanus esse non poterit Imperator.

Petrarch's imagery is a traditional form of imagery for both Church and Empire.[80]

Although Petrarch never questions the overall framework of the myth of the Empire—Charles is clearly Caesar, this Caesar is clearly German, this German Caesar has special duties in Italy—the poet has little liking for the Emperor's nation, *Germania dura* (*PBW*, p. 30). Petrarch, an imperial count palatine (*PBW*, pp. 221ff.), makes a series of extraordinary remarks to Germans concerning things German. It does not seem the most diplomatic utterance, for example, to tell a king that his realm is barbaric. Petrarch does Charles's court chancellor, Johannes of Neumarkt, a great honor by giving him in 1361 the

---

[78] Wolfgang Braunfels, et al., eds., *Karl der Grosse, Werk und Wirkung* (Aachen, 1965), p. 542, item 744.

[79] *PBW*, p. 151.

[80] Cf. Watanabe, *The Political Ideas of Nicholas of Cusa*, p. 62; and Adolf Schmidt and Franz-Josef Schmale, ed. and trans., *Otto von Freising und Rahewin: Die Taten Friederichs . . .*, Book IV.25 (Darmstadt, 1965), pp. 572–73.

first copy of his *Bucolicum Carmen* (p. 125). In it, however, Petrarch denounces Rome's greatest enemies, the baronial tyrants, who are foreigners and come from, among other places, the Rhine.[81] Wherever Petrarch found this strange notion, it could hardly have caused Johannes unalloyed pleasure.

To digress for a moment, I should like to suggest a possible explanation for the supposed Rhenish origin of the Roman baronial families. In a letter to Rienzo and the Roman people, Petrarch warns his readers against several families and mentions there the Colonna who come from the Rhine (*BWR*, III, 65). This was in 1347. Some years before, in 1331, Petrarch wrote a poem to a close and abiding friend who happened to be a member of this Roman family:

> Gloriosa Columna, in cui s'appogia
> Nostra speranza. . . .
>
> [O glorious column against which does lean
> Our . . . hope. . . .][82]

Clearly known to the poet was the accepted etymology of the Colonna name, that connected it with the Column of Trajan, the center of their power in Rome.[83] Why then the Rhine? The similarity between "Colonna" and "Cologne" [*Colonia*] would be flimsy evidence indeed, were it not for two facts. The first is that the Colonna were a traditionally Ghibelline family, in close alliance with the Emperor. The second is that the Archbishop of Cologne was imperial arch-chancellor for Italy, the only one of the three ecclesiastical electors ever to wield real power outside of Germany in his titular province. Petrarch surely knew the title of the Archbishop of Cologne, since it had been in use for several centuries and since Petrarch himself had been in Cologne. The name would also have been refreshed in his memory since he was involved in imperial affairs in behalf of the Visconti in 1356, when

---

[81] Domenico Rossetti, ed., *Francesci Petrarchae Poemata Minora*, 3 vols. (Milan, 1829–34), I, 86. Cf. Konrad Burdach and Paul Piur, eds., *Briefwechsel des Cola di Rienzo*, 5 vols., Vom Mittelalter zur Reformation, II (Berlin, 1912–31), III, 93 [henceforth "*BWR*" with appropriate vol. number].

[82] For the date see I. Fracasetti, ed., *Francisci Petrarchae Epistolae de rebus familiaribus et Variae*, 3 vols. (Milan, 1829–34), I, intro. p. cxxxiii; for text and trans., see Anna Marie Armi and Theodore E. Mommsen, *Petrarch: Sonnets and Songs* (New York, 1946), pp. 10–11.

[83] *BWR*, V, 168. This etymology was common knowledge. The family name was often translated into German as "von der seul"—cf. Theodor von Kern, ed., "Chronik aus Kaiser Sigmund's Zeit bis 1434," *Chroniken der deutschen Städte*, I (Leipzig, 1862), 351 and Rochus von Liliencron, *Die historischen Volkslieder der Deutschen*, I (Leipzig, 1865), 231.

Charles promulgated the Golden Bull in which the title reappears.[84] In general, this is an unimportant issue. If, however, the explanation is correct, it points to a much more tightly knit conception of the loose ends of the imperial myth than one would imagine for four-teenth-century Italians. There may, of course, be an older family tradi-tion with which I am unfamiliar, that may link the Colonna to the Rhine by way of some late Roman administration in the North. Even this would indicate the survival of a generous conception of Romania to include lands which the fourteenth century would have to regard as German. Whatever the explanation, an apparent absence of tact characterizes Petrarch's remarks, openly hostile to Germany in a work presented to a German friend.

Among the great achievements of the Empire listed by Petrarch for German Charles is the defeat of the Cimbri by Marius at Aix-en-Provence (*PBW*, p. 5). By "Empire" he clearly means the Roman state, and by "Cimbri" he clearly means German. In a letter to the young Empress Anna (1358), Petrarch puts *Theutones* and *Cimbri* in direct apposition (*PBW*, p. 77). He wrote Charles, King of the Bohemians as well as Emperor of the Romans, that the Boii (variously Bohemians or Bavarians) have historically been as troublesome as the Galli for imperial, i.e., Italian peace (*PBW*, p. 33). Such incautious remarks would seem rather insulting. On the other hand, for Petrarch the Emperor is Roman regardless of his national origin.[85] Moreover, despite his prejudices, the poet never applies to an individual German the unkind thoughts he has about the Germans at large and about their country.

The same two-sided picture develops in Cola di Rienzo's approach to the Emperor. After the failure of his Roman revolution, Rienzo was in exile and imprisoned by Charles to whom he had fled for support. He wrote from prison, trying to win his freedom, promising to lay all of Italy at Charles's feet (*BWR*, III, 257, 318–19; V, 357, 432). This meant for Rienzo not only the whole of the Apennine peninsula but also Sicily, Sardinia, Corsica, and the Provence. Should Charles support Rienzo, the Emperor would be hailed *barbarorum victor* (*BWR*, III, 230). The Italians certainly counted the Germans among the barbar-ians. Indeed, the Germans agreed (*PBW*, p. 138–39). If Charles ac-cepted Rienzo's policies, Rienzo would be able to say upon his trium-phant entry into Rome, *veni, vidi, vici*, as Caesar said when he was

---

[84] Krammer, *Quellen*, II, 133.

[85] *PBW*, p. 180. Cf. also *BWR*, I, 135, and Paul Piur, ed., *Petrarcas 'Buch ohne Namen' und die päpstliche Kurie*, DVLG Buchreihe, VI (Halle, 1925), p. 87.

victorious over the Germans. In truth, no German victory is associated with those famous words of Caesar. Even if one had been, this hardly seems the right thing to tell a German monarch to win him over to a new plan of action. Rienzo forgot, as Petrarch also did, that the Roman Emperor was simultaneously a German prince.

Rienzo's words were intended to flatter, encourage, and cajole the Emperor to a politically impossible venture. The revolutionary's arguments concealed a terrible vision. In his promise to lay all of Italy at Charles's feet, Rienzo tells the Emperor that he would enter Jerusalem (i.e., Rome) as Solomon, *rex pacificus et securus*. Consider I Thess. V.3:

> For when they shall say to you, peace and security, then shall sudden destruction come upon them. . . .
>
> cum enim dixerint pax, et securitas: tunc repentinus eis superveniet interitus . . .[86]

Pax et securitas are the last words of Antichrist in the *Ludus de Antichristo*.[87] Although Rienzo almost certainly was unfamiliar with the play, he was deeply versed in the strange chiliastic writings which were at its source and which interpreted, along with the Fathers, the Thessalonian Epistles as prophecies concerning Antichrist.[88] Rienzo knew what he was writing and did not accidentally call the Emperor *rex pacificus et securus*. I can only surmise that Rienzo assumed Charles would not understand the concealed wish for the coming of the last age, or that, on the contrary, he wished Charles to share in the great enterprise. Rienzo was in either case fully aware of the crucial position of the Empire in the history of salvation as it had been interpreted from the earliest days of Christianity.

Rienzo's conception of the Empire and his place in it was many-faceted. The Empire was not only Roman and sacred. Rienzo, who had proclaimed himself Roman Tribune, seems sincerely to have believed himself the illegitimate son of Henry VII, and thus twice imperial, as Roman born and as son of the German Emperor.[89] While Roman Tribune, Rienzo assumed the title Severus after Severinus Boethius, whom Rienzo and his age considered the last of the Romans (*BWR*, V, 88). In the mind of Rienzo, Boethius was born of a mother *Boema ex regia stirpe nata* of royal Bohemian, for Rienzo, of German

---

86 English, Douay-Rheims; Latin, Vulgate. Cf. Karl Langosch, ed. and trans., *Geistliche Spiele* (Darmstadt, 1961), pp. 250 and 283.
87 Langosch, pp. 238–39 and cf. pp. 250ff.
88 *BWR*, I, 21ff. and 101.
89 *BWR*, I, 223 and III, 201.

origin. The source of the confusion seems to lie in the name Severinus, which was also borne by the Apostle of Noricum, a missionary in Austria and Bavaria, who was martyred about A.D. 482 (*BWR*, V,326). Rienzo's royal pretensions and flatteries knew no limits. They demonstrate, however, that Rienzo saw the German elements of the Empire and, whether he liked them or not, was forced to accept them. The myth placed the Empire in German hands, and the Tribune explicitly denied that he had ever tried to usurp the rights of its lawful possessors (*BWR*, V, 200–201).

For Petrarch, too, the Empire was in German hands, if not necessarily forever. He had seen in Aachen the great monument to Charlemagne, to be conserved as long as German hands controlled the reins of the Roman Empire (*PBW*, p. 164):

> Quod hodie servatur servabiturque quamdiu Romani frena Imperii
> Theutonica manus aget.

It was also at Aachen that Petrarch heard the tale of Charlemagne's love for his dead lady, much as we saw it in Jansen Enikel (*PBW*, p. 162).

Petrarch contributes one of this period's few examples of matters relating to the German past, but not closely connected to the *Imperium*. In a letter to the Empress, Petrarch inscribes a catalogue of famous women of antiquity. Among them he mentions the ancient Germanic women who were said to be more valorous in battle than their men (*PBW*, p. 17). He praises these same Germanic women in a catalogue that included Lucretia and Virginia. In the "Triumph of Chastity" the poet saw:

> Poi le Tedesche che non aspra morte
> Servaron lor barbarica honestate.
>
> [Then came the German women who chose death
> their own barbaric honor to preserve.][90]

Petrarch had great admiration for German women. While in Cologne in 1333, he was moved to cry out *Dii boni! que forma! quis habitus!*, and to wish he were unattached (*PBW*, p. 169). These women

---

[90] Text ed. by Carl Appel, *Die Triumphe Francesco Petrarcas* (Halle, 1901), p. 233; trans. by Ernst Hatch Wilkins, *The Triumphs of Petrarch* (Chicago, 1962), p. 45. Boccaccio preserves the same story in his book on illustrious women. Boccaccio's Latin was published in Germany in 1473 and 1531; Steinhöwel's German translation appeared in 1479, 1488, and at least four times in the sixteenth century; see Karl Drescher, ed., *Boccaccio: De claris mulieribus Deutsch übersetzt von Stainhöwel*, BLVS, CCV (Tübingen, 1895), pp. IXff., 247ff.

were conjuring the Rhine in what Petrarch recognized as a *pervetustum gentis ritus.* The poet is perhaps the first Renaissance man to express interest in ancient popular ritual in Germany; in no case is he the last.

Taking the intrinsic fascination of such an event for granted, I suggest that Petrarch may have had another reason for recounting the experience of the conjuring. His notebooks of memorable quotations are almost wholly devoid of reference to Germany. The few exceptions include the vignette from Suetonius where Domitian had a German augurer killed for an unfavorable prophecy.[91] These two incidents of interest in pagan Germanic religious practices are of course isolated. However, the only necromancer appearing in the entire correspondence surrounding Rienzo happens to be German.[92] Whether this is simply chance or a new convention is difficult to tell. The widespread popularity of mysterious sects in Germany in this period and such strange tales as those about Frederick II might have given foreigners the feeling of primitive pagan religion in German lands.[93] The memory of northern paganism was certainly much fresher than that of its southern counterpart, particularly since the classical pantheon had long been integrated into acceptable Christian symbolism. Baltic and Slavic peoples were still practicing pagans in these years, and many were within or on the borders of German lands. Germany as a favored setting for magic and witchcraft in literature has, I suspect, some precedent in these traces of interest among the Italians of the fourteenth century.

Minor concerns of Petrarch touch upon other myths of the German past. I have already mentioned the Cimbri in relation to the poet's association with the Emperor. The Cimbri represent the barbaric age for Petrarch. In a verse epistle the poet contrasts the Golden Age and the *Cymbria . . . saecula.*[94] A letter of Petrarch expresses some concern over the ill-treatment of one of Rienzo's emissaries to Avignon, and Petrarch declares that the messenger would have been safer in Germany with the Teutons (or Cimbri) defeated and Marius triumphant:

> Quanto intactior isset in Germaniam, cesis theutonicis et Mario triumphante, quam huc venit, te Romanam ecclesiam filialiter venerante.[95]

---

91 Giuseppe Billanovich, ed., *Rerum Memorandarum Libri* (Florence, n.d. [1943?]), p. 248; cf. "Domitian," ch. XVI, in C. R. Rolfe, ed. and trans., *Suetonius*, 2 vols. Loeb Classical Library (London, 1960), II, 374–75.

92 *BWR*, I, 11; IV, 94; V, 193.

93 Schultheiss, *Die deutsche Volkssage*, pp. 20–21 and 63.

94 Rossetti, *Petrarchae Poemata minora*, II, 220.

95 *BWR*, III, 139–40; Cf. Piur, *Petrarcas 'Buch ohne Namen'*, p. 170.

In the "Triumph of Fame" Petrarch sees the succession of heroes:

> Mario poi, che Jugurtha e Cimbri attera
> E'l tedesco furore. . . .
>
> [Marius then who crushed the German rage,
> Jugurtha, and the Cimbri. . . .][96]

Out of historical antiquity, the defeat of the Cimbri seems to have been virtually the only conflict between "Germans" and Romans that has entered the body of allusions of Petrarch and his friends. The defeat of Varus was known at the time both through the chronicle of Martinus Polonus and through the often cited biographies of Suetonius. The dramatic phrase, *Quintili Vare, legiones redde*, did not go undiscovered in Renaissance Germany. But German national self-consciousness outside of the Empire is non-existent in this period. The Italians had quite enough German trouble without reminding their German neighbors of a victorious pseudo-national past.

The German trouble for the Italians was in Petrarch's lifetime not at all the Empire, but rather the *furor Teutonicus*.[97] The "Great Company" of otherwise unemployed mercenaries under one Werner ravaged Italy in these years.[98] Petrarch's famous song, "Italia mia," mentions these troubles:

> Ben provide natura al nostro stato
> Quando de l'Alpi schermo
> Pose fra noi e la tedesca rabbia. . . .
>
> [Nature did well provide for our weak state
> When she raised like a screen
> The Alps to guard us from the German rage. . . .][99]

Petrarch has applied the all too present fury of the "Great Company" to the Germans at large. His commentator Luigi Marsili makes it quite clear that the "Italia mia" declares the Germans a barbaric

[96] Appel, *Triumphe . . . Petrarcas*, p. 248; Wilkins, *Triumphs of Petrarch*, p. 77.

[97] A complaint as old as Lucan and not forgotten in the Middle Ages: cf. Erwin Panofsky, *Meaning in the Visual Arts* (Garden City, N.Y. 1955), p. 139; and Ernst Dümmler, "Uber den furor teutonicus," *SB der königlichen Preussischen Akademie der Wissenschaften, philosophische-historische Classe*, no. IX (18 February 1897), 111–26.

[98] Edward H. R. Tatham, *Francisco Petrarca, the First Modern Man of Letters*, 2 vols. (London, 1925–26), II, 291ff.

[99] *Ibid.*, pp. 196ff. with commentary. Text and trans. from Armi and Mommsen, pp. 204–5.

nation, one without law.[100] Precisely the same charge appears in connection with the *furor* in the Cortusi's Lombard history.[101] Farther on, in the "Italia mia," Petrarch explains the origins of the beast disturbing the meek flocks:

> Et è questo de seme,
> Per piú dolor, del popol senza legge,
> Al qual, come si legge
> Mario aperse si 'l fianco,
> Che memoria de l'opra anco non langue
> Quando, assetato e stanco,
> Non piú bevve del fiume acqua che sangue.

> [And this comes from the seed
> for greater grief, of the unlawful stocks
> Whose destruction still shocks,
> Whose sides were opened wide
> By Marius, and the memory is still good
> When he, thirsty and tired,
> did not find water in the streams but blood.][102]

What is to be understood by "lawlessness" on one level is clear. It refers to the brigandage perpetrated by the "Great Company." There is, however, another level: the ancient failure of the Germans to abide by Roman law. This was a part of the Italians' objection to them from earliest times.[103] Nonetheless, it is the German Emperor whom Petrarch summons to allay the *transalpinam rabiem*, the *furorem Cimbricum* (*PBW*, pp. 228–29). Rienzo, too, calls upon the *Iuppiter Imperator* to restore order to the South: the *furor theutonicus* is not the mission of the Empire (*BWR*, III, 238–39, 261, 355).

Petrarch and Rienzo had little use for Germany. Except for an occasional pretty lady, a young Empress, a grave gentleman, a surprised reaction to *civilitas* in the barbaric North, a slip about freedom having retreated to the Rhine, the Italians have few good words about their neighbors.[104] This naturally made no difference in their regard for the

---

[100] Burdach, *Aus Petrarcas ... Schülerkreis*, pp. 141–42.

[101] In J. G. Graevius, *Thesaurus antiquitatum et historiarum Italiae*, VI (Leyden, 1722), 41; cf. also cols. 36, 42, and 96 for consistent complaints against the German "furor" to the years 1320, 1323, 1338; similarly in Mussato on the deeds of the Italians, to the year 1328; see L. A. Muratori, *Rerum Italicarum Scriptores*, X (Milan, 1727), 747–48. The term was applied to Otto I in the chronicle of Thomas Tuscus (1278); see E. Ehrenfeuchter, ed., *Gesta imperatorum et pontificum*, MGH SS, XXII, 483–528 (Hannover, 1872), p. 495.

[102] Armi and Mommsen, pp. 204ff.

[103] *BWR*, I, 184 and 189; cf. Piur, *Petrarcas 'Buch ohne Namen'*, p. 27.

[104] *PBW*, p. 168; and Burdach, *Aus Petrarcas ... Schülerkreis*, p. 146.

Empire and the office of Emperor. The myth of the *Imperium* was far stronger than any mere political reality or cultural prejudice.

Petrarch's student Benvenuto Rambaldi condensed the myth of the Empire into a perfectly conventional imperial history (ca. 1387). He proceeds from Julius Caesar over Charlemagne (*adiutor Ecclesiae, protector fidei*), Otto the Great (*post eum soli Teutonici imperauerunt usque ad praesens tempus*), to the reign of Wenceslaus (who holds the *imperium orbis*).[105] The Roman Empire remains German, sacred, and supreme.

The contributions of the fourteenth-century Italians to the creation of the myths of the German past transcend their support of the imperial symbol. That support is unequivocal from Dante over Marsilius of Padua,[106] to Rienzo, Petrarch, and Petrarch's disciples. The later German writers, however, took no small umbrage at Italian condescension. They tried to deny the Italian allegations or to turn them to their own advantage.

To summarize the best opinion of fourteenth-century Italians on things German, I turn again to Petrarch. The poet writes to Boccaccio, in an orgy of national self-criticism. He repeats views that Frederick II is supposed to have expressed about the Germans and the Italians. Still unconcerned about Frederick's reputation as Antichrist and, unaware of the superstitions growing up about him, Petrarch calls him a most prudent prince.[107] The poet probably thinks even more highly of the Emperor, in that Frederick was an Italian by conviction, even though a German by birth. Petrarch uses Frederick's two nationalities to indicate the objectivity and authority of the Emperor's judgements. The two nations are both excellent, indeed the best in the whole world. They differ very much from one another, however. The Italians are better at forebearance, since the Germans impute mercy to fear. Italians must be treated with formality, the Germans with familiarity. The former laugh at anything they disapprove, and consider themselves competent judges of everything. Germans do not condemn friends and quarrel only in a spirit of comradery. Petrarch comments on Fred-

---

[105] Benvenutus de Rambaldis, *Liber Augustalis*, in Marquard Freher and Burkhard G. Struve, eds., *Rerum Germanicarum Scriptores*, 3 vols. (Strassburg, 1717), II, 5–22; esp. pp. 15, 17, and 20. Cf. Potthast, p. 145 (ed. princ., Basel, 1496; another ed. Strassburg, 1505). The work was honored by the Swiss myth makers: Jakob Baechtold, ed., *Die Stretlinger Chronik*, Bibliothek älterer Schriftwerke der deutschen Schweiz, I (Fraunfeld, 1877), p. LXV.

[106] Kusch, *Marsilius von Padua*, II, 865ff., 890ff., and 1078ff.

[107] Frederick had been declared Antichrist by Innocent IV, see Schultheiss, *Die deutsche Volkssage*, p. 11.

erick's criticism of the Italians, saying that it may apply to all Italy, but is surely true of the warring cities (*PBW*, pp. 252–53).

The first generations of Italian humanists had countless interests and universal curiosity. Germany was not one of their primary concerns, but it could not be ignored altogether. Too many Germans inhabited Italy; too many Italian curial interests plagued Germany. However progressive Italian political thought may have been, the thinkers functioned within the all-encompassing ideal state, the Empire. Their connections with German lands and peoples were intimate; their influence among them immediate and widespread. Several minor examples of this will appear in the next pages. These symptoms of the community of European letters in the fourteenth and fifteenth centuries imply numerous cultural cross-currents and, not the least of them, a genuine receptivity abroad for the whims and serious achievements of the Italians.

Petrarch's account of Frederick II's opinions of the Germans and Italians appears in Dietrich of Nieheim's polemic *Viridarium* of Roman Kings and Emperors, published in Rome in 1411 (Lhotsky/ Pivec, pp. 8–9). Dietrich concurs with Petrarch on the judgement that Frederick was a most prudent prince, and goes on to declare that he was a *vir catholicus atque pius et providus imperator* (p. 66). This too is not quite in keeping with the prevailing picture of Frederick II. The only ones who consistently thought well of him were the Teutonic Knights, whom he had endowed with territories extending from Armenia to Latvia.[108] Otherwise, Frederick was feared or venerated as an apocalyptic reformer and as the last Emperor before the end of the world.

THE MYTH OF FREDERICK II had begun with uncertainty about the Emperor's death and continued with open speculation that he still lived. False Fredericks appeared and by their appearance helped substantiate the speculation. The second false Frederick appeared in Germany in 1284 and proved a real threat to Rudolf of Hapsburg. The impostor actually received ambassadors from Italy, much as the false Nero had received recognition from the Parthians.[109] In 1285, Rudolf had the false Frederick and his followers burned at Neuss or

---

[108] Max Toeppen, ed., *Chronicon Terrae Prussiae von Peter von Dusburg* in *Scriptores rerum Prussicarum*, I (Leipzig, 1861), 24–25.

[109] Both false Fredericks are reported by the Thuringian continuator of the *Sächsische Weltchronik* (ca. 1350); cf. Weiland ed., pp. 296 and 303. The same continuator also tells the "three seducers" story (p. 294).

Wetzlar.[110] Other reports indicated that a real Frederick appeared in 1262 and was still alive in 1286, disguised as a mendicant friar.[111]

Many of the chronicles written in Germany in the fourteenth century report something of the real or false Fredericks. The chronicle of Mathias of Neuenburg (ca. 1350) recounts the appearance and execution of the second impostor.[112] The same is reported in an early German prose chronicle (ca. 1349),[113] and by the influential Jacob Twinger of Königshoven (1386–1400).[114] The north German chronicle from Lübeck in its redaction of 1400 relates the appearance of the false Frederick in Lübeck and his burning in the Rhineland, as it was related in the redaction of 1290.[115] Johannes of Winterthur (ca. 1346) conveys similar information and adds the tales told of Frederick's eventual return, his oppression of the Church, and dissolution of the monasteries. He will have the clergy marry and will finally hang his sword (not shield) in a bare tree in the Holy Land.[116] A group of Sibylline texts appear around the year 1361, which seem to verify Johannes's tales.[117] He thinks little of Frederick and sees him in a most unfavorable light. He suspects Frederick of heresy and accuses him of consorting with Mohammedans and schismatics. To prove Frederick's bad character he tells the "three seducers" story.[118] The same story is told in these years (ca. 1362) in the vernacular.[119] A contemporary vernacular author identified as "Oswald der Schrieber" attaches fairy-tale elements to the legend and gives Frederick an asbestos garb from the hands of Prester John, a magic ring, and a secret potion.[120] To help confuse maters utterly, the dead Margrave of Brandenburg, Waldemar,

---

110 Schultheiss, *Die deutsche Volkssage*, pp. 45–48.

111 *Ibid.*, p. 34. Cf. Karl Janicke, ed., *Magdeburger Schöppenchronik,* in *Chroniken der deutschen Städte,* VII (Leipzig, 1869), 153 and 170 [henceforth "Janicke"].

112 Adolf Hofmeister, ed., *Die Chronik des Mathias von Neuenburg,* 2 vols., MGH SS, N.S., IV (Berlin, 1924–40), I, 39, II, 328. This work was known to Cuspinianus: cf. Hofmeister, II, 544.

113 Franz Karl Grieshaber, ed., *Oberrheinische Chronik* (Rastatt, 1850), p. 23.

114 Karl Hegel, ed., *Chroniken der deutschen Städte,* VIII (Leipzig, 1870), 450.

115 Koppmann, *Detmar-Chronik,* p. 367.

116 Friedrich Baethgen, ed., *Die Chronik Johanns von Winterthur* MGH SS, N.S., III (Berlin, 1924), pp. 22 and 28. Johann's autograph was in the possession of the Reformer Bullinger (Baethgen, p. xxxi). Cf. also Schultheiss, *Die deutsche Volkssage,* p. 42.

117 F. Vogt, "Über Sibyllen-weissagung," [Paul's and Braune's] *Beiträge zur Geschichte der deutschen Sprache und Literatur,* IV (1877), 49–100, esp. pp. 45 and 68–69.

118 Baethgen, ed. cit., pp. 6–8.

119 Karl Hegel, ed., "Fritsche (Friedrich) Closeners Chronik," *Chroniken der deutschen Städte,* VIII (Leipzig, 1870), p. 146.

120 Schultheiss, *Die deutsche Volkssage,* p. 51.

seems to have returned from the dead to his old lands in 1348. The Impostor was accredited by the Emperor as long as it was useful, then repudiated, and finally given sanctuary by a sympathetic prince.[121]

Franz Guntram Schultheiss summarizes the myth as it stood in the fourteenth century.[122] Emperor Frederick was a powerful and wise ruler over the Roman Empire in Germany and Italy. He was also King of Sicily by inheritance and King of Jerusalem by virtue of his journey across the sea. Because of his acquaintance with the occult arts, the Saracens were pleased to serve him. He possessed a magic ring, which could make him invisible at will, and a magic potion for rejuvenation. Once, an astrologer assured the Emperor that great dangers were imminent. He advised Frederick to escape them and go into hiding. Frederick has done just that with the aid of his magic ring. Later he appeared at Neuss and Wetzlar to test the people. Rudolf and the pope were hostile. By betrayal he fell into their hands. However, Frederick knew that his time had not yet come, and when he was burned, the flames did not harm him. From time to time he appears to tell someone of his final return, when he will hang his shield on a bare tree in Palestine and reign in Germany and Italy. The power of the popes will crumble, the priests will be humbled, and Frederick will rule in peace as long as he lives.

The Frederick myth was clearly known to DIETRICH OF NIEHEIM, if only in the indications of Alexander of Roes (Lhotsky/Pivec, p. XIII). Dietrich's *Viridarium*, however, reflects none of it in any identifiable fashion. The myth may have passed from learned writing altogether for some years, to become primarily the object of popular tradition. It would thus perhaps have been beneath Dietrich's dignity. These aspects of Frederick's fame may, on the other hand, have been odious to the publicist, who was a pious Christian, however pro-imperial, anti-curial, and reform-minded he may have been. The Frederick myth even in its simplest form was not free of heretical, even pagan overtones. Dietrich's polemic did not require appeal to such questionable authority to make its point. Alexander of Roes and the imperial pub-

---

[121] Hermann Heimpel, *Deutschland im späteren Mittelalter*, Handbuch der Deutschen Geschichte, Leo Just, ed., I.v (Constance, 1957), pp. 57–58 and 62–63. Cf. Janicke, *Magdeburger Schöppenchronik*, p. 4, where it is reported as a resurrection.

[122] Schultheiss, *Die deutsche Volkssage*, pp. 64–65. The first written confusion between Frederick II Stupor Mundi and Frederick I Barbarossa seems to arise in the mid-fourteenth century: Grauert, "Zur deutschen Kaisersage," p. 141. A fairly early learned text preserving the confusion was printed in 1495: Bartoleus Saxoferrato, *De Guelphis et Gebelinis*, where Frederick II is called "Barbarossa."

licistic tradition offered ample quantities of more convincing and less suspect arguments in defense of the Empire.

The binding authority of canon law was a great convenience to the imperial publicists. Dietrich begins the *Viridarium* with a citing of the *Venerabilem*. He shows his debt to the publicistic tradition, and more specifically to Alexander of Roes, by linking to the decretal his identification of Charlemagne as German. A German, Dietrich explains, is one born and buried in Germany. This description is then applied to Charlemagne, with the addition that Charles was educated in Germany as well (Lhotsky/Pivec, pp. 1–2). An explanation that Charles was German carried even more importance than it had for Alexander before him. The convention of regarding Charlemagne as French showed no sign of abating. Dietrich's renowned contemporary, Coluccio Salutati, for example, traces the French royal line back across Lothar and Louis to Charlemagne and Pippin. In the same place, Coluccio relegates the German line to Clovis, whom Pippin and the Carolingians superseded. The tale of Troy is likewise summoned to the cause of French past glories.[123] Whatever distinction Alexander and his immediate imitators made between Frankish and French left little impression on Coluccio or indeed, the larger part of fifteenth-century polemic literature. Dietrich himself sees a *mutacio* of the Empire *de Francis seu Gallicis in Germanos* at the time of Otto (p. 24). Despite the declaration of Charlemagne's German nationality, Dietrich's *mutacio* makes it quite clear that the French once held the Empire. A vernacular chronicler of the same period, Fritsche Closener (fl. 1362), states that with Charlemagne, "das rich kam an die frantzosen."[124] This wording indicates that the very contrast Alexander hoped to preserve was in the process of being totally erased. Even Dietrich, who was presumably more sophisticated and patriotic, could not escape the usage altogether. He certainly places the Empire in the hands of the Germans, but the possession seems to be symbolic from the time of Charlemagne and historic only from the time of Otto.

Although Otto appears almost as often as Charlemagne in imperial polemics, he rarely receives as colorful or extensive treatment. In Dietrich he is given his due. Dietrich quotes in its entirety Boccaccio's history of the scandalous Pope John XII from the *De Casibus Virorum Illustrium*.[125] Otto, the noble Emperor, having liberated the Pope from

---

[123] Francesco Novati, ed., *Epistolario di Coluccio Salutati*, 4 vols. in 5 Fonti per la storia d'Italia, XV–XVIII (Rome, 1891–1911), II, 24.

[124] Hegel, *Chroniken der deutschen Städte*, VIII, 33.

[125] Lhotsky/Pivec, pp. 25ff. Cf. Giovanni Boccaccio, *De Casibus illustrium virorum*, intro. by Louis Brewer Hall (Gainesville, Florida, 1962, from the Paris ed. of 1520), p. 217f. (= fol. CXI^rf., *recte* CV^rf.).

Berengar, is obliged to return to Italy when John's immorality becomes a public blot on his high office. Since the Pope is still quite young, Otto at first does no more than to show him the evil of his ways. When reform is not forthcoming, Otto calls the synod that deposes John. Dietrich tells the story no less than ten times in the course of his works.[126] The tale is superficially a simple *exemplum*, no more offensive to the medieval mind than the pious legend of Pope Joan (who may have been modeled in part on Otto's Pope John), but its repercussions were felt strongly throughout the papal–imperial dispute. Involved were the Emperor's rights over the Papacy as well as his mission as protector of the Church. No less a theorist than Marsilius of Padua had used Otto to demonstrate imperial authority over ecclesiastical matters.[127] Franciscus Toti, adversary of Marsilius and Ludwig the Bavarian, insisted that the synod and not Otto had deposed John.[128] These were the poles of the dispute, and they remained relentlessly at odds well into the Reformation.

In recounting Otto's defeat of Berengar, Dietrich appropriated for the Empire its "fourth wheel," as he expresses it—Lombardy. Along with Alexander of Roes, Dietrich describes the extent of immediate imperial authority to encompass Germany (including Lotharingia), Burgundy (the Kingdom of Arles), Italy, and Lombardy which is distinct from Italy and was won by Otto (Lhotsky/Pivec, pp. 10ff. and 16). Great as Otto I's achievements were, they did not surpass those of his successor Ottos, whose exploits won them the title, "pale death of the Saracens" (p. 48). This Byzantine imperial title had become firmly fixed upon the Ottos by the fourteenth century. Fritsche Closener too calls them "bleicher tot der heiden."[129] The title reflects no historical reality other than the religious aspect of the imperial myth.

Although Dietrich's motives are transparently propagandistic, his bias is largely a simple extension of a belief that transcended partisanship. Not only German publicists professed the myth of the Empire. Coluccio Salutati wrote to Boccaccio of the reception tendered Charles IV during his Italian coronation of 1361. The humanist expressed hope that Charles, "August Caesar," would be the man to free Rome of its oppressors.[130] A contemporary northern chronicler laid great

---

[126] Hermann Heimpel, *Dietrich von Niem*, Veröffentlichungen der historischen Kommission des Provinzialinstituts für Westf. Landes- und Volkskunde: Westfälische Biographien, II (Münster, 1932), p. 85.

[127] Kusch, *Marsilius von Padua*, II, 865ff.

[128] Scholz, *Unbekannte ... Streitschriften*, II, 81; cf. also I, 32, where other publicists join the attack, viz., Andreas of Perugia.

[129] Hegel, *Chroniken der deutschen Städte*, VIII, 35.

[130] Novati, *Epistolario*, I, 85ff. and 88ff.

weight on the presence of Charlemagne's sword in the ceremony of coronation.[131] In short, there were no boundaries to the myth of the Empire, in humanist Italy as in medieval Germany, toward the end of this period as toward the beginning.

Dietrich is very much a part of his time in his views on the dignity of the Empire. In another work, the *Privilegia aut iura imperii*, he declares that all temporal matters are subject to the Emperor. Even the Pope has called the Emperor *suum Dominum*.[132] Some in Dietrich's time declared it heresy to reject the Emperor as monarch and lord of the whole world.[133] Dietrich believes that the Emperor is in a real way minister of God (Schard, *De iurisdictione*, p. 786). The privilege of electing the pope granted to Charlemagne and Otto I was confirmed by popes, cardinals, and the people of Rome. It belongs to the Emperors forever (Schard, p. 789).

In the *Privilegia* as in the *Viridarium*, Dietrich accepts and reconfirms the German character of the Roman Empire, its sanctity and supremacy. The Eastern Empire had been prototypically in the hands of the Germans ever since Saint Helena, mother of Constantine, as she was born and buried in Trier (Schard, *De iurisdictione*, p. 800). The same is true of the Empire in the West. Theodoric the Goth prefigured the German possession first by winning and holding the Empire, and then by marrying into the family of the King of the Franks, who were one day to hold the *Imperium* in truth (Schard, pp. 800–801).

Dietrich's propaganda is largely indistinguishable from the work of his predecessors such as Alexander von Roes and Lupold von Bebenburg. However, he not only points back to the beginnings of the period with his debt to Alexander, but points forward as well to some distinctly new practices. His language did not bear the humanist renovations of the Italians, but his subject matter includes elements that were not to be conventional for years (Lhotsky/Pivec, p. XVII). An example is the excursus on the history of Germanic tribes with which he concludes the *Viridarium* (pp. 100–102). The Vandals (by which Dietrich means Wends or Slavs as well as Vandals) are now living among the Saxons, and extend to the realm of the Goths now called the Swedes. The Goths were divided into five tribes, of which the Ostrogoths and Visigoths were the most important. The Vandals once held Spain, Burgundy, and parts of Gaul. Now they live in Pomerania,

---

131 H. Bresslau, ed., *Chronik Heinrichs Taube von Selbach*, MGH SS, N.S., I (Berlin, 1922), p. 118. This chronicle was known to Meisterlin, Naucler, Trithemius, and Aventinus: Bresslau, p. lxxf.

132 Schard, *De iurisdictione*, p. 785.

133 Zeydel, *Holy Roman Empire*, p. 24 and note 7.

Poland, and near Halberstadt. Their lands are excellent and fertile. The old Vandals were expelled from their original homes in Germany by the invading Saxons, and this is why the Vandals in turn invaded Italy and Africa. The Saxons were fathered by Alexander the Great and are themselves "father of nations": the Angles and the Danes stem from them. Those Saxons who remained pagan after the baptism of their prince, Widukind, fled into Sarmatia and there fathered the Turks.[134] In the *Privilegia* (Schard, *De iurisdictione*, p. 805), Dietrich tells of the Saxons' veneration of Mars in their city *Mons Martis*, Merseburg. While this hardly seems new to the reader of these pages, it must be noted as outside the normal preoccupations of fourteenth-century learned dispute. Such national and provincial pseudo-history appeared in the Middle Ages in learned and popular literature alike. In the learned literature, i.e., Latin, international, written for other scholars, this practice seems to have been abandoned in the fourteenth century. In the popular literature, i.e., vernacular, local, written for anyone who could read or be read to, this practice takes on increasing importance. Not until the Renaissance do the traditions in Germany converge again. In this way, Dietrich is somewhat ahead of his time.

The popular tradition in German historical writing had strong advocates during the rise of Italian humanism and the concomitant learned German preoccupation with polemics. Two vernacular works are the most obvious precedents of the fifteenth-century Latin and German writing of imaginative history. The first is a burgher chronicle, the MAGDEBURGER SCHÖPPENCHRONIK.[135] The motifs are generally familiar. Those of "ancient history" find expression in Julius Caesar's conquest of the north and his endless founding of cities. The city scribe who first composed the chronicle knew of the caesarean foundings of Kyffhäuser and Lüneburg, and includes his own metropolis in the honors. Caesar dedicated a city to the virgin goddess Diana and called it Parthenopolis, which translates into Magdeburg (Janicke, p. 7). The Saxons, who were to populate the city, have their origins in the troops of Petroculus of Cilicia who helped the Queen of Babylon conquer many lands. After the fall of the Babylonian Empire, his men, called "Petroculi" or "little rocks," remained undefeated and joined the forces of Alexander the Great (p. 9). After his fall, they fled in three groups, one to Prussia, one to Denmark, and one to Ocean and thence to the lands of the Wends. Some say the Saxons stem from the army

---

[134] Thus also Rolevinck: Heimpel, *Dietrich von Niem*, pp. 229–30.

[135] Earliest redaction ca. 1367 to 1373. Janicke, *Magdeburger Schöppenchronik* pp. XIII and XIXf. Cf. Potthast, pp. 1002–3.

of Alexander as described; others believe the Saxons come from the Danes; yet others, that they come from Britain. The scribe admits the possibility of correctness for all three accounts (p. 10). His inclination to reconcile conflicting sources is emphatically abandoned by his Renaissance successors.

The chronicler's discussion of German antiquities touches briefly upon pagan Saxon religion: their worship of Mercury among other planets, their sacred groves named after the gods, their veneration of trees, and their interpretation of the flight of birds for prophecy (Janicke, pp. 18–19). The antiquity of the Franks receives passing mention to prepare for the lengthy quarrel between the two tribes. Troy, Valentinian, Priam, and Anthenor all appear, but are given short shrift. The Frankish name means "ferocious," not "free", and the Franks were handed a lasting defeat by the Roman Aristarchus (pp. 10–11). The chronicler's hostility is explainable in two ways: first by Frankish victory in Charlemagne's Saxon wars and second, by the scribe's probable conviction that ancient Franks and modern French were equivalent.

As the chronicle begins its treatment of the less obscure past, the major historical heroes help shape the work. Charlemagne's exploits occupy many pages, highlighted by the embarrassing victory over the Saxons, the destruction of their sacred gold and silver column, the "Hermensul" (p. 24), the appeal to Charles by the multilated pope, and Charles's Roman coronation (pp. 34–35). Since it is a Saxon chronicle, the Ottos enjoy an important place and are honored for their donations to monasteries and hospitals (pp. 8–9), and for their beneficial relations with the papacy as in the deposition of Pope John (p. 51).

The *Magdeburger Schöppenchronik* is a far richer treasury of real and fictitious history than these paragraphs indicate. In addition to its intrinsic merit, it is an important sign of the new directions in German historiography. The monopoly of ecclesiastical and dynastic history is broken once and for all in the fourteenth century, and the *Schöppenchronik* is one of the more readable examples of the new civic histories. It is only predictable that the rising bourgeoisie would wish its own deeds and ancestries preserved in written record. The new trend gains increasing significance through the Renaissance, Baroque, and even to the threshold of modern scientific history in Justus Möser's *Osnabrückische Geschichte* (A.D. 1765ff.).

JACOB TWINGER of Königshoven's chronicle (1400/1415) is in contrast to the *Schöppenchronik* a universal history, hence of the traditional type that was to compete in German historical writing with local history throughout the Renaissance. Despite its traditional form and unoriginal content, Twinger's chronicle also marks an important development in German historiography. It is as secular as historical writing could be in the period, and is self-consciously directed to a large audience. Twinger began writing in Latin and then decided that the instruction of the largest number was preferable to producing yet another chronicle for the learned. He began again and composed the whole work in German. It is filled with real and fictitious history, like most of its predecessors, but unlike them and like the successors, it taps every available source, including the polemical literature of the contemporaries. Twinger is, for example, in great debt to Dietrich of Nieheim.[136] As a consequence, many similarities arise between Twinger's accounts and Dietrich's, but Twinger is less equivocal on certain issues. He tells us that some writers believe the Empire to have been in the hands of the Germans only since Otto the Great. Charlemagne, however, was German.[137] Twinger resolves the dilemma easily by admitting that the Empire was for a time in the hands of the kings of France ("Frangrich"), but at that time, he insists, the kings of France were German (Hegel, p. 404).

The Germans are, moreover, as noble as the Romans from whom they took the Empire. The Franks, who are Germans, came from Troy just as did the Romans (Hegel, p. 624). Those Trojans who married Gallic women ("Walhen") are French; those who remained in German lands are properly called Franks (p. 623). The same incipient patriotism that moved Twinger to rewrite his chronicle in German no doubt also moved him to revive Alexander of Roes's distinctions between Frankish and French. Twinger's home was in Strassburg. As is frequently the case in the extremities of a language area, feelings of difference prevailed which elsewhere had been forgotten or were not to be known for centuries.

Twinger shares with the *Schöppenchronik* some ramblings in German mythical history. He writes of the great battles between Germans and Romans, the severest fought by the Romans since the Punic wars (Hegel, p. 327). The Germans were mightily defeated at the hands of Marius (p. 328), allied themselves with Caesar in his triumph over Rome (p. 332), and soundly returned a defeat at the time of Augustus, when 30,000 Romans fell outside Augsburg (p. 335). Twinger's heroic

---

[136] Heimpel, *Dietrich von Niem*, p. 171.

[137] Karl Hegel, ed., *Chronik des Jacob Twinger von Königshoven, 1400 (1415)*, *Chroniken der deutschen Städte*, VIII.153–498, and all of IX, consecutively paginated (Leipzig, 1870–71), p. 421. Twinger was known to Andreas of Regensburg, Veit Arnpeck, Petermann Etterlin, Schedel, and Trithemius; his chronicle was printed in 1474; see pp. 188–89, 196, 198, and 225 [henceforth "Hegel"].

figures include the familiar leaders of the Troy escape, Anthenor and Priam for example. The myth he emends little, only bringing Prussia and the Maeotian swamps a bit closer together by way of the Sicambri's wanderings (p. 621). Caesar reappears as a founder of cities in Germany (p. 330). He is said also to have built a great temple to Mercury at Eberheimmünster (p. 331). The saints of the Maternus legend find their way into Twinger's chronicle (pp. 709ff.), along with Prester John who died in 1140 A.D. at the advanced age of 361 (p. 439).

Twinger did not make Prester John a German, as did the Alsatian Anonymous of Maximilian's time. But the original audience of the chronicle may well have made the connection between John and Frederick II apropos of the new fairy-tale elements of the Frederick myth. Among the eminent personages of less obscure history Charlemagne appears, distinguished by his service to Church and Empire, such as the construction of the cathedral at Aachen (Hegel, p. 406). Theodoric is given imperial overtones, but has a more important place as a popular hero, whose deeds are celebrated in vernacular song. The songs themselves must have been the perfect blending of history and fiction. Twinger, however, was no minstrel and expressed grave reservations about their veracity (pp. 367–68), reservations as grave as a scientific historian might harbor for Twinger's work. Of ancient religion, Twinger tells us only that Mercury was the most important of the German gods (p. 701).

Not unlike his model in Dietrich of Nieheim, Twinger is a Janus-faced figure in a Janus-faced period. He does not stand at quite the same turning point as the compiler of the *Schöppenchronik*, since universal chronicles were to suffer many more vicissitudes than the younger tradition of civic history. Twinger's is one of the few genuine universal chronicles in German since Jansen Enikel's in the thirteenth century, and it is the first one of any magnitude since Jansen's. To the concept of universal history in the vernacular, he joined his great erudition, a preoccupation with Germanic antiquities, and the same for present publicistic developments. Works of similar character flood the subsequent writing of history in Germany, whether Latin or German, from Gobelinus Persona over Schedel, to the great cosmographies of the sixteenth century. Twinger could be and was simultaneously unoriginal, traditional, even old-fashioned, and pioneering, prophetic, and new.

The terminal event of the period under discussion here is the COUNCIL OF CONSTANCE. It is one of the crossroads of Germany's political and cultural history. Hindsight recognizes the importance of the first great ecclesiastical gathering in the North, including the grant of Prussia to the Hohenzollern and the malingering that would lead inevitably to the Reformation. The Italian wave over Germany uncovered ancient treasures for posterity and swept the North once and for all into the humanistic scholarly tradition. The Council Fathers, whatever their learned avocations, were involved in crucial political discussion. The vocabulary of this discussion is our final evidence for the reality historical myth had in all levels of medieval and Renaissance culture in Germany.[138]

Theodoric the Great was often numbered among the heroic figures of history in the mythical-historical tradition, as for example, in Twinger. The Gothic king also received the attention of canonists and theologians at the Council of Constance. One group of bishops maintained that only the pope and no worldly monarch could call a council. The opposition gave the example of Theodoric (*rex serenissimus a Deo inspirante*) who called a council for ecclesiastical reform. The response held that Theodoric was no better than Julian or Arius and that like them he perished in flames (*Acta*, IV, 376–77).

The documents of the Council generally support the myth of the Empire, whether or not they are written from an imperial point of view. Some say that when Charlemagne won the Empire he won with it the right to name the pope (*Forschungen*, p. 280). Others say that the Roman See kept the power of naming the Emperor when it transferred the Empire from the schismatic Greeks (*Forschungen*, p. 282). In either case, the Emperor was bound to the Pope. In a document prepared specially for the Council, Dietrich of Nieheim repeated his favorite story of John XII's deposition by Otto in order to support the imperial privileges over the papacy (*Acta*, IV, 615). The imperial argument is raised violently in one attack on the popes. They are nothing less than precursors of Antichrist, since they recognize no Emperor after Charles IV and maintain that the Empire ended with him (*Forschungen*, p. 49). The reasoning follows Alexander of Roes on the eschatology of the *Imperium*. This issue dissolved in the first year of the Council (1414), when Sigismund succeeded in having himself crowned Emperor with the insignia of Charlemagne (*Acta*, IV, 447–49). At the Council, the continuity of the German Empire from Rome appeared as taken for granted every time the *Venerabilem* was quoted (e.g., *Acta*, II, 346, among many, many other occasions). Imperial sanc-

---

[138] Heinrich Finke, et al., eds., *Acta Concilii Constanciensis*, 4 vols. (Münster, 1896–1928), II, 125; cf. Finke, *Forschungen und Quellen zur Geschichte des Konstanzer Konzils* (Paderborn, 1889), p. 101 [henceforth "*Acta*" and "*Forschungen*" resp.].

tity and supremacy were often debated bitterly in connection with the
Empire's privileges with the Church, but the very debates assumed the
basic validity of imperial claims, disputing only their application (e.g.,
Forschungen, p. 276).

As in the *Interregnum*, the exigencies of the time of the Council of
Constance largely turned the energies of German men of letters to
pursuits far from the investigation of German antiquities. Also as in
the Interregnum, a few men—like Alexander von Roes then, and
Dietrich and Twinger now—chose to introduce the German mythical
past into their studies of imperial rights. For the first time since the
thirteenth century, some of the older medieval stories begin to reappear. The time elapsed before their reappearance is approximately a
century—from Martinus Polonus (1268/71) to the vernacular chronicles of the 1360s and 1370s. It is a remarkable lacuna in a period of
intense written activity in "national," political, and patriotic matters.
When the Council of Constance brought all variations of historical
argument to a public forum, the German and imperial partisans had
the new beginnings of a nationally inclined mythical history to employ
in their own behalf. Dietrich of Nieheim is a clear instance. His imperially oriented studies led him to investigate national antiquities
and thus to turn attention to conventions that have been dormant for
over a hundred years. Twinger chose him as a model, and the revival
of German antiquities had begun, albeit slowly and haphazardly. The
concentrated interest in these curiosities characteristic of the Renaissance found its first fruits in Gobelinus Persona, with whom we began
our study. He, too, wrote in the wake of the Council of Constance and
was patently in the tradition of Dietrich and Twinger. He was firmly
bound to countless medieval conventions, but just as firmly reached
forward to kinds of historical investigation that were to become typical. The historiographic developments preceding and accompanying
the Council of Constance represent a renewed concern for the national
past and initiated the rapid absorption of mythical history that characterizes German historiography in the Renaissance.

Aside from the developments toward the end of the century, the
major distinguishing feature of the texts discussed in this chapter has
been not the imagination and inventiveness of previous and subsequent
ages, but the consolidation of the myth of the *Imperium*. At the end
of the century, this very interest provided the avenue to the more
limited national subjects. But national history remained inchoate in
this period, and the overwhelming political reality worthy of historical

scrutiny was the Roman Empire. Its nature was presupposed and disputed.

The Troy legend bore witness to the Roman and German characteristics of the Empire. The ancient history of the Germans showed that they were worthy successors to the Empire, first by their parity in age and nobility and then by their heroic relations to ancient Rome. The histories of Charlemagne and Otto contribute to the German aspect of the myth, as well as touching on those of sanctity and supremacy. By his birth, language, death, and burial, Charlemagne is German. He held sway over Germany, Italy, and Gaul. The occasion that brought Charlemagne to the Empire was a summons to protect the Church. Otto the Great was to do the same, and his son was to protect the Church from the Infidel. Emperor Frederick becomes the embodiment of the sacred functions of the Empire. In his person the Empire's place in the history of salvation is preserved, its "holding off" of Antichrist, its sole reign in the last, the Golden Age returned.

The history of salvation suggests one last observation about the historiography of this period and its place in the history of the German mythical past. I think it not too hazardous—and even less original—to maintain that medieval historical writing was an abject servant of the history of salvation. Whatever the national or dynastic bias of a scholar, his work was ultimately an interpretation of God's kingdom. This permitted considerable freedom of inquiry within the obvious limitations. Secular history, particularly the remote past, could receive objective evaluation by a cleric whose theological disposition might keep him sublimely indifferent to worldly sensitivities. The period between the Interregnum and the Council of Constance, I submit, terminated both the relative objectivity of medieval history and the monolithic authority of the history of salvation. A multiplicity of authorities replaced the concept of an ultimate authority. Conflicting authorities were in the Middle Ages typically harmonized or at worst permitted to stand side by side for the reader to judge. In the Renaissance, as we have seen repeatedly, discretion among conflicting authorities, *anasceua*, is the pride of the historian.

Alexander of Roes is an early example of this kind of criticism, which becomes conventional only in the fifteenth century. His criticism is, however, significant of the earlier shift in the concept of authority. Alexander is ostentatiously aware of the history of salvation, but far from sublimely indifferent to worldly sensibilities. Rather, he has subordinated the history of salvation to a secular partisan bias. In that framework, he can no longer accept conflicting authorities: those cordial to his bias he accepts, those uncordial he rejects. The history of salvation certainly survives Alexander as a principle of historical writing, indeed well into the Renaissance and beyond. But it is no longer the ultimate norm, either as an authority to judge the events of history or as a reason for writing history in the first place. The multiplicity of authority which seems to destroy the monopoly of the history of salvation is, however, not the cause but the effect of the change. Scripture, the Fathers, canon law, and traditional history lost their dictatorial powers, not because of the appearance of new authorities, but because of new reasons for historical writing. In Alexander, the defense of the Empire took precedence over the theology of "the city of this world." In early fourteenth-century France, the monarchy took precedence; in later burgher history, the city and the newly powerful social classes became dominant. All these biases failed to supplant the history of salvation, but succeeded in imposing myriad alternatives. The alternatives found certain traditions useful and others repugnant. They were critical and selective, not because of a great new treasury of historical materials, but because of their own prejudices.

The transcending bias of the history of salvation had more room for objective history than early modern historical writing. The roots of modern critical history lie not in some clairvoyant insight into the nature of human events—an insight that exposed the history of salvation as an extrinsic, distorting, and useless category—but rather in a drastic restriction of the aims of history, in a servitude far more abject than any it suffered in the Middle Ages. The panoply of historical prejudice that succeeded the relative harmony and uniformity of medieval historical writing demanded a set of critical tools to construct from the old sources, from the new sources, or *ex nihilo*, a history acceptable to the patron or the private bent of the author. It was only a matter of time before this search for tools would, as it were, discover the principle of anachronism and apply it as the most far-reaching and organic means of historical criticism.

The Renaissance "discovery" of anachronism, I am far from the first to say, paved the way for modern history. But I find myself obliged to reject the notion that awareness of this principle distinguished medieval from modern historical writing. I say "awareness" because actual adherence to the principle is a privilege that always seems reserved to the present generation of historians. The specifically historical faults found in older scholarship are usually offenses against the sense of anachronism prevailing among the fault-finders. But even awareness of the principle distinguishes only a portion of post-medieval history from its forebears. I should like to accuse of anachronism those who maintain that anachronism is the main or essential feature of Renaissance historiography. That view chooses to see in the past only that which has a visible counterpart in the present, rather than to attempt a reconstruction of as much of the past as possible, regardless of present counterparts. In opposition, I suggest that medieval historiographic tradition suffered a serious but not total disruption in the years surrounding the fourteenth century. The disruption resulted in part from the perfection and consequent exhaustion of encyclopedic history, witness Martinus,[139] and in part from the disparity between the relatively stagnant history of salvation and the volatile propagandistic needs of rising political and social forces.

The disruption was only partial and engendered only a partial vacuum. Into the vacuum came the radical incursions on historical scholarship by highly prejudiced publicists. To judge by the unabating use of historical argument in publicistic dispute, the device was considered successful. Success bred success, and historical writing became a primary expression of partisan interests. Some of these interests had never before enjoyed such open access to learned tradition, and learned tradition had previously made little or no room for them. I mean specifically such forces as, among others, newly important dynasties, provinces, and cities. To make room for the new and varied prejudices, the historical tradition was forced to lend its materials to a wide spectrum of innovating interpretations. When it proved inadequate, new materials were sought and found. Old conventions were employed to give the appearance of legitimacy to new entities, and when the old conventions failed, new conventions arose. A virtual anarchy of historical principle, I submit, characterizes the new historical writing and distinguishes between medieval and Renaissance practice. In this anarchy lie the roots of modern scientific history, not in the elimination of bias but rather in its proliferation.

The texts investigated in this chapter give some slight evidence of the change. Alexander, Konrad, Lupold, and Dietrich are all milestones of the subordination of history to political interest. But neither are John of Paris, Dante, Petrarch, Rienzo, or Coluccio to be excluded. Even the Italian provincial chronicles of the fourteenth century, several of which I touched briefly, serve unabashedly patriotic ends. None of the works even mentioned in this chapter is wholly without precedent in the Middle Ages, but equally, none is imaginable as a

---

[139] This cycle was to repeat itself in the Renaissance in a slightly different form (Gerald Strauss, "A Sixteenth-Century Encyclopedia: Sebastian Münster's Cosmography and its Editors," in *From the Renaissance to the Counter-Reformation: Essays in Honor of Garrett Mattingly*, Charles Carter, ed., [New York, 1965], pp. 145–59), and has, in fact, appeared with increasing regularity ever since.

typical historical expression of any medieval generation much before the Interregnum. The shift to worldly history signaled by these authors does not demand a break in the tradition of historical materials. History without tradition is a contradiction in terms. What the shift does imply is selectivity, a concentration of attention on those materials useful to secular historical writing. And precisely that explains the summary of a millennium of imaginative history in little over a century of Renaissance investigation. The period between the Interregnum and the Council of Constance, although almost destitute of dramatic innovations in the content of the myths of the German past, provides the necessary conditions for their flowering in the Renaissance.

VI

Retrospective, perspective, prospective

One obvious presupposition underlies the previous pages: it is the fundamental continuity of learned tradition in the West. The extent of its survival and revival in the Renaissance is amply illustrated in the myths of the German past. Most medieval texts that contributed to the knowledge of real or fabled national history were printed before the death of Aventinus in 1534. In the notes, primarily to the fourth and fifth chapters of this study, I attempted to show that medieval texts were available to Renaissance men. Printed editions and translations of the historical works written by the foremost medieval scholars —from Jerome and Orosius, over Paul the Deacon and Einhard, to Otto von Freising, Saxo Grammaticus, and Lupold von Bebenburg— listed there are but a fraction of the medieval texts known to the Renaissance. Countless others, perhaps not printed, were demonstrably available in manuscript. Trithemius's *Catalogus* alone would suffice to prove it beyond doubt.[1]

The possibility of Renaissance borrowing from the Middle Ages is wholly certain. The likelihood that such possibility was acted upon is almost as certain. Since the survival of ancient texts on matters German was rather limited, the Renaissance had almost no other information but that in medieval histories. Popular sources were, by and large, not considered adequate. The ancient Germanic peoples seem to have preserved their history orally, and as oral tradition gradually passed

---

[1] The *Catalogus* is in part a new redaction of medieval predecessors, although Trithemius not only brought it up to date, but added much first-hand information, confirming immediate and not derivative knowledge of the tradition.

over into written documentation in the Middle Ages, only a few great moments of Germanic antiquity were preserved. I refer specifically to such probable events as the natural catastrophes that moved the Germanic invaders to leave their Scandinavian homeland or, as another example, the intrigues, alliances, battles, and defeats concealed in the *Nibelungenlied*. The actual historical facts behind such popular traditions do not emerge with full clarity even today. In the Renaissance, this obscurity caused popular sources to be used very rarely for information about the German past. The Renaissance, then, had little material from classical antiquity and less from Germanic antiquity to satisfy its interest in the remoter German past. The close attention paid to medieval compilations of history was only to be expected.

Few Renaissance myths of origin are without medieval precedent. The Troy myth of the Franks, the Macedonian origins of the Saxons (and Swabians), the Armenian origins of the Bavarians, the Scandinavian origins of the Goths and Lombards, the founding of the city of Trier, all clearly depend on medieval interpretation, invention, or tradition. The same pertains to the myths of heroes linked to such origins: Priam, Anthenor, Francio, Marcomir, Bavarus, Japhet, Gog, Magog, Trebeta, and Hero. The tales of the exploits of such heroic figures of history as Brennus, Theodoric, Charlemagne, and the Ottos also have their roots as far as the Renaissance knew in the written and predominantly learned tradition of the Middle Ages.

The little that was known in the Renaissance of ancient German religion is also in heavy debt to the medieval texts. Popular oral tradition was effectively upset by the advances of Christianity, especially as it touched pagan practices. The Renaissance learned from Tacitus one interpretation of the ancient religion, including the worship of Mercury, Hercules, Mars, Isis, Nertha, Castor and Pollux, the custom of simple worship in groves, the lack of pretension in funerals, and the prevalence of augury. Tacitus had acquired his information at first or second hand, and conveyed it through his urbane writings to an equally urbane Roman audience. His sources passed through a simple prism that transformed incomprehensible Germanic names and rituals into familiar Roman doctrine. His prism first translated the sources, then formed them into a negative comment on the religious and moral life of his contemporary Rome.

The Middle Ages had a very different disposition toward Germanic religion and had a far more complex prism through which to view it. Although they were closer to the sources than Tacitus, their understanding was more confused. This confusion, in part a product of the medieval understanding of classical antiquity, was passed on to the

Renaissance, and there further confused by the Renaissance syncretistic view of pagan religion. The Middle Ages told the Renaissance of the Germanic veneration for Apollo, Hermes, and Diana on the one hand, and then, of Wotan, Freia, and Thor. The priesthood of the Druids and the Bards was appropriated to the Germans along with the worship in temples of Jupiter and Mars. The Renaissance gratefully accepted the information communicated by the Middle Ages, but ignored the hostility accompanying it in such authors as Paul the Deacon and Saxo Grammaticus.

Ancient and medieval traditions merged in history's judgement of Germanic virtue and vice. Partially out of Tacitus comes the inclination to see the primitives as valorous, just, eloquent, and at the same time quarrelsome, lazy, and self-indulgent. Medieval convention preserves this, adding little besides some pride in legendary ancient German learning. The stereotypes of nations were easily fixed, then as now, and once fixed, not easily changed. No major alterations obscure the continuity of the tradition, although several additions appeared in the new age.

The conventional views of virtue were largely determined by the society which accepted them. Waging war was as important in the reign of Maximilian as in the reign of Augustus or Domitian. The virtue of justice similarly reflects a social orientation, in this case the highly legalistic one that prevailed in the Roman bureaucracy of Tacitus and that structured Germanic tribal organization. The orientation continued to be of greatest importance as the invaders were romanized. One of the later acts of romanization was the imposition of Roman law on all of continental Europe. Renaissance concern with the Roman law helped elicit in Germany a renewed awareness of Germanic law. Here legalistic preoccupation might have been confused for justice, but in this framework justice is logically a focal point of interest. The written tradition of pride in peaceful achievement is minor in the Middle Ages, but offers some remarkable precedents to the somewhat greater Renaissance concern with learning and industry. Otfried von Weissenburg's appeal to the grandeur of the Franks for an independent literary culture seems to have been an isolated cry in the Middle Ages; in the Renaissance, it became a chorus. Joining the chorus were voices espousing and praising peacefulness, artisanship, and artistry. The voices were heard in the cities, and the virtues were found there. As warlike valor was an ideal of the feudal past, industry, art, and learning became ideals of the nation under the influence of the new bourgeoisie. Looking for their past, the burghers found or invented some precedents for their new ideals. The older social order, however, still had the upper hand, and was to keep it for some centuries. With it, the old system of virtues also prevailed, but had to make room for the new, however minimal. Excepting the slight change that was of great importance for the humanists and burghers but few others, the picture of Germanic virtue and vice remains relatively static in the centuries between Tacitus and the Renaissance. The drastic changes in the culture are only dimly reflected.

Equally or more static was the myth of the *Imperium*, which was so constantly present that the Renaissance perceived no fundamental changes in its character. Some of the ultimate sources of the myth are to be found in the history of the Roman Empire from its inception to its first fall in the West. The deification of the Emperors, the extraordinary occurences after the death of Nero, the assumption of political power in the West by Germanic princes after the fall of Augustulus, all find their way into the Renaissance myth of the Empire. The fuller development of the myth had, however, to await the mythical re-establishment of the Empire in the West with Charlemagne. The Renaissance in Germany assumed intact the myth of the Empire as it was developed in the Middle Ages and formulated in the great transitional period between the Interregnum and the Council of Constance. The Emperor was Caesar, was always German, was a charismatic figure, and was head of the world.

The legend of Emperor Frederick as a constituent of the imperial myth was much older than the Emperor himself. The circumstances which permitted the legend to arise were as old as the Roman Empire and the divine attributes of the Emperors. Not a hundred years had passed since the end of the Roman Republic and the foundation of the Empire when the last of the Claudio-Julian line, Nero, was subjected to a legend seminally the same as the legend of Frederick. The appearance of a false Nero and his triumphant reception among the Parthians are two historical "types," of which the Frederick story will represent "anti-types." With Saint Augustine, the additional factors of Nero's resemblance to Antichrist entered tradition, to reappear in the Middle Ages and Renaissance in the figure of Frederick.

Not all Renaissance myths of the German past have such transparent antecedents. Many have only mediate and equivocal sources in antiquity and the Middle Ages. One of the most troublesome examples of this is the Renaissance myth of Swiss origins from the Swedes. The tale as it appears in Eulogius Kiburger is unknown to the written traditions of national origins in Germany. On the other hand, its close similarity to other tales of origin—the early twelfth-century anonymous reports of the origins of the Swabians and the eighth-century report of the origins of the Lombards as found in Paul the Deacon—points to the possibility of a medieval precedent. The story presented by Kiburger or his unknown sources might have been an adaption to new purposes of Paul the Deacon's report, or one similar to the tale of Swabian origins. The basic pattern—starvation in the North, the exodus of a part of the nation, the distinguished leadership, the wars fought on the continent—indicates that the Renaissance myth may not be original, but rather may rely on now untraceable sources in medieval tradition.

The simple outlines of the story may suggest also that the Germanic peoples maintained their own archetypes of historical thought and in this case more specifically of heroic origins. These are generally analogous to the Roman and Jewish traditions in that the Trojans and captive Jews were also divinely favored nations in flight and obliged to battle the natives of their destined homeland. The Germanic version differs somewhat in motive (starvation) and geography (Scandinavia), and could conceivably be rooted in a collective memory of natural disasters common in the North. This must remain pure conjecture, however, precisely because the written tradition is intermittent, obscure, and plagued with enticing analogues.

Of these, the one that most fires the imagination comes from the first book of Herodotus. In the days of King Atys of Lydia, a great famine struck the whole land. When all other measures failed, the King divided the nation by lot, one half to stay, the other to leave with his son, Tyrrhenus. The exiles built themselves ships, and after some peregrination arrived in Umbria, where they laid their name aside and called themselves after their leader, Tyrrhenians. The parallels are too close to admit comfortably of coincidence, but all other explanations lead to wild speculation. Herodotus may have been available to Kiburger in the fifteenth-century Latin redaction, but this leaves the Scandinavian homeland unexplained. The availability or unavailability of Herodotus would seem to pertain still less to the Langobardic origins song. Of course, the Langobardic scop may have known some Roman derivative, considering the lengthy proximity of Langobards and Romans and of Lombardy and Tyrrhenia; but why should he select a rather obscure and unimportant fable of origins from the numerous possibilities? Indeed, the Tyrrhenians, Langobards, Swabians, and Swedes may all have left their homelands in a starvation, but that, I believe, would imply an inordinate instance of national exile by lottery. If Herodotus was preserving some Anatolian song, then the common origins might be sought in the dimmest Indoeuropean antiquity. If the people to whom the song applied were not of Indoeuropean language or culture, directly or indirectly, then the common origins would have to be sought in some utterly indefinite cultural archetype; and then coincidence would be as satisfactory an explanation. The problem, as I suggested, is enticing but leads to little besides wild speculation.

The heroic history of Trithemius rests on similarly but less frustratingly unclear precedents, assuming of course that Hunibald was the author's invention and not his discovery. King Basan's palace on the banks of the Mosel appears to be an attempted explanation of the name Palatinate, like those of Alexander of Roes and Aventinus. Jordanes's Gothic King Burista, with his import of learned men, might possibly have been Trithemius's model for attributing similar activities to Basan. Widukind of Corvey's stress on the alliance of Saxons and Franks might also have served as a model for Trithemius. The pious abbot knew all these works, and more. But his fabrication is so well conceived and executed that all but the most obvious borrowings (the Trojan origin of the Sicambri, the naming of Salic law) defy immediate and unequivocal attribution of source except to the improbable Hunibald.

Nonetheless, Trithemius's history of the Franks is not a mere invention, destitute of its author's great scholastic and humanistic erudition. The *Compendium* is unsatisfactorily described as "a simple anomaly." On the contrary, it is a logical synthesis of medieval materials and Renaissance mentality. Precisely what the medieval materials were, however, awaits intensive study of Trithemius's secular writings in general and his *Compendium* in particular. Uncovering of Trithemius's sources would be interesting in itself but would also prepare the way for significant historical and critical conclusions, viz., his principles of selection and the character of the transformation between medieval chronicle source and Renaissance historical fiction. I suspect that much is to be learned about Renaissance historiography from such an exercise, and perhaps also about Renaissance history, should Trithemius's fiction prove to be a veiled *roman à clef*. This last is again only surmise, but finds support in Trithemius's active participation in imperial affairs, religious reform, and scholarly pursuits. Political allegory was hardly foreign to the Renaissance. The *Compendium* is a distinctly patriotic work. It conveys no reliable information about its purported subject, the prehistory of the Franks; but its author must have meant it to convey something. An elaborate hoax, an outright lie of these dimensions is inconsistent with Trithemius's scholarly gravity and unquestionable piety. His purpose and meaning must reside in an explanation more harmonious with his general character than forgery and mendacity, which are at best superficial evaluations.

The case of Trithemius has a mirror image in Aventinus. Trithemius's imaginativeness has obscured his historical value to modern investigators; Aventinus's historical value has similarly obscured his imaginativeness. Only an evaluation comfortable with both extremes, or apparent extremes, can be genuinely fair. Aventinus's sources are by and large known, except for his equivalent of Hunibald, Frethulphus and Schritovinus (Schreitwein and Freithylph), who have not been successfully identified. All but his most outrageous attempts at etymology ("Weihnachten"—"wine-night") seem to be vaguely traceable to earlier sources as, for example, the German word for hero, "Held," as derivative of the noble ancestor, Helto. Helto seems to have been inspired by Hero, son of the mythical founder of Trier.

The reasons for Aventinus's imaginative etymologies are fairly transparent, even if his sources are occasionally obscure. He sought to fix something as present as a vocabulary item or a native-sounding name in a historical lineage. Words at large and personal and place names in particular were thus not merely conventional locutions, but rather messengers from the past, bursting with historical information. This places him, imaginative or accurate, squarely within the conventions of Renaissance historiography. The Middle Ages, in gentle confusion of past and present, employed eponymy to explain why a present name was this word and no other. The past was serving the present. In Aventinus, as in the rest of the Renaissance etymologizers, this consideration is secondary and its converse is primary. Words were present signs of the past; the past could be learned through them. Aventinus's approach, whether imaginative or accurate, led to history.

The overwhelming prevalence of tradition in the Renaissance's mythical view of German history leads to some doubt whether major anomalies are likely or even tolerable. They are, in fact, neither. The very object of the myths, history as time past, suffers from no such mutability as its interpretations from age to age. Even Annius of Viterbo's forgery is dependent on tradition, mostly on Tacitus, but also on other classical authors and, of course, on scripture. Tradition determines the larger patterns and supplies most of the materials. The individual realization of the patterns and usage of the materials leaves room for variety and even novelty. Minor exceptions have thus to be admitted. When forgery or free imagination works, tradition is bound to suffer to some degree.

The very few Renaissance myths of the German past that are wholly without obvious precedent include such fabrications as the wildest excesses of the Alsatian Anonymous. I have found no earlier claim to Adam's German tongue. Although Prester John himself has medieval origins, his German nationality is not asserted in the Middle Ages. Gebwiler's Tyras, founder of Tyrasburg (Strassburg) seems to be original, although the name was available to Gebwiler in medieval chronicles. Such explanations as the name of Regensburg after "Reginapyrga" and Dietfurt after "Diet" appear also to have no exact visible antecedents. Not many more myths than these are new to the Renaissance. The overall patterns are old, and the vast majority of the myths enjoy, directly or by detour, an ancient or medieval pedigree.

The entire problem of the myths of the German past—the intense frequency of their appearance, their deceptive similarity to older and newer phenomena—requires a setting in the age of the Renaissance, which in turn the myths serve to clarify. Considered unhistorically, the declarations of the Alsatian Anonymous, for example, would seem to indicate a rise of national feeling paralleled only by the almost religious patriotism of the nineteenth century or the fanaticism of the twentieth. Indeed, there are parallels, but they are more obfuscating than enlightening. To seek in the Alsatian Anonymous the prototypes of modern chauvinism is to ignore several essential distinctions. The first is that the Renaissance's inchoate sense of national self-consciousness was primarily the affair of the learned and not a mass popular movement. Secondly, the mythical category of thought was inseparable from Greco-Roman and Biblical antiquity, completely within Western tradition and a powerful affirmation of it. The supposed modern counterpart tried desperately to part mythical backgrounds into national entities and then either to remove them from Western tradition or to claim exclusive development of it. This was in truth a negation of Western tradition. Finally, such a search suggests that the groping for national self-consciousness distinguished one country from another, whereas in fact the mythical reconstruction of the national past was a completely international pastime.

The commonness of such myths outside Germany was implied in

the previous chapters of this study as true of Italy and France, and was no less true of England. The Lombards claimed the monarchy of Italy on the basis of their independent antiquity from Troy and their kingdom in Italy after the fall of Rome. Rienzo's revolution itself was a mythical return to the ancient Roman state. By assuming the titles *Tribunus* and *Augustus*, he applied to himself and to his mission as much as could be borne of the mythical aura of Italy's political antiquity. Rienzo's plan to return pope and emperor to Rome meant a restoration of Italian glory rather than complicity in French papal or German imperial designs in Italy.

In sixteenth-century France, the Troy myth of the Franks received at least as much respect as it did in Germany. There, of course, it served French interests.[2] Some maintained that the inhabitants of Alsatia, despite their German language, were Trojan Franks just as the French were; thus the Alsatians and their land properly belonged to the Frankish, that is, French King (Klippel, p. 51). Francis I was praised for his noble ancestry that included Alexander the Great and Charlemagne (p. 54). The myth of the *Imperium* was also called to French policy, when the transmission of world Empire was traced by way of the Assyrians, Medes, Persians, Macedonians, Romans, and Greeks to the French (p. 71).

The imperial myth in its strictly chiliastic aspects came to England in the seventeenth century. Radical Puritans, spiritual descendents of Joachim of Floris and Thomas Müntzer, sought to establish in England the secular and spiritual successor to the earthly city. For their troubles they were hanged, drawn, and quartered.[3] Less dramatic signs of similar commitment to myth appeared in Tudor England. Polydore Vergil's history of his adoptive homeland was relatively critical in rejecting Geoffrey of Monmouth's more fabulous tales. Nonetheless, the Italian humanist was obliged at least to present the stories of such national heroes as Brutus or Brito, eponymous founder of Britain; King Lear and his youngest daughter; and the British (not Swabian) Brennus, who conquered Rome. Among his contemporaries, however, "for the repudiation of Geoffrey of Monmouth's history, Polydore Vergil was considered almost as a man deprived of reason."[4] There were, we may assume, those in England who adhered more closely to

---

[2] Maria Klippel, *Die Darstellung der fränkischen Trojanersage in Geschichtsschreibung und Dichtung vom Mittelalter bis zur Renaissance in Frankreich* (Marburg, 1936), pp. 49ff.

[3] P. G. Rogers, *The Fifth Monarchy Men* (London, 1966), p. 107 and passim.

[4] Henry Ellis, ed., *Polydore Vergil's English History*, Camden Society Publications, XXXVI (London, 1844), p. x and pp. 27ff., 35–36, 42ff.

the traditional fables of past national glory. The humanist Polydore represents in England much the same spirit of curiosity and attempted critical use of sources that his moderate humanist counterparts in Germany do.

The less moderate utterances of an author like the Alsatian Anonymous have also to be seen in the broader perspective of his contemporary European preoccupations. Outside this perspective, the Alsatian Anonymous and no less his humanist peers appear first to be an outburst of particularly provincial nationalism and second, uniquely German. The pretensions of Rienzo and the Lombard nobility, the French and English origins in Troy, the defamers of Polydore Vergil, and the Fifth Monarchy Men indicate that the outburst was not uniquely German. Among the Alsatians, special political issues do play a part, since they felt pressure from the French on their territory. These issues can explain the fanaticism of the Anonymous, but fail to explain his appearance in the first place. The basic interest in national antiquities extended well beyond Alsatia or similar border territories, and flourished in the absence as in the presence of foreign cultural pressure. The principles underlying this international concern with national antiquities must be sought elsewhere.

It is a truism of Renaissance studies that the new age differs from its predecessor, among other things, by its acquisition of historical perspective. Renaissance historians were aware that when Caesar wrote "miles" he meant "soldier" and not chivalric "knight-errant," as seems to have been the case in the medieval mind. A Lorenzo Valla—but not the Middle Ages before him—could detect in the Donation of Constantine a series of stylistic anachronisms and thus a forgery. History had always been known in its aspect as past time, but it was not always distinguished from the present in style or period. The ability to differentiate raised the best of Renaissance historiography above that of the Middle Ages and classical antiquity. Now the difference in time implied a difference in the style of human affairs. Historical evidence could no longer be evaluated exclusively by analogy to the present. Thus history became more and more "past." The historical consciousness of the Renaissance turned its attention to the distance of events rather than, as in other ages, to an awareness of their proximity.

The effective writing of history depends, of course, on the comprehension of both temporal modes, but distance is the essential critical tool of the historian. Awareness of the proximity of history without the corrective awareness of its distance leads to anachronism, to the assumption that the past was rather like its vestiges in the present.

Recognition of this principle came out of Italy in the *quattrocento* and eventually spread out over all Europe. Whether the Renaissance's consuming interest in history is the cause or the effect of this sophistication is beside the point here. In any case, all Renaissance historical writings are characterized, more or less noticeably, by awareness of historical distance. In its purest forms, this sophistication found expression in the principle of anachronism, which began to be current among the learned and remained with them. The popular chronicles, even those of Italian provenance, did not always share the full clarity of the new perspective. Nonetheless, even they reflected, however dimly or brightly, the age's preoccupation with the past as past. Younger countries, cities, cultures, and classes were all infected with this craving for historicity and sought some identity in the past. In consequence, every conceivable source—no matter how inaccurate and fantastic— was tapped, forgeries were created, and speculation grew rampant.

Since most of the myths are originally medieval, they may seem to represent the same perspective in the Middle Ages as that claimed for the Renaissance. The similarities are no more than superficial. The appearance of the myths in the Middle Ages was sporadic and extrinsic to the larger scheme of theological history. In the Renaissance, they are systematically gathered and become one of the prime interests of practicing historians. When the myths initially appeared in the Middle Ages, they fulfilled specific functions, often political. The seventh-century Troy myth coincides with the rise of the majordomos and Frankish hegemony over most of Roman Europe. The English equivalent is a century or so younger and coincides with Anglo-Saxon hegemony over Britain.[5] In both cases the new nations sought to gain in dignity what they had already gained in might. Some of this may have found its way into the neologizing myths of the Renaissance, particularly those of the cities and burgher families. But legitimation alone cannot explain the Renaissance's concentrated interest in mythical antiquity. Neither the Franks, Bavarians, and Saxons, nor the Hapsburgs required legitimation in the Renaissance. Dignity was indeed at issue, but not by the medieval analogy to a timeless, ever present, Virgilian Rome, whose attraction was not age but fame. Rather, the Renaissance sought to fix its dignity in antiquity, in history as time past.

---

[5] Robert W. Hanning, *The Vision of History in Early Britain* (New York and London, 1966), pp. 103–5, and Domenico Comparetti, *Vergil in the Middle Ages*, E. F. M. Benecke, trans. (1908; reprinted Hamden, Conn., 1966), pp. 179ff. and 244– 45 with notes.

The search proceeded unencumbered through the first third of the sixteenth century. Then new preoccupations and methods began to change historical scholarship in German lands. It would remain a search for history as time past, but under new auspices. The first of these was the Reformation. It required historical legitimation over against the prevailing and hostile Catholic tradition, in much the same way as Christianity at large had required historical legitimation over against the prevailing and hostile pagan tradition in the time of Augustine and Orosius. As a consequence, traditional history had to be rewritten, and Protestant historiography returned to the history of salvation. The declared purposes of historical study remained moralizing, but not as in humanism with the ideal of the wise man (cf. Bebel above), but with the ideal of the right-believing Christian. Melanchthon wrote what might be considered the manifesto of Protestant historiography in his prefaces to the 1532 edition of Carion's chronicle and to Caspar Hedio's 1539 translation of the *Ursberger Chronik*. As a humanist he declares the value of history for its own sake, for it is one of the forms of activity that distinguishes man from the beasts. But his prime concern is that history reveal the wonders of God's work from one point of view: the true Church never vanished from the face of the earth, but was rarely found among those who pretended to it. The heretic of the Middle Ages became the saint of the Reformation.[6]

This is, of course, not the sole distinguishing characteristic of Protestant historiography. The revaluation of theological history in favor of the reform is only one of several such characteristics, and a retrogressive one at that. The implied revaluation of secular history was far more repercussive. The German Reformers extended the ideas of the patriotic humanists, reinterpreting the imperial-papal conflicts of the Middle Ages in the most "modern" terms, viz., as a conflict between a national German monarchy and an intrusive, Italian-based, international empire. Reform historiography records the alliance between nationalism and Protestantism that was to determine much of subsequent European history, from Elizabethan England and the independence of the Netherlands to the "Kulturkampf." It repudiates the international orientation of medieval and earlier Renaissance German historiography.

This dramatic shift of emphasis in historical writing obscures an-

---

6 Heinz Scheible, ed., *Die Anfänge der reformatorischen Geschichtsschreibung: Melanchthon, Sleidan, Flacius und die Magdeburger Zenturien*, Texte zur Kirchen- und Theologiegeschichte, II (Gütersloh, 1966), pp. 14–26, esp. pp. 20–23; cf. also Peter G. Bietentolz, *History and Biography in the Work of Erasmus of Rotterdam*, Travaux d'Humanisme et Renaissance, LXXXVII (Geneva, 1966), pp. 11 and 50.

other development more immediately pertinent to the imaginative disposition underlying the myths of the German past. After the first third of the sixteenth century, German historiography begins to feel the effects of Erasmian philology. It yields its first fruits in Beatus Rhenanus, prospers quietly in the hands of industrious and progressively more discerning editors and translators, and bears a veritable harvest at the end of the century with the normative critical work of Justus Lipsius. Historical writing would never again permit German antiquities the uninhibited fancy they enjoyed in the early Renaissance. The new directions in historiography did not, however, extinguish forever the myths of the German past.

The very sources which supplied the Renaissance with its myths continued to be published, despite some critical awareness of their questionable reliability. Historiographers often forget that the great nineteenth-century century compilations of national antiquities and historical sources followed in an unbroken chain from the sixteenth-century predecessors. The absence of better editions has forced me to use some of the links. I refer to Simon Schard, Margarinus de la Bigne, Marquard Freher, B. G. Struve, Hieronymus Thomas (editor of *Schardius Redivivus*), Henricus Meibom, Johannes Graevius, Leibniz, and Muratori, which takes us to the threshold of the nineteenth century. There are dozens of such works, by no means limited to matters German. This chain is itself sufficient evidence that the majority of sources gathered here was available from the sixteenth century onwards to anyone. Interested readers abounded in numbers sufficient to require edition after edition of individual works and large compilations.

Even several of the lesser-known authors enjoyed popularity in later times, for example, when the eighteenth century anticipated much of the Romantics' interest in German antiquities. Albertus Krantz was the subject of a laudatory biography in 1752.[7] In 1733, Annius of Viterbo's Berosus was incorporated into a German translation of a later sixteenth-century chronicle.[8] Lessing's theological adversary Adolf Klotz published in 1771 an edition with commentary of Saxo Grammaticus.[9] Earlier, Aventinus and his work caught the imagination of several major literary figures. Theobald Hock took citations from Aventinus into his verse (1601).[10] The historian appears in person and

---

[7] Paul Schaerffenberg, *Die Saxonia des Albert Krantz* (Meiningen, 1893), p. 7 note 2.

[8] H. Dannenbauer, *Germanisches Altertum und deutsche Geschichtswissenschaft*, Philosophie und Geschichte, LII (Tübingen, 1935), p. 23.

[9] Hermann Jantzen, trans., *Saxo Grammaticus* (Berlin, 1900), p. XVIf.

[10] Friedrich Gotthelf, *Das deutsche Altertum in den Anschauungen des sechzehnten und siebzehnten Jahrhunderts*, Forschungen zur neueren Litteraturwissenschaft, XIII (Berlin, 1900), p. 37–38.

by frequent borrowing in Moscherosch's *Gesichte Philanders von Sitte-wald* (ca. 1640).[11] The baroque novelist's curiosity about German antiquities was part and parcel of his patriotic political activities. In 1648 he published the German version of Wimpheling's *Germania* to propagandize a German Alsatia against French claims at the end of the Thirty Years' War. His novel displays Widukind, the Saxon chieftain of Charlemagne's time, along with Tuisco, Ariovistus, Arminius, and Siegfried. Aventinus's germanizations of the names are used throughout, e.g., "Tuitscho" for Tuisco, "König Ehrenfest" for Ariovistus. The same heroes appear in the *Adriatische Rosemund* (1645) of Philipp von Zesen, who like Moscherosch widely exploited Aventinus and the whole tradition of Renaissance historiography.[12] Goethe himself studied Aventinus over a long period and mentioned his studies in 1808 and 1818.[13] Among the more surprising survivals is Trithemius's Hunibald, who was still accepted as a credible authority in the nineteenth century by, among others, no less a figure than Görres.[14]

Several isolated but noteworthy examples illustrate the survival into living modern tradition of the hardiest myths and the psychological disposition underlying them. The Trojan origins of the Franks were thought true as late as 1863, and attempts were made to prove the myth to be fact.[15] Also well on into the nineteenth century, research into the Swedish origins of the Swiss was considered a respectable occupation.[16] Among the Swiss, this myth may be heard as unquestionable fact, even today. With due embarrassment I recount the journalistic ramblings of a modern myth-maker, Ian Fleming. His *Thrilling Cities* include Lausanne, Switzerland, where a group of cranks worships Elizabeth II. Apparently, they believe that she descends from King David, that hers is the world *Imperium*, and that she will reign over the millennium.[17] This, of course, proves nothing but the invincibility of human folly.

---

11 Felix Bobertag, ed., *H. M. Moscheroch: Wunderliche und wahrhafte Gesichte Philanders von Sittewald* (1863; reprinted Darmstadt, 1964), pp. 129–38 and 373–99.

12 [*Philipp von Zesen: Ritterholds von Blauen*] *Adriatishe Rosemund*, Max Hermann Jellinek, ed., Neudrucke deutscher Literaturwerke des XVI. und XVII. Jahrhunderts, nos. 160–63 (Halle, 1889), pp. 192–209.

13 *Goethes Tagebücher*, III (Weimar, 1899), 405, and VI (Weimar, 1894), 157 [WA, III, 3 and 6: Goethes Werke herausgegeben im Auftrage der Großherzogin Sophie von Sachsen].

14 K. L. Roth, "Die Trojasage der Franken," [Pfeiffer's] *Germania*, I (1856), 39.

15 Friedrich Zarncke, "Über die s.g. Trojanersage der Franken," *SB Sächsische Gesellschaft der Wissenschaften*, philol-hist. Classe, XVIII (1866), p. 272 and note 7.

16 Jakob Baechtold, ed., *Die Stretlinger Chronik*, Bibliothek älterer Schriftwerke der deutschen Schweiz, I (Frauenfeld, 1877), p. LXXXIIIf.

17 Ian Fleming, *Thrilling Cities* (New York, n.d.), p. 167.

Hardly less foolish is the curious survival into the present of the German Renaissance concept "German" which included everything we recognize today as "Germanic." Modern editions and translations of Tacitus, English as well as German, insist on identifying Tacitus's "Germani" with the Germans of the present. Such an identification suppresses the fact that those whom Tacitus described are ancestors of the modern Germans as much as of the English, the Italian Lombards (Tacitus mentions the Anglii and Langobardi by name in the *Germania*, c. XL), the Frankish French, the Visigothic Spaniards, the Dutch, and the Scandinavians. The implication is that the Germans are linear descendents of Tacitus's "Germani," whereas the English, Italians, or French are mixed with other cultures. This supports the untenable position that German territory and population failed to undergo the same christianization and cultural romanization, the same repeated invasions, and the same spiritual upheavals as the rest of Europe endured. This folly is as invincible among the Germans, who see themselves as Tacitus's noble savages, as it is among the English, who see in Tacitus's war-loving "Germani" the modern Germans rather than ancestors common to both.

The existence of myth in all ages—our own included—is self-evident and hardly requires a great gathering of historical curiosities. These materials and the mythical disposition that supports them do, however, suggest important critical categories. The greater part of the Renaissance myths of the German past was accepted as true by most contemporaries. For credibility, the myths had to parade as fact; they could not very well parade as myth and expect to be believed. The same rules prevail today. In Renaissance historiography, however, the distance of several hundred years, masses of empirical evidence, and a fairly young scientific historical tradition permit the modern investigator to distinguish fact from myth.

That the same distinctions were not made in the Renaissance is more than evident from these pages, but historiography then was by no means uncritical. Only the objects of its criticism differ substantially from our own. This leads to one observation about historiographic study, namely, that critical awareness of the past changes little in itself, but gives the appearance of great change by its application to varying objects. The choice of objects by historical curiosity seems to signify its disposition in any given period. In other words, distinction between myth and fact varies, and the variance is one characteristic of an era's historiography. Ancient historical attention appears to have been directed primarily toward the civilized world. Thus Herodotus and Tacitus could accept or at least be neutral toward the fabulous character of distant times and unfamiliar peoples. This stance was acceptable to the Middle Ages and Renaissance, but is no longer so. The history of salvation seems so to have preoccupied the Middle Ages that it overshadowed all other considerations of fact and fable. Thus medieval historians and poets could mingle their historical and narrative traditions (e.g., *Kaiserchronik* and *Nibelungenlied*). The practice began to lose favor in the Renaissance (e.g., Agrippa von Nettesheim). The Renaissance's discovery of historicity disposed it to credulousness toward documents amicable to its biases and seriously purporting to be ancient (e.g., Pseudo-Berosus and Hunibald but not the Donation of Constantine). The twentieth century is no longer so credulous about the distant past. The recent past is another matter.

Modern historical thought is, I suspect, credulous toward evaluations and generalizations concerning the historical present and the past insofar as it is available to living memory. The historiography of recent events provides numerous examples. Revisionist and re-revisionist historians have placed blame for twentieth-century disasters on every available and remotely likely candidate. The disputes would prove vacuous, were the same principles of distinction applied as are applied by scientific historians to the Crusades or the Roman colonization of Gaul. Allocations of blame rest on emotional and scientifically irrelevant premises. The confidence scientific history feels in its evaluations of distant events is often misapplied, I believe, to more recent times. This polemic has a purpose, but it is not to revise yet again modern historical investigation. Rather, it is to call attention to our historical outlook as no more free of the confusion of myth and fact than that of our intellectual ancestors. Only the areas of confusion differ.

The most proximate parentage of modern Renaissance studies contains a concrete example of the confusion of present myth with past fact. Huizinga's *Waning of the Middle Ages* has remained a basic contribution since its first printing in 1919. The longevity and high esteem accorded it speak well enough for its continuing pertinence to historical and literary study. For this reason, not to mention the work's caution and intrinsic excellence, a serious error in judgement must be attributed to a cause other than slipshod speculation or negligent scholarship. A recent article by Paula S. Fichtner proves beyond doubt that Huizinga made such a serious error in judgement.[18] Central to Huizinga's argument is the spiritual disharmony in fifteenth-century

---

[18] Paula S. Fichtner, "The Politics of Honor: Renaissance Chivalry and Habsburg Dynasticism," *Bibliothèque d'Humanisme et Renaissance*, XXIX (1967), 567–80.

Burgundy signaled by the conflict between the ideals of chivalry and the unworthy behavior of hard politics. This "Zerrissenheit" was supposedly shown by the concept of "honor," which represented an idealistic criterion of behavior, while in practice ruthless expansionism was pursued in its name.

Professor Fichtner's tightly argued essay, employing sound philological methods, shows that honor "embraced a far wider range of meanings [in the fifteenth century] than does its basic modern definition of inner personal integrity" (p. 570). Briefly, "honor" meant "glory, success, and political advantage." Thus no inconsistency prevailed between the neochivalric ideals of the fifteenth century and its opportunistic politics. At least here, "Zerissenheit" was unproved. These meanings of honor were as accessible to Huizinga as they were to Professor Fichtner. They are at the roots of the concept from the darkest Middle Ages through the seventeenth century.[19] Why did then Huizinga give the word a thoroughly anachronistic interpretation? It was not carelessness. I venture to suggest that even the great Dutch scholar had serious difficulty distinguishing between the spirit of his own age and the spirit of his purported subject.[20]

Huizinga's researches, much like Burckhardt's, will stand up for generations in spite of this criticism. The reason is that such work resides in the realm of fact, despite all other limitations. The facts of history are by their very nature extraordinarily unsusceptible to change. They may periodically be purged of impertinencies and augmented by new research. They nonetheless represent a relatively stable principle, "wie es eigentlich gewesen," which remains, from Aristotle to Ranke and beyond, the ideal subject and object of historical researches. Myth parading as fact, on the other hand, is most volatile. The often radical differences in myth from period to period give each new generation of historical consciousness the confidence that it is serving the truth where the previous generation was in error.

---

[19] George Fenwick Jones, *The Ethos of the Song of Roland* (Baltimore, 1963), pp. 46–47.

[20] To have European sensibilities in the first decades of this century—as Huizinga undoubtedly had—meant to watch a tolerably humane political and ethical system perform a self-immolation, to watch a world come tumbling down about one's ears, and to await a wholly unknown successor. Moreover, the descendent of Huizinga's Burgundy, his Netherlands, has stood for centuries as a cultural intermediary between French and German, English and continental, liberal and conservative traditions. This status could well have represented for him the "Zerrissenheit" he detected, I believe, falsely, in fifteenth-century Burgundy. Huizinga's judgements precisely insofar as they are (or may be) evaluations of the historical present have escaped criticism. I believe that this is a case of modern historical consciousness gullibly accepting a myth—here, the faulty equation of present and past—in the guise of fact—the considered judgement of an exacting scholar.

The mere variation, however, in no way vitiates the abiding reality of the mythical disposition, and simple awareness may not be sufficient to free historical reason of it. This freedom may be not at all possible, and if possible, neither necessary nor desirable. These questions, however, belong to the philosophy of history and not to this book. One intention alone inaugurated this excursus on historical attitudes: to facilitate the understanding of the phenomenon this book describes, the mythical disposition of the historical consciousness of the Renaissance in Germany. If the modern can be aware of his own disposition to accept historical myth as fact, then he may consider the Renaissance disposition less entirely foreign or quaint. It is a question of the present informing the past and, while not identifying the two, of letting the familiar open the way to the remote.

The survival of the sources and the mythical disposition is accompanied by a more practical survival. The texts of this study contain many fables and *obiter dicta*; not the stuff of history, to be sure, but very much the stuff of literature—and it is in literature that they have survived most vitally. The standard thematic bibliographies list work after work under their entries on Alaric, Theodoric, Charlemagne, Frederick, the Swiss, Prussia, and many other mythical-historical entities that have become familiar to us. To illustrate this literary survival, let us cast a most cursory glance at select myths in strictly and admittedly imaginative writing. The nature of the borrowings and their poetic metamorphosis are most important for the belles-lettres, but have no place in this study.

The literary utilization of the Arminius myth has undergone several recent investigations.[21] The formidable materials available to the scholars include a massive Baroque novel, Lohenstein's *Arminius* (1689–90), a drama by Johann Elias Schlegel (1743), an epic by Wieland (1751), a trilogy of plays by Klopstock (1769, 1784, 1787), and a national drama by Kleist (1808). Klopstock taps the larger tradition to the extent of selecting from it the names of his characters, who include Theude (Theodo) and Gambriv. Alaric's burial in the Busentus found literary expression in several nineteenth-century ballads, of which the most famous one is by Platen. I have already mentioned Rückert's ballad of Barbarossa and its preservation of the Frederick myth. Achim von Arnim's unfinished novel, *Die Kronenwächter* (1817)—a typical

---

[21] For bibliography, cf. Richard Kuehnemund, *Arminius or the Rise of a National Symbol in Literature*, University of North Carolina Studies in the Germanic Languages and Literatures, VIII (Chapel Hill, 1953), p. XIIIf.

example of German Romantic prose fiction—is based in part on the Frederick myth, specifically the prophecy concerning the branch that is to spring from the tree of Frederick. The repercussions of the Frederick fable and the whole myth of the Empire are wide, extending well beyond literature into the writings of philosophers (Nietzsche) and into concrete political action.

In the Renaissance itself, the myth of the *Imperium* assumed imaginative literary form by way of the Latin school dramas of Nicodemus Frischlin. His *Julius Caesar Redivivus* (1584) plays heavily on the German character of the Empire and incorporates the myths of virtue, piety, and scholarship to make Germany a worthy successor to Rome. The virtue of Germanic women figures in Frischlin's *Hildecarda Magna* (1579), whom he borrowed from the Charlemagne cycle. Charlemagne's antagonist, Widukind of the Saxons, was the subject of an epic poem by the Hamburg opera librettist Christian Heinrich Postel (1658 –1705), which included the destruction of the Irmenseul. German historical subjects, taken largely from Renaissance compilations, frequented the opera stage in the German Baroque.[22] The Scandinavian origins of the Swiss achieved high literary status in Schiller's *Wilhelm Tell* (1804). There Stauffacher tells of the famine in the North, the selection by lot of those to leave, the exodus, and the arrival in the Alps (II.ii, ll. 1167ff.).

The battle of song recounted in Johann Rothe's fifteenth-century Thuringian chronicle found its way into Wagner's *Tannhäuser* (1845). The opera also preserves elements of the imperial myth. To be noted here is that Wagner's production at large is independent of the traditions traced in these pages, with the possible exceptions of *Rienzo*, which relies on Bulwer-Lytton and not the Renaissance accounts, and *Lohengrin*, which relies on medieval romance rather than historiography but which also contains elements of the imperial myth. The antiquity of the *Ring* is predominantly Eddic, and the Renaissance in Germany was poorly informed of the sagas.[23] Wagner's later contemporaries produced a large literature of national and nationalistic theme which often leaned on the Renaissance mythical tradition. Numerous

---

[22] I am indebted to Professor M. G. Flaherty for this information and refer the reader to her forthcoming study, *The Defense of Opera.*

[23] The humanists' involvement with popular heroic literature was slight but far from negligible. Both Celtis and Vadianus at least paid lip-service to its vitality. Vernacular literature preserved more of the heroic tradition, but in the Renaissance it was hopelessly confused with the folk literature of many nations. To the best of my knowledge, the subject is untouched in serious scholarship except in the work of Will-Erich Peuckert, such as *Die Grosse Wende* (1948), 2 vols. (rpt. Darmstadt, 1966), and *Pansophie*, 2nd ed. (Berlin, 1956), and *Gabalia* (Berlin, 1967).

scholars of modest literary talent dipped into Germanic antiquities for the purpose of creating belles-lettres. The result was a new genre—the "Professorenroman." In English, the "professorial novel" accurately suggests the horrors which the neutral German term leaves the unwary reader to discover first-hand. Representative of the less disastrous excursions is the best-seller by the incisive critic Gustav Freytag. His six-volume *Die Ahnen* (1873–81) gave form to the myth of Prussia. A twentieth-century heir of Freytag's interests was Wilhelm Schäfer, who incorporated much mythical material into his work, in its time widely read and highly regarded. Stories of the Cimbri, Arminius, Alaric, Theodoric, Charlemagne, the Ottos, the *Imperium*, and more enrich his *Dreizehn Bücher der deutsche Seele* (1922). Its introduction is an extraordinary document, in part nationalistic and mystic nonsense, in part a moving renunciation of war and a call for the regeneration of his people. Unfortunately, Schäfer later betrayed his better half.

The Grimm brothers' *Deutsche Sagen* (1816–18), much like their more popular collection of fairy-tales, maintain the highest literary standards. The *Sagen* gather together a good many of the Renaissance myths of the German past in a form so accessible as to make them a modern reservoir of these poetic materials. They contain, among others, the tale of Emperor Frederick in the Kyffhäuser (item 23 of the 3rd ed.), the burial of Alaric (373), the origin of the Huns from the Gothic *Alirunae* (378), the death of Theodoric (384), the exodus of the Lombards (388), the naming of the Lombards (390), the origins of the Saxons from Askanius (413) and Macedon (415), the Swabian hero Brenno (421), the Armenian origins of the Bavarians (422), the Trojan origins of the Franks (423), Charlemagne's dead beloved (458), Otto III at Charlemagne's tomb (481), the sainted imperial pair Henry II and Kunigunde (482), and the Swedish origins of the Swiss (514). I realize that a mere listing of corresponding themes is an unsatisfactory exercise. It demands interpretation. That is, however, impossible without the laying of such foundations. Perhaps the critical edifice can soon be built over them.

Some of the myths and the vast majority of the texts in the body of this work usually are neither in the province of the student of literature, nor of interest and importance to a strictly scientific historiographer. The fabrications of Trithemius and the fertile confusions of Aventinus do not serve to enlighten the factual history of Germanic antiquity and are an embarrassment in the supposedly relentless advance of scientific historical writing. Yet neither of them can be called a poet, for what they write is neither "Dichtung" nor "Wahrheit," as it resides on a middle ground between history and literature and shares the incidentals of both but the substance of neither. Or so it seems—but perhaps the distance between historical writing and literature is not so great as to admit of a vast no-man's land which these texts must populate.

The very beginnings of our historical and literary traditions hardly allow radical distinctions. For that, Herodotus is too filled with fiction and Homer with fact. At the wellsprings of the Germanic constituent of our culture—and the Greek as well if we consider Homer or his sources originally historical—poetic and historical composition seem to have been one and the same thing. The growing historical sophistication of antiquity withdrew history from the combination, but let a variant form survive in the epic—such as the epic history of a Lucan or the historical epic of a Virgil. In the prime of Roman historical writing, the variant achieved wholly independent status when the Mediterranean world invented the Alexandrian novel. The novel appeared repeatedly under the fiction of an improvement on history. Dictys and Dares purported to be first-hand witnesses to the Trojan war; Callisthenes, to Alexander's campaigns. In the Middle Ages these novels lived double lives. They helped form the imposing epic tradition of Troy and Alexander novels, and were accepted and cited in the historical literature. Such broad acceptance was surely not the intention of the original authors of the novels. Homer was largely accepted as history and was long available before Dictys and Dares made their fictitious reports. Similarly, the ancient world had several excellent Alexander biographies before Pseudo-Callisthenes appeared in the third century of our era. These fictions were no doubt read by the ancients primarily for entertainment, as the histories were read primarily for information.

The conventions of late antiquity make the distinctions between the disciplines fairly clear. Historical writing diligently attempted to adhere to fact, or at least to the most factually authoritative traditions. Novelistic writing dealt with fact and tradition freely: its prime concern was the creation of an internally consistent imaginative universe.

By ancient and modern standards, the disciplines were not so wholly discrete in the Middle Ages. A strong tradition of factual historical writing did survive classical antiquity in the service of the Church and, secondarily, of the waning Empire. Another tradition, quasi-historical, was brought by the invaders of the Roman world, who preserved their history in heroic song. The songs are lost but left their mark on the historical and epic production of the Middle Ages. Vestiges of Germanic heroic epic remain in Jordanes, Paul the Deacon, and Saxo Grammaticus, among many others. The Theodoric, Nibelungen, Wolfdietrich, Waltharius, and Rother cycles are in similar debt. The writing of ecclesiatical and, secondarily, secular history largely maintained its integrity despite these debts. Its development, however, took it far from its Greco-Roman progenitor. The pious legends of the Middle Ages purposed to be accurate history as they chronicled the triumphs of Christianity. They were the living history, the journalism of the ancient and medieval Church. As they combined with the fairly objective annalistic historical conventions of the Middle Ages, they helped produce the great encyclopedic histories. In Jacobus de Voragine (d. 1298), to take an extreme example, legend and chronicle are virtually indistinguishable. This is not to imply that historical and narrative traditions merged altogether; quite to the contrary, a splendid literature of romance and allegory accompanied historical writing. The literature was, however, intended by its authors and understood by its audience primarily as fiction. Legend and history were intended and understood as fact.

The correspondence between the two disciplines in the late Middle Ages and early Renaissance becomes progressively more complex until history begins to break free and assume its modern appearance. The merger becomes the province of historical fiction in the drama and the novel, more or less repeating the developments of classical antiquity. Petrarch's *Africa* is an example of the Italian Renaissance attempt to produce a work in both genres. The German parallel of this Renaissance conception produced Maximilian's autobiographical neo-chivalric epics. Humanists in imperial service further combined these trends in the largely forgotten Latin epics of the Renaissance (e.g., Bartholini's *Austrias*). At the same time, however, history was in the process of achieving its modern independence with Bruni, Machiavelli, and Guicciardini in Italy, and Beatus Rhenanus, Carion, and Sleidanus in Germany. In subsequent generations, those who wrote history were no longer necessarily attempting to write poetry at the same time. There are exceptions, but they present another and more limited problem. Among those who wrote poetry, however, some did attempt to write history in the same action. World literature knows countless instances, not the least of which are in Shakespeare. Closer to our subject is a Lohenstein who could incorporate into the immense poetic universe of *Arminius* the recent history of the Hapsburgs in the costume of ancient Germans.

From the time distinctions between history and poetry first entered the mind of antiquity, they were never altogether abandoned. Only the objects to which they were applied changed. Most specifically, the conception of historical fact changed. In highly critical Roman historical writing the conception was limited to concrete politics and few mythical entities. In later Roman (e.g., Solinus) and then in medieval historical writing, the conception broadened to include more myth, legend, and miracle. In the Renaissance, legend and miracle began slowly to be eliminated, and objects new to history and less burdened with myth were placed under its scrutiny: art, architecture, literature, and science. Since then, history has served many new disciplines. However broad the focus of history has become, it remained a study of things as they were in real and specific time and place. With a reliable empirical method, the limitations of real and specific time and place have become progressively more stringent. And thus it seems that poetry and history have never been farther apart. In a certain sense, this is true; in another sense, it is not.

The differences between the disciplines can be complex, as the far too superficial argument above might indicate. The similarities are, however, even more difficult, and have been discussed less satisfactorily, as they continue to pose serious and unanswered questions about the comprehension and interpretation of human experience. Happily, at least two aphoristic utterances proclaim—if not explain— the broad common ground. The first, from the pen of Quintilian, states that "history has a certain affinity to poetry and may be regarded as a kind of prose poem."[24] The second is from Francis Bacon's *On the Dignity and Advancement of Learning* (1605), where he promises to treat "under the name of poetry . . . nothing more than imaginary history."[25]

For Quintilian then, history was a form of poetry; for Bacon, poetry was a form of history. Quintilian's utterance is a warning to the orator to be as cautious of history as he is of poetry, since both may be damaging if not subordinated to the demands of rhetoric. Hence his discussion is of little use here. Bacon's is quite the contrary. He makes distinctions between history and poetry (and philosophy) as expressions of the three basic faculties of mind: memory, and imagination (and reason). But the discrete character of the mind's faculties does not carry over into the disciplines. Narrative poetry, for example, "is such an exact imitation of history as to deceive, did it not often carry things beyond probability." "Dramatic poetry," Bacon explains, "is a

---

[24] *Institutio Oratoria*, X.i.31, in H. E. Butler, ed. and trans., *Quintilian*, 4 vols., Loeb Classical Library (London, 1961–63), IV, 21.

[25] II.xiii, in J. E. Creighton, ed., *Francis Bacon* (New York and London, 1900), p. 62. Subsequent quotations are from the same passage.

kind of visible history, giving the images of things as if they were present, whilst history represents them as past." While Bacon is not blind to the differences, his stress is on the similarities. He demonstrates that the growing objectivity of historical awareness in the Renaissance was accompanied by more than an intuition of poetry's consanguinity to history.

It is in the direct tradition of Bacon that Giambattista Vico wrote his *New Science* (3rd ed., 1744).[26] There (par. 819) "memory is the same as imagination." His conclusion is that "the poets must therefore have been the first historians of the nations" (820) and conversely, that the ancient historians were poets (471). Vico's method perhaps left a great deal to be desired. Further, what he considered reliable or certain about antiquity is far from proved by modern standards. His generalizations, however, are a vital insight into the problem of the similarities.

Leaning on my perhaps incomplete understanding of recent discussions,[27] I should like to suggest a characterization of history and poetry, not unfair to the disciplines but broad enough to illuminate their mutual affinity. The stuff of poetry develops in the mind of the creative historian, while poetic imagination can be fruitfully investigated on the evidence of the historiographic tradition. This formulation, I confess, touches closely upon the basic assumptions of this book, and perhaps also on the preserve of the philosopher, in whose labors I disclaim all expertise.

Historical writing and poetry, then, have in common that they are both conscious reconstructions of the meaning of significant human affairs. The choice of object among significant human affairs marks a difference in the disciplines, but that is another matter. History and poetry are both concerned with the creation of consistent universes. In history, it is the uncovery of the likeliest principles to explain the greatest number of facts, in hope that the order thus imposed truly represents the order followed in objective reality. In poetry, the uni-

---

[26] Thomas G. Bergin and Max H. Fisch, trans., *The New Science of Giambattista Vico*, revised edition (Ithaca, N.Y., 1968); references to the text are by paragraph number.

[27] Wilhelm Dilthey, *Pattern and Meaning in History*, H. P. Rickman, ed. (New York, 1962); Benedetto Croce, *History: Its Theory and Practice*, Douglas Ainslie, trans. (New York, 1921); R. G. Collingwood, *The Idea of History*, T. M. Knox, ed. (New York, 1956); E. D. Hirsch, *Validity in Interpretation* (New Haven, Conn., 1967). A stimulating exchange between Maurice Mandelbaum ("A Note on History as Narrative," *History and Theory*, VI [1967], 413–19) and Richard G. Ely, Rolf Gruner, and William H. Dray ("Mandelbaum on Historical Narrative: A Discussion," *History and Theory*, VIII [1969], 275–94) touches repeatedly on the problem but delineates the distinctions rather than the similarities.

verse is an experience ordered by the consciousness of the poet, recreated by him in such a way as to be communicable. Both disciplines are to a certain extent intuitive, imitative, and both require the labors of a giver of order, if we may say so, the labors of a poet.

No matter how much scientific tradition has done to separate the disciplines, their similarities and perhaps even common origins and purpose have a constant reminder in our languages. "Storia" and "storia," "histoire" and "histoire," "Geschichte" and "Geschichte," "story" and "history" declare not the disparity between academic specializations but a unity in humane learning. Ernst Robert Curtius, in league with Arnold Toynbee, conjectured for the foreseeable future a history extending so far beyond its present boundaries that only fiction and poetry would be able to express and comprise it.[28] If Vico was correct about the origins of history and poetry, then we may one day come full circle. The ancients honored history with its own muse, Clio. There is no reason to remove her from the company of her sisters.

---

[28] Ernst Robert Curtius, *European Literature and the Latin Middle Ages*, Willard R. Trask, trans., Bollingen Series, XXXVI (New York, 1953), pp. 6–7.

Appendices

Bibliography and
status of the scholarship

In order to avoid a separate bibliography, I have repeated in each chapter full bibliographical information at the first appearance of a title. I have attempted to keep undecipherable abbreviations to a minimum. Those appearing with greater frequency are:

BLVS—Bibliothek des literarischen Vereins in Stuttgart. 295 vols. in progress. Stuttgart, Tübingen, Leipzig, 1842–1968 and continued.

Chroniken der deutschen Städte—Karl Hegel, et al., eds., *Chroniken der deutschen Städte vom 14. bis ins 16. Jahrhundert.* 36 vols. Leipzig, Stuttgart-Gotha, Stuttgart, 1862–1931 and continued.

MGH—Monumenta Germaniae Historica.

MGH SS—MGH Scriptorum rerum Germanicarum . . . 32 vols. Hannover and Leipzig, 1826–1934; in the presence of further bibliographical information, "Scriptores."

PL—Jacques-Paul Migne. *Patriologiae cursus completus . . . Series Latina.* 221 vols. Paris, 1841–1903.

Significant efforts have been made toward explaining the Renaissance concept of Germany and its past. Paul Joachimsen's *Geschichtsauffassung und Geschichtschreibung in Deutschland unter dem Einfluss des Humanismus,* Beiträge zur Kulturgeschichte des Mittelalters und der Renaissance, VI (Leipzig and Berlin, 1910) remains the most important study of the historiography of the Renaissance in Germany. Virtually everything written since on the subject begins with and often merely repeats Joachimsen's findings. Joachimsen presents exceedingly useful introductions to most of the German humanists who turned to the writing of history. He is interested first and foremost in the development among the German humanists of a critical approach to the historical discipline. The consequence is that he passes over with some displeasure the more imaginative products of a Trithemius (pp. 55–56) or an Annius of Viterbo (p. 95). Among the many virtues of Joachimsen's work, the greatest seems to me the recognition of the importance of the newly discovered medieval sources. This aspect of the humanists' historical study has been much underestimated, despite Joachimsen. Even with this recognition, Joachimsen usually fails to trace Renaissance commonplaces back beyond the fifteenth century. He accredits Aeneas Sylvius as the source for one etymology of the word German (p. 95), where in fact it is traceable to Isidore, whom Joachimsen, curiously, mentions in another connection on the next page. The new is, however, more important to Joachimsen than the old.

Although Joachimsen touches upon some myths of the German past (e.g., Irenicus's "Gothentheorie," p. 175), his main interest lies in critical approaches to history. Thus the larger part of the myths among the German humanists is left without mention. By limiting his subject to the humanists, he passes over most of the vernacular sources, an even richer storehouse of fabulous tales about German antiquity. But this was not his subject, and the lacuna is no flaw in his work.

Indulging somewhat more in the Renaissance's less critical study of the German past is Friedrich Gotthelf's *Das deutsche Altertum in den Anschauungen des sechzehnten und siebzehnten Jahrhunderts,* Forschungen zur neureren Litteraturgeschichte, XIII (Berlin, 1900). The title excludes the traditions and inventions of the earlier fifteenth century, and does not claim to trace sources into the Middle Ages. Gotthelf limits himself in the sixteenth-century section, for all practical purposes to Annius of Viterbo in the work of Aventinus. Even with that limitation, Gotthelf ignores some of Aventinus's most delicious confabulations. Gotthelf does, however, begin to fill in some of the imaginative gaps left by Joachimsen's critical interests. His is a tolerably good introduction to the Renaissance myths of the German past, but he leaves the impression that the sixteenth- and seventeenth-century view of German antiquities was almost altogether fabulous. This is not the case, despite the direction of my own study. Certainly by the beginning of the seventeenth century, almost as much was known about Germanic antiquities as is known today, and they were much more a current item in an educated person's reservoir of knowledge.

A large number of humanists are examined for their contributions to folklore by Erich Schmidt in his *Deutsche Volkskunde im Zeitalter des Humanismus und der Reformation,* Historische Studien, XLVII (Berlin, 1904). As far as he goes, Schmidt has fascinating and often amusing matters to bring to light, such as an exceedingly nasty catalogue of German provincial vices. Mysteriously, Schmidt ignores the vernacular literature of his period, which was of course rich in folklore. There is the whole question of the myth of Emperor Frederick and the habits, beliefs, and superstitions of the Prussians in Simon Grunau's chronicle of about 1526.

Schmidt explains (p. 17) that medieval tradition did not permit tales heard first-hand to enter writing without previous written authority. The authority principle in the Middle Ages is well known, but there are enough exceptions to warrant a search for the sources of what appears to be folk tradition. Schmidt, then, like most of the other authors here, ignores most medieval antecedents. Hans Tiedemann's *Tacitus und das Nationalbewusstsein der deutschen Humanisten am Ende des 15. und Anfang des 16. Jahrhunderts* (Berlin, 1913) is, after Joachimsen's, the most excellent work touching on the subject. Tiedemann gives fair coverage to numerous humanists, not all German. Despite his primary concern with the revival of classical learning in Renaissance study of the German past, Tiedemann turns again and again to medieval sources known or revived in the Renaissance. He points out interest in the Carolingian flowering (p. 72 and note 11), for example, Beatus Rhenanus's admiration of the ninth-century German Gospel harmony by Otfried von Weissenburg (p. 81). Tiedemann is aware that the German humanists devoured medieval sources on Germanic antiquity, as in twelfth-century reports of ancient battles between barbaric tribes and Roman legions (p. 113).

Tiedemann's search into the Middle Ages is, however, not exhaustive by any standards. His task, on the other hand, was not to trace the Middle Ages in the thought of the Renaissance. He was concerned with Tacitus's influence, which he covers very well indeed.

Theobald Bieder's *Geschichte der Germanenforschung, Erster Teil 1500–1806* (Leipzig and Berlin, 1921) is almost entirely dependent on Joachimsen for the Renaissance section. He repeats most of Joachimsen's weaknesses and adds a good many of his own. When he recedes to the Middle Ages, Bieder inclines to be misleading. While relating an interesting little fact, that Jordanes's Gothic history entered some thirteenth-century Spanish poetry, Bieder suggests that such an influence is unusual. Jordanes was in truth widely read in the Middle Ages, remained available in numerous extracts in other chronicles, and was preserved in a remarkably large number of manuscripts.

Bieder has, however, a great many fascinating observations on the later survival of uncritical beliefs about German antiquities. Leibnitz, for example, is supposed to have considered German the "Urspache" of Europe, the basis of all European vernaculars (p. 69). Leibnitz has this in common with the Alsatian Anonymous, of all people. Bieder also mentions (p. 67) an etymology fantastic enough to have been made in the Middle Ages or Renaissance: "Titan" and "Teuton" are made cognate. Actually, this derivation is a nineteenth-century invention and has, to the best of my knowledge, no earlier tradition. Bieder's work is certainly useful, but its strength does not lie in its sections on the Renaissance. Joachim Wagner, in his most readable dissertation for the University of Leipzig, *Nationale Strömungen am Ausgange des Mittelalters* (Weida in Thüringen, 1929), performs some real services. His is the first general work that touches more closely on the vernacular manifestations of the myths. His main sources are the folk song, Jacob Twinger von Königshoven, and the Alsatian Anonymous. The only serious fault of the essay is that it omits a geat many texts that deserve attention. It stands alone in ignoring the Latin contemporaries, which is a definite virtue; its greatest virtue is not repeating previous findings, particularly those of Joachimsen.

This virtue is not shared by the otherwise splendid dissertation of Hedwig Riess for the University of Freiburg in Breisgau, *Motive des patriotischen Stolzes bei den deutschen Humanisten* (Berlin, 1934). It concentrates on select problems in select authors: the concepts of the *Imperium* and German political prerogatives in the works of Hermann Peter of Andlau, Heinrich Bebel, Johannes Naucler, Conrad Celtis, Ulrich von Hutten, and Aventinus. The findings are correct and often exciting. An extremely convenient compilation of pertinent texts intelligently selected constitutes the appendix (pp. 45ff.). The work fills in some of the many outlines in Joachimsen, but like him fails to consider the Middle Ages.

Paul Hans Stemmermann's Heidelberg dissertation, *Die Anfänge der deutschen Vorgeschichtsforschung* (Quackenbrück, 1934) is a curious combination of completely new and completely old material. Stemmermann's work is exciting when it discusses an almost unknown collector of inscriptions, Nicolaus Marescalcus Thurius (d. 1525). But all too often it is simply a repetition of what is to be found in Joachimsen, all properly accredited, but not new. One would imagine that Stemmermann would find delight in finding the medieval sources of the Renaissance's work on German pre-history. On the contrary, Stemmermann insists (p. 7) that the Middle Ages are desert territory for prehistorical investigations. Scholastic dependence on dogma and the absolute absence of historical perception in the Middle Ages are the reasons, according to Stemmermann. Be that as it may, Renaissance views which, Stemmermann thinks, exemplify the beginnings of prehistorical study are, as often as not, simple continuations of medieval tradition. He points out (p. 17) that Hartmann Schedel had German tribes descending from Noah over Japhet. He traces the utterance back to Meisterlin; in truth, it lies at least as far back as Saint Jerome. Other examples could show that his work satisfies as a study of pre-history in the Renaissance, but not of the beginnings of this study, as his title implies.

The inaugural address by H. Dannenbauer upon his appointment to the chair of History at the University of Tübingen in 1935, *Germanisches Altertum und deutsche Geschichtswissenschaft*, Philosophie und Geschichte, LII (Tübingen, 1935) has some distressing elements occasioned by the political situation of the time. But Dannenbauer did not let politics invade the facts of his presentation. Considering the limitations imposed by a lecture, he does considerable justice to the more important Renaissance conceptions of German antiquity. He does not regard their factual accuracy, and so touches closely on some myths of the German past. His concern is primarily with the Pseudo-Berosus of Annius of Viterbo. Dannenbauer examines its influence among the German Humanists, such as Naucler, Celtis, Irenicus, Franck, and Aventinus. He has some new information on the survival of Berosus into the eighteenth century. If one is not too distracted by the political disgressions,

Dannenbauer's work is a useful introduction to the subject of Renaissance myths of the German past.

Among the very best monographs that touch our subject is Ulrich Paul's *Studien zur Geschichte des deutschen Nationalbewusstseins im Zeitalter des Humanismus und der Reformation*, Historische Studien, CCXCVIII (Berlin, 1936). He traces the influence of Aeneas Sylvius, Pseudo-Berosus, and Trithemius's Hunibald through the other humanists in Germany. It is refreshing to read in Paul that the humanists were a confusion of medieval and modern (p. 12). But alas, he does not go back to the medieval, and just like Joachimsen before him, traces the origins of humanist imagination about the German past only as far as Aeneas Sylvius. He also ignores most vernacular works, except the translations of Aventinus.

Paul of course discusses Renaissance thought from the point of view of growing German national self-consciousness, as his title states. But he himself admits that there is hardly any German national self-consciousness to speak of at the time, that Germans still lived in the aura of the Empire, of the *Res Publica Christiana* (pp. 14ff.). The medieval sources of the imperial myth failed to entice Paul. His failings are, however, small in contrast to the success with which he captures many Renaissance ideas and traces their distribution among the German scholars of the time.

To be used with extreme caution is Ludwig Sponagel's *Konrad Celtis und das deutsche Nationalbewusstsein*, Bausteine zur Volkskunde und Religionswissenschaft, XVIII (Bühl/Baden, 1939). I mention it here because of its treatment of the myths of the German past, and not so much because of its treatment of Celtis, which is occasionally unfortunate. Sponagel's presentation of the myths as they emanate from Celtis is interesting but somewhat one-sided, as though Celtis would never think of criticizing his countrymen. He does mention Celtis's interest in the Middle Ages (pp. 74, 81–82) but fails to follow his example. Apart from Sponagel's transparent and opportunistic politics, his essay suffers from few major flaws not yet met with in titles discussed already. In his favor is the work's free investigation of the most unrealistic flights of Celtis and his followers.

A recent and thoroughly superior study of Renaissance historiography is Gerald Strauss's *Sixteenth-Century Germany, Its Topography and Topographers* (Madison, Wis., 1959). The work has command of the vast bibliography. It touches on the myths of the German past (pp. 29ff.), but primarily from the point of view of the history of geography. Its concern for sources is largely reserved for the rediscovered classical texts. Strauss inclines to subdue the fantastic statements of his authors. He writes (p. 76) of Felix Fabri and his *Tractatus de Civitate Ulmensi*, "he soon leaves [the] world of fantasy for more substantial matters." Although there is in Fabri's tract, I suppose, a great deal of "substance" (which is of little interest here), there is as well a great deal of fantasy. Strauss's work is nonetheless one of the most useful tools for the study of German humanist cosmographical interests. Just as a Renaissance cosmography was not merely a geography, but rather an encyclopedia of the culture, customs, history, and legends of a nation or place, Strauss's book goes well beyond topography. That he does not dwell on myths or medieval sources is certainly not a failing. They are not his task.

The best study of any single myth of the German past is James Bryce's classic, *The Holy Roman Empire* (1904; reprinted New York, 1966). My own investigations into the imperial myth do nothing but reconfirm his findings. His evocation of this influential political idea has been attacked by historians of political realities. The controversy has, however, subsided in favor of a compromise between political history and the history of an idea. Both Bryce's book and the controversy offer valuable insights into the workings of the past and, incidentally, of the present as well.

Chronology

Years connected by dashes normally represent approximate or conjectured lifetime; single date or years connected by virgule represent *floruit*.

485–425 B.C.	Herodotus	730–804	Alcuin
70–19	Virgil	770–840	Einhard
10 B.C.–A.D. 30	Velleius Paterculus	784–856	Hrabanus Maurus
1st century A.D.	Dares	800	Dungal "Hibernicus
23–79	Pliny the Elder		Exul"
39–65	Lucan	808–849	Walahfrid Strabo
55–120	Tacitus	844	Origin of the Franks
69–140	Suetonius	863	Rudolf von Fulda
2nd or 3rd		865	Otfried von
century	Dictys		Weissenburg
260–339	Eusebius	840–912	Notker Balbulus
353–400	Ammianus Marcellinus	867/896	Genealogy of Frankish
364/378	Eutropius		Kings
348–420	Jerome	883	Pseudo-Isidore
354–430	Augustine	9th century	Waltharius
390–440	Orosius	900	Eutropius the
534	Marcellinus Comes		Lombard
490–555	Cassiodorus	906	Regino von Prüm
551	Jordanes	920–972	Liutprand of Cremona
538–594	Gregory of Tours	925–973	Widukind von Corvey
540–604	Gregory the Great	935–1000	Hrotswitha von
570–636	Isidore of Seville		Gandersheim
660	Fredegarius	1000	Landulfus Sagax
664	Vita of Saint	975–1018	Thietmar von
	Columban		Merseburg
670	Origin of the	1004–1081	Aimonius of Fleury
	Lombards	1049	Wipo
8th century	Liber Historiae	1013–1054	Hermann von
	Francorum		Reichenau
8th century	Aethicus Hyster	11th century	Excerpta ex Gallica
672–735	Venerable Bede		Historica
720–797	Paul the Deacon	1025–1081	Lampert von Hersfeld

1028–1082	Marianus Scotus
1030–1112	Sigebert of Gembloux
1066/1081	Adam von Bremen
1086/1090	Benzo of Alba
1103	Frutolf
1125	Ekkehard von Aura
12th century	Origin of the Swabians
1079–1142	Abelard
1080–1137	Honorius of Autun
1120	Hugo of Fleury
1132	Gesta Trevirorum
1139	Annalista Saxo
1098–1179	Hildegard von Bingen
1111–1158	Otto von Freising
Mid-12th century	Pseudo-Turpin
Mid-12th century	Kaiserchronik
Mid-12th century	Ordines for Imperial Coronation
1160	Archipoeta
1160	Ludus de Antichristo
1186	Robertus de Monte
1125–1192	Gotfried of Viterbo
1200	Saxo Grammaticus
1202	*Venerabilem*
1160–1215	Sicardus of Cremona
1220/1248	Eike von Repgow
1220/1254	Rudolf von Ems
1225/1250	Bartholomeus Anglicus
1228–1298	Jacobus de Voragine
1244/1264	Vincent of Beauvais
1261	Erfurt Anonymous
1270	Annales Austriae
1275	Jansen Enikel
1276	Detmar Chronik
1277	Martinus Polonus
1277/1287	Gotfrid Hagen
1278	Thomas Tuscus
1287	Girardus of Arvernia
1281/1288	Alexander von Roes
1292	Flores Temporum
1236–1326	Ptolemy of Lucca
1243–1316	Aegidius Romanus
1250–1321	Pierre du Bois
1261–1329	Mussato
1265–1321	Dante
1275–1349	Alvarus Pelagius
1300	Reinfrid von Braunschweig
1304	*Historiae Patavienses et Cremifanenses*
1306	John of Paris
1307	Sigfrid von Balnhusen
1308	Tractatus Anonymus
1312/1318	Ottokar

1275–1343	Marsilius of Padua
1290–1350	William of Occam
1297–1363	Lupold von Bebenburg
1300–1350	Johannes von Winterthur
1304–1374	Petrarch
1309–1374	Konrad von Megenberg
1310–1380	Johannes von Neumarkt
1313–1354	Cola di Rienzo
1313–1375	Boccaccio
1320–1373	Heinrich von Mügeln
1320	Landulfus Colonna
1328	Franciscus Toti
1331–1406	Coluccio Salutati
1340–1418	Dietrich von Nieheim
1346–1420	Jacob Twinger von Königshoven
1350	Mathias von Neuenburg
1361	Sibylline Prophecies
1362	Fritsche Closener
1364	Heinrich Taube
1364	Cortusi Chronicle
1372	Magdeburg Schöppenchronik
1385/1391	Benvenuto Rambaldi
1358–1421	Gobelinus Persona
1414/1438	Ulrich von Richenthal
1418	Thomas Prischuh
1401–1464	Nicolaus Cusanus
1428	Mühldorfer Annalen
1428	Nicolaus Grill
1405–1464	Aeneas Sylvius Piccolomini
1421/1440	Endres Tucher
1434	Chronik aus Kaiser Sigmunds Zeit
1434/1440	Johannes Rothe
1437/1442	Der Küchlin
1439	Andreas von Regensburg
1448/1462	Felix Hemmerlin
1450/1484	Hermann Peter aus Andlau
1450/1498	Eulogius Kiburger
1454/1491	Sigismund Meisterlin
1462	Thomas Lirer
1469	Augsburg Anonymous
1471/1477	Antonio Campano
1474	Prophetic Folk Song
1425–1502	Werner Rolevinck
1440–1514	Hartmann Schedel
1441–1502	Felix Fabri
1445–1517	Albertus Krantz
1450–1513	Hans Folz

1450–1521	Erasmus Stella	1513	Zwölff Sibyllen
1450–1528	Jakob Wimpheling		Weissagung
1456/1509	Alsatian Anonymous	1515/1520	Paulus Langius
1458–1521	Sebastian Brant	1519	Barbarossa Chapbook
1459–1508	Conrad Celtis	1519	Johannes Adelphus
1462–1516	Trithemius		Muling
1482/1520	Jacobus Foresta	1473–1545	Hieronymus Gebwiler
1488/1496	Veit Arnpeck	1475–1537	Thomas Murner
1495/1516	Riccardo Bartholini	1477–1534	Aventinus
1498/1502	Annius of Viterbo	1479–1522	Cochlaeus
1462–1535	Jodocus Badius	1482–1511	Matthias Ringman
1465–1547	Conrad Peutinger		Philesius
1470–1530	Willibald Pirckheimer	1484–1551	Vadianus
1470–1531	Simon Grunau	1485–1547	Beatus Rhenanus
1472–1518	Heinrich Bebel	1486–1535	Agrippa
1499	*Koelhoffische Chronik*	1488–1563	Henricus Glareanus
1501	Chronik der	1489–1552	Sebastian Münster
	Pfalzgrafen	1495–1559	Franciscus Irenicus
1506	Coccinius	1498–1564	Andreas Althamer
1510	Naucler	1505–1572	Aegidius Tschudi

Index

Ronsard, Pierre, 25
Roschildia, 139
Rosicrucians, 118
Rostock, 136
Rothar, 195
Rothe, Johann, 49–52, 55, 66, 261 n, 320
Rother, 323
Rückert, Friedrich, 153 n, 319
Rudolf I, emperor, 51, 95, 140, 244, 252, 275, 286, 288
Rudolf III, King of Burgundy, 123, 232
Rudolf von Ems, 244
Rudolf von Fulda, 208, 218, 223, 225
Rügen, 31
Rumo, 65
Rumulus, Duke of Swabia, 82–83
Russia(ns), 29, 92
Ruther, 274. *See also* Rothar; Rother

Sacrifice, 158–59, 179; animal, 145, 158–59, 179; human, 20, 122, 129, 133, 140, 145, 158–59, 189, 218, 225. *See also* Religion
Saint Denis, 114
Saint Gall, 126, 161
Saladin, 101
Salagast(us), 121, 132, 133, 221, 230, 275
Salagastald, 19, 131, 133
Salegast, 46, 197, 223, 237. *See also* Salagast(us)
Salgast, 236. *See also* Salagast(us)
Salic law, 46, 121, 132, 223, 230. *See also* Law, givers of; Salagast(us); Salegast; Salgast
Salutati, coluccio, 289, 290, 300
Sappho, 107
Saracens, 65, 103, 275, 288; pale death of, title, 48, 212, 231, 237, 290
Sarmatia(ns), 72, 89–90, 168, 194
Satraps, Saxon, 74, 199
Saturburg, 139
Saturn, 36, 56, 138, 139; son of Noah, 120. *See also* Religion
Saturnia tempora, 72. *See also* Golden Age
Saul, 49
Saxo Grammaticus, 12 n, 218, 238–40, 302, 304, 314, 323
Saxoferrato, Bartoleus, 288 n
Saxons, 71–72, 93, 122, 132, 134, 139–40, 157, 165, 203, 211, 212, 231; in ancestry of Amazons, 117; in ancestry of Danes, 292; in ancestry of English, 273, 292; in ancestry of Swiss, 121; in ancestry of Turks, 121; biblical origins of, 49; in Britain, 18, 73, 81, 94, 137, 208, 218, 223–24, 242;

brothers of the Franks, 128–30; Danish origins of, 145; language of, 31, 37, 141, 194; Macedonian origins of, 18, 24, 31, 55, 100–11, 137, 162, 213, 223, 242, 303, 321; Norman origins of, 145; Sicambrian origins of, 168; Trojan origins of, 128, 133
Saxony, 29, 113, 128, 138
Saz, 161
Scandinavian origins, 225, 267. *See also* Amazons; Burgundians; Danes; Gepidae; Goths; Hungarians; Huns; Lombards; Scythians; Swabians; Swiss; Vandals; Winili
Schardius, Simon, 3, 10
Schäfer, Wilhelm, 321
Schedel, Hartmann, 96, 104, 123, 197 n, 219 n, 256 n, 294 n, 330; chronicle of, 77 n, 80, 84–86, 91, 116, 120, 295
Scheier, 169
Schgolopotius, 62. *See also* Scolopetius
Schiller, Friedrich, 320
Schiri, 169
Schlegel, Friedrich and August Wilhelm, 3
Schlegel, Johann Elias, 319
Schleswig, 225
Schorio, 169
Schreitwein, 91, 170, 308. *See also* Fictitious authority
Schritovinus, 308. *See also* Schreitwein
Schwab, King, 170. *See also* Suevus
Schweyg, 65, 138. *See also* Senner
Schwyter, 65, 138
Schwyz, 64, 65, 125, 138
Scierer, 169
Sclavonia, 30. *See also* Slavs
Scolopetius, 185, 223. *See also* Schgolopotius
Scotland, 166
Scoto, Duke, 137
Scots, 111, 137, 205
Scytha, 90
Scythae, 168, 183
Scythes, 167
Scythia(ns), 29, 78, 101, 120, 185, 193, 194, 230; as German, 14; as Gothic, 72, 137, 182, 189; and the Huns, 124, 125; invaded by Goths, 30, 31, 188, 223; Scandinavian origins of, 209
Sedanus, 129
Seifridt, 49. *See also* Siegfried
Selgenstadt, 132
Sem, 76, 104, 236
Semiramis, 19, 44, 55, 117, 120, 167, 226–27, 230, 236. *See also* Trier

THE JOHNS HOPKINS PRESS

Composed in Baskerville text and display
by Monotype Composition Company

Printed on 60-lb (P & S, R) Sebago MF
by Universal Lithographers, Inc.

Bound in Bancroft Kennett
by L. H. Jenkins, Inc.